70 Canadian Poets

70 Canadian Poets

Fifth Edition | EDITED BY Gary Geddes

with Di Brandt, Anne Compton, & Carmine Starnino

OXFORD
UNIVERSITY PRESS

OXFORD
UNIVERSITY PRESS

Oxford University Press is a department of the University of Oxford. It furthers the University's objective of excellence in research, scholarship, and education by publishing worldwide. Oxford is a registered trade mark of Oxford University Press in the UK and in certain other countries.

Published in Canada by
Oxford University Press
8 Sampson Mews, Suite 204,
Don Mills, Ontario M3C 0H5 Canada

www.oupcanada.com

First Edition published in 1970 under title: 15 Canadian poets.
Second Edition published in 1978 under title: Canadian poets plus 5.
Third Edition published in 1998 under title: 15 Canadian poets times 2.
Fourth Edition published in 2001 under title: 15 Canadian poets times 3.

Library and Archives Canada Cataloguing in Publication

70 Canadian poets / edited by Gary Geddes. — Fifth edition.
Includes index.

Preceded by: 15 Canadian poets X3 / edited by Gary Geddes. 4th ed. 2001.

ISBN 978-0-19-900190-3 (pbk.)

1. Canadian poetry (English)—20th century. 2. Canadian poetry (English)—21st century. I. Geddes, Gary, 1940-, writer of introduction, editor of compilation II. Title: Seventy Canadian poets.

PS8291.F53 2014 C811'.5408 C2013-907173-3

Oxford University Press is committed to our environment. Wherever possible, our books are printed on paper which comes from responsible sources.

Printed and bound in the United States of America

1 2 3 4 — 17 16 15 14

Contents

Introduction

In the fall of 1970, I was living in London, United Kingdom, working on my doctoral thesis, trying to write poetry, and recovering from two long bouts of what I now see as a bad case of *anthologitis*. Margaret Atwood had invited Phyllis Bruce and me to dinner at the flat she shared with her then-husband Jim Polk. I had given her in advance a batch of my poems, which she had generously offered to peruse. After dinner, we sat on the floor in the living room while she unceremoniously went through the manuscript, poem by poem, dropping them in piles: A (good), B (workable), and C (doubtful, a.k.a. rubbish). I do not recall many poems winding up in pile A, but several made it to pile B, and the bulk earned an ignominious burial in pile C. To change the subject, and cover the embarrassment of the moment, she asked me when I planned to edit my next anthology. My collection *20th Century Poetry and Poetics* had been published in 1969, and the release of *15 Canadian Poets* was imminent.

"Never," I replied, rather too quickly. I was painfully aware of what it had cost me, in terms of time and creativity, spending so much time writing notes and poring over the work of other poets rather than struggling to write my own. "Atrophy of the right hemisphere," I added, thinking of all the poems I might have written during those three years, not to mention the unfinished thesis. Still, there was plenty to be learned about the craft by reading so many good poems and having to think about what made one more engaging than another.

"Once an anthologist, always an anthologist," she said, with that wonderful acumen and wicked smile that have become so familiar to Canadians. It was a prophetic moment, for both of us. Atwood went on to publish several more anthologies, and I, at the point when I should be sailing or sipping martinis in Fiji, am still hard at it.

Yes, *anthologitis*, a recurring disease.

* * * *

In previous editions of this anthology, I was keen to set the record straight for teachers and students who might not realize that Canadian poetry experienced a liberating renaissance during the sixties and seventies, overcoming colonial notions of inferiority, including the view that the only worthwhile writing had to be produced, or at least heavily influenced, by the mother country. As it happened, we had many mothers to consider. Thanks to A.J.M. Smith, Milton Wilson, Northrop Frye, Eli Mandel, and other critics, we came to see that "eclectic detachment," the ability to learn from and assimilate a host of influences—English, European, American, Asian,

African, Arabian, Persian, and Latin American—rather than imposing a single, dominant mode, might turn out to be our strength. I think that prediction has proven true.

I want to reiterate my view that poetry is a subversive force. Like music and the other arts, it has the capacity to fly beneath the radar, to enter our bodies and change the way we think and feel. Some still argue, taking the wrong cue from W.H. Auden's elegy on the death of Yeats, that "poetry makes nothing happen." Auden made his own position on the subject quite clear in his essays, insisting that "the mere making of a work of art is itself a political act" because it bears witness, because it reminds the management that we are human beings with rights and feelings, not just cogs in the machinery. We are in perilous times, with resource wars everywhere, ideological skirmishes, environmental disasters, severe economic disparities both nationally and internationally, and the continuing rape of indigenous peoples. So we need more than ever the subversive capacities of poetry, one of which is its ability to shake us up; the other, its power to heal. Dylan Thomas, who suffered from alcoholism and other demons, was making a similar point when he wrote: "Out of the inevitable conflict of images—inevitable because of the creative, recreative, destructive, and contradictory nature of the motivating centre, the womb of war—I try to make that momentary peace which is a poem."

Content, or what Wallace Stevens called "pressure of the real," is only part of the formula for good poetry, Canadian or otherwise. Whether the poet is engaged with domestic, social, political, environmental, spiritual, or philosophical issues, to write anything worth reading and of lasting value requires an intense involvement with the language. Avoiding the Scylla of cliché and the Charybdis of triteness requires time, thought, and verbal attention. An image is only as good as the letters, syllables, and stress patterns that embody it; in other words, an image will only knock a reader's socks off if it has the right music, which may require an extra syllable here, a denser concentration of recurring vowels and consonants there, or a simple alteration in the pattern of stress to make the phrase nest in the ear.

If, as I like to argue, poetry is our first language—a primary process language learned in infancy, more concerned with sound than sense, a kind of substitute umbilical cord, or bridge, that reconnects us to our mothers and to the rest of the human species—then its place in the educational system ought to be important and obvious. Yet this has not always been the case, and, in current times, while the influence of poetry grows in the streets and on the Internet, it seems to be losing ground in the academy, at least in English departments. I was fortunate to have high school teachers who did not feel it was their duty to make me analyze poems and struggle to dredge out "meanings." Most of their efforts involved celebrating poetry's music and economy, its capacity to pack so much into so few words. It seemed more important to enjoy poems, and to learn as many of them as possible by heart, than to count syllables or list the metaphors and figures of speech. We did not, as Wordsworth warned, "murder to dissect." I am glad my education happened that way, as it left the door open for me to experience, later, at university, a genuine hunger for the secrets and techniques of this singular craft.

While competing interests in English departments, including queer, ethnic, cultural, feminist, postcolonial, film, and a host of other studies, have pushed poetry to the academic sidelines, creative writing programs are booming. Poetry readings, residencies, slams, and prizes abound; workshops and festivals are much in demand; literary presses continue to publish more books of poetry; and poems appear on public transit, on billboards, and as song lyrics. In other words, poetry continues to speak to large numbers of Canadians. At Concordia University, where I taught for 20 years, creative writing courses initially had a low profile, and were regarded with some suspicion by many of my colleagues. However, when it gradually became obvious that creative writing students in the graduate program were winning most of the entrance fellowships and, later, when those students began to accumulate prizes and recognition, an attitudinal sea change took place. Now, academic study and the practice of writing poetry go hand in hand.

* * * *

While Canada's early poets devoted considerable attention to nation building, I think it is fair to say that their contemporary equivalents are less likely to be writing pan-Canadian poems than to be addressing local and international concerns. In other words, now that the muses have become acclimatized, and poets feel at home in this vast land, their attentions have shifted to the inner life (the noosphere), and to larger political realities. While major concerns—war, pollution, degradation of the planet—loom large in the contemporary consciousness, poets come to these issues from a personal vantage point, writing out of place, or locale, rather than out of region, province, or nation. A greater intimacy with the objects, creatures, and phenomena of our daily lives is being sought and achieved, and this is reflected in the verse. It is no longer enough to speak of birds or trees; the generic has been replaced by specific names, and micro-history has largely replaced the study of great men and events. As Seamus Heaney has cautioned, "We are no longer innocent, we are no longer just parishioners of the local, yet a sense of place is central to collective and poetic continuity."

The loss of innocence makes the search for meaning in the local, the personal, so much more challenging and intense. It also involves a more sustained and sophisticated critique of the social and economic values at home and abroad that shape, or disfigure, the modern world: the continuing impacts of the Industrial and Electronic Revolutions, the widening gap between rich and poor, the loss of meaningful employment, and a myriad of smaller but no less troubling effects of globalization, all efforts to tame, control, and Americanize the planet. The poets have stepped up to the challenge to sing and to critique their world, giving their work great power, urgency, and healing potential.

I am not a slave to Ezra Pound's dictum that poets must bend over backwards to "make it new." Nor do I adhere to the view of so-called experimental work expressed by that reprobate artist Gully Jimson, living on a houseboat on the Thames in Joyce Cary's *The Horse's Mouth*, who, when asked about the avant-garde, replied: "all this amateur stuff is like farting Annie Laurie through a keyhole. It may be clever but is it worth the trouble?" The debate between neo-formalists and proponents of free verse and organic form continues apace, but it always reminds me of Robinson Jeffers's dismissal of the work of his contemporaries and his lament about the losses poetry had suffered in his time—rhyme, metre, story, image, metaphor and what he called "recognizable emotions"—leaving the impression that the only route ahead was "originality by amputation," a path he refused to take. Would words themselves be next to go, then consonants and vowels?

As for making it new, which many poets take to mean art for art's sake, I say that life and art are inseparable, and, since life is constantly changing, art will do the same. Franz Kafka, D.H. Lawrence, and Aldous Huxley each spoke of art as a way of breaking out of the prisons that engulf us, of finding ways to say what has to be said. This is dangerous and Plato knew it. He refused poets admission to the ideal republic because they were always inventing new rhythms that upset the status quo. Rather than set formalists against free verse poets, I share Camus's view in *The Rebel* that the pendulum of taste is constantly swinging back and forth between extremes of form and formlessness. While these shifts are as often temperamental as ideological, it is obvious that the impenetrability of extreme form can become distasteful and life-denying; so, too, can the near absence of form—as found in greeting-card verse, soap operas, formulaic novels, and clichéd landscape paintings—because its excessive familiarity and lack of challenge will inevitably bore.

To forge a revolutionary poetics—which some might call an instructive redundancy—has required all of the emotional, intellectual, and technical resources available to poets, as well as the invention of a few new ones. Contemporary poets have not only embraced ancient forms such as the Persian ghazal, but also availed themselves of the self-reflexive mode of post-modernism and the humour and irony it unleashes. The battle is no longer between open and closed form. Most poets agree with Eliot that "No verse is free for the poet who wants to do a good job"—a useful reminder that, regardless of the building materials or the architectural design, the making of a poem is serious work. Otherwise, where is the fun?

Michael Ondaatje has said many things about poetic form, but one of the most interesting is this comment from "The gate in his head," a poem about his friend and fellow poet Victor Coleman:

> And that is all this writing should be then.
> The beautiful formed things caught at the wrong moment
> so they are shapeless, awkward
> moving to the clear.

This is the space poetry inhabits, the cut, the ragged edge, the borderblur, or along a treacherous tightrope. Poems emerge from that mysterious terrain between sleep and waking, thought and feeling, reality and dream, where past and present and so much else contend for our attention. And the best of them draw us, as readers, to the cut, the dissolve, and out along the razor's edge. It is an important but not always a safe or comfortable place to be, as Milan Kundera reminds us in *The Book of Laughter and Forgetting*:

> It takes so little, so infinitely little, for a person to cross the border beyond which everything loses meaning: love, conviction, faith, history. Human life—and herein lies the secret—takes place in the immediate proximity of that border, even in direct contact with it; it is not miles away, but a fraction of an inch.

* * * *

In my not so humble view, every good poem is an experiment, because it has achieved a successful fusion of content and form. That is, it has mustered just the right technical chops to create an imaginative shape for an object, feeling, idea, or situation that will claim the reader's, or listener's, attention. In the course of reading a decade's worth of new poetry books, and rereading the work of many poets I had previously passed over, it was obvious to me that I was faced with an embarrassment of riches, a veritable cornucopia. There are at least another hundred poets out there whose work merits serious attention and might easily have graced these pages. It caused me no end of discomfort to realize I could not celebrate them all. I do not pretend to have absolute criteria or a magical formula for selection. My choices, I confess, are subjective, though hopefully informed by a lifetime of reading, writing, and teaching. I have always been drawn to poems that engage me in terms of sight, sound, and idea; I also have to confess a bias for narrative modes and an inadequate appreciation of conceptual poetry. However, now and then a poem struck me as so damned clever that I was prepared to overlook its lack of density and patterning; at other times, engaging music, or a compelling image, made me embrace an otherwise unexacting poem. And, of course, there were other non-aesthetic considerations. For an anthology to be useful to teachers and students in a country as big and diverse as Canada, I also had to consider region, gender, ethnicity, and, of course, some of the bolder challenges to what poetry is, and what it can do.

All of this said, I still wanted a broader perspective on the editing process than my own. To compensate for my aesthetic and temperamental blinkers, I not only asked many poets to recommend new additions, but enlisted the help of three advisory editors—Di Brandt, Anne Compton, and Carmine Starnino—to make suggestions and bring me up to speed on new or neglected voices in their regions. Though the advice I received was invaluable, the choices I made remain my own responsibility. I am not alone as a poet in feeling the competing pull of story and song, or lyric and narrative, as this comment by Robert Bringhurst suggests:

> I don't live in a world in which the short poem is a welcome or sensible object. What can I do with one if I write it except send it to the editor of some morose or flippant little magazine—or worse, sell it for money to the editor of some hopped-up monthly, where it will function as an ornament between two columns of racy prose and a four-colour ad for Scotch whisky? The short poem is welcome grace in an ordered life. We do not lead ordered lives. We live in a catastrophic world—a world which the short poem can't convincingly address. A world, therefore, in which, if someone does read a poem, he is likely to read it too earnestly and all wrong, or too quickly, too lightly, and equally wrong. The temptation in such a world is to create an island of answering: to reinvent everything, to write another obese, eccentric monument, in spite of one's best intentions.

Although this is how many poets have felt over the last half century, most instructors, if they teach poetry at all, still prefer the lyric for its economy and intensity, and perhaps because they cannot afford the time or sustained attention required by long poems. In order to make room for new poets, I have regretfully surrendered the space previously devoted to Robert Kroetsch's *Seed Catalogue* and Anne Carson's "The Glass Essay" in their entirety. Those two wonderful long poems, both in print, should be on the course list of every Canadian poetry instructor, along with *The Titanic*, *The Journals of Susanna Moodie*, *The Collected Works of Billy the Kid*, *The T.E. Lawrence Poems*, and *The Martyrology*. However, I have managed to include a brief excerpt from *Seed Catalogue* and a somewhat shorter poem sequence by Anne Carson, "The Truth about God," which should give readers a taste of this wonderfully elastic and ruminative form.

* * * *

Canon-making is not the aim of this edition, nor was it of the previous incarnations. My main concern here has been to produce an exciting and representative teaching anthology. However, while I was keen to add many new poets, I was faced with certain restrictions that made this an extremely difficult task. The anthology had to be cut from 622 to 520 pages to make it smaller and more affordable, which meant performing radical surgery on the original selections. Still, I am pleased to have retained a generous selection of the original poets and poems; to have been able to include a large number of poets who have emerged in the last couple of decades, including Lisa Robertson, Karen Solie, Anne Compton, and Ken Babstock; and also to have gathered A.J.M. Smith, Milton Acorn, John Thompson, Dennis Lee, Susan Musgrave, and Tom Wayman belatedly into the fold. It is my hope that excerpts from longer works included here will encourage students to seek out poem sequences, narratives, and book-length poems by Pratt, Livesay, Reaney, Macpherson, MacEwen, Atwood, Nichol, Lee, Kroetsch, Beissel, Carson, McKinnon, and many others. So, too, will I be pleased if the delight to be found in the new works included stimulates an appetite for lyric poets such as Brian Bartlett, Marilyn Bowering, George McWhirter, Mary di Michele, Barry Dempster, Anne Simpson, Michael Crummey, Eve Joseph, Evelyn Lau, Carla Funk, Phil Hall, George Murray, Stephanie Bolster, Tim Bowling, Kate Braid, Jeffery Donaldson, John Terpstra, Evan Jones, and Steven Price, to name just a few of the many poets I admire. I hope, too that the work of bpNichol, Erín Moure, Lisa Robertson, and Sina Queyras will generate interest in the technical explorations of Colin Browne, Rita Wong, Christian Bök, and other poets working on that extreme edge where, as Roland Barthes suggests, "the death of language is glimpsed." From First Nations and Métis poets, working in and against the oral tradition, and those poets mining the riches and serious challenges of ethnicity more generally, poems by Gregory Scoffield, Marilyn Dumont, Kevin Paul, Roy Miki, Carolyn Souaid, and John Asfour and would have been a welcome addition to these pages.

I would like to thank the poets included in this anthology for their advice on the notes and their help in finding and choosing selections from their own work. My thanks also go out to my editor Meagan Carlsson, astute copy editor Helen Guri, and production coordinator Lisa Ball; to the staff at Oxford who felt this new edition important enough to champion; and to the many academics who offered advice: Jenny Penberthy, Alexis Kienlen, Mark Harris, Ruth Panofsky, Travis Mason, Manina Jones, Rob Zacharias, Neil Querengesser, Crystal Hurdle, Margery Fee, Linda Morra, Emily Wall, Matthew Gruman, Dean Irvine, Susie deCoste, Sue Sorensen, Rita Wong, Alan Hill, Kit Dobson, Faye Hammill, Klaus Martens, and Jesse Ferguson. Given that so much biographical and bibliographical information is now available on the Internet, it was possible to be more spare and selective in my notes on the poets. And, finally, I hope that this anthology will renew interest amongst teachers of Canadian literature (poetry in particular), and reverse the tendency toward course packs which, to me, seems based on a false economy. In trying to save a few dollars, instructors may be shortchanging their students, denying them a broader perspective and a range of engaging voices that will be available in their personal libraries long after classes end.

Gary Geddes
Thetis Island
2013

E.J. Pratt

(1883–1964)

Edwin John Pratt was born in Western Bay, Newfoundland. After graduating from St John's Methodist College, he spent four years as a teacher and minister in coastal villages before entering the University of Toronto. A succession of degrees followed—BA in philosophy (1911), MA (1912), BD (1913), and Ph.D. in theology (1917)—after which he taught in the English department of Victoria College until his retirement in 1953. Pratt was an enthusiastic and respected teacher, as well as an active force in the social and intellectual community of the university. He was also editor of *Canadian Poetry Magazine* from 1936 to 1942.

Pratt's critical reputation has been uneven, depending on the whims and fluctuations of the literary stock market in Canada. He began writing long poems in an age that valued brevity and economy; he espoused humanistic values—such as courage, endurance, and solidarity—when the dominant mode was irony and understatement, and the chief expression was a tight-lipped dismissal of society and its destructive ways. Yet Pratt was never naively optimistic; human weakness and vanity come up for regular drubbings in his work. Although Poe has called the long poem "a contradiction in terms," and the English critic B.S. Johnson describes the narrative poet as a "literary flat-earther," the long poem still remains an important force in Canada, and Pratt is its chief architect. His verse narratives restored drama, psychological depth, structural complexity, intelligence, and verbal texture to a form that had lost its energy and direction.

Pratt almost single-handedly upheld the expansive tradition in Canadian poetry, arguing for a poetry that is "a grand binge" rather than a snack at a funeral. His use of rhyme, metrics, and blank verse has often blinded readers to the spare brilliance of his early poems (such as "The Shark"), and the rich contribution he has made to poetic diction, ushering in—with the scholar's resourcefulness and the child's delight—whole new vocabularies from science, technology, and anthropology. Earle Birney, in "E.J. Pratt and his Critics," calls him "a man whose capacity for feeling is so great he is like a smelter furnace demanding stacks of raw material for fuel."

As Pratt wrote in the *Canadian Poetry Magazine* in 1936:

> Poetry is an exacting, difficult craft, and it takes years of hard work, and education and a sense of the language. Rhyme and metre do not make a poem; they produce by themselves nothing but doggerel. The real flesh and blood of poetry lies in turns of phrases, vivid images, new and unusual thoughts and manners of expressing them. A good poem is good because it is an unusual, imaginative, arresting way of writing English. We do not speak in poetry, except at rare moments; and if a poet writes so simply as to give the effect of spoken language, that effect is all the more startling and novel.
>
> To be able to use this language one must learn it, and that takes, among other things, reading. Practically all the great poets of our language were very highly educated, and the majority were scholars of enormous learning, commanding a large number of languages living and dead. Shakespeare, Burns and Keats are usually regarded as proving the contrary, but their capacity to respond to the books they did read was tremendous, and of no great poet is it untrue to say that his genius would have starved to death without books, for all his observations and experience of life.

Pratt also prepared the way for Atwood, Kroetsch, Ondaatje, and Nichol by parodying in *Towards the Last Spike* both the epic form and the values it traditionally espoused—nationhood, heroism, and reason. Milton Wilson fully understood the importance of Pratt: "I have the notion that the problems involved in *Towards the Last Spike* are going to be the central problems in the poetry of our future. . . . [Pratt writes] narratives, no doubt, but discontinuous narratives which are always turning, on the one side, into documents, letters, and jokes, and on the other, into pure lyrics."

Pratt's many publications include *Newfoundland Verse* (1923), *The Witches' Brew* (1925), *Titans* (1926), *The Iron Door* (1927), *The Roosevelt and the Antinoe* (1930), *The Titanic* (1935), *Still Life and Other Verse* (1943), *Dunkirk* (1941), *Behind the Log* (1947), *Brébeuf and His Brethren* (1940), and *Towards the Last Spike* (1952). Pratt's *Collected Poems* appeared in 1944 and again in 1958, this time with a long introduction by Northrop Frye. *Complete Poems*, edited by Sandra Djwa and R.G. Moyles, appeared in 1989; and *Selected Poems*, edited by Sandra Djwa, W.J. Keith, and Zailig Pollock, in 1999.

The Shark

He seemed to know the harbour,
So leisurely he swam;
His fin,
Like a piece of sheet-iron,
Three-cornered,
And with knife-edge,
Stirred not a bubble
As it moved
With its base-line on the water.

His body was tubular
And tapered
And smoke-blue,
And as he passed the wharf
He turned,
And snapped at a flat-fish
That was dead and floating.
And I saw the flash of a white throat,
And a double row of white teeth,
And eyes of metallic grey,
Hard and narrow and slit.

Then out of the harbour,
With that three-cornered fin
Shearing without a bubble the water
Lithely,
Leisurely,
He swam—
That strange fish,
Tubular, tapered, smoke-blue,
Part vulture, part wolf,
Part neither—for his blood was cold.

Sea-Gulls

For one carved instant as they flew,
The language had no simile—
Silver, crystal, ivory
Were tarnished. Etched upon the horizon blue.
The frieze must go unchallenged, for the lift

And carriage of the wings would stain the drift
Of stars against a tropic indigo
Or dull the parable of snow.

Now settling one by one
Within green hollows or where curled
Crests caught the spectrum from the sun,
A thousand wings are furled.
No clay-born lilies of the world
Could blow as free
As those wild orchids of the sea.

Erosion

It took the sea a thousand years,
A thousand years to trace
The granite features of this cliff,
In crag and scarp and base.

It took the sea an hour one night,
An hour of storm to place
The sculpture of these granite seams
Upon a woman's face.

The Man and the Machine

By right of fires that smelted ore
Which he had tended years before,
The man whose hands were on the wheel
Could trace his kinship through her steel,
Between his body warped and bent
In every bone and ligament,
And this "eight-cylinder" stream-lined,
The finest model yet designed.
He felt his lesioned pulses strum
Against the rhythm of her hum,
And found his nerves and sinews knot
With sharper spasm as she climbed
The steeper grades, so neatly timed
From storage tank to piston shot—
This creature with the cougar grace,
This man with slag upon his face.

from The Titanic

Harland & Wolff Works, Belfast, May 31, 1911

The hammers silent and the derricks still,
And high-tide in the harbour! Mind and will
In open test with time and steel had run
The first lap of a schedule and had won.
Although a shell of what was yet to be
Before another year was over, she,
Poised for the launching signal, had surpassed
The dreams of builder or of navigator.
The Primate of the Lines, she had out-classed
That rival effort to eliminate her
Beyond the North Sea where the air shots played
The laggard rhythms of their fusillade
Upon the rivets of the *Imperator.*
The wedges in, the shores removed, a girl's
Hand at a sign released a ribbon braid;
Glass crashed against the plates; a wine cascade,
Netting the sunlight in a shower of pearls,
Baptized the bow and gave the ship her name;
A slight push of the rams as a switch set free
The triggers in the slots, and her proud claim
On size—to be the first to reach the sea—
Was vindicated, for whatever fears
Stalked with her down the tallow of the slips
Were smothered under by the harbour cheers,
By flags strung to the halyards of the ships.

March 31, 1912

Completed! Waiting for her trial spin—
Levers and telegraphs and valves within
Her intercostal spaces ready to start
The power pulsing through her lungs and heart.
An ocean lifeboat in herself—so ran
The architectural comment on her plan.
No wave could sweep those upper decks—unthinkable!
No storm could hurt that hull—the papers said so.
The perfect ship at last—the first unsinkable,
Proved in advance—had not the folders read so?
Such was the steel strength of her double floors
Along the whole length of the keel, and such

The fine adjustment of the bulkhead doors
Geared to the rams, responsive to a touch,
That in collision with iceberg or rock
Or passing ship she could survive the shock,
Absorb the double impact, for despite
The bows stove in, with forward holds aleak,
Her aft compartments buoyant, watertight,
Would keep her floating steady for a week.
And this belief had reached its climax when,
Through wireless waves as yet unstaled by use,
The wonder of the ether had begun
To fold the heavens up and reinduce
That ancient *hubris* in the dreams of men,
Which would have slain the cattle of the sun,
And filched the lightnings from the fist of Zeus.
What mattered that her boats were but a third
Of full provision—caution was absurd:
Then let the ocean roll and the winds blow
While the risk at Lloyds remained a record low.

Dorothy Livesay

(1909–1996)

Dorothy Livesay was born in Winnipeg, but raised mostly in Ontario. She graduated from the University of Toronto in 1931 and then studied at the Sorbonne, exploring the influence of the French Symbolists on modern English poetry. During the Depression she was a social worker in Toronto, Montreal, and New Jersey. After 1936 she lived in Vancouver, where she worked at the YWCA, taught, and contributed to political and literary magazines, including Alan Crawley's *Contemporary Verse*. When her husband died, Livesay returned to Paris, where she worked for UNESCO before being posted to Zambia for three years. She taught widely and was a writer-in-residence at various Canadian universities, including the University of Manitoba, where she founded *CV/II*, a periodical of poetry and reviews.

Livesay's many poetry publications include *Green Pitcher* (1928), *Signpost* (1932), *Day and Night* (1944), *Selected Poems* (1957), *The Unquiet Bed* (1967),

Collected Poems: The Two Seasons (1972), *The Phases of Love* (1983), *The Self-Completing Tree: Selected Poems* (1986, 1999), and *The Woman I Am* (1991). Her non-fiction work includes two memoirs, *A Winnipeg Childhood* (1975) and *Journeys with My Selves* (1991), and a gathering of prose pieces, *Right Hand Left Hand: A True Life of the Thirties* (1977) edited by David Arnason and Kim Todd. She edited *The Collected Poems of Raymond Knister* (1949) and two anthologies of poetry by women: *Forty Women Poets of Canada* (1972) and *Woman's Eye* (1974). Livesay was twice the recipient of Governor General's Awards for poetry and received the Lorne Pierce Medal for Literature in 1947. She was productive to the last, publishing *Beginnings* (1988), *The Husband* (1990, a novella), and *Awakenings* (1991).

"I suppose that all my life I have fought against obscurantism!" Livesay said in "Song and Dance" (*Canadian Literature*, No. 41, summer 1969). "For me, the true intellectual is a simple person who knows how to be close to nature and to ordinary people. I therefore tend to shy away from academic poets and academic critics. They miss the essence." The constant fact in her art, as in her life, was the struggle to reconcile her need for privacy and her need for community. At times Livesay likened this struggle to the search for the "perfect dancing partner" or the perfect muse. As she says in "Song and Dance," writing is "Not a dance of touch, but one where the rhythm itself created an unseen wire holding two people together in the leap of movement."

Livesay describes "Call My People Home" as her "most thoroughly documented 'public' poem," one that is able to create a "dialectic between the objective facts and the subjective feelings of the poet" ("The Documentary Poem: A Canadian Genre," *Contexts of Canadian Criticism*, edited by Eli Mandel, 1971).

Livesay rejects the elegiac preoccupations of much modern writing. "We are optimists," she says in "Song and Dance,"

> Blakean believers in the New Jerusalem. We cannot see man's role as tragic but rather as divine comedy. We are alone—so what? We are not always lonely. Laughter heals, the dance captures, the song echoes forth from the tree-top. I won't stop believing this until every tree in Canada's chopped down; I thumb my nose at those who say that nature, and with it human nature, is becoming "obsolete."

Spain

When the bare branch responds to leaf and light
Remember them: it is for this they fight.
It is for haze-swept hills and the green thrust
Of pine, that they lie choked with battle dust.
You who hold beauty at your finger-tips

Hold it because the splintering gunshot rips
Between your comrades' eyes; hold it across
Their bodies' barricade of blood and loss.

You who live quietly in sunlit space
Reading The Herald after morning grace
Can count peace dear, when it has driven
Your sons to struggle for this grim, new heaven.

Comrade

Once only did I sleep with you;
A sleep and love again more sweet than I
Have ever known; without an aftertaste.
It was the first time; and a flower could not
Have been more softly opened, folded out.
Your hands were firm upon me: without fear
I lay arrested in a still delight—
Till suddenly the fountain in me woke.

My dear, it's years between; we've grown up fast
Each differently, each striving by itself.
I see you now a grey man without dreams,
Without a living, or an overcoat:
But sealed in struggle now, we are more close
Than if our bodies still were sealed in love.

from Call My People Home

A Documentary Poem for Radio or Choral Presentation

First Fisherman

Home was my boat: T.K. 2930—
Wintering on the Skeena with my nets
Cast up and down the river, to lure and haul
The dogfish. (His oil, they said, was needed overseas
For children torn from home, from a blitzed town.)
We made good money, and the sockeye run
That summer had outdone all the remembered seasons.
Now I could own my boat, *Tee Kay*, the Gillnetter
The snug and round one, warm as a woman
With her stove stocked at night and her lanterns lit

And anchor cast, brooding upon the water
Settled to sleep in the lap of the Skeena.

Now after thirty years, come from an island
To make a home near water: first on a sailing vessel
Towed, each season, to the fishing grounds:
Then the small gasboat, the gillnetter, that belonged
Not to the man who fished, but to the cannery.
Now after thirty years a free man, naturalized,
A man who owned his boat! I smelt the wind
Wetting my face, waves dashing against the *Tee Kay*'s sides
The grey dawn opening like a book
At the horizon's rim. I was my own master—
Must prove it now, today! Stooping over the engine
Priming the starter, opening the gas valve,
I felt her throbbing in answer; I laughed
And grasped the fly wheel, swung her over.
She churned off up the river—my own boat, my home.
That was before Pearl Harbor: before a December day
Spent on a restless sea; then anchor in the dusk
And down to bunk to have a bowl of rice.
By lantern light I turned the battery set
To hear brief messages from fishermen
From boat to shore, to learn the weather forecast.
Must have been dozing when I woke up sharp—
What was he saying? Some kind of government order?
"All fishing craft on the high seas must head at once
To the nearest port, report to authorities."
Did they not want our fish, the precious oil?
"No," said the voice, "Our boats were to be examined, searched
For hidden guns, for maps, for treachery . . ."
I heard, but could not understand. Obeyed,
But as a blind man. The numb fear about my boat,
Tee Kay, found no release in port, off shore,
Rubbing against a fleet of trollers, frail gillnetters
All heading down the Inverness and Tusk
All in the dark, with rumour flying fast.
No one knew more than his fear whispered,
No one explained.
We thought: perhaps it's all a mistake
Perhaps they'll line us up and do a search

Then leave us free for Skeena, Ucluelet—
The time is ripe, the season's fish are running.

* * *

Christmas at sea. The bitterest for me
That any year had given. Even so
Some had a celebration, pooled their funds
And bought the only chicken left in Alert Bay.
Others boiled cabbages in salt sea water,
Pulled out the playing cards and shrugged, and laughed.
As we set sail at midnight, now a thousand boats
Chained to the naval escort, steadily south
Into familiar waters where the forests cooled their feet
At rocks'-end, mountains swam in mist—
As we set sail for home, the young ones, born here, swore
Not softly, into the hissing night. The old men wept.

The rest takes little telling. On the fifteenth night
We passed Point Grey's low hulk, our long line wavered shoreward.
Dirty and hungry, sleep lying like a stone
Stuck in our heads, we nosed our broken craft
Into the wharf at Steveston, "Little Tokyo."
The crowd on the dock was silent. Women finding their men
Clung to them searchingly, saying never a word,
Leading them home to the *ofuro** and supper.
Others of us, like me, who knew no one,
Who had no place near the city's centre
Stood lonely on the wharf, holding the *Tee Kay*'s line
For the last time, watching the naval men
Make a note of her number, take my name.
That was the end of my thirty years at the fishing
And the end of my boat, my home.

**ofuro*—the bath

The Unquiet Bed

The woman I am
is not what you see
I'm not just bones
and crockery

the woman I am
knew love and hate
hating the chains
that parents make

longing that love
might set men free
yet hold them fast
in loyalty

the woman I am
is not what you see
move over love
make room for me

Bartok and the Geranium

She lifts her green umbrellas
Towards the pane
Seeking her fill of sunlight
Or of rain;
Whatever falls
She has no commentary
Accepts, extends,
Blows out her furbelows,
Her bustling boughs;
And all the while he whirls
Explodes in space,
Never content with this small room:
Not even can he be
Confined to sky
But must speed high and higher still
From galaxy to galaxy,
Wrench from the stars their momentary notes
Steal music from the moon.

She's daylight
He is dark
She's heaven-held breath
He storms and crackles
Spits with hell's own spark.

Yet in this room, this moment now
These together breathe and be:
She, essence of serenity,
He in a mad intensity
Soars beyond sight
Then hurls, lost Lucifer,
From heaven's height.

And when he's done, he's out:
She leans a lip against the glass
And preens herself in light.

Without Benefit of Tape

The real poems are being written in outports
on backwoods farms
in passageways where pantries still exist
or where geraniums
nail light to the window
while out of the window boy in the flying field
is pulled to heaven on the keel of a kite.

Stories breed in the north:
men with snow in their mouths
trample and shake at the bit
kneading the woman down under blankets of snow
icing her breath, her eyes.

The living speech is shouted out
by men and women leaving railways lines
to trundle home, pack-sacked
just company for deer or bear—
    Hallooed
across the counter, in a corner store
it booms upon the river's shore:
on midnight roads where hikers flag you down
speech echoes from the canyon's wall
    resonant
    indubitable.

Ralph Gustafson

(1909–1995)

Ralph Gustafson was born of Anglo-Swedish stock in Lime Ridge, Quebec, and raised in Sherbrooke. He graduated from Bishop's University in Lennoxville, then studied at Oxford. After a brief stint of teaching at St Alban's School in Brockville, Ontario, he returned to the UK in 1933 and remained there until 1939, publishing his first two books of poetry. Gustafson lived in New York City from 1939 until 1963, working during the war for British Information Services. Afterward, he returned to Canada, living in North Hatley and serving as poet-in-residence and a professor of English at Bishop's until his retirement in 1977.

Gustafson's many poetry collections include *The Golden Chalice* (1935), *Flight into Darkness* (1944), *Rivers among Rocks* (1960), *Rocky Mountain Poems* (1960), *Sift in an Hourglass* (1966), *Selected Poems* (1972), *Fire on Stone* (1974), *Corners in the Glass* (1977), *Landscape with Rain* (1980), *Gradations of Grandeur* (1982), *The Moment Is All: Selected Poems* (1983), *The Collected Poems of Ralph Gustafson* (1987), *Shadows in the Grass* (1991), *Tracks in the Snow* (1994), and *Visions Fugitive* (1996). He won a Governor General's Award in 1974 for *Fire on Stone* and was the recipient of the A.J.M. Smith Prize. He edited three anthologies for Penguin, including the early *Penguin Book of Canadian Verse* (1942), published for the troops in Europe, and the later, more inclusive versions, (1958, 1967, and 1984). He also published two collections of short stories: *The Brazen Tower* (1974) and *The Vivid Air* (1980).

Gustafson's early poems are measured, compressed closed lyrics, a sort of wise talk that can be richly meditative. At times they are dense, angular, syncopated, labyrinthine, and given to large-scale pronouncements and generalizations about historical events and human motivations. Inside their tortured syntax, the poet/journalist is often at odds with the man who feels; and the singer, with the thinking man. But in the fifties, a sea change occurs in Gustafson's poetry; new energies are released, and new landscapes and experiences appear that demand an opening out toward longer, more discursive and narrative modes. This new sense of emotional and physical space—far removed from the claustrophobic bed-sitters and flats of London and the garrets of Manhattan, and doubtless his reading of recent American poetics and decision to return home—pushed Gustafson toward extended forms, particularly the poem sequence, to which he brought lyric skills, outrageous wit, and an eye for significant detail.

Although in his essays he celebrated the ironic and meditative advantages of the sequence, Gustafson seems to have felt most comfortable with the short lyric or impromptu poem, the "inspired accident" or "devil in a halo": "The structuring, invisible, cogent, is from learning; the vitality of its cadence is from metrical control; the verbal music is from the tuned ear" (*Plummets and Other Partialities*, 1987).

"S.S.R., Lost at Sea." The *Times*

What heave of grapnels will resurrect the fabric
Of him, oceans drag, whereof he died,
Drowning sheer fathoms down, liquid to grab on—
Sucked by the liner, violence in her side?
Of no more sorrow than a mottled Grief
In marble. There fantastic in the murk,
Where saltwhite solitary forests leaf,
He swings: the dark anonymously works.
For who shall count the countless hands and limbs
In ditch and wall and wave, dead, dead
In Europe: touch with anguished name and claim
And actual tear, what must be generally said?
O let the heart's tough riggings salvage him,
Only whose lengths can grapple with these dead.

S.S. *Athenia*
September 3, 1939

Now at the Ocean's Verge

After great expectations, what
It is the time of life declares, that
Was there, is as the ebbtide shows:
These miles of sand packt and under a slant
Moon, the piling granite throw of surf,
Nothing but the beauty of itself.
Conch and shell and tugged weed cling
To the wave and are thrown.
        I turn to the seamark,
Climb descensions of pebbles and under the moon
Sit arms on knees, the night of stars,
Each in apportioned stance, intolerable before

The initialling mind. Indigence is all.
Concrete heaven only must suffice,
What expectation thought was possible:
Packt sand; a grasp, whorled and beautiful
Tossed by the tide, this accessible,
Reached for, empty shell.

The Newspaper

That photo of the little Jew in the cap,
Back to the gun held by the Nazi
With splay feet aware of the camera,
The little boy his hands in the air,
I turn over, I don't want to see it.
As a member of the human race. I am
Civilized. I am happy. I flap the
Newspaper with the picture over
So that when it is picked up to be taken
Down cellar to be put with the trash
I won't see it. I am sensitive.
The little boy is dead. He went
Through death. The cap is his best one.
He has brown eyes. He does not
Understand. Putting your hands
Up in front of a carbine prevents
The bullet. He is with the others.
Some of them he knows, so
It is all right. I turn
The paper over, the picture face
Down.

Wednesday at North Hatley

It snows on this place
And a gentleness obtains.
The garden fills with white,
Last summer's hedgerow
Bears a burden and birds
Are scarce. The grosbeak
Fights for seeds, the squirrel
Walks his slender wire.
There is a victory;
The heart endures, the house

Achieves its warmth and where
He needs to, man in woollen
Mitts, in muffler, without
A deathwish, northern, walks.
Except he stop at drifts
He cannot hear this snow,
The wind has fallen, and where
The lake awaits, the road
Is his. Softly the snow
Falls. Chance is against him.
But softly the snow falls.

In the Yukon

In Europe, you can't move without going down into history.
Here, all is a beginning. I saw a salmon jump,
Again and again, against the current,
The timbered hills a background, wooded green
Unpushed through; the salmon jumped, silver.
This was news, was commerce, at the end of the summer
The leap for dying. Moose came down to the water edge
To drink and the salmon turned silver arcs.
At night, the northern lights played, great over country
Without tapestry and coronations, kings crowned
With weights of gold. They were green,
Green hangings and great grandeur, over the north
Going to what no man can hold hard in mind,
The dredge of that gravity, being without experience.

Ramble on What in the World Why

Making a meaning out of everything that has happened,
The there-it-is, plainsong, pitch and pinnacle:
All is blanket-plucking otherwise. My father
Lighted a pipe out in a rowboat on the lake
When he fished and brought up Leviathan on a wormy
Hook, Ahab's pegleg in the belly,
So the watching boy said. Brahms
Percolated coffee, something to fiddle with,
The cup, the pot, the burner, to duck having
To write down music. Meaning is wearying, hammers,
Level, hacking out hunks of marble to raise
Cathedrals. I travel to get out of it to walk in them—
And run slambang into gospels of course,

Pegasus loose and the barndoor slammed.
Berryman took poems and jumped off a bridge.
It all comes down to making oneself one
With sea-slime. Knowing what is OK,
It's the why we've got to, the prehensile toes
And the rest of it, slops, jade and Jesus,
Venice, murder, virgins and music, that counts.

The Arrival of Wisdom

Of course the truth is there's no design,
Just process: which settles all-seeing God for good
And Him as a chemist mixing combinations
To get what He could declare without it,
Wanting to be worshipped, pitching beginnings
With a Bang into teleological void.

Truth goes on solving nothing, gluons
And quarks combine, come apart, not caring, stars
Go out, suns come on, the clutter ever
Expanding; sheep on the meadow chew, chew,
Man makes mince, until his neck-thongs shrivel
And breath departs lugging its baggage
Of unaccomplished dreams. What a celestial
Tautology to get there! fun in the dreaming,
Irony in choice, tragedy in the waste,
Getting nowhere with injustice.

Faith is an ignorance. Love without hurt
The only choice.

State of Affairs

This is a world of small boys with legs off.
Hip. Hip. They walk the world grown up.
Bitterness is not unknown.

Of course always there have been legs off
In a manner of speaking, taking legs off
To stand for eyes out,

But that is expected—the previous century is barbaric,
Few university degrees were granted,
TV was unknown.

It is too bad since we have so many computers,
So many carbines and combines that we have
So many legs off

But it can't be helped, boys must hop as best
They can, bitterness or not, there must be legs off
So there can be progress,

That is to say democratic election,
Culture for the collectivity and les
In the future legs off.

A.M. Klein

(1909–1972)

Abraham Moses Klein was born in Ratno, in the Ukraine, and the following year his family moved to Montreal. He began writing seriously as a student at McGill University (1926–30), where he first met A.J.M. Smith, F.R. Scott, Leon Edel, and Leo Kennedy. In 1930 he entered law school at the University of Montreal and received his LLB in 1933. He became editor of the *Canadian Jewish Chronicle* in 1938; the following year he began a long association with Sam Bronfman, as a speech writer and public relations adviser. While his literary reputation grew over the years—with the winning of a Governor General's Award in 1949 for *The Rocking Chair and Other Poems* (1948) and the great critical success of his novel *The Second Scroll* (1951)—Klein was never quite satisfied and was easily distracted into causes and kinds of writing for which he was neither gifted nor temperamentally disposed. He was a lawyer with the spirit and instincts of a poet and scholar; an employee of big business, but with a socialist's vision and conscience; and a deeply religious, though not orthodox, Jew struck by a growing horror at what had unfolded during the war in Europe. While these pressures and contradictions contributed to his eventual breakdown and long silence, it must be said that his unusual burdens fired a remarkable talent and inspired a body of work unique in vision and seldom surpassed in craft.

In his "Portrait of the Poet as Landscape," Klein speaks of the poet as someone compulsively engaged in naming, cataloguing, deciphering. Klein's tools included French, English, Latin, Yiddish, and Hebrew, and a love of language that expressed itself in infectious wit, outrageous pedantry, freewheeling wordplay, and a propensity for exotic vocabularies and frequent allusions to religious and literary classics. His biographer, Usher Caplan, calls attention in *Like One That Dreamed* to Klein's earthy humour and Joycean playfulness, qualities also noticed by his friend and fellow poet P.K. Page:

> His puns were unbelievable—he just couldn't resist them. Language was marvellously flexible on his tongue, he could bend it any way at all, make it do anything. Klein had that sense of the child in him, to delight in language and play with it. His joyfulness, his delight in things—he was so alive to the world.

Klein's devotion to craft and his love of language helped him rise above the causes and the occasions that triggered much of his poetry, so that he could make coexist, in a single literary context, the ridiculousness and the horror of Nazism, the sacredness and profanity of French-Canadian culture, and the sublimity and folly of artistic ambition and endeavour.

Klein's publications include *Hath Not a Jew* (1940), *The Hitleriad* (1944), *Poems* (1944), and *Collected Poems* (1974), edited with an introduction by Miriam Waddington. As Waddington points out, Klein's influence among Canadian poets has more to do with the later work, where "he put into poetry his double and sometimes triple tradition, extending ancient biblical metaphors to include modern grain elevators in a northern landscape, and finding a new metaphysic in such folk objects as rocking chairs and spinning wheels."

Klein had little use for prescriptive poetics:

> You know such questions elicit only the sheerest of arrogant balderdash. What shall I say in reply: "I sing because I must!"—How phoney! Or that I wish to improve the world with my rhyme!—How ridiculous! . . . I will have none of that cant. Simply expressed, I write poetry only to reveal my civilization, my sensitivities, my craftsmanship. This, however, is not to be quoted. (*Like One That Dreamed: A Portrait of A.M. Klein*, edited by Usher Caplan, 1982)

Heirloom

My father bequeathed me no wide estates;
No keys and ledgers were my heritage;
Only some holy books with *yahrzeit* dates
Writ mournfully upon a blank front page—

Books of the Baal Shem Tov, and of his wonders;
Pamphlets upon the devil and his crew;
Prayers against road demons, witches, thunders;
And sundry other tomes for a good Jew.

Beautiful: though no pictures on them, save
The scorpion crawling on a printed track;
The Virgin floating on a scriptural wave,
Square letters twinkling in the Zodiac.

The snuff left on this page, now brown and old,
The tallow stains of midnight liturgy—
These are my coat of arms, and these unfold
My noble lineage, my proud ancestry!

And my tears, too, have stained this heirloomed ground,
When reading in these treatises some weird
Miracle, I turned a leaf and found
A white hair fallen from my father's beard.

Autobiographical

Out of the ghetto streets where a Jewboy
Dreamed pavement into pleasant Bible-land,
Out of the Yiddish slums where childhood met
The friendly beard, the loutish Sabbath-goy,
Or followed, proud, the Torah-escorting band,
Out of the jargoning city I regret,
Rise memories, like sparrows rising from
The gutter-scattered oats,
Like sadness sweet of synagogal hum,
Like Hebrew violins
Sobbing delight upon their Eastern notes.

Again they ring their little bells, those doors
Deemed by the tender-year'd, magnificent:
Old Ashkenazi's cellar, sharp with spice;
The widows' double-parloured candy-stores
And nuggets sweet bought for one sweaty cent;
The warm fresh-smelling bakery, its pies,
Its cakes, its navel'd bellies of black bread;
The lintels candy-poled
Of barber-shop, bright-bottled, green, blue, red;

And fruit-stall piled, exotic,
And the big synagogue door, with letters of gold.

Again my kindergarten home is full—
Saturday night—with kin and compatriot:
My brothers playing Russian card-games; my
Mirroring sisters looking beautiful,
Humming the evening's imminent fox-trot;
My uncle Mayer, of blessed memory,
Still murmuring Maariv, counting holy words;
And the two strangers, come
Fiery from Volhynia's murderous hordes—
The cards and humming stop.
And I too swear revenge for that pogrom.

Occasions dear: the four-legged aleph named
And angel pennies dropping on my book;
The rabbi patting a coming scholar-head;
My mother, blessing candles, Sabbath-flamed,
Queenly in her Warsovian perruque;
My father pickabacking me to bed
To tell tall tales about the Baal Shem Tov—
Letting me curl his beard.
Oh memory of unsurpassing love,
Love leading a brave child
Through childhood's ogred corridors, unfear'd!

The week in the country at my brother's—(May
He own fat cattle in the fields of heaven!)
Its picking of strawberries from grassy ditch,
Its odour of dogrose and of yellowing hay—
Dusty, adventurous, sunny days, all seven!—
Still follow me, still warm me, still are rich
With the cow-tinkling peace of pastureland.
The meadow'd memory
Is sodded with its clover, and is spanned
By that same pillow'd sky
A boy on his back one day watched enviously.

And paved again the street: the shouting boys,
Oblivious of mothers on the stoops,
Playing the robust robbers and police,

The corncob battle—all high-spirited noise
Competitive among the lot-drawn groups.
Another day, of shaken apple trees
In the rich suburbs, and a furious dog,
And guilty boys in flight;
Hazelnut games, and games in the synagogue—
The burrs, the Haman rattle,
The Torah dance on Simchas-Torah night.

Immortal days of the picture calendar
Dear to me always with the virgin joy
Of the first flowering of senses five,
Discovering birds, or textures, or a star,
Or tastes sweet, sour, acid, those that cloy;
And perfumes. Never was I more alive.
All days thereafter are a dying off,
A wandering away
From home and the familiar. The years doff
Their innocence.
No other day is ever like that day.

I am no old man fatuously intent
On memoirs, but in memory I seek
The strength and vividness of nonage days,
Not tranquil recollection of event.
It is a fabled city that I seek;
It stands in Space's vapours and Time's haze;
Thence comes my sadness in remembered joy
Constrictive of the throat;
Thence do I hear, as heard by a Jewboy,
The Hebrew violins,
Delighting in the sobbed Oriental note.

For the Sisters of the Hotel Dieu

In pairs,
as if to illustrate their sisterhood,
the sisters pace the hospital garden walks.
In their robes black and white immaculate hoods
they are like birds,
the safe domestic fowl of the House of God.

O biblic birds,
who fluttered to me in my childhood illnesses
—me little, afraid, ill, not of your race,—
the cool wing for my fever, the hovering solace,
the sense of angels—
be thanked, O plumage of paradise, be praised.

Portrait of the Poet as Landscape

I

Not an editorial-writer, bereaved with bartlett,
mourns him, the shelved Lycidas.
No actress squeezes a glycerine tear for him.
The radio broadcast lets his passing pass.
And with the police, no record. Nobody, it appears,
either under his real name or his alias,
missed him enough to report.

It is possible that he is dead, and not discovered.
It is possible that he can be found some place
in a narrow closet, like the corpse in a detective story,
standing, his eyes staring, and ready to fall on his face.
It is also possible that he is alive
and amnesiac, or mad, or in retired disgrace,
or beyond recognition lost in love.

We are sure only that from our real society
he has disappeared; he simply does not count,
except in the pullulation of vital statistics—
somebody's vote, perhaps, an anonymous taunt
of the Gallup poll, a dot in a government table—
but not felt, and certainly far from eminent—
in a shouting mob, somebody's sigh.

O, he who unrolled our culture from his scroll—
the prince's quote, the rostrum-rounding roar—
who under one name made articulate
heaven, and under another the seven-circled air,
is, if he is at all, a number, an x,
a Mr Smith in a hotel register,—
incognito, lost, lacunal.

II

The truth is he's not dead, but only ignored—
like the mirroring lenses forgotten on a brow
that shine with the guilt of their unnoticed world.
The truth is he lives among neighbours, who, though they will allow
him a passable fellow, think him eccentric, not solid,
a type that one can forgive, and for that matter, forgo.

Himself he has his moods, just like a poet.
Sometimes, depressed to nadir, he will think all lost,
will see himself as throwback, relict, freak,
his mother's miscarriage, his great-grandfather's ghost,
and he will curse his quintuplet senses, and their tutors
in whom he put, as he should not have put, his trust.

Then he will remember his travels over that body—
the torso verb, the beautiful face of the noun,
and all those shaped and warm auxiliaries!
A first love it was, the recognition of his own.
Dear limbs adverbial, complexion of adjective,
dimple and dip of conjugation!

And then remember how this made a change in him
affecting for always the glow and growth of his being;
how suddenly was aware of the air, like shaken tinfoil,
of the patents of nature, the shock of belated seeing,
the lonelinesses peering from the eyes of crowds;
the integers of thought; the cube-roots of feeling.

Thus, zoomed to zenith, sometimes he hopes again,
and sees himself as a character, with a rehearsed role:
the Count of Monte Cristo, come for his revenges;
the unsuspected heir, with papers; the risen soul;
or the chloroformed prince awaking from his flowers;
or—deflated again—the convict on parole.

III

He is alone; yet not completely alone.
Pins on a map of a colour similar to his,
each city has one, sometimes more than one;
here, caretakers of art, in colleges;
in offices, there, with arm-bands, and green-shaded;
and there, pounding their catalogued beats in libraries,—

everywhere menial, a shadow's shadow.
And always for their egos—their outmoded art.
Thus, having lost the bevel in the ear,
they know neither up nor down, mistake the part
for the whole, curl themselves in a comma,
talk technics, make a colon their eyes. They distort—

such is the pain of their frustration—truth
to something convolute and cerebral.
How they do fear the slap of the flat of the platitude!
Now Pavlov's victims, their mouths water at bell,
the platter empty.
                                See they set twenty-one jewels
into their watches; the time they do not tell!

Some, patagonian in their own esteem,
and longing for the multiplying word,
join party and wear pins, now have a message,
an ear, and the convention-hall's regard.
Upon the knees of ventriloquists, they own,
of their dandled brightness, only the paint and board.

And some go mystical, and some go mad.
One stares at a mirror all day long, as if
to recognize himself; another courts
angels,—for here he does not fear rebuff;
and a third, alone, and sick with sex, and rapt,
doodles him symbols convex and concave.

O schizoid solitudes! O purities
curdling upon themselves! Who live for themselves,
or for each other, but for nobody else;
desire affection, private and public loves;
are friendly, and then quarrel and surmise
the secret perversions of each other's lives.

IV

He suspects that something has happened, a law
been passed, a nightmare ordered. Set apart,
he finds himself, with special haircut and dress,
as on a reservation. Introvert.
He does not understand this; sad conjecture
muscles and palls thrombotic on his heart.

He thinks an imposter, having studied his personal biography,
his gestures, his moods, now has come forward to pose
in the shivering vacuums his absence leaves.
Wigged with his laurel, that other, and faked with his face,
he pats the heads of his children, pecks his wife,
and is at home, and slippered, in his house.

So he guesses at the impertinent silhouette
that talks to his phone-piece and slits open his mail.
Is it the local tycoon who for a hobby
plays poet, he so epical in steel?
The orator, making a pause? Or is that man
he who blows his flash of brass in the jittering hall?

Or is he cuckolded by the troubadour
rich and successful out of celluloid?
Or by the don who unrhymes atoms? Or
the chemist death built up? Pride, lost impostor'd pride,
it is another, another, whoever he is,
who rides where he should ride.

V

Fame, the adrenalin: to be talked about;
to be a verb; to be introduced as *The:*
to smile with endorsement from slick paper; make
caprices anecdotal; to nod to the world; to see
one's name like a song upon the marquees played;
to be forgotten with embarrassment; to be—
to be.

It has its attractions, but is not the thing;
nor is it the ape mimesis who speaks from the tree
ancestral; nor the merkin joy . . .
Rather it is stark infelicity
which stirs him from his sleep, undressed, asleep
to walk upon roofs and window-sills and defy
the gape of gravity.

VI

Therefore he seeds illusions. Look, he is
the nth Adam taking a green inventory
in world but scarcely uttered, naming, praising,

the flowering fiats in the meadow, the
syllabled fur, stars aspirate, the pollen
whose sweet collision sounds eternally.

For to praise
the world—he, solitary man—is breath
to him. Until it has been praised, that part
has not been. Item by exciting item—
air to his lungs, and pressured blood to his heart,—
they are pulsated, and breathed, until they map,
not the world's, but his own body's chart!

And now in imagination he has climbed
another planet, the better to look
with single camera view upon this earth—
its total scope, and each afflated tick,
its talk, its trick, its tracklessness—and this,
this, he would like to write down in a book!

To find a new function for the *déclassé* craft
archaic like the fletcher's; to make a new thing;
to say the word that will become sixth sense;
perhaps by necessity and indirection bring
new forms to life, anonymously, new creeds—
O, somehow pay back the daily larcenies of the lung!

These are not mean ambitions. It is already something
merely to entertain them. Meanwhile, he
makes of his status as zero a rich garland,
a halo of his anonymity,
and lives alone, and in his secret shines
like phosphorus. At the bottom of the sea.

Earle Birney

(1904–1995)

Earle Birney's life was as colourful as his art—and as controversial. He was born in Calgary, but spent most of his youth in Banff and in Creston, BC. He graduated from the University of British Columbia in 1926. His graduate studies in California were interrupted by difficulties, mostly financial, which took him to Utah to teach, and to New York to work for the Trotskyites. With a grant from the Royal Society, he completed his doctoral studies in London, United Kingdom, and at the University of Toronto, where he lectured for several years and served as literary editor of the *Canadian Forum*. During the Second World War, he was a personnel selection officer overseas, and then, for a short time, supervisor of foreign language broadcasts to Europe for the CBC. Later he joined the English department at the University of British Columbia, where he founded and briefly headed the department of creative writing. He served as writer-in-residence at the University of Toronto and travelled widely throughout Asia, Europe, South America, and the United States.

His many poetry books include *David and Other Poems* (1942) and *Now Is Time* (1945), for each of which he won a Governor General's Award, *The Strait of Anian: Selected Poems* (1948), *Trial of a City and Other Verse* (1952), *Ice Cod Bell or Stone* (1962), *Near False Creek Mouth* (1964), *Selected Poems* (1966), *Rag and Bone Shop* (1970), *The Collected Poems of Earle Birney* (1975), and *Last Makings* (1991). He published two novels, *Turvey* (1949) and *Down the Long Table* (1955); two books on the creative process, *The Creative Writer* (1966) and *The Cow Jumped Over the Moon* (1972); and an autobiographical work, *Spreading Time, Book One, 1940–1949* (1980). *Words on Waves: The Selected Radio Plays of Earle Birney*, edited by Howard Fink and John Jackson, appeared in 1985.

In *The Creative Writer*, Birney speaks eloquently of the situation of the writer in Canada:

> It seems to me that the effective writer is one who is inwardly sure of the entire naturalness of his creative act. For instance, he must be aware that he is writing not merely because he is neurotic. Everybody's a bit queer and slightly mad, but I'm sure that my compulsion to construct more and more unprofitable verses isn't anywhere near as screwball as the compulsion of businessmen to

> make more and more money. But the writer who does not believe this is hamstrung from the start, haunted by a false diagnosis of his society, and driven either into a permanent state of apology and mock-modesty for his abnormality, or into snarling hatred for the nastiness of the normal.

Birney believed in the possibility of moral progress, but the scarred battleground of his own century troubled him deeply, driving him to satire or causing him to lash out in anger at human cruelty and indifference, and to despair at his own guilt and complicity. These responses reflect the Marxism of a generation caught in two world wars and a depression as well as the Puritanism of Birney's heritage. In addition to writing his major work, the narrative poem "David," Birney reinvented what I call the manic-depressive ode, building on the examples of Wordsworth, Keats, and Shelley. Down in the mouth, or disturbed by some personal dilemma, the poet's spirit is lifted by a landscape, a work of art, or a simple human gesture. The ode informs "A Walk in Kyoto" and a number of Birney's travel poems, which, in turn, influenced many of Al Purdy's poems.

"Living art," Birney says, "like anything else, stays alive only by changing." His own verse has travelled from the most traditional beginnings—including narratives, meditative lyrics, satires, nature poems, and odes—through years of experiment with typography and orthography, down the long road to concrete and performance poetry. He was a constant reviser of poems and a contributor to little magazines. "I don't know exactly where the literary Dew Line is this moment," he says, "but I'm sure it lies somewhere in the complicated world of today's little-little magazines and small-press chapbooks."

From the Hazel Bough

I met a lady
        on a lazy street
hazel eyes
        and little plush feet

her legs swam by
        like lovely trout
eyes were trees
        where boys leant out

hands in the dark and
        a river side
round breasts rising
        with the fingers' tide

she was plump as a finch
    and live as a salmon
gay as silk and
    proud as Brahmin

we winked when we met
    and laughed when we parted
never took time
    to be brokenhearted

but no man sees
    where the trout lie now
or what leans out
    from the hazel bough

David

I

David and I that summer cut trails on the Survey,
All week in the valley for wages, in air that was steeped
In the wail of mosquitoes, but over the sunalive week-ends
We climbed, to get from the ruck of the camp, the surly

Poker, the wrangling, the snoring under the fetid
Tents, and because we had joy in our lengthening coltish
Muscles, and mountains for David were made to see over,
Stairs from the valleys and steps to the sun's retreats.

II

Our first was Mount Gleam. We hiked in the long afternoon
To a curling lake and lost the lure of the faceted
Cone in the swell of its sprawling shoulders. Past
The inlet we grilled our bacon, the strips festooned

On a poplar prong, in the hurrying slant of the sunset.
Then the two of us rolled in the blanket while round us the cold
Pines thrust at the stars. The dawn was afloating
Of mists till we reached to the slopes above timber, and won

To snow like fire in the sunlight. The peak was upthrust
Like a fist in a frozen ocean of rock that swirled

Into valleys the moon could be rolled in. Remotely unfurling
Eastward the alien prairie glittered. Down through the dusty

Skree on the west we descended, and David showed me
How to use the give of shale for giant incredible
Strides. I remember, before the larches' edge,
That I jumped a long green surf of juniper flowing

Away from the wind, and landed in gentian and saxifrage
Spilled on the moss. Then the darkening firs
And the sudden whirring of water that knifed down a fern-hidden
Cliff and splashed unseen into mist in the shadows.

III

One Sunday on Rampart's arête a rainsquall caught us,
And passed, and we clung by our blueing fingers and bootnails
An endless hour in the sun, not daring to move
Till the ice had steamed from the slate. And David taught me

How time on a knife-edge can pass with the guessing of fragments
Remembered from poets, the naming of strata beside one,
And matching of stories from schooldays. . . . We crawled astride
The peak to feast on the marching ranges flagged

By the fading shreds of the shattered stormcloud. Lingering
There it was David who spied to the south, remote,
And unmapped, a sunlit spire on Sawback, an overhang
Crooked like a talon. David named it the Finger.

That day we chanced on the skull and the splayed white ribs
Of a mountain goat underneath a cliff face, caught
On a rock. Around were the silken feathers of hawks.
And that was the first I knew that a goat could slip.

IV

And then Inglismaldie. Now I remember only
The long ascent of the lonely valley, the live
Pine spirally scarred by lightning, the slicing pipe
Of invisible pika, and great prints, by the lowest

Snow, of a grizzly. There it was too that David
Taught me to read the scroll of coral in limestone

And the beetle-seal in the shale of ghostly trilobites,
Letters delivered to man from the Cambrian waves.

V

On Sundance we tried from the col and the going was hard.
The air howled from our feet to the smudged rocks
And the papery lake below. At an outthrust we baulked
Till David clung with his left to a dint in the scarp,

Lobbed the iceaxe over the rocky lip,
Slipped from his holds and hung by the quivering pick,
Twisted his long legs up into space and kicked
To the crest. Then grinning, he reached with his freckled wrist

And drew me up after. We set a new time for that climb.
That day returning we found a robin gyrating
In grass, wing-broken. I caught it to tame but David
Took and killed it, and said, "Could you teach it to fly?"

VI

In August, the second attempt, we ascended The Fortress.
By the forks of the Spray we caught five trout and fried them
Over a balsam fire. The woods were alive
With the vaulting of mule-deer and drenched with clouds
all the morning,

Till we burst at noon to the flashing and floating round
Of the peaks. Coming down we picked in our hats the bright
And sunhot raspberries, eating them under a mighty
Spruce, while a marten moving like quicksilver scouted us.

VII

But always we talked of the Finger on Sawback, unknown
And hooked, till the first afternoon in September we slogged
Through the musky woods, past a swamp that quivered
with frog-song,
And camped by a bottle-green lake. But under the cold

Breath of the glacier sleep would not come, the moon-light
Etching the Finger. We rose and trod past the feathery
Larch, while the stars went out, and the quiet heather
Flushed, and the skyline pulsed with the surging bloom

Of incredible dawn in the Rockies. David spotted
Bighorns across the moraine and sent them leaping
With yodels the ramparts redoubled and rolled to the peaks,
And the peaks to the sun. The ice in the morning thaw

Was a gurgling world of crystal and cold blue chasms,
And seracs that shone like frozen saltgreen waves.
At the base of the Finger we tried once and failed. Then David
Edged to the west and discovered the chimney; the last

Hundred feet we fought the rock and shouldered and kneed
Our way for an hour and made it. Unroping we formed
A cairn on the rotting tip. Then I turned to look north
And the glistening wedge of giant Assiniboine, heedless

Of handhold. And one foot gave. I swayed and shouted.
David turned sharp and reached out his arm and steadied me,
Turning again with a grin and his lips ready
To jest. But the strain crumbled his foothold. Without

A gasp he was gone. I froze to the sound of grating
Edge-nails and fingers, the slither of stones, the lone
Second of silence, the nightmare thud. Then only
The wind and the muted beat of unknowing cascades.

VIII

Somehow I worked down the fifty impossible feet
To the ledge, calling and getting no answer but echoes
Released in the cirque, and trying not to reflect
What an answer would mean. He lay still, with his lean

Young face upturned and strangely unmarred, but his legs
Splayed beneath him, beside the final drop,
Six hundred feet sheer to the ice. My throat stopped
When I reached him, for he was alive. He opened his grey

Straight eyes and brokenly murmured "over . . . over."
And I, feeling beneath him a cruel fang
Of the ledge thrust in his back, but not understanding,
Mumbled stupidly, "Best not to move," and spoke

Of his pain. But he said, "I can't move. . . . If only I felt
Some pain." Then my shame stung the tears to my eyes

As I crouched, and I cursed myself, but he cried,
Louder, "No, Bobbie! Don't ever blame yourself.

I didn't test my foothold." He shut the lids
Of his eyes to the stare of the sky, while I moistened his lips
From our water flask and tearing my shirt into strips
I swabbed the shredded hands. But the blood slid

From his side and stained the stone and the thirsting lichens,
And yet I dared not lift him up from the gore
Of the rock. Then he whispered, "Bob, I want to go over!"
This time I knew what he meant and I grasped for a lie

And said, "I'll be back here by midnight with ropes
And men from the camp and we'll cradle you out." But I knew
That the day and the night must pass and the cold dews
Of another morning before such men unknowing

The ways of mountains could win to the chimney's top.
And then, how long? And he knew . . . and the hell of hours
After that, if he lived till we came, roping him out.
But I curled beside him and whispered, "The bleeding will stop.

You can last." He said only, "Perhaps. . . . For what? A wheelchair,
Bob?" His eyes brightening with fever upbraided me.
I could not look at him more and said, "Then I'll stay
With you." But he did not speak, for the clouding fever.

I lay dazed and stared at the long valley,
The glistening hair of a creek on the rug stretched
By the firs, while the sun leaned round and flooded the ledge,
The moss, and David still as a broken doll.

I hunched to my knees to leave, but he called and his voice
Now was sharpened with fear. "For Christ's sake push me over!
If I could move. . . . Or die. . . ." The sweat ran from his forehead,
But only his eyes moved. A hawk was buoying

Blackly its wings over the wrinkled ice.
The purr of a waterfall rose and sank with the wind.
Above us climbed the last joint of the Finger
Beckoning bleakly the wide indifferent sky.

Even then in the sun it grew cold lying there. . . . And I knew
He had tested his holds. It was I who had not. . . . I looked
At the blood on the ledge, and the far valley. I looked
At last in his eyes. He breathed, "I'd do it for you, Bob."

IX

I will not remember how nor why I could twist
Up the wind-devilled peak, and down through the chimney's empty
Horror, and over the traverse alone. I remember
Only the pounding fear I would stumble on It

When I came to the grave-cold maw of the bergschrund . . . reeling
Over the sun-cankered snowbridge, shying the caves
In the névé . . . the fear, and the need to make sure It was there
On the ice, the running and falling and running, leaping

Of gaping greenthroated crevasses, alone and pursued
By the Finger's lengthening shadow. At last through the fanged
And blinding seracs I slid to the milky wrangling
Falls at the glacier's snout, through the rocks piled huge

On the humped moraine, and into the spectral larches,
Alone. By the glooming lake I sank and chilled
My mouth but I could not rest and stumbled still
To the valley, losing my way in the ragged marsh.

I was glad of the mire that covered the stains, on my ripped
Boots, of his blood, but panic was on me, the reek
Of the bog, the purple glimmer of toadstools obscene
In the twilight. I staggered clear to a firewaste, tripped

And fell with a shriek on my shoulder. It somehow eased
My heart to know I was hurt, but I did not faint
And I could not stop while over me hung the range
Of the Sawback. In blackness I searched for the trail by the creek

And found it. . . . My feet squelched a slug and horror
Rose again in my nostrils. I hurled myself
Down the path. In the woods behind some animal yelped.
Then I saw the glimmer of tents and babbled my story.

I said that he fell straight to the ice where they found him,
And none but the sun and incurious clouds have lingered

Around the marks of that day on the ledge of the Finger,
That day, the last of my youth, on the last of our mountains.

Bushed

He invented a rainbow but lightning struck it
shattered it into the lake-lap of a mountain
so big his mind slowed when he looked at it

Yet he built a shack on the shore
learned to roast porcupine belly and
wore the quills on his hatband

At first he was out with the dawn
whether it yellowed bright as wood-columbine
or was only a fuzzed moth in a flannel of storm
But he found the mountain was clearly alive
sent messages whizzing down every hot morning
boomed proclamations at noon and spread out
a white guard of goat
before falling asleep on its feet at sundown

When he tried his eyes on the lake   ospreys
would fall like valkyries
choosing the cut-throat
He took then to waiting
till the night smoke rose from the boil of the sunset

But the moon carved unknown totems
out of the lakeshore
owls in the beardusky woods derided him
moosehorned cedars circled his swamps and tossed
their antlers up to the stars
Then he knew   though the mountain slept   the winds
were shaping its peak to an arrowhead
poised

And now he could only
bar himself in and wait
for the great flint to come singing into his heart

1951

A Walk in Kyoto

all week the maid tells me bowing
her doll's body at my mat is Boys' Day
also please Man's Day and gravely
bends deeper the magnolia sprig in my alcove
is it male The old discretions of Zen
were not shaped for my phallic western eye
there is so much discretion
in this small bowed body of an empire
(the wild hair of waterfalls combed straight
in the ricefields the inn-maid retreating
with the face of a shut flower) i stand hunched
and clueless like a castaway in the shoals of my room

when I slide my parchment door to stalk awkward
through lilliput gardens framed & untouchable
as watercolours the streets look much as everywhere
men are being pulled past on the strings
of their engines the legs of the boys
are revolved by a thousand pedals
& all the faces are taut & unfestive as Moscow's
or Toronto's or mine

Lord Buddha help us all there is vigour enough
in these islands & in all islands reefed & resounding
with cities but the pitch is high high as the ping
of cicadas (those small strained motors concealed
in the propped pines by the dying river) & only male
as the stretched falsetto of actors mincing the roles
of kabuki women or female only as the lost heroes
womanized in the Ladies' Opera—
where in these alleys jammed with competing waves
of signs in two tongues & three scripts
can the simple song of a man be heard?

by the shoguns' palace the Important Cultural Property
stripped for tiptoeing schoolgirls i stare
at the staring penned carp that flail
on each other's backs to the shrunk pool's edge
for the crumb this non-fish tossed
is this the Day's one parable

or under that peeling pagoda the 500 tons
of hermaphrodite Word?

At the inn i prepare to surrender again
my defeated shoes to the bending maid   but suddenly
the closed lotus opens to a smile & she points
to where   over my shoulder   above the sagging tiles
tall in the bare sky & huge as Gulliver
a carp is rising   golden & fighting
thrusting its paper body up from the fist
of a small boy on an empty roof   higher
& higher   into the endless winds of the world

1958

The Bear on the Delhi Road

Unreal   tall as a myth
by the road the Himalayan bear
is beating the brilliant air
with his crooked arms
about him two men   bare
spindly as locusts   leap

One pulls on a ring
in the great soft nose   His mate
flicks   flicks with a stick
up at the rolling eyes

They have not led him here
down from the fabulous hills
to this bald alien plain
and the clamorous world   to kill
but simply to teach him to dance

They are peaceful both   these spare
men of Kashmir   and the bear
alive is their living   too
If   far on the Delhi way
around him galvanic they dance
it is merely to wear   wear
from his shaggy body the tranced
wish forever to stay

only an ambling bear
four-footed in berries

It is no more joyous for them
in this hot dust to prance
out of reach of the praying claws
sharpened to paw for ants
in the shadows of deodars
It is not easy to free
myth from reality
or rear this fellow up
to lurch   lurch with them
in the tranced dancing of men

Srinagar 1958—Ile des Porquerolles 1959

A.J.M. Smith

(1902–1980)

Arthur James Marshall Smith was born and raised in Montreal. After spending time in the UK as a teenager, he took the Cambridge Local Examinations, failing all but English and history. As an undergraduate at McGill University, he co-edited the *McGill Daily Literary Supplement* and, with F.R. Scott, co-founded the *McGill Fortnightly Review*, whose Modernist bent attracted writers such as A.M. Klein, Leo Kennedy, and Leon Edel. His own poems appeared in *Dial* shortly before that influential magazine folded. After completing a doctorate in 1931, Smith co-edited with Kennedy and Scott what for Canada was a groundbreaking anthology, *New Provinces*.

Smith then took a position in the English department at Michigan State University, in East Lansing, where he remained until retirement. He spent his summers in North Hatley, Quebec, and continued to be active as a poet and critic, editing *The Book of Canadian Poetry* in 1943 and numerous anthologies of poetry and criticism, including *Masks of Poetry: Canadian Critics on Canadian Verse* (1962), *The Blasted Pine: An Anthology of Satire, Invective and Disrespectful Verse* (1957), and *Modern Canadian Verse in English and French* (1967). His many works of poetry include *News of the Phoenix and Other Poems* (1943), *A Sort of Ecstasy* (1957), *Poems New and Collected* (1967), and a critical edition, *The Complete Poems of A.J.M. Smith*, edited by Brian Trahearne (2006).

To glimpse the ongoing debate over Smith's importance as a poet, it is worth reading Milton Wilson's "Second and Third Thoughts about Smith" (*Canadian Literature,* No. 15, winter 1963) and Sandra Djwa's article, "A.J.M. Smith: Of Metaphysics and Dry Bones" (*Studies in Canadian Literature*, Vol. 3, No. 1, 1978). The former argues that Smith often lacks the thrust and dynamism of Donne and the Metaphysical poets of the seventeenth century, and the latter makes a case for Smith's "extraordinary versatility." Smith suggests his poems should be viewed as part of the depersonalization poetic: "None of them is reverie, confession, or direct self-expression. . . . The 'I' of the poem, the protagonist of its tragedy or the clown of its pantomime, is not me. As Rimbaud said, *Je est un autre*, I is another." Djwa argues that Smith brings an ironic Modernist sensibility to bear on the spirit/flesh dichotomies that trouble the Metaphysical poets.

Smith's best poems are complex, densely knit constructs that require thought, even some knowledge of literature and the classics, if their allusions and wordplay are to be fully understood. Yet even the most difficult poems exhibit a prosodic elegance that can be appreciated by anyone who loves language. A witty and ironic social critic, Smith addressed the materialism, loss of faith, and disillusionment of the postwar period with grace, urbanity, and the well-tuned ear of a lyric poet, using a host of personas, his steely intelligence, and largely formal verse not always able to mask a deeply emotional, Romantic sensibility.

Like an Old Proud King in a Parable

A bitter king in anger to be gone
From fawning courtier and doting queen
Flung hollow sceptre and gilt crown away,
And breaking bound of all his counties green
He made a meadow in the northern stone
And breathed a palace of inviolable air
To cage a heart that carolled like a swan,
And slept alone, immaculate and gay,
With only his pride for a paramour.

O who is that bitter king? It is not I.

Let me, I beseech thee, Father, die
From this fat royal life, and lie

As naked as a bridegroom by his bride,
And let that girl be the cold goddess Pride:

And I will sing to the barren rock
Your difficult, lonely music, heart,
Like an old proud king in a parable.

A Hyacinth for Edith

Now that the ashen rain of gummy April
Clacks like a weedy and stain'd mill,

So that all the tall purple trees
Are pied porpoises in swishing seas,

And the yellow horses and milch cows
Come out of their long frosty house

To gape at the straining flags
The brown pompous hill wags,

I'll seek within the wood's black plinth
A candy-sweet sleek wooden hyacinth—

And in its creaking naked glaze,
And in the varnish of its blaze,

The bird of ecstasy shall sing again,
The bearded sun shall spring again—

A new ripe fruit upon the sky's high tree,
A flowery island in the sky's wide sea—

And childish cold ballades, long dead, long mute,
Shall mingle with the gayety of bird and fruit,

And fall like cool and soothing rain
On all the ardour, all the pain

Lurking within this tinsel paradise
Of trams and cinemas and manufactured ice,

Till I am grown again my own lost ghost
Of joy, long lost, long given up for lost,

And walk again the wild and sweet wildwood
Of our lost innocence, our ghostly childhood.

The Lonely Land

Cedar and jagged fir
uplift sharp barbs
against the gray
and cloud-piled sky;
and in the bay
blown spume and windrift
and thin, bitter spray
snap
at the whirling sky;
and the pine trees
lean one way.

A wild duck calls
to her mate,
and the ragged
and passionate tones
stagger and fall,
and recover,
and stagger and fall,
on these stones—
are lost
in the lapping of water
on smooth, flat stones.

This is a beauty
of dissonance,
this resonance
of stony strand,
this smoky cry
curled over a black pine
like a broken
and wind-battered branch
when the wind
bends the tops of the pines
and curdles the sky
from the north.

This is the beauty
of strength
broken by strength
and still strong.

The Plot against Proteus

This is a theme for muted coronets
To dangle from debilitated heads
Of navigation, kings, or riverbeds
That rot or rise what time the seamew sets
Her course by stars among the smoky tides
Entangled. Old saltencrusted Proteus treads
Once more the watery shore that water weds
While rocking fathom bell rings round and rides.

Now when the blind king of the water thinks
The sharp hail of the salt out of his eyes
To abdicate, run thou, O Prince, and fall
Upon him. This cracked walrus skin that stinks
Of the rank sweat of a mermaid's thighs
Cast off, and nab him; when you have him, call.

News of the Phoenix

They say the Phoenix is dying, some say dead.
Dead without issue is what one message said,
But that has been suppressed, officially denied.

I think myself the man who sent it lied.
In any case, I'm told, he has been shot,
As a precautionary measure, whether he did or not.

Prothalamium

Here in this narrow room there is no light;
The dead tree sings against the window pane;
Sand shifts a little, easily; the wall
Responds a little, inchmeal, slowly, down.

My sister, whom my dust shall marry, sleeps
Alone, yet knows what bitter root it is
That stirs within her; see, it splits the heart—

Warm hands grown cold, grown nerveless as a fin,
And lips enamelled to a hardness—
Consummation ushered in
By wind in sundry corners.

This holy sacrament was solemnized
In harsh poetics a good while ago—
At Malfy and the Danish battlements,
And by that preacher from a cloud in Paul's.

No matter: each must read the truth himself,
Or, reading it, reads nothing to the point.
Now these are me, whose thought is mine, and hers,
Who are alone here in this narrow room—
Tree fumbling pane, bell tolling,
Ceiling dripping and the plaster falling,
And Death, the voluptuous, calling.

The Wisdom of Old Jelly Roll

How all men wrongly death to dignify
Conspire, I tell. Parson, poetaster, pimp,
Each acts or acquiesces. They prettify,
Dress up, deodorize, embellish, primp,
And make a show of Nothing. Ah, but metaphysics
laughs: she touches, tastes, and smells
—Hence knows—the diamond holes that make a net.
Silence resettled testifies to bells.
"Nothing" depends on "Thing," which is or was:
So death makes life or makes life's worth, a worth
Beyond all highfalutin' woes or shows
To publish and confess. "Cry at the birth,
Rejoice at the death," old Jelly Roll said,
Being on whisky, ragtime, chicken, and the scriptures fed.

Al Purdy

(1918–2000)

Purdy was born in Wooler, Ontario, and educated at Albert College in Belleville. At 16 he dropped out of school and began his wanderings, working at odd jobs, putting in time with the RCAF in British Columbia, and trying his hand at writing. He could not support himself by writing until he sold a script to the CBC in 1955, after which he moved to Montreal. He built a cabin at Roblin Lake in Ameliasburgh, Ontario, travelling from there to the Cariboo, Newfoundland, Baffin Island, Cuba, Greece, and the UK, and serving as writer-in-residence at various Canadian universities. "I write poems like spiders spin webs," he said, "and perhaps for much the same reason, to support my existence . . . unless one is a stone one doesn't sit still. And perhaps new areas of landscape awaken old areas of one's self."

Purdy's development was haphazard and independent, a product of his continuous experimentation and discovery of interesting poets. He objected as much to the "sweetness and iambic smoothness" of academic poets as to the "togetherness . . . of the Duncan-Creeley-Olson bunch." "I have no one style," he said in a letter to Charles Bukowski, "I have a dozen: have got to be virtuoso enough so I can shift gears like a hot-rod kid—I doubt that my exact combo ever came along before. Unlike some, I have no ideas about being a specific kind of poet. I mean, I don't make rules and say THIS is what a poet HAS to be. I don't know what the hell a poet is or care much. I do know what he isn't sometimes."

Despite these protests, Purdy developed a poetic voice that is unmistakable, characterized by a mixture of profundity and self-deprecating chattiness, homely observation and historical allusion. Poetry, his "umbilical cord with the world and other people," should, he said, resemble prose but make it "suddenly glow like coloured glass in a black and white world." Structurally, his verse is equally recognizable. His poems are often open-ended, the apparent subjects deliberately unresolved. There is no fixed subject outside the poem other than the perceiving consciousness of the poet; in other words, the subject of the poem is the *process itself*. In his best work, wit, erudition, and self-mockery rescue him from the pitfalls of such indeterminacy. Of poetic process, Purdy said:

> There ought to be a quality in a good poet beyond any analysis, the part of his mind that leaps from one point to another, sideways, backwards, ass-over-electric-kettle. This quality is not logic, and the result may not be consistent with the rest of the poem when it happens, though it may be.... And when this happens, or when you think it does, that time is joyous, and you experience something beyond experience. Like discovering you can fly, or that relative truth may blossom into an absolute. And the absolute must be attacked again and again, until you find something that will stand up, may not be denied, which becomes a compass point by which to move somewhere else.... And sometimes—if you're lucky—a coloured fragment may slip through into the light when you're writing a poem.

His poetry publications include the modest, self-published *The Enchanted Echo* (1944), *Poems for All the Annettes* (1962), *The Cariboo Horses* (1965, Governor General's Award), *North of Summer* (1967), *Wild Grape Wine* (1968), *Love in a Burning Building* (1970), *Selected Poems* (1972), *Sex and Death* (1973), *The Poems of Al Purdy* (1976), *The Stone Bird* (1981), *Piling Blood* (1984), *The Collected Poems of Al Purdy* (1986, Governor General's Award), and *Rooms for Rent in the Outer Planets* (1996), which contains a medley of his critical comments on poetry gathered by Sam Solecki. Purdy edited *Storm Warning* (1971), *Storm Warning II* (1976), and a collection of Canadian views of the United States called *The New Romans* (1968). He published a novel, *A Splinter in the Heart* (1990); a memoir, *Reaching for the Beaufort Sea* (1993); and *Starting from Ameliasburgh: The Collected Prose of Al Purdy* (1995).

Home-Made Beer

I was justly annoyed 10 years ago
in Vancouver: making beer in a crock
under the kitchen table when this
next-door youngster playing with my own
kid managed to sit down in it and
emerged with one end malted—
With excessive moderation I yodelled
at him
          "Keep your ass out of my beer!"
          and the little monster fled—
Whereupon my wife appeared from the bathroom
where she had been brooding for days
over the injustice of being a woman and
attacked me with a broom—

With commendable savoir faire I broke
the broom across my knee (it hurt too) and
then she grabbed the breadknife and made
for me with fairly obvious intentions—
I tore open my shirt and told her calmly
with bared breast and a minimum of boredom
"Go ahead! Strike! Go ahead!"
Icicles dropped from her fiery eyes as she
snarled
"I wouldn't want to go to jail
for killing a thing like you!"
I could see at once that she loved me
tho it was cleverly concealed—
For the next few weeks I had to distribute
the meals she prepared among neighbouring
dogs because of the rat poison and
addressed her as Missus Borgia—
That was a long time ago and while
at the time I deplored her lack of
self-control I find myself sentimental
about it now for it can never happen again—

Sept. 22, 1964: PS, I was wrong—

The Country North of Belleville

Bush land scrub land—
Cashel Township and Wollaston
Elzevir McClure and Dungannon
green lands of Weslemkoon Lake
where a man might have some
opinion of what beauty
is and none deny him
for miles—

Yet this is the country of defeat
where Sisyphus rolls a big stone
year after year up the ancient hills
picnicking glaciers have left strewn
with centuries' rubble
backbreaking days
in the sun and rain

when realization seeps slow in the mind
without grandeur or self-deception in
                    noble struggle
of being a fool—

A country of quiescence and still distance
a lean land
                    not like the fat south
with inches of black soil on
                    earth's round belly—
And where the farms are
                    it's as if a man stuck
both thumbs in the stony earth and pulled
                                        it apart
                                        to make room
enough between the trees
for a wife
                    and maybe some cows and
                    room for some
of the more easily kept illusions—
And where the farms have gone back
to forest
                    are only soft outlines
                    shadowy differences—

Old fences drift vaguely among the trees
                    a pile of moss-covered stones
gathered for some ghost purpose
has lost meaning under the meaningless sky
                    —they are like cities under water
and the undulating green waves of time
                    are laid on them—

This is the country of our defeat
                    and yet
during the fall plowing a man
might stop and stand in a brown valley of the furrows
                    and shade his eyes to watch for the same
                    red patch mixed with gold
                    that appears on the same
                    spot in the hills
                    year after year
                    and grow old

plowing and plowing a ten-acre field until
the convolutions run parallel with his own brain—

And this is a country where the young
          leave quickly
unwilling to know what their fathers know
or think the words their mothers do not say—
Herschel Monteagle and Faraday
lakeland rockland and hill country
a little adjacent to where the world is
a little north of where the cities are and
sometime
we may go back there
          to the country of our defeat
Wollaston Elzevir and Dungannon
and Weslemkoon lake land
where the high townships of Cashel
          McClure and Marmora once were—
But it's been a long time since
and we must enquire the way
          of strangers—

The Cariboo Horses

At 100 Mile House the cowboys ride in rolling
stagey cigarettes with one hand reining
half-tame bronco rebels on a morning grey as stone
—so much like riding dangerous women
      with whiskey coloured eyes—
such women as once fell dead with their lovers
with fire in their heads and slippery froth on thighs
—Beaver and Carrier women maybe or
     Blackfoot squaws far past the edge of this valley
on the other side of those two toy mountain ranges
      from the sunfierce plains beyond—

But only horses
               waiting in stables
hitched at taverns
               standing at dawn
pastured outside the town with
jeeps and fords and chevvys and
busy muttering stake trucks rushing

importantly over roads of man's devising
over the safe known roads of the ranchers
families and merchants of the town—
                    On the high prairie
are only horse and rider
                    wind in dry grass
clopping in silence under the toy mountains
dropping sometimes and
                    lost in the dry grass
                    golden oranges of dung—

Only horses
        no stopwatch memories or palace ancestors
not Kiangs hauling undressed stone in the Nile Valley
and having stubborn Egyptian tantrums or
Onagers racing thru Hither Asia and
the last Quagga screaming in African highlands
        lost relatives of these
        whose hooves were thunder
the ghosts of horses battering thru the wind
whose names were the wind's common usage
whose life was the sun's
        arriving here at chilly noon
        in the gasoline smell of the
        dust and waiting 15 minutes
        at the grocer's—

Wilderness Gothic

Across Roblin Lake, two shores away,
they are sheathing the church spire
with new metal. Someone hangs in the sky
over there from a piece of rope,
hammering and fitting God's belly-scratcher,
working his way up along the spire
until there's nothing left to nail on—

Perhaps the workman's faith reaches beyond:
touches intangibles, wrestles with Jacob,
replacing rotten timber with pine thews,
pounds hard in the blue cave of the sky,
contends heroically with difficult problems of
gravity, sky navigation and mythopoeia,

his volunteer time and labour donated to God,
minus sick benefits of course on a non-union job—

Fields around are yellowing into harvest,
nestling and fingerling are sky and water borne,
death is yodelling quiet in green woodlots,
and bodies of three young birds have disappeared
in the sub-surface of the new county highway—

That picture is incomplete, part left out
that might alter the whole Dürer landscape:
gothic ancestors peer from medieval sky,
dour faces trapped in photograph albums escaping
to clop down iron roads with matched greys:
work-sodden wives groping inside their flesh
for what keeps moving and changing and flashing
beyond and past the long frozen Victorian day.
A sign of fire and brimstone? A two-headed calf
born in the barn last night? A sharp female agony?
An age and a faith moving into transition,
the dinner cold and new-baked bread a failure,
deep woods shiver and water drops hang pendant,
double-yolked eggs and the house creaks a little—
Something is about to happen. Leaves are still.
Two shores away, a man hammering in the sky.
Perhaps he will fall.

Arctic Rhododendrons

They are small purple surprises
in the river's white racket
and after you've seen them
a number of times
in water-places
where their silence seems
related to river-thunder
you think of them as "noisy flowers"
Years ago
it may have been
that lovers came this way
stopped in the outdoor hotel
to watch the water floorshow
and lying prone together

where the purged green
boils to a white heart
and the shore trembles
like a stone song
with bodies touching
flowers were their conversation
and love the sound of a colour
that lasts two weeks in August
and then dies
except for the three or four
I pressed in a letter
and sent whispering to you

Lament for the Dorsets

(Eskimos extinct in the 14th century A.D.)

Animal bones and some mossy tent rings
scrapers and spearheads carved ivory swans
all that remains of the Dorset giants
who drove the Vikings back to their long ships
talked to spirits of earth and water
—a picture of terrifying old men
so large they broke the backs of bears
so small they lurk behind bone rafters
in the brain of modern hunters
among good thoughts and warm things
and come out at night
to spit on the stars

The big men with clever fingers
who had no dogs and hauled their sleds
over the frozen northern oceans
awkward giants
                                   killers of seal
they couldn't compete with little men
who came from the west with dogs
Or else in a warm climatic cycle
the seals went back to cold waters
and the puzzled Dorsets scratched their heads
with hairy thumbs around 1350 A.D.
—couldn't figure it out

went around saying to each other
plaintively
                    "What's wrong? What happened?
                    Where are the seals gone?"
And died

Twentieth century people
apartment dwellers
executives of neon death
warmakers with things that explode
—they have never imagined us in their future
how could we imagine them in the past
squatting among the moving glaciers
six hundred years ago
with glowing lamps?
As remote or nearly
as the trilobites and swamps
when coal became
or the last great reptile hissed
at a mammal the size of a mouse
that squeaked and fled

Did they ever realize at all
what was happening to them?
Some old hunter with one lame leg
a bear had chewed
sitting in a caribou skin tent
—the last Dorset?
Let's say his name was Kudluk
carving 2-inch ivory swans
for a dead grand-daughter
taking them out of his mind
the places in his mind
where pictures are
He selects a sharp stone tool
to gouge a parallel pattern of lines
on both sides of the swan
holding it with his left hand
bearing down and transmitting
his body's weight
from brain to arm and right hand

and one of his thoughts
turns to ivory
The carving is laid aside
in beginning darkness
at the end of hunger
after a while wind
blows down the tent and snow
begins to cover him
After 600 years
the ivory thought
is still warm

F.R. Scott

(1899–1985)

Frank Scott was born and raised in Quebec City, where his father was an Anglican minister and a poet. He graduated from Bishop's College in Lennoxville, was a Rhodes scholar at Oxford, and then studied law at McGill University, where he graduated and joined the faculty in 1928. He was dean of law from 1961 to 1964 and retired from McGill in 1968. He was active in founding the League for Social Reconstruction in 1932 and the Co-operative Commonwealth Federation (the CCF, which eventually became the NDP), drafting its Regina Manifesto and acting as the CCF's national chairman from 1942 to 1950. He contributed to *Social Planning for Canada* (1935), wrote *Canada and the United States* (1941), edited *Canada Today: A Study of Her National Interests and National Policy* (1943), and co-edited with Michael Oliver *Quebec States Her Case* (1964). Scott not only became an expert on international law and constitutional affairs, but also defended D.H. Lawrence's *Lady Chatterley's Lover* in the courts and won a case against the notorious Padlock Law of the Duplessis government. He published *Essays on the Constitution: Aspects of Canadian Law and Politics* (1977, Governor General's Award), *A New Endeavour: Selected Political Essays, Letters, and Addresses* (1986), and numerous translations, including *St. Denys Garneau and Anne Hébert* (1978).

"What is my personal conception of poetry?" Scott wrote. "If I could define it, it would not be too different from my conception of life itself. The making of something new and true. An exploring of the frontiers of the world inside and the world outside man. And a kind of umbilical contemplation from within the poem itself of its own dynamic and central structure." His examination of the non-human world began with a number of imagistic poems about nature, particularly related to the northernness of Canada, its remote lakes and vast rock formations, such as the Canadian Shield; this early work, in terms of its subject matter and visual intensity, has much in common with the work of the Group of Seven. Against the serene and austere aspects of nature in Canada, Scott pits the human work of building and "civilizing," though he does this in terms that are not entirely romantic; he admires the work of human hands where it constructs, by way of its "cabin syllables," art and language, and such human enterprises as education, medicine, and government. However, his keen intellect and training in law gave him sufficient insight to identify, and the wit to parody, all that is bogus and destructive in human affairs, so that even a largely affirmative poem such as "Laurentian Shield" ends with the ambivalent phrase, "the long sentence of their exploitation."

After the financial crash of 1929 and the Depression, Scott turned to politics and to satire. His lively poetic diatribes against hypocrisy and waste in government, or prudery and racism in society, are seldom without redeeming humour and infectious wordplay, making generous use of puns and double entendre.

Editor of the *McGill Fortnightly Review* in 1925, Scott was not widely noticed for his writing until it appeared in *New Provinces: Poems of Several Authors* (1936), co-edited with his friend and fellow poet A.J.M. Smith. Scott was co-founder of *Preview* in 1942, which merged three years later with *First Statement*; 1945 also saw the publication of *Events & Signals*. Then came Scott's *Overture* (1954), *The Eye of the Needle* (1957), *The Blasted Pine: An Anthology of Satire, Invective, and Disrespectful Verse, Chiefly by Canadian Writers*, co-edited with A.J.M. Smith (1957), *Signature* (1964), *Selected Poems* (1966), and *The Collected Poems of F.R. Scott* (1981, Governor General's Award).

Lakeshore

The lake is sharp along the shore
Trimming the bevelled edge of land
To level curves; the fretted sands
Go slanting down through liquid air
Till stones below shift here and there
Floating upon their broken sky
All netted by the prism wave
And rippled where the currents are.

I stare through windows at this cave
Where fish, like planes, slow-motioned, fly.
Poised in a still of gravity
The narrow minnow, flicking fin,
Hangs in a paler, ochre sun,
His doorways open everywhere.

And I am a tall frond that waves
Its head below its rooted feet
Seeking the light that draws it down
To forest floors beyond its reach
Vivid with gloom and eerie dreams.

The water's deepest colonnades
Contract the blood, and to this home
That stirs the dark amphibian
With me the naked swimmers come
Drawn to their prehistoric womb.

They too are liquid as they fall
Like tumbled water loosed above
Until they lie, diagonal,
Within the cool and sheltered grove
Stroked by the fingertips of love.

Silent, our sport is drowned in fact
Too virginal for speech or sound
And each is personal and laned
Along his private aqueduct.

Too soon the tether of the lungs
Is taut and straining, and we rise
Upon our undeveloped wings
Toward the prison of our ground
A secret anguish in our thighs
And mermaids in our memories.

This is our talent, to have grown
Upright in posture, false-erect,
A landed gentry, circumspect,
Tied to a horizontal soil
The floor and ceiling of the soul;

Striving, with cold and fishy care
To make an ocean of the air.

Sometimes, upon a crowded street,
I feel the sudden rain come down
And in the old, magnetic sound
I hear the opening of a gate
That loosens all the seven seas.
Watching the whole creation drown
I muse, alone, on Ararat.

Laurentian Shield

Hidden in wonder and snow, or sudden with summer,
This land stares at the sun in a huge silence
Endlessly repeating something we cannot hear.
Inarticulate, arctic,
Not written on by history, empty as paper,
It leans away from the world with songs in its lakes
Older than love, and lost in the miles.

This waiting is wanting.
It will choose its language
When it has chosen its technic,
A tongue to shape the vowels of its productivity.

A language of flesh and roses.

Now there are pre-words,
Cabin syllables,
Nouns of settlement
Slowly forming, with steel syntax,
The long sentence of its exploitation.

The first cry was the hunter, hungry for fur,
And the digger for gold, nomad, no-man, a particle;
Then the bold commands of monopoly, big with machines,
Carving its kingdoms out of the public wealth;
And now the drone of the plane, scouting the ice,
Fills all the emptiness with neighbourhood
And links our future over the vanished pole.

But a deeper note is sounding, heard in the mines,
The scattered camps and the mills, a language of life,
And what will be written in the full culture of occupation
Will come, presently, tomorrow,
From millions whose hands can turn this rock into children.

Overture

In the dark room, under a cone of light,
You precisely play the Mozart sonata. The bright
Clear notes fly like sparks through the air
And trace a flickering pattern of music there.

Your hands dart in the light, your fingers flow.
They are ten careful operatives in a row
That pick their packets of sound from steel bars
Constructing harmonies as sharp as stars.

But how shall I hear old music? This is an hour
Of new beginnings, concepts warring for power,
Decay of systems—the tissue of art is torn
With overtures of an era being born.

And this perfection which is less yourself
Than Mozart, seems a trinket on a shelf,
A pretty octave played before a window
Beyond whose curtain grows a world crescendo.

Charity

A code of laws
Lies written
On this beggar's hand.

My small coin
Lengthens
The harsh sentence.

Saturday Sundae

The triple-decker and the double-cone
I side-swipe swiftly, suck the coke-straws dry.
Ride toadstool seat beside the slab of morgue—
Sweet corner drug-store, sweet pie in the sky.

Him of the front-flap apron, him I sing,
The counter-clockwise clerk in underalls.
Swing low, sweet chocolate, Oh swing, swing,
While cheek by juke the jitter chatter falls.

I swivel on my axle and survey
The latex tintex kotex cutex land.
Soft kingdoms sell for dimes, Life Pic Look Click
Inflate the male with conquest girly grand.

My brothers and my sisters, two by two,
Sit sipping succulence and sighing sex.
Each tiny adolescent universe
A world the vested interests annex.

Such bread and circuses these times allow,
Opium most popular, life so small and slick,
Perhaps with candy is the new world born
And cellophane shall wrap the heretic.

Bonne Entente

The advantages of living with two cultures
Strike one at every turn,
Especially when one finds a notice in an office building:
"This elevator will not run on Ascension Day";
Or reads in the *Montreal Star*:
"Tomorrow being the Feast of the Immaculate Conception,
There will be no collection of garbage in the city";
Or sees on the restaurant menu the bilingual dish:

DEEP APPLE PIE
TARTE AUX POMMES PROFONDES

For Bryan Priestman

(Drowned while attempting to save a child.)

The child fell, turning slowly with arms outstretched like a doll,
One shrill cry dying under the arches,
And floated away, her time briefer than foam.

Nothing was changed on the summer's day. The birds sang,
The busy insects followed their fixed affairs.
Only a Professor of Chemistry, alone on the bridge,

Suddenly awoke from his reverie, into the intense moment,
Saw all the elements of his life compounded for testing,
And plunged with searching hands into his last experiment.

This was a formula he had carried from childhood,
That can work but once in the life of a man.
His were the labels of an old laboratory,
And the long glass tubes of the river.

Irving Layton

(1912–2006)

Irving Layton was born in Romania. While still a child he immigrated with his parents to Montreal. He studied agricultural science at Macdonald College and economics at McGill University, and taught in a boys' private school before taking up his teaching position at Sir George Williams University. In the forties he was associated with Louis Dudek and John Sutherland in the editing of *First Statement*, the controversial literary magazine that later merged with *Preview* to become *Northern Review*. In the fifties he co-founded Contact Press. Career launched, he taught, travelled widely, edited books, read his poetry on campuses across the country, and was an active commentator on current affairs. He taught English at several universities, including Concordia and York, but spent his final days in Montreal.

Layton was a man of contradictions. He presented himself as a rebel and outsider, a brawling, irreverent, wild-eyed poet with no use for conservative values. As he says in the preface to *The Laughing Rooster*:

> In this country the poet has always had to fight for his survival. He lives in a middle-class milieu whose values of money-getting, respectability, and success are hostile to the kind of integrity and authenticity that is at the core of his endeavour. His need to probe himself makes him an easy victim for those who have more practical things to do—to hold down a job, amass a fortune, or to get married and raise children. His concern is to change the world; at any rate, to bear witness that another besides the heartless, stupid, and soul destroying one men have created is possible.

His barbs were not limited to the middle class. He was critical of educational institutions, rejecting high culture as "that underarm perspiration odour of impotent old men" and describing good taste as "something to wipe our unstodgy behinds with."

Despite his swagger, Layton was neither a primitive nor a sensualist. His satire, bombast, and erotica are the masks for a fine, beleaguered sensibility. His need to project an image of controversy made him espouse issues and causes that seem inconsistent with his expressed poetic vision, with the vision of poetry as freedom. And it is a comment on our country, rather than on Layton, that his second-rate poems of social invective should attract more attention than his refined verse.

Like Whitman in the United States, Layton did much to stimulate interest in poetry and to unbutton its shirt collar. He reminded us that there are no inherently unpoetic subjects. Poetry, he said, is "a self authenticated speaking, a reaching down into the roots of one's being." The poet is someone who knows "the terror and ecstasy of living daily beyond one's psychic means." A meticulous craftsman, Layton insisted that "without the material given the poet when his Unconscious (soul) is stirred into activity by a powerful emotion, his intelligence and craftsmanship are of no use to him whatever." His best poems are a perfect blend of passion and restraint, of a conscious and an unconscious ordering of materials.

About poetry in general Layton has this to say: "I like poems that are subtle and circular—the perfect form of a serpent swallowing its own tail and rolling towards Eternity. A meditative music, the feelings open as the sky. Formless poems give me the pips. If ideas, I want to see them dance" (*Poet's Choice*, 1966).

His more than 52 poetry publications include *Here and Now* (1945), *The Improved Binoculars* (1956), *A Red Carpet for the Sun* (1959, Governor General's Award), *Balls for a One-Armed Juggler* (1963), *The Laughing Rooster* (1964), *Periods of the Moon* (1967), *For My Brother Jesus* (1976), *The Covenant* (1977), *Final Reckoning: Poems 1984–1987* (1987), *Fortunate Exile* (1987), *A Wild Peculiar Joy 1945–1989* (1989), and *Fornalutx: Selected Poems, 1928–1990* (1992).

Look, the Lambs Are All Around Us!

Your figure, love,
curves itself
into a man's memory;
or to put it the way
a junior prof
at Mount Allison might,
Helen with her thick
absconding limbs

about the waist
of Paris
did no better.

Hell, my back's sunburnt
from so much love-making
in the open air.
The Primate (somebody
made a monkey of him)
and the Sanhedrin
(long on the beard, short
on the brain)
send envoys to say
they don't approve.
You never see them, love.
You toss me in the air
with such abandon,
they take to their heels and run.
I tell you
each kiss of yours
is like a blow on the head!

What luck, what luck to be loved
by the one girl
in this Presbyterian
country
who knows how to give
a man pleasure.

The Cold Green Element

At the end of the garden walk
the wind and its satellite wait for me;
their meaning I will not know
    until I go there,
but the black-hatted undertaker

who, passing, saw my heart beating in the grass,
is also going there. Hi, I tell him,
a great squall in the Pacific blew a dead poet
    out of the water,
who now hangs from the city's gates.

Crowds depart daily to see it, and return
with grimaces and incomprehension;
if its limbs twitched in the air
    they would sit at its feet
peeling their oranges.

And turning over I embrace like a lover
the trunk of a tree, one of those
for whom the lightning was too much
    and grew a brilliant
hunchback with a crown of leaves.

The ailments escaped from the labels
of medicine bottles are all fled to the wind;
I've seen myself lately in the eyes
    of old women,
spent streams mourning my manhood,

in whose old pupils the sun became
a bloodsmear on broad catalpa leaves
and hanging from ancient twigs,
    my murdered selves
sparked the air like the muted collisions

of fruit. A black dog howls down my blood,
a black dog with yellow eyes;
he too by someone's inadvertence
    saw the bloodsmear
on the broad catalpa leaves.

But the furies clear a path for me to the worm
who sang for an hour in the throat of a robin,
and misled by the cries of young boys
    I am again
a breathless swimmer in that cold green element.

Whatever Else Poetry Is Freedom

Whatever else poetry is freedom.
Forget the rhetoric, the trick of lying
All poets pick up sooner or later. From the river,
Rising like the thin voice of grey castratos—the mist;

Poplars and pines grow straight but oaks are gnarled;
Old codgers must speak of death, boys break windows;
Women lie honestly by their men at last.

And I who gave my Kate a blackened eye
Did to its vivid changing colours
Make up an incredible musical scale;
And now I balance on wooden stilts and dance
And thereby sing to the loftiest casements.
See how with polish I bow from the waist.
Space for these stilts! More space or I fail!

And a crown I say for my buffoon's head.
Yet no more fool am I than King Canute,
Lord of our tribe, who scanned and scorned;
Who half-deceived, believed; and, poet, missed
The first white waves come nuzzling at his feet;
Then damned the courtiers and the foolish trial
With a most bewildering and unkingly jest.

It was the mist. It lies inside one like a destiny.
A real Jonah it lies rotting like a lung.
And I know myself undone who am a clown
And wear a wreath of mist for a crown;
Mist with the scent of dead apples,
Mist swirling from black oily waters at evening,
Mist from the fraternal graves of cemeteries.

It shall drive me to beg my food and at last
Hurl me broken I know and prostrate on the road;
Like a huge toad I saw, entire but dead,
That Time mordantly had blacked; O pressed
To the moist earth it pled for entry.
I shall be I say that stiff toad for sick with mist
And crazed I smell the odour of mortality.

And Time flames like a paraffin stove
And what it burns are the minutes I live.
At certain middays I have watched the cars
Bring me from afar their windshield suns;
What lay to my hand were blue fenders,

The suns extinguished, the drivers wearing sunglasses.
And it made me think I had touched a hearse.

So whatever else poetry is freedom. Let
Far off the impatient cadences reveal
A padding for my breathless stilts. Swivel,
O hero, in the fleshy groves, skin and glycerine,
And sing of lust, the sun's accompanying shadow
Like a vampire's wing, the stillness in dead feet—
Your stave brings resurrection, O aggrievèd king.

The Fertile Muck

There are brightest apples on those trees
    but until I, fabulist, have spoken
they do not know their significance
or what other legends are hung like garlands
    on their black boughs twisting
like a rumour. The wind's noise is empty.

Nor are the winged insects better off
    though they wear my crafty eyes
wherever they alight. Stay here, my love;
you will see how delicately they deposit
    me on the leaves of elms
or fold me in the orient dust of summer.

And if in August joiners and bricklayers
    are thick as flies around us
building expensive bungalows for those
who do not need them, unless they release
    me roaring from their moth-proofed cupboards
their buyers will have no joy, no ease.

I could extend their rooms for them without cost
    and give them crazy sundials
to tell the time with, but I have noticed
how my irregular footprint horrifies them
    evenings and Sunday afternoons:
they spray for hours to erase its shadow.

How to dominate reality? Love is one way;
imagination another. Sit here
beside me, sweet; take my hard hand in yours.
We'll mark the butterflies disappearing over the hedge
with tiny wristwatches on their wings:
our fingers touching the earth, like two Buddhas.

Berry Picking

Silently my wife walks on the still wet furze
Now darkgreen the leaves are full of metaphors
Now lit up is each tiny lamp of blueberry.
The white nails of rain have dropped and the sun is free.

And whether she bends or straightens to each bush
To find the children's laughter among the leaves
Her quiet hands seem to make the quiet summer hush—
Berries or children, patient she is with these.

I only vex and perplex her; madness, rage
Are endearing perhaps put down upon the page;
Even silence daylong and sullen can then
Enamour as restraint or classic discipline.

So I envy the berries she puts in her mouth,
The red and succulent juice that stains her lips;
I shall never taste that good to her, nor will they
Displease her with a thousand barbarous jests.

How they lie easily for her hand to take,
Part of the unoffending world that is hers;
Here beyond complexity she stands and stares
And leans her marvellous head as if for answers.

No more the easy soul my childish craft deceives
Nor the simpler one for whom yes is always yes;
No, now her voice comes to me from a far way off
Though her lips are redder than the raspberries.

Keine Lazarovitch 1870–1959

When I saw my mother's head on the cold pillow,
Her white waterfalling hair in the cheeks' hollows,

I thought, quietly circling my grief, of how
She had loved God but cursed extravagantly his creatures.

For her final mouth was not water but a curse,
A small black hole, a black rent in the universe,
Which damned the green earth, stars and trees in its stillness
And the inescapable lousiness of growing old.

And I record she was comfortless, vituperative,
Ignorant, glad, and much else besides; I believe
She endlessly praised her black eyebrows, their thick weave,
Till plagiarizing Death leaned down and took them for his mould.

And spoiled a dignity I shall not again find,
And the fury of her stubborn limited mind;
Now none will shake her amber beads and call God blind,
Or wear them upon a breast so radiantly.

O fierce she was, mean and unaccommodating;
But I think now of the toss of her gold earrings,
Their proud carnal assertion, and her youngest sings
While all the rivers of her red veins move into the sea.

P.K. Page

(1916–2010)

"I am a traveller," P.K. Page wrote in "Traveller, Conjuror, Journeyman,"

> I have a destination but no maps. Others will have reached that destination already, still others are on their way. But none has had to go from here before—nor will again. One's route is one's own. One's journey unique. What I will find at the end I can barely guess. What lies on the way is unknown. How to go? Land, sea or air? What techniques to use? What vehicle?

Patricia Kathleen Page was a traveller in both her life and art. She was born in the United Kingdom but raised in Calgary and Winnipeg, where her father was stationed with the Strathcona Horse. She said she "first came to writing by being an adolescent, which is enough to make anyone write." After living briefly in the Maritimes, she moved to Montreal, where she worked as a scriptwriter for the National Film Board and became associated with Patrick Anderson and F.R. Scott in the editing of *Preview* magazine. Her first major publication was in *Unit of Five* (1944), an anthology of five poets edited by Ronald Hambleton. Page lived abroad for many years, in Mexico, Australia, and Brazil, where she began to draw and paint under her married name, P.K. Irwin. Her latter years were spent in Victoria, BC.

Page's search for the technique with which to make her spiritual and aesthetic journey is a fascinating study. Her early poetry, which she came to describe as "clotted with images," explores the contradictions that underlie everyday experience: the terrible and explosive beauty of childhood; the haunting presence of boredom and madness associated with the deadly routine of jobs; the vanity and self-delusion that infect the most charitable and earnest of actions and statements. Such subjects lend themselves readily to a richly textured and highly allusive style, in which the interplay of elements of prosody and figurative language serve to heighten the sense of irony and paradox. Detail and stylization give imaginative expression to the problem of workers alienated from the product of their labours as no Marxist treatises could do. Page does not glorify or romanticize the secretaries or miners, but her metaphors leave no doubt that such conditions are, ultimately, dehumanizing.

Time and travel altered Page's conception of life and art, shifting her attention from social and political surfaces to internal psychological states. Her parallel development as a visual artist serves as a useful analogy for her poetic progress. The shock of learning another language, as she says in "Questions and Images" (*Canadian Literature,* No. 41, summer 1969), was like being born a second time, growing from silence through a linguistic childhood and adolescence toward a radically altered adulthood, in which all her perceptions underwent a subtle shift. Since she could not write poetry, she began to draw, going first through a realist phase in which she had to "see with the eye of an ant" in order to appropriate the new and exotic environment; then, she says, "the pen began dreaming. It began a life of its own," to the point where the painter could look into the macaw's eye and be "drawn through its vortex into a minute cosmos which contained all the staggering dimensions of outer space."

Here poet and painter speak the same language, both being concerned, as she says in "Stories of Snow," with that "area behind the eyes / where silent, unrefractive whiteness lies." No other Canadian poet has been so intensely concerned with exploring the nature of visual perception. Eyes abound in her poems, as do lenses, cameras, field glasses. Perspectives are almost always unusual; compositional elements play an important part; images may be blurred, superimposed, surprisingly juxtaposed, viewed through distorting lenses. These perceptual elements, including an attention to colour and light and shade, combine with an imagistic precision that recalls her experience of film. As Munro Beattie has observed, "Several of her poems might serve as scripts for little experimental films for 'art' theatres. Action flows into action, image melts, 'by a slow dissolve,' into image."

After Canada, which she has described as a "whim-oriented culture," Page found the cultural symbols in Mexico liberating. She came to believe that art was not an end in itself so much as a means to an end, a path to wisdom, a technique of transformation or metamorphosis, a vehicle for conducting us on that route that leads through the looking glass, beyond the senses to "some unseen centre." "Poetry," she insists, is "more than ever in the perceiving" and "without magic the world is not to be borne. A good writer or painter understands these laws and practices conjuration."

Page published a novel, *The Sun and the Moon*, in 1944, under the pseudonym Judith Cape. It was reprinted with eight short stories in 1973, under the title *The Sun and the Moon and Other Fictions*. Her books of poetry include *As Ten As Twenty* (1946), *The Metal and the Flower* (1954, Governor General's Award), *Cry Ararat!* (1967), *Poems Selected and New* (1974), *Leviathan in a Pool* (1974), *Evening Dance of the Grey Flies* (1981), *The Glass Air: Selected Poems* (1985, 1991), *Hologram: A Book of Glosas* (1994), and *The Hidden Room: Collected Poems, Volumes One and Two* (1997), which is graced with her own unique drawings. She also published the autobiographical *Brazilian Journal* (1986) and many works for young readers.

The Stenographers

After the brief bivouac of Sunday,
their eyes, in the forced march of Monday to Saturday,
hoist the white flag, flutter in the snow-storm of paper,
haul it down and crack in the mid-sun of temper.

In the pause between the first draft and the carbon
they glimpse the smooth hours when they were children—
the ride in the ice-cart, the ice-man's name,
the end of the route and the long walk home;

remember the sea where floats at high tide
were sea marrows growing on the scatter-green vine
or spools of grey toffee, or wasps' nests on water;
remember the sand and the leaves of the country.

Bell rings and they go and the voice draws their pencil
like a sled across snow; when its runners are frozen
rope snaps and the voice then is pulling no burden
but runs like a dog on the winter of paper.

Their climates are winter and summer—no wind
for the kites of their hearts—no wind for a flight;
a breeze at the most, to tumble them over
and leave them like rubbish—the boy-friends of blood.

In the inch of the noon as they move they are stagnant.
The terrible calm of the noon is their anguish;
the lip of the counter, the shapes of the straws
like icicles breaking their tongues, are invaders.

Their beds are their oceans—salt water of weeping
the waves that they know—the tide before sleep;
and fighting to drown they assemble their sheep
in columns and watch them leap desks for their fences

and stare at them with their own mirror-worn faces.
In the felt of the morning the calico-minded,
sufficiently starched, insert papers, hit keys,
efficient and sure as their adding machines;

yet they weep in the vault, they are taut as net curtains
stretched upon frames. In their eyes I have seen
the pin men of madness in marathon trim
race round the track of the stadium pupil.

Landlady

Through sepia air the boarders come and go,
impersonal as trains. Pass silently
the craving silence swallowing her speech;
click doors like shutters on her camera eye.

Because of her their lives become exact:
their entrances and exits are designed;
phone calls are cryptic. Oh, her ticklish ears
advance and fall back stunned.

Nothing is unprepared. They hold the walls
about them as they weep or laugh. Each face
is dialled to zero publicly. She peers
stippled with curious flesh;

pads on the patient landing like a pulse,
unlocks their keyholes with the wire of sight,
searches their rooms for clues when they are out,
pricks when they come home late.

Wonders when they are quiet, jumps when they move,
dreams that they dope or drink, trembles to know
the traffic of their brains, jaywalks their street
in clumsy shoes.

Yet knows them better than their closest friends:
their cupboards and the secrets of their drawers,
their books, their private mail, their photographs
are theirs and hers.

Knows when they wash, how frequently their clothes
go to the cleaners, what they like to eat,
their curvature of health, but even so
is not content.

And like a lover must know all, all, all.
Prays she may catch them unprepared at last
and palm the dreadful riddle of their skulls—
hoping the worst.

Stories of Snow

Those in the vegetable rain retain
an area behind their sprouting eyes
held soft and rounded with the dream of snow
precious and reminiscent as those globes—
souvenir of some never-nether land—
which hold their snow-storms circular, complete,
high in a tall and teakwood cabinet.

In countries where the leaves are large as hands
where flowers protrude their fleshy chins

and call their colours,
an imaginary snow-storm sometimes falls
among the lilies.
And in the early morning one will waken
to think the glowing linen of his pillow
a northern drift, will find himself mistaken
and lie back weeping.
And there the story shifts from head to head,
of how in Holland, from their feather beds
hunters arise and part the flakes and go
forth to the frozen lakes in search of swans—
the snow-light falling white along their guns,
their breath in plumes.
While tethered in the wind like sleeping gulls
ice-boats wait the raising of their wings
to skim the electric ice at such a speed
they leap jet strips of naked water,
and how these flying, sailing hunters feel
air in their mouths as terrible as ether.
And on the story runs that even drinks
in that white landscape dare to be no colour;
how flasked and water clear, the liquor slips
silver against the hunters' moving hips.
And of the swan in death these dreamers tell
of its last flight and how it falls, a plummet,
pierced by the freezing bullet
and how three feathers, loosened by the shot,
descend like snow upon it.
While hunters plunge their fingers in its down
deep as a drift, and dive their hands
up to the neck of the wrist
in that warm metamorphosis of snow
as gentle as the sort that woodsmen know
who, lost in the white circle, fall at last
and dream their way to death.

And stories of this kind are often told
in countries where great flowers bar the roads
with reds and blues which seal the route to snow—
as if, in telling, raconteurs unlock
the colour with its complement and go
through to the area behind the eyes
where silent, unrefractive whiteness lies.

Photos of a Salt Mine

How innocent their lives look,
how like a child's
dream of caves and winter, both combined;
the steep descent to whiteness
and the stope
with its striated walls
their folds all leaning as if pointing to
the greater whiteness still,
that great white bank
with its decisive front,
that seam upon a slope,
salt's lovely ice.

And wonderful underfoot the snow of salt
the fine
particles a broom could sweep,
one thinks
muckers might make angels in its drifts
as children do in snow,
lovers in sheets,
lie down and leave imprinted where they lay
a feathered creature holier than they.

And in the outworked stopes
with lamps and ropes
up miniature matterhorns
the miners climb
probe with their lights
the ancient folds of rock—
syncline and anticline—
and scoop from darkness an Aladdin's cave:
rubies and opals glitter from its walls.

But hoses douse the brilliance of these jewels,
melt fire to brine.
Salt's bitter water trickles thin and forms,
slow fathoms down,
a lake within a cave,
lacquered with jet—
white's opposite.
There grey on black the boating miners float

to mend the stays and struts of that old stope
and deeply underground
their words resound,
are multiplied by echo, swell and grow
and make a climate of a miner's voice.

So all the photographs like children's wishes
are filled with caves or winter,
innocence
has acted as a filter,
selected only beauty from the mine.
Except in the last picture,
it is shot
from an acute high angle. In a pit
figures the size of pins are strangely lit
and might be dancing but you know they're not.
Like Dante's vision of the nether hell
men struggle with the bright cold fires of salt,
locked in the black inferno of the rock:
the filter here, not innocence but guilt.

After Rain

The snails have made a garden of green lace:
broderie anglaise from the cabbages,
chantilly from the choux-fleurs, tiny veils—
I see already that I lift the blind
upon a woman's wardrobe of the mind.

Such female whimsy floats about me like
a kind of tulle, a flimsy mesh,
while feet in gum boots pace the rectangles—
garden abstracted, geometry awash—
an unknown theorem argued in green ink,
dropped in the bath.
Euclid in glorious chlorophyl, half drunk.

I none too sober slipping in the mud
where rigged with guys of rain
the clothes-reel gauche
as the rangy skeleton of some
gaunt delicate spidery mute
is pitched as if
listening;

while hung from one thin rib
a silver web—
its infant, skeletal, diminutive,
now sagged with sequins, pulled ellipsoid,
glistening.

I suffer shame in all these images.
The garden is primeval, Giovanni
in soggy denim squelches by my hub
over his ruin,
shakes a doleful head.
but he so beautiful and diademmed,
his long Italian hands so wrung with rain
I find his ache exists beyond my rim
and almost weep to see a broken man
made subject to my whim.

O choir him, birds, and let him come to rest
within this beauty as one rests in love,
till pears upon the bough
encrusted with
small snails as pale as pearls
hang golden in
a heart that knows tears are a part of love.

And choir me too to keep my heart a size
larger than seeing, unseduced by each
bright glimpse of beauty striking like a bell,
so that the whole may toll,
its meaning shine
clear of the myriad images that still—
do what I will—encumber its pure line.

Planet Earth

It has to be spread out, the skin of this planet,
has to be ironed, the sea in its whiteness;
and the hands keep on moving,
smoothing the holy surfaces.
In Praise of Ironing, Pablo Neruda

It has to be loved the way a laundress loves her linens,
the way she moves her hands caressing the fine muslins
knowing their warp and woof,

like a lover coaxing, or a mother praising.
It has to be loved as if it were embroidered
with flowers and birds and two joined hearts upon it.
It has to be stretched and stroked.
It has to be celebrated.
O this great beloved world and all the creatures in it.
It has to be spread out, the skin of this planet.

The trees must be washed, and the grasses and mosses.
They have to be polished as if made of green brass.
The rivers and little streams with their hidden cresses
and pale-coloured pebbles
and their fool's gold
must be washed and starched or shined into brightness,
the sheets of lake water
smoothed with the hand
and the foam of the oceans pressed into neatness.
It has to be ironed, the sea in its whiteness

and pleated and goffered, the flower-blue sea
the protean, wine-dark, grey, green, sea
with its metres of satin and bolts of brocade.
And sky—such an O! overhead—night and day
must be burnished and rubbed
by hands that are loving
so the blue blazons forth
and the stars keep on shining
within and above
and the hands keep on moving.

It has to be made bright, the skin of this planet
till it shines in the sun like gold leaf.
Archangels then will attend to its metals
and polish the rods of its rain.
Seraphim will stop singing hosannas
to shower it with blessings and blisses and praises
and, newly in love,
we must draw it and paint it
our pencils and brushes and loving caresses
smoothing the holy surfaces.

Raymond Souster

(1921–2012)

Raymond Souster was born in Toronto and, except for the war years, spent most of his life there. "I suppose I am truly an unrepentant regionalist. . . . All the experiences one is likely to encounter in Paris can be found in this city. Toronto has a flavour all its own. . . . My roots are here, this is the place that tugs at my heart when I leave it and fills me with quiet relief when I return to it," he said of his hometown. Until his retirement, Souster was employed for four decades by the Canadian Imperial Bank of Commerce in downtown Toronto. He was an enabling presence in the literary community; editor of a mimeographed magazine called *Combustion* (1957–60), the anthologies *New Wave Canada: The New Explosion in Canadian Poetry* (1966), and *Generation Now* (1970); a founder-editor of the poets' co-operative Contact Press; and a founding member of the League of Canadian Poets.

Souster's numerous books of poetry include *When We Are Young* (1946), *Shake Hands with the Hangman* (1953), *The Colour of the Times* (1964, Governor General's Award), *Ten Elephants on Yonge Street* (1965), *So Far So Good* (1969), *Selected Poems* (1972), *On Target* (1973), *Collected Poems* in 10 volumes (1980 ff.), *Asking for More* (1988), *Running Out the Clock* (1991), *Riding the Long Black Horse* (1993), *Old Bank Notes* (1993), *No Sad Songs Wanted Here* (1995), *Close to Home* (1996), and a steady output of new work in his final years.

Souster might be viewed as a poet of content, primarily concerned with giving imaginative expression to the disenfranchised, the down-and-out, and to our struggle with the inequalities and fleetingness of modern life. But the aesthetic concerns in his work are as strong as the sociological. He sees the poet as a recorder or photographer of the human condition at a particular moment in history; or rather—and perhaps this is the main function—as an entertainer able to divert attention away from the sources of despair. The short poem is itself a function of the poet's view of the impermanence of all things; and, as Frost suggests, the good poem provides "a momentary stay against confusion."

In terms of form and prosody, Souster owes a certain allegiance to the theories and practice of Ezra Pound and William Carlos Williams, especially their commitment to the image. He wrote a number of excellent imagist poems, verbal snapshots, such as "Study: The Bath" and "The Six-Quart Basket," that have the clarity and economy of the haiku. He preferred the shifting rhythms of speech to the monotony of the metronome. The poems of lyrical reflection testify to Souster's integrity as a man and as a poet; they are beautifully turned and reveal a quiet concern, or empathy, that is always surprising, at times deeply moving.

Young Girls

With the night full of spring and stars we stand
here in this dark doorway and watch the young
girls pass, two, three together, hand in hand.
Like flowers they are whose fragrance has not sprung
or awakened, whose bodies dimly feel
the flooding upward welling of the trees;
whose senses, caressed by the wind's soft fingers, reel
with a delirium that makes them ill at ease.

They lie awake at night unable to sleep
and walk the streets kindled by strange desires;
they steal glances at us, unable to keep
control upon those subterranean fires.
We whistle after them, then laugh, for they
stiffen, not knowing what to do or say.

Lagoons, Hanlan's Point

Mornings
before the sun's liquid
spilled gradually, flooding
the island's cool cellar,
there was the boat
and the still lagoons,
with the sound of my oars
the only intrusion
over the cries of birds
in the marshy shallows,
or the loud thrashing
of the startled crane
rushing the air.

And in one strange
dark, tree-hung entrance,
I followed the sound
of my heart all the way
to the reed-blocked ending,

with the pads of the lily
thick as green-shining film
covering the water.

And in another
where the sun came
to probe the depths
through a shaft of branches,
I saw the skeletons
of brown ships rotting
far below in their burial-ground,
and wondered what strange fish
with what strange colours
swam through these places
under the water. . . .

A small boy
with a flat-bottomed punt
and an old pair of oars
moving with wonder
through the antechamber
of a waking world.

Downtown Corner News Stand

It will need all of death to take you from this corner.
It has become your world, and you its unshaved
bleary-eyed, foot stamping king. In winter
you curse the cold, huddled in your coat from the wind,
you fry in summer like an egg hopping on a griddle;
and always the whining voice, the nervous-flinging arms,
the red face, shifting eyes watching, waiting
under the grimy cap for God knows what
to happen. (But nothing ever does, downtown Toronto
goes to sleep and wakes the next morning
always the same, except a little dirtier.)
And you stand with your armful of Stars and Telys,
the peak of your cap well down against the sun,
and all the city's restless seething river
surges besides you, but not once do you plunge
into its flood, are carried or tossed away:
but reappear always, beard longer than ever, nose running,
to catch the noon editions at King and Bay.

Study: The Bath

In the almost dim light
of the bathroom a woman
steps from white tub
towel around her shoulders.

Drops of water glisten
on her body, slight buttocks,
neck, tight belly,
fall at intervals
from the slightly plumed
oval of crotch.

Neck bent forward
eyes collected
her attention gathered
at the ends of fingers

as she removes
dead skin from her nipples.

All This Slow Afternoon

All this slow afternoon
the May winds blowing
honey of the lilacs,
sounds of waves washing
through the highest branches
of my poplar tree.

Enough in such hours
to be simply alive;
I will take death tomorrow
without bitterness.

Today all I ask
is to be left alone
in the wind
in the sunshine,
with the honey of lilacs
down the garden;

to fall asleep tired
of small birds' gossip,
of so much greenness
pushed behind my eyes.

The Six-Quart Basket

The six-quart basket
one side gone
half the handle torn off

sits in the centre of the lawn
and slowly fills up
with the white fruits of the snow.

Somalia

In the time it takes
to say Mogadishu,

a five-year-old
playing in the mud
has both arms blown away.

The militiamen call him
Little-One-Who-Can't-Fly.

Phyllis Webb

(b. 1927)

Readers caught up in Phyllis Webb's early work are often startled by the subject matter—suicide, betrayal, violence, death—and may need to be reminded that, whatever its ostensible content, good poetry is an affirmation of the human spirit, of the power of the imagination to confront and reshape reality. As Albert Camus argues in his famous treatise, *The Rebel*, there is no such thing as a nihilistic work of art; even if literature "describes nostalgia, despair, frustration, it still creates a form of salvation. To talk of despair is to conquer it. Despairing literature is a contradiction in terms." I'm not sure why it should be necessary to say this, in an age of concentration camps, forced migrations, ethnic cleansing—subjects which the artist ignores at her (and our) peril—but it is. What's important to celebrate in Webb's poetry is the style, the way in which she imposes *form* on whatever elements from reality she uses.

As is evident in her poems and in the emphasis her critical writings place on the poetic line, the creative process, and the genesis of poems, Webb is extremely conscious of even the smallest nuance of rhythm or sound. Her dissatisfaction with the verbosity and heavy-handedness of conventional rhetoric led her, in the mid-sixties, toward the minimalism of *Naked Poems* (1965), with their short lines and abbreviated manner; the same questing and curiosity led her, in the eighties, to explore the eighth-century Persian form called the *ghazal*, whose discrete but tonally linked couplets accommodated themselves particularly well, in *Water and Light* (1984), to the verbal dexterity and imaginative leaping that are Webb's hallmarks.

To fully appreciate the importance Webb places on form, it is instructive to read "Up the Ladder: Notes on the Creative Process" and "The Crannies of Matter: Texture in Robin Blaser's Later *Image-Nations*" (*Nothing But Brush Strokes*), where she scrutinizes, with great wit and linguistic playfulness, her own creative processes and those of a fellow poet:

> I used to think of texture in poetry as mainly a sound apparition produced by an intricate play of vocables whose plosives, dentals, labials, fricatives, hoots, whistles, yells and chuckles, sighs, murmurs, phonemic and syllabic interactions could scuff up or smooth out the surface of a poem. . . . When we speak of texture in poetry

> we're in the land of mixed metaphors, or, more accurately, in the surreal world of synaesthesia where sensory perceptions seem to be cross-wired and the sky today is high C, or the high C sounds like cerulean blue. . . . When we sound a poem aloud the synaesthesic transfer that takes place to give us a sense of texture occurs because—simplicity itself—words are formed inside the chest and head, inside the mouth.

In "Seeking Shape, Seeking Meaning: An Interview with Phyllis Webb" conducted by Smaro Kamboureli (*West Coast Line*, 6, fall/winter 1991–92), Webb talks at length about how she employs an associative process in writing poetry; the need not so much for passivity on the part of the poet, as for "fertile silence" and "active attention" to what the language is revealing; aspiring to a "speakeasy" frame of mind; her resistance to poetic theory and dogma; how the prose poem upsets the "logical expectations" of prose; the "death of the lyric poem"; and how, in seeking to move outside the individual ego . . . . "I think we must trust that primal creativity, trust its slow-motion urge toward order and enlightenment."

Webb was born in Victoria, BC, and raised there and in Vancouver. She studied English and philosophy at UBC from 1945 to 1949 and ran unsuccessfully as a candidate for the CCF (Co-operative Commonwealth Federation, a precursor to the NDP), in the provincial elections. She worked briefly as a secretary in Montreal, where she also attended McGill and came into contact with F.R. Scott and John Sutherland. Her poems were first published in *Trio*, along with those of Eli Mandel and Gael Turnbull. For the next 14 years she lived intermittently in the UK, Montreal, Paris, Vancouver, and Toronto, where she was co-creator and executive producer of the CBC *Ideas* program. She lives on Salt Spring Island.

Her poetry books include *Even Your Right Eye* (1956), *The Sea Is Also a Garden* (1962), *Naked Poems* (1965), *Wilson's Bowl* (1980), *The Vision Tree: Selected Poems* (1982, Governor General's Award), *Water & Light: Ghazals and Anti-Ghazals* (1982; 1984), and *Hanging Fire* (1991). Her critical writings appear in *Talking* (1982) and *Nothing But Brush Strokes: Selected Prose* (1995), which includes a number of her own photocollages. See also John Hulcoop's *Phyllis Webb and Her Works* (1991) and Pauline Butling's *Seeing in the Dark: The Poetry of Phyllis Webb* (1996).

Love Story

It was easy to see what he was up to,
the grey, bundled ape,
as he sidled half-playfully
up to the baby

and with a sly look behind
put his hands onto the crib
and leapt in.

The child's pink, beginning face
stared up as the hair-handed monkey
explored the flesh, so soft, of our infant race.
The belly spread like plush to the monkey's haunch,
he settled, heavy and gay, his nuzzling
mouth at the baby's neck.

But, no answer accurate to a smile,
he bit, tasted time, maddened,
and his nails rooted sudden fire in the ribs of Adam,
towered, carnivorous, for aim
and baby face, ears, arms
were torn and taken in his ravaging.

And so the killing, too-late parents came,
hysteric, after their child's
futile pulse had stopped its beating.
Only the half-pathetic, half-triumphant
monkey peered out from the crib,
bobbed nervously on the dead infant's belly,
then stopped, suddenly paralyzed on that soft tomb.

Was it the donkey Death brayed out at him
from the human mother's eyes,
or did his love for her in that pause
consume him?

The jealous ape's death was swift
and of natural cause. "Died of shame,"
some said, others, "of shock."
But his death was Othello's death,
as great, as picayune,
he died of envy, lacking the knack of wisdom.

Sitting

The degree of nothingness
is important:
to sit emptily

in the sun
receiving fire
that is the way
to mend
an extraordinary world,
sitting perfectly
still
and only
remotely human.

Poetics Against the Angel of Death

I am sorry to speak of death again
(some say I'll have a long life)
but last night Wordsworth's "Prelude"
suddenly made sense—I mean the measure,
the elevated tone, the attitude
of private Man speaking to public men.
Last night I thought I would not wake again
but now with this June morning I run ragged to elude
The Great Iambic Pentameter
who is the Hound of Heaven in our stress
because I want to die
writing Haiku
or, better,
long lines, clean and syllabic as knotted bamboo. Yes!

Eschatology of Spring

Death, Judgement, Heaven, Hell,
and Spring. The Five Last Things,
the least of which I am, being in
the azaleas and dog-toothed violets
of the South of Canada. Do not tell me
this is a cold country. I am also in
the camellias and camas of early, of
abrupt birth.
We are shooting up for the bloody
judgement of the six o'clock news.
Quick, cut us out from the deadlines
of rotting newspapers, quick, for the
tiny skeletons and bulbs will tell you
how death grows and grows in Chile and

Chad. Quick, for the small bones pinch
me and insects divulge occult excrement
in the service of my hyacinth, my trailing
begonia. And if you catch me resting
beside the stream, sighing against
the headlines of this pastoral, take
up your gun, the flowers blossoming
from its barrel, and join this grief, this
grief: that there are lambs, elegant black-
footed lambs in this island's eschatology,
Beloved.

Prison Report

The eye of Jacobo Timerman looks through the hole and sees
another eye looking through a hole.

These holes are cut into steel doors in prison cells in Argentina.

Both eyes are wary.
They disappear.

Timerman rests his cheek on the icy door,
amazed at the sense of space he feels—the joy.

He looks again: the other's eye is there,
then vanishes like a spider.

Comes back, goes, comes back.

This is a game of hide-and-seek.
This is intelligence with a sense of humour.
Timerman joins the game.

Sometimes two eyes meet at exactly the same moment.

This is music.   This is love
playing in the middle of a dark night
in a prison in Argentina.

My name is Jacobo one eye says.
Other eye says something, but Jacobo can't quite catch it.

Now a nose appears in the vision-field
of Timerman. It rubs cold edges of the hole,
a love-rub for Jacobo.

This is a kiss, he decides, a caress,
an emanation of solitude's tenderness.

In this prison everything is powered electrically
for efficiency and pain. But tenderness is also
a light and a shock.

An eye, a nose, a cheek resting against a steel door
in the middle of the dark night.
These are parts of bodies, parts of speech,
saying,
I am with you.

Treblinka Gas Chamber

"Klostermayer ordered another count of the children. Then their stars were snipped off and thrown into the center of the courtyard. It looked like a field of buttercups."

—*A Field of Buttercups* by Joseph Hymans

fallingstars
    'a field of
        buttercups'

        yellow stars
            of David
                falling

the prisoners
    the children
        falling

    in heaps
        on one another
            they go down

Thanatos
showers
his dirty breath
they must breathe
him in

they see stars
behind their
eyes

David's
'a field of
buttercups'

a metaphor
where all that's
left lies down

Peacock Blue: An Anti-Ghazal

Peacock blue. Words fail me,
Fishstar, for the packed, inbred

splendour of this bird. His strut,
the cock of his head, a royal courtier

in the barnyard. Essex. See how the
Fabulous points into the spectrum, pecks out

accurately a blue-green scream for Elizabeth.
It is morning. It is the first morning

of creation, an absurd idea, but I tell you,
Fishstar, the colour of chaos was not

Peacock blue.

Cornflowers & Saffron Robes Belittle the Effort

Ssh, sigh, silence is coming, the night time blues. Hark. Ahem. Sir? I lift my arm, the wind chimes through my holy raiment. Mesmeric bells reduce the flies to slumber. Pajama party. The end of the Raj.

Leonard Cohen

(b. 1934)

Leonard Cohen's imagination was shaped not only by his Jewish heritage and the Catholic milieu of Montreal, but also by the literary values and antics of the beat generation, whose bohemianism embodied anew the Blakean notion that the road of excess is the path to wisdom. His earliest poems in *Let Us Compare Mythologies* (1956), and *Spice-Box of Earth* (1961), which are witty, exuberant, and richly embroidered, reveal a fascination with eroticism and violence as means of spiritual transcendence, a theme that finds its fullest expression in his novel *Beautiful Losers* (1966). *Flowers for Hitler* (1964) announces a deepening and maturing of vision; the tone of joyous celebration gives way to darker imaginings. The poet descends morally and imaginatively into the fiery furnaces of Belsen and Auschwitz, where, like Conrad's Marlow, he comes face to face with his own emptiness and potential for evil. The poems move toward the greater simplicity of form delineated in "Style," where Cohen hints at the potential for brotherhood and harmony that might be possible beyond the trappings of ego, culture, and nationalism. "Well, you know, you get wiped out," he said. "And the deeper the wipe-out, the deeper the reluctance to use ornament or to use any other faculties that brought you to the wipe-out."

Parasites of Heaven (1966) and *The Energy of Slaves* (1972) give full expression to Cohen's rejection of many of the values and strategies of conventional poetry. The books consist mainly of anti-poems, gestures of refusal, indicating a belief that the act of writing may itself be a betrayal. By the time he published *Parasites and Slaves*, Cohen was already internationally known for his folk songs. He could afford to announce his demise as a writer; he may also have had serious doubts, given the demands of his musical career and the lessons to be learned in the public arena, about both his poetic talent and the efficacy of poetry as a means of communication. However, there is in Cohen's most serious pronouncements a redeeming degree of humour and self-mockery, so it is not surprising to find, after a six-year silence, that he published a new collection of poems called *Death of a Ladies' Man* (1978), a sort of dialogue of self and soul, in which the poet and his alter ego debate the meaning of art, love, politics, and nation.

Sainthood and renunciation figure prominently in *Death of a Ladies' Man*, as they do in *Beautiful Losers*. However, the sharing of spiritual wisdom, as he says in an interview with Michael Harris in *Duel*, requires special discipline and talent:

> I think that a decent man who has discovered valuable secrets is under some obligation to share them. But I think that the technique of sharing them is a great study. Now, you can reveal secrets in many ways. One way is to say this is the secret discovered. I think that this way is often less successful because when that certain kind of conscious mind brings itself to bear on this information, it distorts it, makes it very inaccessible. Sometimes, it's just in the voice, sometimes just in the style, in the length of the paragraph; it's in the tone rather than in the message.

As Cohen's musical career blossomed, his private life was characterized more and more by solitude, simplicity, and meditation. *Book of Mercy* (1984) is in the form of 50 prayers and incantations that recall the Old Testament Psalms, the Sermon on the Mount, and the tradition of religious verse.

Cohen was born in Montreal, and studied at McGill University. He tried graduate studies for three weeks at Columbia, but returned to Montreal to read in clubs, write his unpublished novel *Ballet of Lepers*, and do a stint in the family clothing business. A Canada Council grant enabled him to travel to the UK, where he wrote *The Favourite Game* (1963), then to the island of Hydra in Greece, where he wrote much of his poetry and fiction. In Montreal and New York and at various monasteries, he pursued his writing, music, and spiritual journeying. And the rest is showbiz history. Additional poetry titles include *Stranger Music: Selected Poems and Songs* (1993), *God Is Alive: Magic is Afoot* (2000), and *Book of Longing* (2006).

Elegy

Do not look for him
In brittle mountain streams:
They are too cold for any god;
And do not examine the angry rivers
For shreds of his soft body
Or turn the shore stones for his blood;
But in the warm salt ocean
He is descending through cliffs
Of slow green water
And the hovering coloured fish
Kiss his snow-bruised body
And build their secret nests
In his fluttering winding-sheet.

You Have the Lovers

You have the lovers,
they are nameless, their histories only for each other,
and you have the room, the bed and the windows.
Pretend it is a ritual.
Unfurl the bed, bury the lovers, blacken the windows,
let them live in that house for a generation or two.
No one dares disturb them.
Visitors in the corridor tip-toe past the long closed door,
they listen for sounds, for a moan, for a song:
nothing is heard, not even breathing.
You know they are not dead,
you can feel the presence of their intense love.
Your children grow up, they leave you,
they have become soldiers and riders.
Your mate dies after a life of service.
Who knows you? Who remembers you?
But in your house a ritual is in progress:
it is not finished: it needs more people.
One day the door is opened to the lovers' chamber.
The room has become a dense garden,
full of colours, smells, sounds you have never known.
The bed is smooth as a wafer of sunlight,
in the midst of the garden it stands alone.
In the bed the lovers, slowly and deliberately and silently,
perform the act of love.
Their eyes are closed,
as tightly as if heavy coins of flesh lay on them.
Their lips are bruised with new and old bruises.
Her hair and his beard are hopelessly tangled.
When he puts his mouth against her shoulder
she is uncertain whether her shoulder
has given or received the kiss.
All her flesh is like a mouth.
He carries his fingers along her waist
and feels his own waist caressed.
She holds him closer and his own arms tighten around her.
She kisses the hand beside her mouth.
It is his hand or her hand, it hardly matters,
there are so many more kisses.
You stand beside the bed, weeping with happiness,
you carefully peel away the sheets

from the slow-moving bodies.
Your eyes are filled with tears, you barely make out the lovers.
As you undress you sing out, and your voice is magnificent
because now you believe it is the first human voice
heard in that room.
The garments you let fall grow into vines.
You climb into bed and recover the flesh.
You close your eyes and allow them to be sewn shut.
You create an embrace and fall into it.
There is only one moment of pain or doubt
as you wonder how many multitudes are lying beside your body,
but a mouth kisses and a hand soothes the moment away.

As the Mist Leaves No Scar

As the mist leaves no scar
On the dark green hill,
So my body leaves no scar
On you, nor ever will.

When wind and hawk encounter,
What remains to keep?
So you and I encounter,
Then turn, then fall to sleep.

As many nights endure
Without a moon or star,
So will we endure
When one is gone and far.

Now of Sleeping

Under her grandmother's patchwork quilt
a calico bird's-eye view
of crops and boundaries
naming dimly the districts of her body
sleeps my Annie like a perfect lady

Like ages of weightless snow
on tiny oceans filled with light
her eyelids enclose deeply
a shade tree of birthday candles
one for every morning
until the now of sleeping

The small banner of blood
kept and flown by Brother Wind
long after the pierced bird fell down
is like her red mouth
among the squalls of pillow

Bearers of evil fancy
of dark intention and corrupting fashion
who come to rend the quilt
plough the eye and ground the mouth
will contend with mighty Mother Goose
and Farmer Brown and all good stories
of invincible belief
which surround her sleep
like the golden weather of a halo

Well-wishers and her true lover
may stay to watch my Annie
sleeping like a perfect lady
under her grandmother's patchwork quilt
but they must promise to whisper
and to vanish by morning—
all but her one true lover.

The Genius

For you
I will be a ghetto jew
and dance
and put white stockings
on my twisted limbs
and poison wells
across the town

For you
I will be an apostate jew
and tell the Spanish priest
of the blood vow
in the Talmud
and where the bones
of the child are hid

For you
I will be a banker jew
and bring to ruin
a proud old hunting king
and end his line

For you
I will be a Broadway jew
and cry in theatres
for my mother
and sell bargain goods
beneath the counter

For you
I will be a doctor jew
and search
in all the garbage cans
for foreskins
to sew back again

For you
I will be a Dachau jew
and lie down in lime
with twisted limbs
and bloated pain
no mind can understand

Style

I don't believe the radio stations
of Russia and America
but I like the music and I like
the solemn European voices announcing jazz
I don't believe opium or money
though they're hard to get
and punished with long sentences
I don't believe love
in the midst of my slavery I
do not believe
I am a man sitting in a house
on a treeless Argolic island

I will forget the grass of my mother's lawn
I know I will
I will forget the old telephone number
Fitzroy seven eight two oh
I will forget my style
I will have no style
I hear a thousand miles of hungry static
and the old clear water eating rocks
I hear the bells of mules eating
I hear the flowers eating the night
under their folds
Now a rooster with a razor
plants the haemophilia gash across
the soft black sky
and now I know for certain
I will forget my style
Perhaps a mind will open in this world
perhaps a heart will catch rain
Nothing will heal and nothing will freeze
but perhaps a heart will catch rain
America will have no style
Russia will have no style
It is happening in the twenty-eighth year
of my attention
I don't know what will become
of the mules with their lady eyes
or the old clear water
or the giant rooster
The early morning greedy radio eats
the governments one by one the languages
the poppy fields one by one
Beyond the numbered band
a silence develops for every style
for the style I laboured on
an external silence like the space
between insects in a swarm
electric unremembering
and it is aimed at us
(I am sleepy and frightened)
it makes toward me brothers

The Music Crept by Us

I would like to remind
the management
that the drinks are watered
and the hat-check girl
has syphilis
and the band is composed
of former SS monsters
However since it is
New Year's Eve
and I have lip cancer
I will place my
paper hat on my
concussion and dance

D.G. Jones

(b. 1929)

Doug Jones was born in Bancroft, Ontario. He earned his BA at McGill, where he began writing and won several prizes, and went on to earn his MA at Queen's University. His early work was encouraged and ultimately published, in magazines and in book form, by Louis Dudek and Raymond Souster at Contact Press. Jones taught English at the Ontario Agricultural College in Guelph and, later, for many years, at the University of Sherbrooke, where with Sheila Fischman he co-edited *Ellipse*, a quarterly review designed to present the work of French- and English-Canadian writers in reciprocal translation. He has published numerous books of poetry, including *Frost on the Sun* (1957), *The Sun Is Axeman* (1961), *Phrases from Orpheus* (1967), *Under the Thunder the Flowers Light Up the Earth* (1977, Governor General's Award), *Balthazar and Other Poems* (1988), *The Floating Garden* (1995), *Grounding Sight* (1999), and *The Stream Exposed with All Its Stones: Collected Poems* (2010). In addition to reviews and critical articles, Jones published a major analysis of image and theme in Canadian literature, *Butterfly on Rock* (1970). He also edited *Esprit de Corps: Québec Poetry of the Late Twentieth Century in Translation* (1997) and has done separate translations of the poetry of Emile Martel, Gaston Miron, and Paul-Marie Lapointe. His translation of Normand de Bellefeuille's *Categorics One, Two and Three* received the Governor General's Award for translation in 1993. Jones is also a two-time recipient of the A.M. Klein Award for poetry. He lives in North Hatley, Quebec.

There is a passage in *Butterfly on Rock* that is both an acute comment on the state of poetry in Canada and a useful summary of Jones's own poetic development: "Having reached the Pacific, Canadians have begun to turn back on themselves, to create that added dimension Teilhard de Chardin calls the noosphere. . . . More than ever before, we have arrived at a point where we recognize, not only that the land is ours, but that we are the land's." His first three volumes of poetry represent the stages in his own journey toward a "true" landscape. In *The Sun Is Axeman*, a hostile nature is presented, one that is stunted and barren, mute and unsympathetic, unlike anything in the pastoral world of his earlier poems. In *Phrases from Orpheus*, the poet experiences a dark night of the soul, in which he asks, "how shall I love / this earth, / which is my certain death?"

As important as locating his own noosphere is Jones's discovery of the means to give it imaginative expression. In "Clotheslines" he argues that "the most common things / clothes hung out to dry / serve as well as kings / for your imagery." The metaphors here are organic, drawing the reader toward, rather than away from, the subject; and the poetry makes its appeal more through the senses than through the intellect. In a letter to me he explains his method: "It is always a case of seeing through a conventional pattern or faded myth to something more immediate, vital or violent, and the renewal of the old or the creation of a new myth more adequate to that immediate experience."

In the later work, using his twin viewpoints—his garden as a window on the natural world and television as a window on the world of society and politics—Jones combines metaphors of growth and decay, love and violence, to create poems that attain great lyrical intensity. He distances himself, as a poet, from logic and rhetorical persuasion, for reasons he makes clear in this interview with Philip Lanthier (*Matrix*, No. 50):

> More and more it's a question of leaps, a question of not getting locked in. You want to have some kind of rigour, but logical rigour, even metaphysical rigour, can be so bloody boring. . . . One of the images I have of a poem and of living is broken-field running. The thing is to keep going and not fall flat on your face with whatever comes up: bumps, holes, ups and downs, winds, logs. You keep going up and over and around. You negotiate all these things and to get there you also have to digest them. That's what people do in living.

Beautiful Creatures Brief as These

For Jay Macpherson

Like butterflies but lately come
From long cocoons of summer
These little girls start back to school
To swarm the sidewalks, playing-fields,
And litter air with colour.

So slight they look within their clothes,
Their dresses looser than the Sulphur's wings,
It seems that even if the wind alone
Were not to break them in the lofty trees,
They could not bear the weight of *things*.

And yet they cry into the morning air
And hang from railings upside down
And laugh, as though the world were theirs
And all its buildings, trees, and stones
Were toys, were gifts of a benignant sun.

For Françoise Adnet

It is that time of day, time
To chop the beans, to peel
Potatoes for the evening meal.

The fullness of time
Grows, at this hour,
Like the shadows on the crockery.

Mademoiselle's mauve gloves,
Alone, tell of the afternoon, the dried
Flowers, the delicate hands among the stalks.

For once things are what they are,
Until my little girl
Comes in from outdoors, the melting snow

Cool in her nostrils,
Sky, blue without clouds,
Behind her eyes.

But even these dissolve.
Fingering an orange
She lets her bare legs dangle.

Time is space, it glows
Like the white tablecloth,
The breadboard where I slice the onions.

The kitchen floats in my tears—
And the sun
In its brazier of urban trees.

These Trees Are No Forest of Mourners

They had dragged for hours.
The weather was like his body,
Cold, though May. It rained.

It had rained for three days—
In the grass, in the new leaves,
In the black boughs against the sky.

The earth oozed,
Like the bottom of the lake—
Like a swamp. They stared

At the drowned grass, at the leaves
That dripped in the water—aware
Of their own death, heavy

As the black boughs of the spruce
Moving in a current under the grey
Surface of the sky—aware

Of a supreme ugliness, which seemed
In its very indifference,
Somehow, to defy them:

The sodden body of the world
And of their only son.

Let them be. Oh hear me,

Though it cannot help you. They exist
Beyond your grief; they have their own
Quiet reality.

The Stream Exposed with All Its Stones

The stream exposed with all its stones
Flung on a raw field
Is covered, once again,

With snow.

It is not hidden. It
Still flows.

The houses in the valley, standing
Motionless below,
Seem wrapped in sunlight like a snow

And are deceptive. Even stones
Deceive us.

The creator goes
Rampaging through our lives: winter
Is a masquerade.

I tell you
Nakedness is a disguise: the white
Is dark below

The silence is the water's cry.

I tell you in those silent houses girls
Are dancing like the stones.

Words From the Aviary

For Monique

I would clothe you in feathers

You are too bare
in your long bones when the wind
sighs in the snow

You are a movement of birds

I would clothe you in voices
appellations, words
spare as the mirror of a young girl

or raw, and deliquescent as the crow's
cawing over chill fields

It is not a clothing but a call

of voices, nameless
gone into the still air

of the small birds that drift
above a river running among stones
in the Haute-Savoie

above the grasses of the steppe, and in the small
trees of the taiga

in the summer forest
north
along the Ottawa

I would surround you with a guard
of heron like a tall
smoke, I would surround you with a choir
of unrecorded waterbirds, exiguous
emerging from a wall

beyond the Nile

I would have you smile, and see the sun
arrested, rest among your bones

as glistening

you move within the garden of your names, diaphanous
innumerable

You walk as you have always walked
through desert yards, the cold
spaces where the night

sighs among the stars

the sunken orchard where the wind
sighs in the snow

You are an overture. You come

like a migration
like the first waters of the world
with their entelechy of flowers

And then your naked summer
silences my words

Alden Nowlan

(1933–1983)

Alden Nowlan was born in the Nova Scotia backwoods. He left school at age 12 and worked as a farm labourer, a sawmill helper, the manager of a country music band, and editor of the *Hartland Observer*, finally joining the *Telegraph-Journal* of Saint John, New Brunswick. He engaged in various freelance writing projects, and was writer-in-residence at the University of New Brunswick from 1969 until his death. Nowlan wrote plays including *Frankenstein* (1967) and *One Dollar Woman* (1971), both with Walter Learning, and an unpublished work about Sherlock Holmes. His more than 25 published collections of poetry include *The Rose and the Puritan* (1958), *A Darkness in the Earth* (1959), *Wind in a Rocky Country* (1960), *Under the Ice* (1961), *The Things Which Are* (1962), *Bread, Wine and Salt* (1967, Governor General's Award), *the mysterious naked man* (1969), *Playing the Jesus Game* (1970), *Between Tears and Laughter* (1971), *I'm a Stranger Here Myself* (1974), *Smoked Glass* (1977), *I Might Not Tell Everybody This* (1982), *An Exchange of Gifts: Poems New and Selected* (1985), *Selected Poems* (1996, edited by Patrick Lane and Lorna Crozier), and *Between Tears and Laughter: Selected Poems* (UK, 2004). Some of his short stories are collected in *Miracle at Indian River* (1968); an autobiographical novel, *Various Persons Named Kevin O'Brien*, appeared in 1973, and a second novel, *The Wanton Troopers*, appeared in 1988. *Road Dancers*, a gathering of journalistic pieces, was published in 1999.

"I am a product," Nowlan said, "of a culture that fears any display of emotion and attempts to repress any true communication. . . . In my childhood and early youth I experienced the kind of poverty that scarifies and warps the soul." His is a dark world indeed, a world brutalized by destitution, ignorance, fear, greed, and lust. Anyone familiar with the fictional world of Hugh MacLennan's *Each Man's Son* or David Adams Richards's Miramichi novels will recognize Nowlan's landscapes at once.

Poetry for Nowlan was a means of establishing communication; like the atheist's prayer, it was a "reaching out in fear and gentleness." Though not a moralist, he is capable of fine moral discriminations, as in "In Those Old Wars" where he reflects on the degrading effects of power and the (sometimes) ennobling effects of defeat. Nowlan claimed that his work as a journalist gave him the sense of writing for an audience. "You learn a great respect for the audience when you do newspaper work," he said. "And, another thing, it made me very aware of people." He brought to poetry the journalist's disarming directness and nose for story, the novelist's gift of characterization, and the capacity to embody a feeling or idea in an image of action. "I don't like hypocrisy and I don't like fakes," he said in a typically candid fashion. "I think the most important division in the world is between the people who are real and the people who are fakes." Journalism also left its mark on his style, where the pressure to "get things said" seemed to preclude rhetoric, ornament.

As Robert Bly suggests in the prefatory note to *Playing the Jesus Game*, Nowlan is a poet entangled not in words, but in the universe. "Human feeling is all that counts," Nowlan said. "To hell with literature . . . it's a kind of reassurance that there are people out there, listening. Makes me sort of visualize my poems wandering all over the place tapping people on the shoulder and saying: 'Hi there, I'm Alden Nowlan, who are you?'" In response to being labelled a regionalist poet, Nowlan replied: "I don't write about Maritime people in capital letters, as if they were some special species. I have certain feelings and responses—I could well have these same feelings and responses if I lived in Montreal, but I'd write about them in a different way, simply because I'd have a different experience and see different things if I lived in Montreal."

Beginning

From that they found most lovely, most abhorred,
my parents made me: I was born like sound
stroked from the fiddle to become the ward
of tunes played on the bear-trap and the hound.

Not one, but seven entrances they gave
each to the other, and he laid her down
the way the sun comes out. Oh, they were brave,
and then like looters in a burning town.

Their mouths left bruises, starting with the kiss
and ending with the proverb, where they stayed;
never in making was there brighter bliss,
followed by darker shame. Thus I was made.

Warren Pryor

When every pencil meant a sacrifice
his parents boarded him at school in town,
slaving to free him from the stony fields,
the meagre acreage that bore them down.

They blushed with pride when, at his graduation,
they watched him picking up the slender scroll,
his passport from the years of brutal toil
and lonely patience in a barren hole.

When he went in the Bank their cups ran over.
They marvelled how he wore a milk-white shirt
work days and jeans on Sundays. He was saved
from their thistle-strewn farm and its red dirt.

And he said nothing. Hard and serious
like a young bear inside his teller's cage,
his axe-hewn hands upon the paper bills
aching with empty strength and throttled rage.

And He Wept Aloud, So That the Egyptians Heard It

In my grandfather's house
for the first time in years,
houseflies big as bumblebees
playing crazy football
in the skim-milk-coloured windows,

leap-frogging from
the cracked butter saucer
to our tin plates of

rainbow trout and potatoes, catching the bread
on its way to our mouths,
        mounting one another
        on the rough deal table.

It was not so much their filth
as their numbers and persistence and—
oh, admit this, man, there's no point in poetry
if you withhold the truth
once you've come by it—
        their symbolism:
        Baal-Zebub,
god of the poor and outcast,

that enraged me, made me snatch the old man's
Family Herald, attack them like a maniac,
lay to left and right until the window sills
over-flowed with their smashed corpses,
until bits of their wings
stuck to my fingers,
until the room buzzed with their terror . . .

And my grandfather, bewildered and afraid,
came to help me:
        "never seen a year
        when the flies were so thick"
as though he'd seen them at all before I came!

His voice so old and baffled and pitiful
that I threw my club into the wood box and sat down
        and wanted to beg his forgiveness
as we ate on in silence broken only
by the almost inaudible humming
of the flies rebuilding their world.

The Mysterious Naked Man

A mysterious naked man has been reported
on Cranston Avenue. The police are performing
the usual ceremonies with coloured lights and sirens.
Almost everyone is outdoors and strangers are conversing excitedly
as they do during disasters when their involvement is peripheral.
"What did he look like?" the lieutenant is asking.

"I don't know," says the witness. "He was naked."
There is talk of dogs—this is no ordinary case
of indecent exposure, the man has been seen
a dozen times since the milkman spotted him and now
the sky is turning purple and voices
carry a long way and the children
have gone a little crazy as they often do at dusk
and cars are arriving
from other sections of the city.
And the mysterious naked man
is kneeling behind a garbage can or lying on his belly
in somebody's garden
or maybe even hiding in the branches of a tree,
where the wind from the harbour
whips at his naked body,
and by now he's probably done
whatever it was he wanted to do
and he wishes he could go to sleep
or die
or take to the air like Superman.

For Claudine Because I Love Her

Love is also
my finding this house
emptier than a stranger
ever could.

Is it the sound of your movements
enlivening the chairs
although I hear nothing, is it the weight
of your small body moving the house
so little no machine
could ever assess it,
though my mind knows,
is it some old
wholly animal instinct
that fills every room with you,
gently, so I am aware of it only

when I come home
and there is nothing here.

Ypres: 1915

The age of trumpets is passed, the banners hang
like dead crows, tattered and black,
rotting into nothingness on cathedral walls.
In the crypt of St Paul's I had all the wrong thoughts,
wondered if there was anything left of Nelson
or Wellington, and even wished
I could pry open their tombs and look,
then was ashamed
of such morbid childishness, and almost afraid.

I know the picture is as much a forgery
as the Protocols of Zion, yet it outdistances
more plausible fictions: newsreels, regimental histories,
biographies of Earl Haig.
              It is always morning
and the sky somehow manages to be red
though the picture is in black and white.
There is a long road over flat country,
shell holes, the debris of houses,
a gun carriage overturned in a field,
the bodies of men and horses,
but only a few of them and those
always neat and distant.
              The Moors are running
down the right side of the road.
The Moors are running
in their baggy pants and Santa Claus caps.
The Moors are running.
              And their officers,
Frenchmen who remember
Alsace and Lorraine,
are running backwards in front of them,
waving their swords, trying to drive them back,
weeping
   at the dishonour of it all.
The Moors are running.
And on the left side of the same road,
the Canadians are marching
in the opposite direction.

The Canadians are marching
in English uniforms behind
a piper playing "Scotland the Brave."

The Canadians are marching
in impeccable formation,
every man in step.

The Canadians are marching.

And I know this belongs
with Lord Kitchener's mustache
and old movies in which the Kaiser and his general staff
seem to run like the Keystone Cops.

That old man on television last night,
a farmer or fisherman by the sound of him,
revisiting Vimy Ridge, and they asked him
what it was like, and he said,
There was water up to our middles, yes
and there was rats, and yes
there was water up to our middles
and rats, all right enough,
and to tell you the truth
after the first three or four days
I started to get a little disgusted.
Oh, I know they were mercenaries
in a war that hardly concerned us.
I know all that.

Sometimes I'm not even sure that I have a country.

But I know they stood there at Ypres
the first time the Germans used gas,
that they were almost the only troops
in that section of the front
who did not break and run,
who held the line.

Perhaps they were too scared to run.
Perhaps they didn't know any better
—that is possible, they were so innocent,

those farmboys and mechanics, you have only to look
at old pictures and see how they smiled.
Perhaps they were too shy
to walk out on anybody, even Death.
Perhaps their only motivation
was a stubborn disinclination.

Private MacNally thinking:
You squareheaded sons of bitches,
you want this God damn trench
you're going to have to take it away
from Billy MacNally
of the South End of Saint John, New Brunswick.

And that's ridiculous, too, and nothing
on which to found a country.
Still
It makes me feel good, knowing
that in some obscure, conclusive way
they were connected with me
and me with them.

Eli Mandel

(1922–1992)

Eli Mandel was born in Estevan, Saskatchewan, and lived in that province until he joined the Army Medical Corps in 1943 and went overseas. When he returned from the war, he completed his MA at the University of Saskatchewan and taught at the Collège Militaire Royale de St Jean. He earned a Ph.D. in English at the University of Toronto, taught at the University of Alberta, and became a professor in the fine arts and humanities departments at York University. His first poems were published in *Trio* (1954), with those of Gael Turnbull and Phyllis Webb. His numerous published books of poetry include *Fuseli Poems* (1960), *Black and Secret Man* (1964), *An Idiot Joy* (1967, Governor General's Award), *Crusoe: Poems Selected and New* (1973), *Stony*

Plain (1973), *Out of Place* (1977), *Life Sentence* (1981), *Dreaming Backwards: The Selected Poetry of Eli Mandel, 1954–1981* (1981), and *The Family Romance* (1986). Mandel was also an important critic and anthologist, who had an unusual talent for critical synthesis. He published a series of broadcasts for the CBC: *Criticism: The Silent Speaking Word* (1966), *Contexts of Canadian Criticism* (1971), and *Another Time* (1977). Mandel also edited *Poetry '62* (with Jean-Guy Pilon), *Five Modern Canadian Poets* (1970), *Poets of Contemporary Canada: 1960–1970* (1972), and, with David Tarus, *A Passion for Identity: Introduction to Canadian Studies* (1987).

Mandel's early poetry was admired for its use of classical mythology as a means of exploring experience obliquely. His "Minotaur Poems" and many of the Fuseli poems were written under the critical inspiration of Northrop Frye. In the early poems there is a lyrical poet caged and threatening to break out. In *Black and Secret Man* the work turned personal, inward. Mandel was "a man in search of himself" and his voyage of discovery took him into difficult, troubled waters, through the ranks of his own ghosts, his files of guilt and suffering.

The form of Mandel's verse changed radically over the years, from a rational ordering of materials to fragmentation and logical discontinuity, from language that is heavily rhetorical to a more colloquial idiom. He left behind "the poise and thrust of speech" that "gleams like polished steel" for rougher, more halting, and at times almost incoherent forms of expression. His later poems echo the last speeches of Samuel Beckett's characters in combining grunts, non sequiturs, and erratic description with philosophical profundities and lyrical outpourings. As a Jew, and as a person who had read and absorbed the critical theories of George Steiner in *Language and Silence*, he understood the limitations of rational discourse and the dangers inherent in an indiscriminate use of language.

Mandel was fond of perceptual tricks—unexpected shifts in tone, diction, or point of view that startle the reader into consciousness—although his later verse always seems personal, affective. He uses alienating devices to give another dimension to his poetry. In "Pictures in an Institution" the three self-consciously comic and anti-poetic "notices" in the poem seem at first designed to conceal the poet's embarrassment at the deeply personal nature of the materials. However, it is well to remember that poets are good liars, creatures with a "forked tongue," to use Mandel's phrase, and that the "notices" can also be regarded as devices to heighten the personal emphasis by trying to shift attention to the banal or the merely comic.

For Mandel, the poet is an escape artist, a Houdini, continually seeking newer and more difficult emotional and verbal nets from which to extricate himself. "I am crazed by poetry," Mandel admits, a man "reeling with messages." There is in his poetry and critical utterances a passionate intensity that reminds one at times of W.B. Yeats, his earliest and most obvious influence.

Thief Hanging in Baptist Halls

After a Sculpture by George Wallace

Amid the congratulations of summer,
polite vegetation, deans, a presbyterian sun,
brick minds quaintly shaped in gothic and glass,
here where the poise and thrust of speech
gleams like polished teak
I did not expect to see myself.
But there he hangs
shrugging on his huge lines,
soft as a pulped fruit or bird
in his welded soft suit of steel.

I wish he would not shrug
and smile weakly at me
as if ashamed that he is hanging there,
his dean's suit fallen off, his leg cocked
as if to run
or (too weak, too tired, too undone)
to do what can be done
about his nakedness.

Why should he hang there,
my insulting self, my deanship, all undone?

He dangles while the city bursts in green and steel,
black flower in the mouth of speech:
the proud halls reel,
gothic and steel melt in the spinning sun.

Pictures in an Institution

I

Notice: all mirrors will be covered
the mailman is forbidden to speak
professors are confined to their offices
faculties no longer exist.

II

I speak of what I know,
how uncle Asher, spittle on his lips,
first typed with harvest hands the fox

across a fence and showing all good men
come to their country's aid rushed off to Israel
there to brutalize his wife and son

how step-grandfather Barak wiped
sour curds out of his curly beard
before he roared the Sabbath in my ears
what Sara, long his widow, dreamed
the night she cried: God, let him die at last,
thinking perhaps of Josef who had lost
jewels in Russia where the Cossack rode
but coughed his stomach out in Winnipeg

Your boredom does not matter. I take,
brutal to my thoughts, these lives, defy
your taste in metaphor; the wind-break
on the farm that Barak plowed to dust
makes images would ruin public poetry.

The rites of love I knew:
how father cheated brother, uncle, son,
and bankrupt-grocer, that we might eat
wrote doggerel verse, later took his wife,
my mother, in the English way beside my bed.
Why would he put his Jewishness aside?
Because there was no bread?
                                        Or out of spite
that doctors sliced his double rupture,
fingered spleen, and healed his bowel's ache?

Lovers lie down in glades, are glad.
These, now in graves, their headstones sunk,
knew nothing of such marvels, only God, his ways,
owning no texts of Greek or anthropology.

III

Notice: the library is closed to all who read
any student carrying a gun
registers first, exempt from fines,
is given thirteen books per month,
one course in science, one in math,

two options
campus police
will see to co-eds' underwear

IV

These names I rehearse:
Eva, Isaac,
Charley, Yetta, Max
now dead
or dying or beyond my lies

till I reeling with messages
and sick to hold again their bitter lives
put them, with shame, into my poetry.

V

Notice: there will be no further communication
lectures are cancelled
all students are expelled
the reading of poetry is declared a public
crime

On the 25th Anniversary of the Liberation of Auschwitz

Memorial Services, Toronto, YMHA, Bloor & Spadina, January 25, 1970

the name is hard
a German sound made out of
the gut guttural throat
y scream yell ing open
voice mouth growl
and sweat

the only way out of Auschwitz
is through the chimneys
of course
that's second hand that's told
again Sigmund Sherwood (Sobolewski)
twisting himself into that sentence
before us on the platform
the poem

shaping itself late in the after
noon later than it would be:

Penderecki's "Wrath of God"
moaning electronic Polish theatric
the screen silent
                    framed by the name
looking away from/pretending not there
no   name   no not   name   no

Auschwitz
     in GOTHIC lettering
                          the hall
a parody a reminiscence a nasty memory
the Orpheum in Estevan before Buck Jones
the Capital in Regina before Tom Mix
waiting for the guns
waiting for the cowboy killers
one two three
                  Legionnaires
Polish ex-prisoners Association
Legions
          their medals their flags

so the procession, the poem gradually
insistent beginning to shape itself
with the others
                    walked with them
into the YMHA Bloor & Spadina
thinking apocalypse shame degradation
thinking bones and bodies melting
thickening thinning melting bones and bodies
thinking not mine/speak clearly
the poet's words/Yevtyshenko at Baba-Yar

there   this January   snow
heavy wet   the wind   heavy wet
the street grey white slush melted concrete
bones and bodies melting slush
                                    saw
with the others
                    the prisoner

in the YMHA hall Bloor & Spadina
arms wax stiff body stiff unnatural
coloured face blank eyes
walked
with the others toward the screen
toward the pictures
SLIDES
this is mother
this is father
this is
the one who is
waving her arms like that
is the one who
like
I mean running with her breasts bound
ing
running
with her hands here and there
with her here and
there
hands
that that is

the poem becoming the body
becoming the faint hunger
ing body
prowling
through
words the words words the words
opening mouths ovens
the generals smiling saluting
in their mythic uniforms god-like
generals uniforms with the black leather
with the straps and intricate leather
the phylacteries the prayer shawl
corsets and the boots and the leather straps
and the shining faces of the generals in their boots
and their stiff wax bodies their unnatural faces
and their blank eyes and their hands their stiff hands
and the generals in their straps and wax and stiff
staying standing

melting bodies and thickening
quick flesh on flesh handling
hands

the poem flickers, fades
the four Yarzeit candles guttering one
each four million lights dim
my words drift
smoke from chimneys and ovens
a bad picture, the power failing
pianist clattering on and over and through
the long Saturday afternoon in the Orpheum
while the whitehatted star spangled cowboys
shot the dark men and shot the dark men
and we threw popcorn balls and grabbed
each other and cheered:
me jewboy yelling
for the shot town and the falling men
and the lights come on
and
with the others
standing in silence

the gothic word hangs
over us on a shroud-white screen
and we drift away
to ourselves
to the late Sunday *Times*

the wet snow
the city

a body melting

Milton Acorn

(1923–1986)

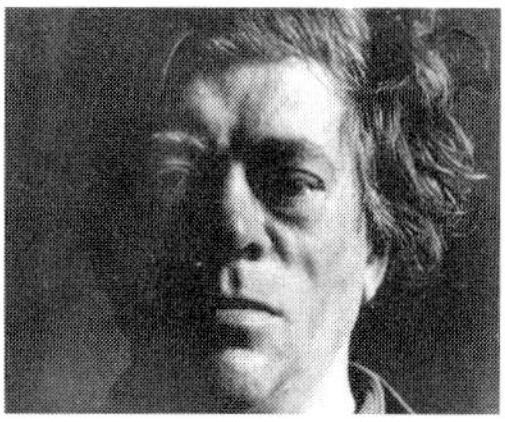

Milton Acorn was born and died in Charlottetown, Prince Edward Island, but he travelled extensively in Canada, spending time in Montreal, Toronto, and Vancouver. In Montreal, he found encouragement and support from poets such as F.R. Scott and A.M. Klein, but he seems to have felt more comfortable amongst the Contact Press group in Toronto, which included Raymond Souster, John Robert Colombo, Irving Layton, and younger poets such as Joe Rosenblatt, Dennis Lee, and Gwendolyn MacEwen, to whom Acorn was married briefly. In Vancouver, he fell in with Dorothy Livesay, Pat Lane, and Bill Bissett, founding an alternative newspaper called *The Georgia Straight*, which is still in operation. Back in Toronto, Acorn was active in art and politics, co-founding Steel Rail Publishing, and so beloved as a literary mentor and role model that he was referred to by many as "The People's Poet."

His philosophy and poetics may be extracted from *Hundred Proof Earth* (1988, edited by James Deahl), where he speaks of poetry as a spiritual exercise, an existential choice that manifests itself in lifting the community to a higher level of caring and consciousness. An admirer of many poetic paths, Acorn chose that of celebration and social engagement:

> Now I am a poet who writes about politics. I don't cover it up with any half-apologetic double-talk about "angelic ravings," I call it politics. Politics in this present day, especially in what is laughably called the "free world," is a mess—and I don't blame any young poet who feels it is a mess and therefore tries to steer clear of it altogether. But, in the most creative moments of history, politics is the focus where all human aspirations meet and struggle for fulfilment. Furthermore, politics is a subject with which most intelligent and sensitive persons are concerned, even if their concern is expressed in a periodic refusal to vote for any of the hopeless fart-faced goons the political machine periodically presents to us in order that we may exercise our "free franchise."

In terms of technique, Acorn favours descriptive image and conversational speech, but argues for personal choice in matters of subject and form. He believed that to achieve so-called timelessness, poetry should be timely, and he believed that the poet needs to address issues such as hunger, poverty, corruption, greed, and loneliness in a personal manner, partisan on behalf of humanity, not some rigid ideology. His books include *In Love and Anger* (1956), *Jawbreakers* (1963), *The Brain's the Target* (1960, edited by Al Purdy), *I've Tasted My Blood* (1969), *More Poems for People* (1972), *The Island Means Minago* (1975), *Jackpine Sonnets* (1977), *Dig Up My Heart* (1983), *Whisky Jack* (1986), and *The Edge of Home: Milton Acorn from the Island* (2002, edited by Anne Compton).

Offshore Breeze

The wind, heavy from the land, irons the surf
to a slosh on silver-damp sand.
The sea's grey and crocheted with ripples;
but shadows, the backs of waves,
lengthen and lapse in the dim haze,
hinting of farther, rougher doings.

The boats went out early, but now
come worm-slow thru haze and distance.
Their gunnels invisible, the men and engines
dots moving on a spit of foam,
they travel past my vision, past
that red jag of a headland, to harbour.

Charlottetown Harbour

An old docker with gutted cheeks,
time arrested in the used-up-knuckled hands
crossed on his lap, sits
in a spell of the glinting water.

He dreams of times in the cider sunlight
when masts stood up like stubble;
but now a gull cries, lights,
flounces its wings ornately, folds them,
and the waves slop among the weed-grown piles.

The Island

Since I'm Island-born home's as precise
as if a mumbly old carpenter,
shoulder-straps crossed wrong,
laid it out,
refigured to the last three-eighths of shingle.

Nowhere that plough-cut worms
heal themselves in red loam;
spruces squat, skirts in sand;
or the stones of a river rattle its dark
tunnel under the elms,
is there a spot not measured by hands;
no direction I couldn't walk
to the wave-lined edge of home.

In the fanged jaws of the Gulf,
a red tongue.
Indians say a musical God
took up His brush and painted it;
named it, in His own language,
"The Island."

Knowing I Live in a Dark Age

Knowing I live in a dark age before history,
I watch my wallet and
am less struck by gunfights in the avenues
than by the newsie with his dirty pink chapped face
calling a shabby poet back for his change.

The crows mobbing the blinking, sun-stupid owl;
wolves eating a hamstrung calf hindend first,
keeping their meat alive and fresh . . . these
are marks of foresight, beginnings of wit:
but Jesus wearing thorns and sunstroke
beating his life and death into words
to break the rods and blunt the axes of Rome:
this and like things followed.

Knowing that in this advertising rainbow
I live like a trapeze artist with a headache,
my poems are no aspirins . . . they show
pale bayonets of grass waving thin on dunes;
the paralytic and his lyric secrets;
my friend Al, union builder and cynic,
hesitating to believe his own delicate poems
lest he believe in something better than himself:
and history, which is yet to begin,
will exceed this, exalt this
as a poem erases and rewrites its poet.

The Natural History of Elephants

In the elephant's five-pound brain
The whole world's both table and shithouse
Where he wanders seeking viandes, exchanging great farts
For compliments. The rumble of his belly
Is like the contortions of a crumpling planetary system.
Long has he roved, his tongue longing to press the juices
From the ultimate berry, large as
But tenderer and sweeter than a watermelon;
And he leaves such signs in his wake that pygmies have fallen
And drowned in his great fragrant marshes of turds.

In the elephant's five-pound brain
The wind is diverted by the draughts of his breath,
Rivers are sweet gulps, and the ocean
After a certain distance is too deep for wading.
The earth is trivial, it has the shakes
And must be severely tested, else
It'll crumble into unsteppable clumps and scatter off
Leaving the great beast bellowing among the stars.

In the elephant's five-pound brain
Dwarves have an incredible vicious sincerity,
A persistent will to undo things. The beast cannot grasp
The convolutions of destruction, always his mind
Turns to other things—the vastness of green
And of frangibility of forest. If only once he could descend
To trivialities he'd sweep the whole earth clean of his tormentors
In one sneeze so mighty as to be observed from Mars.

In the elephant's five-pound brain
Sun and moon are the pieces in a delightfully complex ballgame
That have to do with him . . . never does he doubt
The sky has opened and rain and thunder descend
For his special ministration. He dreams of mastodons
And mammoths and still his pride beats
Like the heart of the world, he knows he could reach
To the end of space if he stood still and imagined the effort.

In the elephant's five-pound brain
Poems are composed as a silent substitute for laughter,
His thoughts while resting in the shade

Are long and solemn as novels and he knows his companions
By names differing for each quality of morning.
Noon and evening are ruminated on and each overlaid
With the taste of night. He loves his horny perambulating hide
As other tribes love their houses, and remembers
He's left flakes of skin and his smell
As a sign and permanent stamp on wherever he has been.

In the elephant's five-pound brain
The entire Oxford dictionary'ld be too small
To contain all the concepts which after all are too weighty
Each individually ever to be mentioned;
Thus of course the beast has no language
Only an eternal pondering hesitation.

In the elephant's five-pound brain
The pliable trunk's a continuous diversion
That in his great innocence he never thinks of as perverse,
The pieces of the world are handled with such a thrilling
Tenderness that all his hours
Are consummated and exhausted with love.
Not slow to mate every female bull and baby
Is blessed with a gesture grandly gracious and felt lovely
Down to the sensitive great elephant toenails.

And when his more urgent pricking member
Stabs him on its horrifying season he becomes
A blundering mass of bewilderment. . . . No thought
But twenty tons of lust he fishes madly for whales
And spiders for copulation. Sperm falls in great gouts
And the whole forest is sticky, colonies of ants
Are nourished for generations on dried elephant semen.

In the elephant's five-pound brain
Death is accorded no belief and old friends
Are continually expected, patience
Is longer than the lives of glaciers and the centuries
Are rattled like toy drums. A life is planned
Like a brushstroke on the canvas of eternity,
And the beginning of a damnation is handled
With great thought as to its middle and its end.

I've Tasted My Blood

If this brain's over-tempered
consider that the fire was want
and the hammers were fists.
I've tasted my blood too much
to love what I was born to.

But my mother's look
was a field of brown oats, soft-bearded;
her voice rain and air rich with lilacs:
and I loved her too much to like
how she dragged her days like a sled over gravel.

Playmates? I remember where their skulls roll!
One died hungry, gnawing grey porch-planks;
one fell, and landed so hard he splashed;
and many and many
come up atom by atom
in the worm-casts of Europe.

My deep prayer a curse.
My deep prayer the promise that this won't be.
My deep prayer my cunning,
my love, my anger,
and often even my forgiveness
that this won't be and be.
I've tasted my blood too much
to abide what I was born to.

Margaret Avison

(1918–2007)

In 1941 Margaret Avison outlined a modest poetic: "Literature," she wrote, "results when: (a) every word is written in the full light of all the writer knows; (b) the writer accepts the precise limits of what he knows, i.e., distinguishes unerringly (while writing) between what he knows, and what he merely knows about, by reputation or reflected opinion." This view, which she endorsed again in 1962, reflects not only the seriousness with which she approached her craft, but also her view of poetry as a vehicle of discovery. She was a philosophical, not a descriptive, poet, interested, as she explains in "Voluptuaries and Others," in "that other kind of lighting up / That shows the terrain comprehended." "Nobody stuffs the world in at your eyes," she writes in "Snow." "The optic heart must venture: a jailbreak / And re-creation." In order to make this jailbreak, the optic heart must see through the pollution of body and mind that produces a society of unconscious grey men and clapboard suburbs, and "this communal cramp of understanding" ("The World Still Needs"). In a world where salesmanship is valued more than a fine ear, where limited imaginations triumph, the poet can find little that is worth her attention and respect. The landscapes of *Winter Sun* (1960) are bleak and imprisoning, like the landscapes of Eliot's early poetry; like Eliot also, Avison is often forced to search the past for significant moments of illumination—hence her interest in great scientists whose imaginative leaps have opened up new worlds of knowledge and experience. "History makes the spontaneous jubilation at such moments less and less likely though," she laments.

Many poems in *Winter Sun* are characterized by rapid shifts of perspective, a kind of poetic equivalent of the use of multiple lenses and camera angles in filmmaking. To write in the "full light of all the writer knows" involves dispensing with all formal notions of time and space. Like the stream-of-consciousness novel, Avison's poetry often leaves the reader hard-pressed to find a centre of gravity, a fixed point of reference. It is as though, in this world of continuous change, the only certainty is the act of perception itself. Each new poem, for poet and reader alike, is analogous to the swimmer's moment at the whirlpool; if both "dare knowledge," they will perhaps discover "the silver reaches of the estuary."

The austere winter terrain of her first book gives way to the gentler landscapes and warmer climates in *The Dumbfounding* (1966), marking a deepening of religious experience as a Christian. There is also reconciliation with the physical world that results in poetry at once more concrete and sensuous. These poems are characterized by a careful observation of minutiae, such as the faces of loiterers and the industry of ants; it is the work of a poet fully absorbed in actuality. Here Avison leaves behind most of the rhetorical and esoteric elements that trouble her earlier verse; her sensitivity to the subtleties of language now encompasses the sound of raindrops, "letting the ear experience this / discrete, delicate / clicking."

Margaret Avison was born in Galt, Ontario, and was educated at the University of Toronto. She worked as a librarian, a secretary, a research worker, a lecturer in English literature, and a social worker at a religious mission in downtown Toronto. During the forties and fifties she contributed to Sid Corman's *Origin*, along with Charles Olson, Denise Levertov, and Robert Creeley. Although remaining at the edges of the literary arena in Canada, Avison was an enthusiastic supporter of other writers and a translator of poems from Hungarian, which appear in *The Plough and the Pen: Writings from Hungary, 1930–1956* (1963), edited by Ilona Duczynska and Karl Polanyi. Her poetry books include *Winter Sun* (1960, Governor General's Award), *The Dumbfounding* (1966), *Sunblue* (1978), *No Time* (1998), *Selected Poems* (1991, Governor General's Award), *Not Yet But Still* (1997), and *Concrete and Wild Carrot* (2002, Griffin Poetry Prize).

Snow

Nobody stuffs the world in at your eyes.
The optic heart must venture: a jail-break
And re-creation. Sedges and wild rice
Chase rivery pewter. The astonished cinders quake
With rhizomes. All ways through the electric air
Trundle candy-bright disks; they are desolate
Toys if the soul's gates seal, and cannot bear,
Must shudder under, creation's unseen freight.
But soft, there is snow's legend: colour of mourning
Along the yellow Yangtze where the wheel
Spins an indifferent stasis that's death's warning.
Asters of tumbled quietness reveal
Their petals. Suffering this starry blur
The rest may ring your change, sad listener.

To Professor X, Year Y

The square for civic receptions
Is jammed, static, black with people in topcoats
Although November
Is mean, and day grows late.

The newspapermen, who couldn't
Force their way home, after the council meeting
&c., move between windows and pressroom
In ugly humour. They do not know
What everybody is waiting for
At this hour
To stand massed and unmoving
When there should be—well—nothing to expect
Except the usual hubbub
Of city five o'clock.

Winter pigeons walk the cement ledges
Urbane, discriminating.

Down in the silent crowd few can see anything.
It is disgusting, this uniformity
Of stature.
If only someone climbed in pyramid
As circus families can . . .
Strictly, each knows
Downtown buildings block all view anyway
Except, to tease them,
Four narrow passages, and ah
One clear towards open water
(If "clear"
Suits with the prune and mottled plumes of
Madam night).

Nobody gapes skyward
Although the notion of
Commerce by air is utterly
familiar

Many citizens at this hour
Are of course miles away, under
Rumpus-room lamps, dining-room chandeliers,
Or bound elsewhere.

One girl who waits in a lit drugstore doorway
North 48 blocks for the next bus
Carries a history, an ethics, a Russian grammar,
And a pair of gym shoes.

But the few thousand inexplicably here
Generate funny currents, zigzag
Across the leaden miles, and all suburbia
Suffers, uneasily.

You, historian, looking back at us,
Do you think I'm not trying to be helpful?
If I fabricated cause-and-effect
You'd listen? I've been dead too long for fancies.
Ignore us, hunched in these dark streets
If in a minute now the explosive
Meaning fails to disperse us and provide resonance
Appropriate to your chronicle.

But if you do, I have a hunch
You've missed a portent.
("Twenty of six." "Snow?—I wouldn't wonder.")

The Swimmer's Moment

For everyone
The swimmer's moment at the whirlpool comes,
But many at that moment will not say
"This is the whirlpool, then."
By their refusal they are saved
From the black pit, and also from contesting
The deadly rapids, and emerging in
The mysterious, and more ample, further waters.
And so their bland-blank faces turn and turn
Pale and forever on the rim of suction
They will not recognize.
Of those who dare the knowledge
Many are whirled into the ominous centre
That, gaping vertical, seals up
For them an eternal boon of privacy,
So that we turn away from their defeat
With a despair, not for their deaths, but for
Ourselves, who cannot penetrate their secret

Nor even guess at the anonymous breadth
Where one or two have won:
(The silver reaches of the estuary).

Voluptuaries and Others

That Eureka of Archimedes out of his bath
Is the kind of story that kills what it conveys;
Yet the banality is right for that story, since it is not a
    communicable one
But just a particular instance of
The kind of lighting up of the terrain
That leaves aside the whole terrain, really,
But signalizes, and compels, an advance in it.
Such an advance through a be-it-what-it-may but take-it-not-
    quite-as-given locale:
Probably that is the core of being alive.
The speculation is not a concession
To limited imaginations. Neither is it
A constrained voiding of the quality of immanent death.
Such near values cannot be measured in values
Just because the measuring
Consists in that other kind of lighting up
That shows the terrain comprehended, as also its containing
    space,
And wipes out adjectives, and all shadows
    (or, perhaps, all but shadows).

The Russians made a movie of a dog's head
Kept alive by blood controlled by physics, chemistry, equip-
    ment, and
Russian women scientists in cotton gowns with writing tablets.
The heart lay on a slab midway in the apparatus
And went phluff, phluff.
Like the first kind of illumination, that successful experiment
Can not be assessed either as conquest or as defeat.
But it is living, creating the chasm of creation,
Contriving to cast only man to brood in it, further.

History makes the spontaneous jubilation at such moments
    less and less likely though,
And that story about Archimedes does get into public school
    textbooks.

Pace

"Plump raindrops in these
faintly clicking groves,
the pedestrian's place, July's
violet and albumen
close?"

"No. No. It is perhaps the conversational side-effect
among the pigeons; behold
the path-dust is nutmeg powdered and
bird-foot embroidered."

        The silk-fringed hideaway
        permits the beechnut-cracking
        squirrels to plumply
        pick and click and
        not listen.

Pedestrians linger
striped stippled sunfloating
    at the rim of the
        thin-wearing groves

letting the ear experience this
discrete, delicate
clicking.

Black-White Under Green: May 18, 1965

This day of the leafing-out
speaks with blue power—
among the buttery grassblades
white, tiny-spraying spokes on the end of a weed-stem
and in the formal beds, tulips
and invisible birds inaudibly hallooing,
enormous, their beaks out wide, throats bulging, aflutter,
eyes weeping with speed
where the ultraviolets play and the scythe of the jets
flashes, carrying
the mind-wounded heartpale person, still a boy, a pianist, dying
        not

of the mind's wounds (as they read the x-rays) but
dying, fibres separated, parents ruddy and
American, strong, sheathed in the cold of
years of his differentness, clustered by two at
the nether arc of his flight.

This day of the leafing-out is one to remember
        how the ice crackled among
                stiff twigs. Glittering strongly
                        the old trees sagged. Boughs
                abruptly unsocketed. Dry, orange gashes
the dawn's fine snowing discovered and powdered over.

. . . to remember the leaves ripped loose
the thudding of the dark sky-beams
and the pillared plunging sea
shelterless. Down the centuries
a flinching speck
        in the white fury found of itself—and another—
the rich blood spilling, mother to child, threading
the perilous combers, marbling
the surges, flung
out, and ten-fingered, feeling for
the lollop, the fine-wired
music, dying skyhigh
still between carpets and the
cabin-pressuring windows
on the day of the leafing.

Faces fanned by
rubberized, cool air
are opened; eyes wisely
smile.
The tulips, weeds, new leaves
neither smile nor are scorning to smile nor uncertain,
dwelling in light.
A flick of ice, fire, flood,
far off from
the day of the leafing-out I knew
when knee-wagon small, or from my
father's once at a horse-tail silk-shiny
fence-corner or this

day when the runways wait
white in the sun, and a new leaf is
metal, torn out of that blue
afloat in the dayshine.

In a Season of Unemployment

These green painted park benches are
all new. The Park Commissioner had them
planted.
Sparrows go on
having dust baths at the edge of
the park maple's shadow, just where
the bench is cemented down, planted
and then cemented.

Not a breath moves
this newspaper.
I'd rather read it by the Lapland sun at midnight. Here we're
bricked in early by a
stifling dark.

On that bench a man in a
pencil-striped white shirt
keeps his head up and steady.

The newspaper-astronaut says
"I feel excellent under the condition of weightlessness."
And from his bench a
scatter of black bands in the hollow-air
ray out—too quick for the eye—
and cease.

"Ground observers watching him on a TV circuit said
At the time of this report he
was smiling," Moscow ra-
dio reported.
I glance across at him, and mark that
he is feeling
excellent too, I guess, and
weightless and
"smiling."

Gwendolyn MacEwen

(1941–1987)

Gwendolyn MacEwen rejected self-indulgent, therapeutic poetry and the "terribly cynical and 'cool' poetry written today." She wrote with the conviction that she had discovered things sayable, and worth saying. "I write basically to communicate joy, mystery, passion," she said, "not the joy that naïvely exists without knowledge of pain, but that joy which arises out of and conquers pain. I want to construct a myth."

MacEwen's poetry might well be discussed in terms of the peculiar ground it inhabits, between the "realists" and the "mythmakers" in Canadian poetry. From the beginning she repudiated the actual world for one that is ancient and mythic, believing that imagination can reconcile the antinomies in life. "I believe there is more room inside than outside," she says in the introduction to *A Breakfast for Barbarians*. "And all the diversities which get absorbed can later work their way out into fantastic things, like hawk-training, IBM programming, mountain-climbing, or poetry."

"I am involved with writing as a total profession, not as an aesthetic pursuit," she said, an opinion borne out by her lifelong commitment and willingness to survive on the barest essentials. "My prime concern has always been with the raw materials from which literature is derived, not with literature as an end in itself." Of course one of the primary sources of raw material for the writer is literature. Although her usual method was to begin with names, to decode language for what it may reveal about the human condition, MacEwen appears, in *The Shadow-Maker*, to be moving more in the direction of realism. Although she employs the passionate more than the normal aspects of speech, she often, like Yeats, combines the oracular and the vernacular in a single poem. She favours the dramatic gesture and direct speech of the actor or storyteller. Hers is also, at times, a poetry of chant or incantation.

Gwendolyn MacEwen was born in Toronto. She first published poetry when she was 15, in *Canadian Forum*. At 18 she left school to take up a full-time career as a writer. After receiving her first Canada Council grant to research a historical novel in Egypt, she went on to receive the CBC New Canadian Writing Contest Award, the Borestone Mountain Poetry Award, and other prizes. She translated, prepared plays and talks for radio, read poetry in clubs, universities, and schools, and was writer-in-residence at the University of Toronto in 1986. She died in November 1987.

Her publications include *Selah* (1961), *The Drunken Clock* (1961), *The Rising Fire* (1963), *A Breakfast for Barbarians* (1966), *The Shadow-Maker* (1969), *The Armies of the Moon* (1972), *Magic Animals: Selected Poems Old and New* (1974), *The Fire-Eaters* (1976), *The T.E. Lawrence Poems* (1982), *Earth Light: Selected Poetry* (1982), *Afterworlds* (1987, Governor General's Award), and a work for juvenile readers, *Dragon Sandwiches* (1987). Her works of adult fiction include *Julian the Magician* (1963), *King of Egypt, King of Dreams* (1971), *Noman* (1972), and *Noman's Land* (1985). Her work is discussed and celebrated in Rosemary Sullivan's *Shadow-Maker: The Life of Gwendolyn MacEwen* (1995).

Manzini: Escape Artist

now there are no bonds except the flesh; listen—
there was this boy, Manzini, stubborn with
gut stood with black tights and a turquoise
leaf across his sex

and smirking while the big
brute tied his neck arms legs, Manzini
naked waist up and white with sweat

struggled. Silent, delinquent, he
was suddenly all teeth and knee, straining slack
and excellent with sweat, inwardly

wondering if Houdini would take as long
as he; fighting time and the drenched
muscular ropes, as though his tendons were worn
on the outside—

as though his own guts were the ropes
encircling him; it was beautiful; it was thursday; listen—
there was this boy, Manzini

finally free, slid as snake from
his own sweet agonized skin, to throw his entrails
white upon the floor
with a cry of victory—

now there are no bonds except the flesh,
but listen, it was thursday, there was this boy,
Manzini—

Poem Improvised around a First Line*

the smoke in my bedroom which is always burning
worsens you, motorcycle Icarus;
you are black and leathery and lean and
you cannot distinguish between sex and nicotine

anytime, it's all one thing for you—
cigarette, phallus, sacrificial fire—
all part of that grimy flight
on wings axlegreased from Toronto to Buffalo
for the secret beer over the border—

now I long to see you fullblown and black
over Niagara, your bike burning and in full flame
and twisting and pivoting over Niagara
and falling finally into Niagara,
and tourists coming to see your black leather wings
hiss and swirl in the steaming current—

now I long to give up cigarettes
and change the sheets on my carboniferous bed;
O baby, what Hell to be Greek in this country—
without wings, but burning anyway

*The first line around which it was improvised has disappeared.

Memoirs of a Mad Cook

There's no point kidding myself any longer,
I just can't get the knack of it; I suspect
there's a secret society which meets
in dark cafeterias to pass on the art
from one member to another.
Besides,
it's so *personal* preparing food for someone's
insides, what can I possibly know
about someone's insides, how can I presume
to invade your blood?
I'll try, God knows I'll try
but if anyone watches me I'll scream
because maybe I'm handling a tomato wrong

how can I *know* if I'm handling a tomato wrong?

something is eating away at me
with splendid teeth

Wistfully I stand in my difficult kitchen
and imagine the fantastic salads and soufflés
that will never be.
Everyone seems to grow thin with me
and their eyes grow black as hunter's eyes
and search my face for sustenance.
All my friends are dying of hunger,
there is some basic dish I cannot offer,
and you my love are almost as lean
as the splendid wolf I must keep always
at my door.

The Child Dancing

there's no way I'm going to write about
the child dancing in the Warsaw ghetto
in his body of rags

there were only two corpses
on the pavement that day
and the child I will not write about
had a face as pale and trusting
as the moon

(so did
the boy with a green belly full of dirt
lying by the roadside
in a novel of Kazantzakis
and the small girl T.E. Lawrence wrote about
who they found after the Turkish massacre
with one shoulder chopped off, crying:
"don't hurt me, Baba!")

I don't feel like slandering them with poetry.

the child who danced
in the Warsaw ghetto
to some music no one else could hear

had moon-eyes, no
green horror and no fear
but something worse

a simple desire to please
the people who stayed
to watch him shuffle back and forth,
his feet wrapped in the newspapers
of another ordinary day

from The T.E. Lawrence Poems

Apologies

I did not choose Arabia; it chose me. The shabby money
That the desert offered us bought lies, bought victory.
    What was I, that soiled Outsider, doing
Among them? I was not becoming one of them, no matter
What you think. They found it easier to learn my kind
    of Arabic, than to teach me theirs.
And they were all mad; they mounted their horses and camels
    from the right.

But my mind's twin kingdoms waged an everlasting war;
The reckless Bedouin and the civilized Englishman
    fought for control, so that I, whatever I was,
Fell into a dumb void that even a false god could not fill,
    could not inhabit.

The Arabs are children of the idea; dangle an idea
In front of them, and you can swing them wherever.
    I was also a child of the idea; I wanted
    no liberty for myself, but to bestow it
Upon them. I wanted to present them with a gift so fine
    it would outshine all other gifts in their eyes;
    it would be *worthy*. Then I at last could be
Empty.

You can't imagine how beautiful it is to be empty.
Out of this grand emptiness wonderful things must surely
    come into being.
When we set out, it was morning. We hardly knew
That when we moved we would not be an army, but a world.

Nitroglycerine Tulips

We planted things called tulip bombs to knock out
    Turkish trains, or curl up the tracks;
    the Turks were so stupid, it sometimes
    seemed to me too easy. How could they
    expect a proper war
If they gave us no chance to honor them?

I called myself Emir Dynamite, and became quite deft
    at the whole business of organized
    destruction. In the back of one train
    which I derailed, was a carriage full of
    dying men; one whispered Typhus,
So I wedged the door closed and left them in.

Another time I straightened out the bodies of dead Turks,
    placing them in rows to look better;
    I was trying, I think, to make it
    a neat war. Once there were three hundred
    of them, with their clothes stripped off,
And I wanted nothing more than to lie down with them,

And die, of course—and think of nothing else but
    raspberries cold with rain, instead of
    sending currents into blasting gelatin
    and watching the sad old trains
    blow sky high
With Turks in little bits around everywhere.

Deraa

I started to write something like:
The citadels of my integrity were lost, or
quo vadis from here, Lawrence?
                                        How pathetic.

I may as well tell you that as a boy my best castle
    was besieged and overcome by my brothers.

What happened of course was that I was raped at Deraa,
    beaten and whipped and reduced to shreds
    by Turks with lice in their hair, and VD,
    a gift from their officers, crawling all over
    their bodies.

I had thought that the Arabs were
Bad enough. Slicing the soles of a prisoner's feet
so that when they let him return to his men,
he went very, very slowly;
but they were merciful.

Imagine, I could never bear to be touched by anybody;
I considered myself a sort of flamboyant monk, awfully
intact, yet colorful.
Inviolable is the word.
But everything is shameful, you know; to have a body
is a cruel joke. It is shameful to be under
an obligation to anything, even an animal;
life is shameful; I am shameful. There.

So what part of me lusted after death, as they smashed
knees into my groin and turned a small knife
between my ribs? Did I cry out or not when
they held my legs apart and one of them rode
upon me, laughing, and splitting open
a bloody pathway through my soul?
I don't remember.
They beat me until something, some
primal slime spilled out of me, and fire
shot to my brain.
On a razor edge of reality,
I knew I would come out of this, bleeding and broken,
and singing.

They lean on the horizon, insolent and wise.

Ghazala's Foal

Ghazala was the second finest camel in all Arabia, and
She did not know it.
She had absolutely no mission in life
and no sense of honor or of shame; she was
almost perfect.
I've seen so many camels die
that it doesn't matter—the females going on
until they foundered and died in their tracks,
the males roaring and flinging themselves down
and dying unnecessarily out of sheer rage, those
we scooped out of the snow at Tafileh—but

Mostly I remember Ghazala's foal, getting up and walking
when it was three hours old, then falling down
again, in a little heap of slippery limbs.

One of the men skinned it, and Ghazala cried and sniffed
the little hide.
Then we marched again, and often
she stopped short, and looked around wildly,
remembering something that was terribly important
then lapsing into a blank, dazed stare.
Only
when the poor, tiny piece of skin was placed
before her on the ground would she
Murmur something, nudge it, ponder a while, and walk on.

Tall Tales

It has been said that I sometimes lie, or bend the truth
to suit me. Did I make that four hundred mile
trip alone in Turkish territory or not?
I wonder if it is anybody's business
to know. Syria is still there,
and the long lie that the war was.

Was there a poster of me offering money for my capture,
and did I stand there staring at myself,
daring anyone to know me? Consider
truth and untruth, consider why they call them
the theatres of war. All of us
played our roles to the hilt.

Poets only play with words, you know; they too
are masters of the Lie, the Grand Fiction.
Poets and men like me who fight for something
contained in words, but not words.

What if the whole show was a lie, and it bloody well was—
would I still lie to you? Of course I would.

Notes from the Dead Land

I have died at last, Feisal. I have been lying
On this hospital bed for five days, and I know
that I am dead. I was going back home

on my big bike, and I wasn't doing more
than sixty when this black van, death camel,
Slid back from the left side of my head, and ahead,
Two boys on little bikes were biking along, and
something in my head, some brutal music
played on and on. I was going too fast,
I was always going too fast for the world,
So I swerved and fell on my stupid head, right
In the middle of the road. I addressed myself
to the dark hearts of the tall trees
and nothing answered.

The Arabs say that when you pray, two angels stand
On either side of you, recording good and bad deeds,
and you should acknowledge them.
Lying here, I decide that now
the world can have me any way it pleases.
I will celebrate my perfect death here. *Maktub*:
It is written. I salute both of the angels.

John Newlove

(1938–2003)

John Newlove's poetry is damnably engaging. The alienation and "wearied intellectuality" he refers to in "In This Reed" predominates in his early work, whose tone recalls postwar British poets such as Philip Larkin. Newlove's poems are peopled with derelicts, hitchhikers, sex workers, outsiders of all sorts. The poet appears as an outsider wandering in a no man's land between the vanishing past and a never-to-be realized future. Memory is another country he inhabits frequently, but in Newlove's cosmos even memory breaks down. The vision of *Black Night Window* is dark indeed, but *The Cave's* landscape is even more desolate. He moves from the bleakness of the Prairies and the unending highway to a more primal landscape of swamps and sea. It is a book of terse confessions, tortured examinations of failed relationships and breakdowns in communication, cynical meditations on history and "progress." The poet experiences not only the disintegration of personality, of identity, but also the collapse of the objective world; he is a man caught between the engine and the sea.

Newlove often writes in a halting, disjunctive, matter-of-fact manner, his resistance to the poetic process evident. As vision darkens there is a corresponding paring down of language. The poems become like etchings, painstakingly made, distillations of complex thoughts and feelings: "I am too tense / decline to dance / verbally." Why, then, given the bleakness of its ostensible content, is Newlove's poetry so breathtaking and exhilarating? A comment of Margaret Atwood's (from an interview with Geoff Hancock in *Canadian Fiction* magazine) seems particularly apt here: "When I finish a book I really like, no matter what the subject matter, or see a play or film like Kurosawa's *Ran*, which is swimming in blood and totally pessimistic, but so well done, I feel very good. I do feel hope. It's the well-doneness that has that effect on me. Not the conclusion—not what is said, per se." A master craftsman with a near perfect ear, Newlove not only knew how to use the tools of poetry, but also had an exceptional gift for rhythm and cadence.

"Ride off Any Horizon" is a good example of his lyricism and range of poetic materials. The poem is interesting first of all because it demonstrates one of the primary ways in which Newlove's imagination works. To ride off any horizon is to let the mind follow any idea or feeling for which there is an appropriate sound pattern, to let the mind be carried along by the verbal associations. The various sections contain almost all of the areas of experience that concern Newlove in his poetry: the vast, untamed Prairies barely touched by the forces of industrialization; the landscapes of the Depression; the destruction of the First Nations that finds its most powerful expression in "The Pride"; the place of boyhood and family memories and emotional relationships; and, finally, the lonely crowds and concrete wilderness of the city. These images are held together by a hypnotic refrain, syntactical recurrence and a subtle patterning of sound.

"Poetry is the shortest distance between two points; prose, the longest," Newlove insists. He writes with directness, candour, and economy about personal relationships and seldom stops short of a precise, rhythmical expression of feeling. Where he cannot find the measure to control a feeling, he will occasionally turn on a gentle but perfectly pitched irony.

Newlove was born in Regina and lived for a number of years in Russian farming communities on the eastern edges of Saskatchewan, where his mother was a teacher. He also lived and worked in Vancouver, Toronto, Ottawa, and Terrace, BC. He served as a publisher's editor, technical writer for government, and writer-in-residence at several Canadian universities. His publications include *Grave Sirs* (1962), *Elephants, Mothers & Others* (1963), *Moving In Alone* (1965), *Notebook Pages* (1966), *What They Say* (1967), *Black Night Window* (1968), *The Cave* (1970), *The Fat Man* (1977), *The Night the Dog Smiled* (1986), and *Apology for Absence: Selected Poems 1962–1992* (1993).

Then, If I Cease Desiring

Then, if I cease desiring,
you may sing a song
of how young I was.

You may praise famous moments,
all have them, of the churches
I broke into for wine,

not praise, the highways
I travelled drunkenly
in winter, the cars I stole.

You may allow me moments,
not monuments, I being
content. It is little,
but it is little enough.

Crazy Riel

Time to write a poem
or something.
Fill up a page.
The creature noise.
Huge massed forces of men
hating each other.
What young men do not know.
To keep quiet,
contemporaneously.
Contempt. The robin diligently
on the lawn sucks up worms,
hopping from one to another.
Youthfully. Sixteen miles
from my boyhood home
the frogs sit in the grassy marsh
that looks like a golf course
by the lake. Green frogs.
Boys catch them for bait or sale.
Or caught them. Time.
To fill up a page.
To fill up a hole.
To make things feel better. Noise.

The noise of the images
that are people I will never understand.
Admire them though I may.
Poundmaker. Big Bear. Wandering Spirit,
those miserable men.
Riel. Crazy Riel. Riel hanged.
Politics must have its way.
The way of noise. To fill up.
The definitions bullets make,
and field guns.
The noise your dying makes,
to which you are the only listener.
The noise the frogs hesitate
to make as the metal hook
breaks through the skin
and slides smoothly into place
in the jaw. The noise
the fish makes caught in the jaw,
which is only an operation
of the body and the element,
which a stone would make
thrown in the same water, thrashing,
not its voice.
The lake is not displaced
with one less jackfish body.
In the slough that looks like a golf course
the family of frogs sings. Metal throats.
The images of death hang upside-down.
Grey music.
It is only the listening for death,
fingering the paraphernalia,
the noise of the men you admire.
And cannot understand.
Knowing little enough about them.
The knowledge waxing.
The wax that paves hell's road,
slippery as the road to heaven.
So that as a man slips
he might as easily slide
into being a saint as destroyer.
In his ears the noise magnifies.
He forgets men.

Verigin, Moving In Alone,

(fatherless, 250 people,
counting dogs and gophers
we would say, Jmaeff's grocerystore,
me in grade 4, mother
principal of the 2-building,
3-room, 12-grade school,)

a boy sitting on the grass
of a small hill, the hot fall,
speaking no russian, an airgun
my sister gave me making me envied.

I tried all fall, all spring
the next ominous year, to kill
a crow with it, secretly glad
I could not, the men
in winter shooting the town's
wild dogs, casually tossing
the quick-frozen barely-bleeding
head-shot corpses onto
the street-side snowbanks,

the highway crews cutting their way
through to open the road with what
I was sure was simply
some alternate of a golden summer's
wheat-threshing machine, children
running through the hard-tossed spray,
pretending war from the monster's snout,

leaping into snowbanks from
Peter The Lordly Verigin's
palace on the edge of town
in a wild 3-dimensional
cubistic game of cops and robbers,

cold spring swimming
in Dead Horse Creek and farmers'
dugouts and doomed fishing
in beastless ponds, strapped
in school for watching a fight,

coldly holding back tears
and digging for drunken father's
rum-bottle, he had finally
arrived, how I loved him,
loved him, love him, dead, still.

My mad old brother chased me
alone in the house with him
around and around
the small living room, airgun
rifle in hand, silently,
our breaths coming together—

all sights and temperatures
and remembrances,
as a lost gull screams now
outside my window,
a 9-year-old's year-long
night and day in tiny
magnificent prairie Verigin:

the long grey cat we got,
the bruised knees, cut fingers,
nails in feet, far walks
to watch a horse's corpse
turn slowly and sweetly to bone,
white bone, and in the late spring,
too, I remember the bright
young bodies of the boys,

my friends and peers and enemies,
till everything breaks down.

Ride off any horizon

and let the measure fall
where it may—

on the hot wheat,
on the dark yellow fields
of wild mustard, the fields

of bad farmers, on the river,
on the dirty river full
of boys and on the throbbing

powerhouse and the low dam
of cheap cement and rocks
boiling with white water,

and on the cows and their powerful
bulls, the heavy tracks
filling with liquid at the edge

of the narrow prairie
river running steadily away.

*

Ride off any horizon
and let the measure fall
where it may—

among the piles of bones
that dot the prairie

in vision and history
(the buffalo and deer,

dead indians, dead settlers
the frames of lost houses

left behind in the dust
of the depression,

dry and profound, that
will come again in the land

and in the spirit, the land
shifting and the minds

blown dry and empty—
I have not seen it! except

in pictures and talk—
but there is the fence

covered with dust, laden,
the wrecked house stupidly empty)—

here is a picture for your wallet,
of the beaten farmer and his wife
leaning toward each other—

sadly smiling, and emptied of desire.

*

Ride off any horizon
and let the measure fall
where it may—

off the edge
of the black prairie

as you thought you could fall,
a boy at sunset

not watching the sun
set but watching the black earth,

never-ending they said in school,
round: but you saw it ending,

finished, definite, precise—
visible only miles away.

*

Ride off any horizon
and let the measure fall
where it may—

on a hot night the town
is in the streets—

the boys and girls
are practising against

each other, the men
talk and eye the girls—

the women talk and
eye each other, the indians
play pool: eye on the ball.

*

Ride off any horizon
and let the measure fall
where it may—

and damn the troops, the horsemen
are wheeling in the sunshine,
the cree, practising

for their deaths: mr poundmaker,
gentle sweet mr bigbear,
it is not unfortunately

quite enough to be innocent,
it is not enough merely
not to offend—

at times to be born
is enough, to be
in the way is too much—

some colonel otter, some
major-general middleton will
get you, you—

indian. It is no good to say,
I would rather die
at once than be in that place—

though you love that land more,
you will go where they take you.

*

Ride off any horizon
and let the measure fall—

where it may;
it doesn't have to be

the prairie. It could be
the cold soul of the cities
blown empty by commerce

and desiring commerce
to fill up emptiness.

The streets are full of people.

It is night, the lights
are on; the wind

blows as far as it may. The streets
are dark and full of people.

Their eyes are fixed as far as
they can see beyond each other—

to the concrete horizon, definite,
tall against the mountains,
stopping vision visibly.

Such Fun, Such Fun

When the poets stopped writing poetry
I thought they were dead
and I went about and tried to describe my country
not leaf by leaf but soul by soul
and I found that though my soul was obscure
it was common. Liquor cured me or calmed me
and pain and long lying lines.

And the poets came back to life and said I was a poet too
and I was astonished!
I hadn't thought they'd known so much
or that I had cared so much.

And the booze tastes good even if the body aches
and the end is shame—but the sheer pleasure
of the gift, of a few gloomy words—

This is prose, this is a ghost with a steel chisel
sneaking another letter onto the stone.

Such fun, such fun. I guess you would have to pay attention
to someone besides yourself. It's better to celebrate
your funeral before you die.

Thank you, thank you.

Robin Blaser

(1925–2009)

Robin Blaser was born in Denver, Colorado. He studied at Northwestern University, College of Idaho, and Berkeley, and was a librarian at Harvard before emigrating from San Francisco to Vancouver to teach English at Simon Fraser University. He became a Canadian citizen in 1972 and gradually published *Cups* (1960), *The Moth Poem* (1964), *Les Chimères* (1964), *Image-Nation 1–12* (1974), *Syntax* (1983), *The Faerie Queene & The Park* (1988), *Pell Mell* (1988), and *Exody* (1993), all part of the lifelong writing project that would be published as *The Holy Forest* (1993).

In league with Jack Spicer, Blaser claimed to be engaged in a "battle for the real," which he considered a narrative of the spirit:

> I'm interested in a particular kind of narrative—what Jack Spicer and I agreed to call in our own work the serial poem—this is a narrative which refuses to adopt an imposed story line, and completes itself only in the sequence of poems, if, in fact, a reader insists upon a definition of completion which is separate from the activity of the poems themselves. The poems tend to act as a sequence of energies.

As a statement of poetics to accompany "The Moth Poem," which appeared in Sharon Thesen's *The New Long Poem Anthology*, Robin Blaser wrote:

> I have found in the serial poem a way to work from my displaced, uncentered "I" in order to be found among things—relational, at least, to what I can. Recent theory tells us writers that the author is gone from his/her authority. That seemed real enough to me before theory ever hit home. And, without authority, a conversation went on. . . . I don't know how to write any more. The covers won't close. I asked a scholar friend of these matters, "What do you say when asked about the serial poem and how it works?" Miriam Nichols answered, "The serial poem builds worlds that are provisional, and those worlds are specific, but not limited, in place and time—the result: plural worlds." So, I guess, "The Moth Poem," though back there, is still working at my initial sense of the multiplicity of times, persons, gods, things, thoughts, places and stuff—folding—

Blaser prefers a poetry open to both the old elegance and to all other forms of language and content, so his work shifts easily from high style to colloquialism—"listen, kid, / there isn't anything but art"—slang, scatological reference, snippets of autobiography, love letters, jokes, and graffiti. In terms of form, it encompasses lyric, anecdote, meditation, elegy, ode, imagist poem, and the occasional professorial aside. He admires the workings of chance in art, which "enters the mind, willy-nilly to unfold our form."

Although the dominant stance here is that of one poet talking to another—through his lyrical, gossipy, or scholarly "notations" and asides, his serial jottings—rather than to some mythical common reader, there is plenty to learn, enjoy, and admire for the eavesdropper in Blaser's salon. As he says in "First Love":

> These poems may seem quirky, even hermetic. They are not. But they do reflect a lifetime of scholarship which gave me, first, pleasure, and then, a cosmos, and then, happiness. I hope that scholarship and the joy of it—the helpless quotation of it—gave greater generosity, a love of this one and that one, who turned up as helpless as I am.

Blaser's love of language and serendipity embrace a scrap of graffiti found in a Gastown washroom: "Artists are the deodorant pucks in the urinals of life." He even incorporates an unflattering personal note from Charles Olson: "I'd trust you anywhere with image, but you've got no syntax."

Winter Words

O fountains, where the throat
is a silent partnership,   part of

the folklore of birds,
the news is

these sorrows
on a dream tree

rigged and actual

(the diaries of friendships
    have almost won a nest for themselves

the life in art fashions itself,
returns, gazes upon the traffic

(has the cold caught
    my hand in the game

    torn

an invisible entertainment
somehow
falls upon all things

Dreams, April, 1981

so it is death is the
condition of infinite form—
the rebellion of particulars,
ourselves and each thing,
even ideas, against that infinitude,
is the story of finitude—the
dream of the children harvested
in a harvester-machine
there are the real voice
and the voice imagined
and both have a reality,
but the latter is out of it
the ladder things

never accept gifts from the gods
—Hesiod's bitter-sweet sense of it—
rings true and doesn't
settle the sea-shore down
to where the *heart breaks or is bronzed*
"I am happy," the man said,
"because the toad of the morning
is the worst thing I'll find today"
and CBC's TV critic says, "television
is the Shakespeare of the 20th century"
red lilies fall on the carpet
and Art Tatum, drawing his art
out of hymns, wanted more dissonance
perfect

there are knives in the air
all around the poorly loved
their lives follow life back
into stone and they dream
a sweeter consonance at the centre
the art of a screaming and
demented oyster is not theirs

The Iceberg

for Michael Ondaatje

I want no summer to melt you
I want no tip to disappear where
I find you—and the largeness
out there, wanders, incomplete,
a constant creation to leap into

"Love" wanders, the speechless
mind of it, all that cost of the
flowers and statues—all that
city of delighted streets and
whimpers   O, the locked heaven
whose gate jangles   I wonder
at the steep of it

then wait, astonished that
the sweet heart grows in some
root or depth—and turns

into ceremonies   there are
the losses of the heartland, light,
sleepless forms against themselves
I repeat you, endlessly—

common, sorrowing, old,
and gigantic
                    this waits
and spits the bird image that
began icily in the distance to
save us, unaware that it lifted,
or was said to, the tip of ourselves

Home for Boys and Girls

the silvery dark, the cry of it,
writing, the couching lion and the
jokes thereof, playing marbles with
jasper—one was how close do
you get to the wall, or the other,
fall into the pit, steelies will get
you out with losses, keeping the marbles,
glassies were resplendent, butterflies,
monarchs of black and near-gold bronze,
clay balls are the cheapest, used if
you're going to lose—or let's play
conkers, polish with shoe-polish,
harden the chestnuts, string them
and swing, hitting the other, spring
games and fall games, of free
children, the unwanted, sent
from England, 1880–1920, Dr. Barnardo's,
when the child first came, he was taken
to a thawing field and told to bury
the dead cow, he dug all day and
used a crow-bar to push the cow
in, buried her, but the legs stuck
up—stiff and everlasting—he
was given an axe, told to return
to the spot and chop the legs off,
the pieces under the thaw and mud,
in the child's mind, everlasting—
and the true gleam of Wordsworth's

children and Coleridge's answer
in the wind's scream, widening loss
and joyance given I repeat:
steelies, pits, jasper and
resplendent glassies

For Barry Clinton, D. 17 June, 1984, of AIDS

a circle of bricks beneath Lucretius' tall
Aphrodite who holds her shell among plum
branches—and iris, columbine—your favourite—
primula Florindae, again to surprise you—pale
blues and bright yellows—white poppies are not
available here—hail! dear blue-eyed
painter

Praise to Them, December 30, 1984

the robins, returned to
the holly-tree   snow-
covered unusually, search
for red berries   joined by
flames—and larger—a
Common Flicker, "red-
shafted," speckled fawn-
breast, long beak of
Picus—the first in
fourteen years—eating
berries in this city-
garden

Of the Land of Culture

I flew too far into the future: a horror assailed me

think of it as fissiparous

an Other who is no longer God or the muse, but anonymous

a CBC interview on China: "Business is above politics"   thereby:
beyondness   and "politics" seeks equality in *kakistocracy* and
its professions

the psychiatric patient said, No, I don't want to go back there—
the place is full of fallen angels trapped in human form

strangers in the existing order, which the ordinary woman or man
can't narrate, though h/she is the most recent and only narrator
left to an anonymous culture   and is promissory

she said, someone broke in last night and stole my sexual organs,
I've called the police again and again, but they won't do any-
thing   the doctor said gently, let's have a look, and he told
her he'd found them where they should be   and she left without
even a thank-you

was her thought of the loss really of the burglar, for whom most
of us wait?

age deepens politics and the wonderful world—oh, dear! body's
and mind's it-ain't-what-it-used-to-be decays in cliché, and is
beside the point—because it never was—in order to say, your
smile is true at the cut

how many centuries has Christianity had in *kind* hands our other-
ness, one to one, here & there, & beyondness?   "christians"—
now manifesting—should all get together and play patty-cake, for
that is the size of their cultural heaven

everyone said, thank you for your bright and careless eyes

Ethan Mordden said, *it could not be that paranoid Old Testament*
sheik with the plagues and tantrums   stopped by briefly, doing all
        over
again goodness

a song on the radio today sang, "To our God we are in debt," so
to describe the deficit

the shills said, confidentially, cultural haven is under one of
these three walnut shells, named O.T., N.T., and materialism—
try your luck!

Hustle, eyes watering, bent over the tabula rasa and his hand
trembled

Then I flew back, homeward—and faster and faster I flew: and so
I came to you, you men of the present, and to the land of culture
I laughed and laughed, while my foot still trembled and my heart
as well: "Here must be the home of all the paint-pots!" I said

You are half-open doors at which grave-diggers wait. And this is
your reality: "Everything is worthy of perishing"

it's amazing to be pushed out of shape a lot of the time, and the
amazement is a cultural gift

someone said, the stones of ______________ [fill in the name of
your own home town] are saturated with poetry

(Nietzsche whispering

George Bowering

(b. 1935)

George Bowering's work has been closely associated with the *Tish* group of poets, who, in reaction to prescribed texts and dominant literary forebears, rejected much of the formalism of Modernist poetry in favour of a poetry that was more personal, more clearly rooted in region or place, and committed to a greater degree of open-endedness. Under the influence mainly of American models, such as William Carlos Williams, Charles Olson, Robert Creeley, and Jack Spicer, these young poets came to regard the poem less as a set piece, or well-made artifact, and more as a process, a sustained moment of discovery. The poet begins with the physical fact of being; thus a preoccupation with breathing, the body, nearby objects and persons. The poem, the created thing, becomes an object in its own right, with laws, a fusion of form and content, a unit of energy passed from writer to reader.

Rather than depending on the metrics and syllabics of closed form, Bowering aims to find and intensify the rhythms of the speaking voice, to be attentive to the music inherent in language, and to reinterpret and invigorate such traditional literary forms as the elegy, the biography, the epistle, the journal, and the thematically based sequence. He has also found congenial the example of earlier poets, such as Rilke. While appearing to drift between form and formlessness, he is struggling to resolve the issue of voice. "Not just Wordsworth's vague idea of using common speech," he says, "but *how to get your own voice on the page*." In his book *Al Purdy* (1970), Bowering explains the notion of finding your own voice as "a writing-school aphorism that inadequately describes the process whereby the poet comes to avail himself of ways to get the individualities of his speech habits into his prosody." As for being a "packrat of the trivial," he insists "there is something in post-modernist composition that welcomes the stray material and resists absorption."

Bowering prefers the notion of dictated writing, letting language rather than content drive the poem—"We are priests, not monarchs. We have no subjects. A gift from the gods is not a licence to rule"—and favours what he calls *tapinosis*, "the saying of very serious things in offhand language, in vernacular, even in slang." He also makes a distinction between those whom he calls the heavy-duty "male" manipulators of language—shapers, power-brokers—and those "girlish priests . . . insect collectors, roadside talkers," like himself, who seek out music, serve rather than master language, and rejoice in "a multiplicity in order." So, it's no surprise that he rejects poetic *aboutists*, insisting that Daphne Marlatt's long poem *Steveston* is not *about* the immigrant or work experiences, though it may allude to them: "A poem such as that, with its devotion to the words, is speaking for poetry, not for the poet."

Bowering was born in Penticton, BC, and was educated at the University of British Columbia, where he received his BA in history and MA in English. In addition to being a co-editor of *Tish*, he edited *Imago* (a magazine devoted to the publication of the long poem), was a contributing editor to *Open Letter*, and edited various anthologies. He taught in Calgary and Montreal before joining the English department at Simon Fraser University in Burnaby, BC. He lives in Vancouver.

An extremely prolific writer, Bowering has published at least 27 books of poetry, including *Sticks & Stones* (1963), *The Man in Yellow Boots* (1965), the two books *Rocky Mountain Foot* and *The Gangs of Kosmos* (1969, which together won a Governor General's Award), *George Bowering: Selected Poems 1961–1992* (1993), *George, Vancouver* (1970), *Autobiology* (1972), *Kerrisdale Elegies* (1984), *His Life: A Poem* (2000), and *Vermeer's Light: Poems 1996–2006* (2006). Bowering has also written several books of criticism, including *A Way With Words* (1982), *The Mask in Place: Essays on Fiction in North America* (1983), *Imaginary Hand: Essays* (1988), and a book of poetics in verse form, *Errata* (1988). He is also author of various works of fiction, including *Protective Footwear* (1978), *Burning Water* (1980, Governor General's Award), *Caprice* (1987), and *Standing on Richards* (2004). His non-fiction works include *Bowering's BC: A Swashbuckling History* (1996), *Egotists and Autocrats: The Prime Ministers of Canada* (1999), and *A Magpie Life: Growing a Writer*. He was appointed Canada's first Parliamentary Poet Laureate in 2002.

Grandfather

Grandfather
                    Jabez Harry Bowering
strode across the Canadian prairie
hacking down trees
                                and building churches
delivering personal baptist sermons in them
leading Holy holy holy lord god almighty songs in them
red haired man squared off in the pulpit
reading Saul on the road to Damascus at them
Left home
                big walled Bristol town
at age eight
                  to make a living
buried his stubby fingers in root snarled earth
for a suit of clothes and seven hundred gruelly meals a year
taking an anabaptist cane across the back every day
for four years till he was whipped out of England

Twelve years old
                          and across the ocean alone
to apocalyptic Canada
                                    Ontario of bone bending child labor
six years on the road to Damascus till his eyes were blinded
with the blast of Christ and he wandered west
to Brandon among wheat kings and heathen Saturday nights
young red haired Bristol boy shoveling coal
in the basement of Brandon college five in the morning

Then built his first wooden church and married
a sick girl who bore two live children and died
leaving several pitiful letters and the Manitoba night

He moved west with another wife and built children and churches
Saskatchewan Alberta British Columbia Holy holy holy
lord god almighty
                           struck his labored bones with pain
and left him a postmaster prodding grandchildren with crutches
another dead wife and a glass bowl of photographs
and holy books unopened save the bible by the bed

Till he died the day before his eighty fifth birthday
in a Catholic hospital on sheets white as his hair

Bones along Her Body

Bones along her body show
art is never far below,
reason offers equal space
bones that glimmer in her face;
art is never far from where
reason offers up its chair—
art is never far away.

Phones ring out in open air,
ears deduce a message there,
noises all fall into place,
tones that need no special grace;
letting half her reason go,
art is never far from so,
never far when she will play
dancing bones on reason's day.

from Kerrisdale Elegies

Elegy One[1]

If I did complain, who among my friends
would hear?
                    If one of them
amazed me with an embrace
he would find his arms empty, his own face
staring from a mirror.

Beauty is the first prod of fear,
                                        we must
live our lives in.
                        We reach for her,
we think we love her, because she holds the knife
a knife-edge from our throat.

---

[1] The stanzas of this poem were originally separated by page breaks, represented here by bullets.

Every fair heart
is frightful.
Every rose petal
exudes poison in bright sunlight.

•

So I close my mouth, and my cry
makes dark music in my belly.
Who would listen
who could amaze?
Friends and beauty
lie waiting in poems, and the god
whose life we once wrote has left us
to muck in a world we covered with grease.

Maybe I should watch the blossoms
turn to toasted flakes on my cherry tree.
Maybe I should walk along 41st Avenue
where mothers in velvet jogging suits push prams
and imitate the objects of my first lyrics.
Maybe I should comb my hair
the way I did in high school.

•

In the night the wind slides in from the sea
and eats at our faces;
that sweetheart,
she would do anything you ask her,
ask her,
she'll lie down for a lonely heart.
Night-time's for lovers, maybe, closing their eyes
and pretending tomorrow will be splendid.

You should know that, you adult;
why dont you fling your arms wide
into the juicy air, chuck your ardent loneliness,
bump birds out of their dark paths
homeward to their grieving chicks.

•

Be grateful—
sadness makes music, cruel
April tuned a string for you.

Moons
whirled around planets waiting for you to spot them.
The middle of the Pacific prepared a wave
to plash ashore at your visit.
A radio
switched to a melody as you walked by
a neighbour's window.

You should know by now,
the world waited
to come alive at your step—
could you handle that?
Or did you think this was love,
movie music
introducing a maiden you could rescue?
Where were you going to keep her,
and keep her
from seeing those dreams you were already
playing house with?

•

When your heart hungers,
sing a song of six-
teen, remember your own maidenly love
and the girls that aroused it,
make them famous.
Remember their plain friends who danced so well
because they never got into a back seat.
Bring them all back, become a lyric poet again.
Identify with heroes who die for love
and a terrific image,
you'll live forever
in your anguished exalted metaphors.
Oh yeah.

•

But remember nature?
She takes back all
worn-out lovers,
two lie in the earth, one moulders
above-ground;
nature is an exhausted mom,
she cant go on forever,

this is late
in the machine age.
Can you think of one woman
who gave up on the stag line and turned
to God and a peaceful lawn?

•

Isnt it about time we said to hell with agony?
Shouldnt we be rich with hit parade love by now?
Arent we really free to choose joy over drama,
and havent we come through looking pretty good,
like a line-drive off a perfect swing
in the ninth inning?
It leaves the bat faster
than it came to the plate.
Taking that pitch
and standing still in the batter's box is nowhere.

•

Somebody's talking.
Listen, stupid Kerrisdale heart,
the way your dead heroes listened, till
they were lifted out of their shoes,
but they couldnt hear it all, they thought
they were standing on earth.
No,
you're not going to hear the final clap of truth;
that would kill you in two heart-beats.

•

But listen to the wind in the chestnut trees,
the breath of autumn's bleeding,
the death
of your young heroes.
You recall the breeze
across from the station in Florence,
where you saw an amazing name by the door?
Remember the clouds pulled off the face
of Mt. Blanc you saw from the morning window?
Why would the wind reach down to me?

Am I supposed to translate that swishy voice
into some kind of modern law?
Make me their liar even as the chestnuts are?

Deesse dans l'air repandue,
flamme dans notre souterrain!

•

Yes, I know, it is odd to be away from the world,
dropping all the habits you learned so well;
never bending to look at a rose face to face,
throwing your name away,
free of hands that held you fiercely,
laughing at what you once ached for,
watching all the old connections unravel in space.

•

Being dead is no bed of roses,
you have so much work piled up in front of you
before the long weekend.
But the folks who are still alive are too quick
to make their little decisions.
The spooks, they tell me, cant tell whether they're moving
among corpses or the fretful living.
The everlasting universe of things rolls
through all minds of all ages in every back yard,
and none of them can hear themselves think.

The ones who left early dont need our voices;
they're weaned from this ground as neatly
as we're diverted from mom's tit. But
what about us?
                    We need the mystery, we need
the grief that makes us long for our dead friends,
we need that void for our poems.
We'd be dead without them.

•

Queen Marilyn made silly movies, but she's
the stuff our words are made from.
                                        Her meaning
struts along the lines of a hundred lovely books.
Her music may be heard in the gaps in the traffic
of 41st Avenue.
                    Her shiny breasts
fill the hands of our weeping poets.

Fred Wah

(b. 1939)

Born in Swift Current, Saskatchewan, Fred Wah grew up in the West Kootenay area of British Columbia, a region his work is steeped in, and where he later edited *Scree*, taught at Selkirk College, and was active in founding the writing program at David Thompson University Centre. As he says in an afterword to his *Selected Poems: Loki Is Buried at Smoky Creek* (1976):

> Writing has a lot to do with "place," the spiritual and spatial localities of the writer. I see things from *where* I am, my view point, and I measure and imagine a world from there. . . . I live in the "interior" of British Columbia and such a qualification affects my particular sense of what the world looks like. . . . In the particularity of a place the writer finds revealed the correspondences of a whole world.

While at the University of British Columbia studying music and English literature, Wah became a founding editor of *Tish*, a poetry newsletter influenced by the American Black Mountain poets. To the magazine's celebration of place and formal experimentation in art, Wah added his own musical and linguistic concerns, developing a work that is uniquely grounded, spare, improvisational, and rooted in the vernacular. His graduate study in literature and linguistics at the University of New Mexico and the State University of New York at Buffalo deepened his interest in words as both sign and sound, little units of acoustic energy that have their own agenda, tricks to play, and surprises to offer. Words, he feels, are intimately linked to the body, fuelled or fired by our breathing, and gaining speed, momentum, and coloration from the delivering pulse and nervous system.

While teaching at the University of Calgary, Wah's attention shifted to the remembered places of childhood and family, exploring the contours, the scree and flora, of his Chinese and Caucasian background. Less interested in strict autobiography, he explores instead the word-fields of family, Chinese café, small town, conducting an ongoing dialogue with his dead father, whimsically deconstructing his former selves and the conventions of autobiographical writing, and, of course, experimenting with the long or serial poem. As he explains in a statement written for Sharon Thesen's *The New Long Poem Anthology*:

> Length in poetry seems useful as a means by which to investigate the possibilities of a content, formally, and, further, to extend the inquiry into contiguous aspects of the content. Such a process of composition offers generative resources that extend the dynamics of the poem (rhythm, repetition, shape, etc.) that not so much avoid cadence as configure it in different ways (cadence as shapely settling, not closure).

In "Music, Heart, Thinking," a fascinating interview conducted by Lola Tostevin (*Line*, 12, 1988), Wah speaks not only of "place as a stain, the stain the world makes on a person," but also of more formal considerations, including Victor Shklovsky's theory of "making strange," which Wah explains in this way:

> No, you hold the perception by making it strange. He said that the purpose of art was to make the stone stony. We don't pay attention to the fact that the stone is stony. It's a quality that's given, so it doesn't enter our perception. It's not something that we knowingly experience—but if I make the stone strange, so that somehow you can experience its stoniness, then there's a perception of something that wasn't there before.

In the same interview, Wah argues that "good poetry should bring language to the fore" and speaks of the poet's language as a sort of psychic DNA, an externalization of the music at the heart of the poet's thinking/feeling. He comes back, again and again, to music and cadence:

> I like the discord, the dissonant, because it pushes toward the edge and doesn't fall. . . . What you do when you're a musician or artist is you play the expectation of randomness against the predictability of form that starts to occur. . . . Music by and large operates on cadence and I've always been interested in language as a cadential structure, even minutely, in terms of phrases and clauses.

Wah's other titles include *Lardeau* (1965), *Among* (1967), *Tree* (1974), *Earth* (1974), *Pictograms from the Interior of BC* (1980), *Breathin' My Name with a Sigh* (1981), *Waiting for Saskatchewan* (1985, Governor General's Award), *Music at the Heart of Thinking* (1989), *So Far* (1991), *Sentenced to Light* (2008), *The False Laws of Narrative: The Poetry of Fred Wah* (2009), a prose bio-fiction called *Diamond Grill* (1996), and a collection of critical writing titled *Faking It: Poetics & Hybridity* (2000). He served as Parliamentary Poet Laureate from 2011 to 2013.

from Pictograms from the Interior of BC

Under and over
I see myself rocking
boat/cradle
cave to swim into
over and over again
home again
home

from Waiting for Saskatchewan

Waiting for Saskatchewan
and the origins grandparents countries places converged
europe asia railroads carpenters nailed grain elevators
Swift Current my grandmother in her house
he built on the street
and him his cafes namely the "Elite" on Center
looked straight ahead Saskatchewan points to it
Erickson Wah Trimble houses train station tracks
arrowed into downtown fine clay dirt prairies wind waiting
for Saskatchewan to appear for me again over the edge
horses led to the huge sky the weight and colour of it
over the mountains as if the mass owed me such appearance
against the hard edge of it sits on my forehead
as the most political place I know these places these strips
laid beyond horizon for eyesight the city so I won't have to go
near it as origin town flatness appears later in my stomach why
why on earth would they land in such a place
mass of pleistocene
sediment plate wedge
arrow sky beak horizon still waiting for that
I want it back, wait in this snowblown winter night
for that latitude of itself its own largeness
my body to get complete
it still owes me, it does

Elite 2

Do you remember how living on the prairies was like living in water, in an ocean or a large lake. Movements, decisions, fortunes were made by undercurrent, a sense of sliding along a large floor, in the night. The night I was with you on a trip, just before we moved out to BC, it felt like that, the way we moved, probably by train, through unknown territory. Always you had an "intent." You were on business of some sort and the others we met were all Chinese. You could talk to them. They gave me candy and pinched me. You and they talked and talked. Chinese always sounds so serious, emotional, angry. I napped on the couch in some Chinese store in some Alberta town. The old men played dominoes and smoked and drank tea. In the window dusty plants in porcelain bowls and some goldfish. Does it seem strange to you now to see this in words? Do you remember the trip I'm talking about? Late at night somewhere you played Mah Jong. From outside the sound of the click-clack of the pieces being shuffled over the tabletop under the hum of the men's voices, a real music I felt comfortable with. Even though you stayed late you always came back, going somewhere. We moved that night through this subcontinent of prairie landscape, it was summer and the water was warm and hazy, the possible distances, distant.

Father/Mother Haibun 4

Your pen wrote Chinese and your name in a smooth swoop with flourish and style, I can hardly read my own tight scrawl, could you write anything else, I know you could read, nose in the air and lick your finger to turn the large newspaper page pensively in the last seat of those half-circle arborite counters in the Diamond Grill, your glass case bulging your shirt pocket with that expensive pen, always a favourite thing to handle the way you treated it like jewellry, actually it was a matched pen and pencil set, Shaeffer maybe (something to do with Calgary here), heavy, silver, black, gold nib, the precision I wanted also in things, that time I conned you into paying for a fountain pen I had my eye on in Benwell's stationery store four dollars and twenty cents Mom was mad but you understood such desires in your cheeks relaxed when you worked signing checks and doing the books in the back room of the cafe late at night or how the pen worked perfectly with your quick body as you'd flourish off a check during a busy noon-hour rush the sun and noise of the town and the cafe flashing.

High muck-a-muck's gold-toothed clicks ink mark red green
on lottery blotting paper, 8-spot (click, click)

Father/Mother Haibun 11

Mother somewhere you flying over me with love and close careless caress from Sweden your soft smooth creme skin only thoughts from your mother without comparison the lightness of your life/ blood womaness which is mine despite language across foetalness what gods of northern europe bring out of this sentence we say and live in outside of the wife of the storm god's frictive battle with the "story" our names

Rain washes first snow, old words here on the notepad,
"Where did Odysseus go?"

Music at the Heart of Thinking 90

On the weekend I got into anger talk about landscape and the hunger of narrative to eat answer or time but space works for me because place got to be more spiritual at least last felt now this watery genetic I suspect passions like anger suprafixed to simply dwells I mean contained as we speak of it believe me I'd like to find a new word-track for feeling but language and moment work out simply as simultaneous occurences so I don't think you should blame words for time-lapse tropism eg ethics is probably something that surrounds you like your house it's where you live.

Hamill's Last Stand[1]

for Gladys McLeod

1.

Our concern is tree-murder, harvest
of the forest (she's worried
they call it "timber") timber sale A04292
        structure wood
could be a rough political situation,
                                        could be
we speak as trees,
                        innocent understanding of ourselves

[1] Hamill refers to the watershed forest around Hamill Creek, at the north of Kootenay Lake.

as things or places too, maybe farming
but for the mess
left on the smouldering hillsides
and silting the creeks
maybe a new crop another lifetime, no care
for the names Hemlock, Balsam, Spruce
undone words from our own mouths,
no flowers anymore but
cubic feet seven million two hundred
and thirty-eight
thousand Cedar, Larch, White Bark Pine,
trunk roots and
limbs scrapped trash-wood fuel
for the bush-fires dirty
orange summer skyline, Lodgepole,
White Pine, Other
Species, in other words
strip it, all the growth
for structure wood
core of our eyes to see and say it,
won't be taken
care of, hearts lost in the language
of public auction
only "profit" in the names, no talk
left about it, so set now
there is no argument, choices gone,
nothing left to say
Forest Ranger.

2.

house of structure wood all leaky
roof this morning in the rain

sits in the chimney flashing seeps
through to the roof joists and drips

still upright tree wood (branches?)
from the floor sill to cross-beams

what cells left without the bark, root-
less timbers stand in the doorways

and window frames its ok the house
is "appropriate," our real needs

do not profit us, the hillside trees
also leak the rain down to their roots.

3.

I admit the industry of it, hot
summer work, sweat and mosquitoes
in the headband of the hardhat, chain-oil,
whine of the diesel among the spruce
ehrrrrrehrrr of the saw
to the heart-wood, I admit
the hi-bailer works for a new pickup
each year, weekends in town
I admit his skill, I admit that he makes
a life of his own from it, with a grip
on the throttle lever, admit it

4.

Probably the trees are warming in the sun
the mud dries up and hardens on the roads
streams are full and muddy now in runoff
a whole forest stretches out the new rings
probably it all just stands there, amazed
with the steam rising up from clay banks
gravel shoulders glisten
                                        in the morning light
bridge planks shed roofs ditches a contour
part of a scene, probable and amazing
for the sun,
            warmer now towards the end of March,
a forest moves towards the light.

Margaret Atwood

(b. 1939)

Margaret Atwood, whose career has spanned five decades, is Canada's most celebrated writer, recipient of the Governor General's Award, the Man Booker Prize, France's *Chevalier dans l'Ordre des Arts et des Lettres*, and many others. A literary survivor herself, she champions the survival of individuals in the face of social pressures, of women in a male-dominated society, of communities faced with various threats, and of nature struggling to survive the technologies that dominate it—a degradation that, carried to its extreme, will ensure the extinction of the human species.

Atwood's early poems often depict pioneers confronting a new environment, where "unstructured / space is a deluge." Like the artist, the settler struggles to shape the chaos, render it manageable. *The Journals of Susanna Moodie* (1970) is her most ambitious exploration of this motif. Threats to Canadian sovereignty and cultural survival addressed in our literature—posed by postcolonial attitudes and the increasing dominance of the United States—are wittily explored in *Survival: A Thematic Guide to Canadian Literature* (1972).

Manifestations of greed and power have long interested Atwood. Her work addresses poverty, women's issues, torture, human rights violations, totalitarianism, and racism, presenting the writer as reluctant witness and provocateur. Though these concerns find their fullest dramatic expression in her novels, the poems of *Procedures for Underground* (1970) and *Power Politics* (1973) explore these various battlegrounds in bizarre parables and mordant satires.

In an interview with Christopher Levenson in *Manna*, Atwood said, "I don't think what poetry does is express emotion. What poetry does is evoke emotion from the reader, and that is a very different thing. As someone once said, if you want to express emotion, scream. If you want to evoke emotion it's more complicated." Her use of anomaly and other dislocating devices keeps the reader involved in the poetic process. Non sequiturs, shifts of perspective, misdirections—the surface of an Atwood poem is rarely solid. She loves to explode traditional romantic stances; instead of lyrical overkill and displays of rhetorical sonority, she prefers understatement, the creation of a wry and prosaic voice, and the shock value of surreal images.

Atwood insists that

> every poem has a texture of sound which is at least as important to me as the "argument." This is not to minimize "statement." But it does annoy me when [people] ask, "What is the poet trying to say?" It implies that the poet is some kind of verbal cripple who can't quite "say" what he "means" . . . Poetry is where the language is renewed. If poetry vanished, language would become . . . embalmed. . . . If you think of language as a series of concentric circles, poetry is right in the centre.

Atwood was born in Ottawa and spent much of her childhood in the woods of northern Quebec. She studied at the University of Toronto and Harvard. Her poetry books include *The Circle Game* (1966), *The Animals in That Country* (1968), *You Are Happy* (1974), *Two-Headed Poems* (1978), *True Stories* (1981), *Interlunar* (1984), *Good Bones* (1992), *Morning in the Burned House* (1995), and *The Door* (2007). She has written 13 novels, 10 collections of short fiction, several children's books, and many non-fiction works, including *Moving Targets* (2005), *Negotiating with the Dead: A Writer on Writing* (2002), *Second Words: Selected Critical Prose* (1982), *Payback: Debt and the Shadow Side of Wealth* (2008), and *In Other Worlds: SF and the Human Imagination* (2011). She lives in Toronto.

Progressive Insanities of a Pioneer

I

He stood, a point
on a sheet of green paper
proclaiming himself the centre,

with no walls, no borders
anywhere; the sky no height
above him, totally un-
enclosed
and shouted:

Let me out!

II

He dug the soil in rows,
imposed himself with shovels.
He asserted

into the furrows, I
am not random.

The ground
replied with aphorisms:

a tree-sprout, a nameless
weed, words
he couldn't understand.

III

The house pitched
the plot staked
in the middle of nowhere.

At night the mind
inside, in the middle
of nowhere.

The idea of an animal
patters across the roof.

In the darkness the fields
defend themselves with fences
in vain:
        everything
        is getting in.

IV

By daylight he resisted.
He said, disgusted
with the swamp's clamourings and the outbursts
of rocks,
      This is not order
      but the absence
      of order.

He was wrong, the unanswering
forest implied:

      It was
      an ordered absence

V

For many years
he fished for a great vision,
dangling the hooks of sown
roots under the surface
of the shallow earth.

It was like
enticing whales with a bent
pin. Besides he thought

in that country
only the worms were biting.

VI

If he had known unstructured
space is a deluge
and stocked his log house-
boat with all the animals

even the wolves,

he might have floated.

But obstinate he
stated, The land is solid
and stamped,

watching his foot sink
down through stone
up to the knee.

VII

Things
refused to name themselves; refused
to let him name them.

The wolves hunted
outside.

On his beaches, his clearings,
by the surf of under-
growth breaking

at his feet, he foresaw
disintegration
                    and in the end
through eyes
made ragged by his
effort, the tension
between subject and object,

the green
vision, the unnamed
whale invaded.

They Eat Out

In restaurants we argue
over which of us will pay for your funeral

though the real question is
whether or not I will make you immortal.

At the moment only I
can do it and so

I raise the magic fork
over the plate of beef fried rice

and plunge it into your heart.
There is a faint pop, a sizzle

and through your own split head
you rise up glowing;

the ceiling opens
a voice sings Love Is A Many

Splendoured Thing
you hang suspended above the city

in blue tights and a red cape
your eyes flashing in unison.

The other diners regard you
some with awe, some only with boredom:

they cannot decide if you are a new weapon
or only a new advertisement.

As for me, I continue eating;
I liked you better the way you were,
but you were always ambitious.

Death of a Young Son by Drowning

He, who navigated with success
the dangerous river of his own birth
once more set forth

on a voyage of discovery
into the land I floated on
but could not touch to claim.

His feet slid on the bank,
the currents took him;
he swirled with ice and trees in the swollen water

and plunged into distant regions,
his head a bathysphere;
through his eyes' thin glass bubbles

he looked out, reckless adventurer
on a landscape stranger than Uranus
we have all been to and some remember.

There was an accident; the air locked,
he was hung in the river like a heart.
they retrieved the swamped body,

cairn of my plans and future charts,
with poles and hooks
from among the nudging logs.

It was spring, the sun kept shining, the new grass
lept to solidity;
my hands glistened with details.

After the long trip I was tired of waves.
My foot hit rock. The dreamed sails
collapsed, ragged.

I planted him in this country
like a flag.

Notes toward a Poem That Can Never Be Written

For Carolyn Forché

i

This is the place
you would rather not know about,
this is the place that will inhabit you,
this is the place you cannot imagine,
this is the place that will finally defeat you

where the word *why* shrivels and empties
itself. This is famine.

ii

There is no poem you can write
about it, the sandpits
where so many were buried
& unearthed, the unendurable
pain still traced on their skins.

This did not happen last year
or forty years ago but last week.
This has been happening,
this happens.

We make wreaths of adjectives for them,
we count them like beads,
we turn them into statistics & litanies
and into poems like this one.

Nothing works.
They remain what they are.

iii

The woman lies on the wet cement floor
under the unending light,
needle marks on her arms put there
to kill the brain
and wonders why she is dying.

She is dying because she said.
She is dying for the sake of the word.
It is her body, silent
and fingerless, writing this poem.

iv

It resembles an operation
but it is not one

nor despite the spread legs, grunts
& blood, is it a birth.

Partly it's a job
partly it's a display of skill
like a concerto.

It can be done badly
or well, they tell themselves.

Partly it's an art.

v

The facts of this world seen clearly
are seen through tears;
why tell me then
there is something wrong with my eyes?

To see clearly and without flinching,
without turning away,
this is agony, the eyes taped open
two inches from the sun.

What is it you see then?
Is it a bad dream, a hallucination?
Is it a vision?
What is it you hear?

The razor across the eyeball
is a detail from an old film.
It is also a truth.
Witness is what you must bear.

vi

In this country you can say what you like
because no one will listen to you anyway,
it's safe enough, in this country you can try to write
the poem that can never be written,
the poem that invents
nothing and excuses nothing,
because you invent and excuse yourself each day.

Elsewhere, this poem is not invention.
Elsewhere, this poem takes courage.
Elsewhere, this poem must be written
because the poets are already dead.

Elsewhere, this poem must be written
as if you are already dead,
as if nothing more can be done
or said to save you.

Elsewhere you must write this poem
because there is nothing more to do.

1981

A Women's Issue

The woman in the spiked device
that locks around the waist and between
the legs, with holes in it like a tea strainer
is Exhibit A.

The woman in black with a net window
to see through and a four-inch
wooden peg jammed up
between her legs so she can't be raped
is Exhibit B.

Exhibit C is the young girl
dragged into the bush by the midwives
and made to sing while they scrape the flesh
from between her legs, then tie her thighs
till she scabs over and is called healed.
Now she can be married.
For each childbirth they'll cut her
open, then sew her up.
Men like tight women.
The ones that die are carefully buried.

The next exhibit lies flat on her back
while eighty men a night
move through her, ten an hour.
She looks at the ceiling, listens
to the door open and close.
A bell keeps ringing.
Nobody knows how she got here.

You'll notice that what they have in common
is between the legs. Is this
why wars are fought?
Enemy territory, no man's
land, to be entered furtively,
fenced, owned but never surely,
scene of these desperate forays
at midnight, captures
and sticky murders, doctors' rubber gloves
greasy with blood, flesh made inert, the surge
of your own uneasy power.

This is no museum.
Who invented the word love?

Patrick Lane

(b. 1939)

In an essay entitled "To the Outlaw," first published in John Gill's *New: American & Canadian Poetry* (1971), the young Patrick Lane wrote passionately of the poet as an outsider, a half-mad fugitive who inhabits the margins of society, the darkest corners. Appropriately, images of confinement—jails, cages, rooms, attitudes, roles, social classes, political systems—abound in his poems. Animals—creatures that ought to exist outside the mental and physical prisons man makes, but which are constantly being trapped, victimized, or rendered extinct—stalk through the pages of Lane's books, especially birds, those exotic reminders of our earthbound nature and our deepest yearnings for escape.

Writing from the margins and committed to the working class, Lane identified with Chilean poet Pablo Neruda and the plight of Third World peoples, advocating a poetry along lines suggested in Neruda's essay "Towards an Impure Art": "A poetry impure as the clothing we wear, soup-stained, soiled with our shameful behaviour, our wrinkles and vigils and dreams."

The form and content of most of Lane's early work falls within such "impure" bounds. His messages are not pretty; they are full of guilt and suffering, separation and loss. Gradually, however, the image of the tight-lipped loner who inhabits these poems gives way to a wiser, more reflective persona, capable of greater understanding and a broader historical reference. Whether he is writing about love, nature, the destruction of native cultures, or the castration of a ram, Lane is capable of a delicate but biting lyricism. While his early work was largely anecdotal, Lane moved steadily toward *significant form*, which has more to do with the resources of language than with sensational events. His considerable metaphorical gifts, which had seemed unsuited to an age committed to understatement and economy, became increasingly capable of profound and startling effects.

Ultimately there is a degree of poetic learning and a real commitment to literature in Lane's work that has a more enduring resonance than his outlaw stance. As he works with the longer line and explores certain metrical and syllabic possibilities, Lane learns to appropriate other voices, other times. He speaks more often of tradition and learning from the old masters. In "Meditation 6" of his teaching notes, he explains: "It was simply that I had chosen too narrow a field to work in. I broke away from my contemporaries and spent the next five years studying the masters. If I wanted to be a good writer, I thought back then, I have much to learn." Lane's sense of prosody owes a good deal to Irving Layton, Gwendolyn MacEwen and, perhaps surprisingly, to the prose of writers such as Ernest Hemingway and Raymond Carver. He pays tribute to a wide range of poets, including Jack Gilbert, Robert Hass, Elizabeth Bishop, and Al Purdy.

Lane was born in Nelson, BC, and lived intermittently in the Interior and in Saskatchewan before returning to the west coast. His travels have taken him to Europe, China, and South America. As his poems indicate, he tried his hand at a wide variety of jobs, mostly manual. He was co-founder, with Bill Bissett, of Very Stone House, a small publishing venture operating in transit out of a series of doomed Volkswagen vans, and has been writer-in-residence at Concordia, the University of Manitoba, and the University of Alberta. Before retiring, he taught part-time in the department of creative writing at the University of Victoria. His many books of poetry include *Letters from a Savage Mind* (1966), *The Sun Has Begun to Eat the Mountains* (1972), *Passing into Storm* (1973), *Beware the Months of Fire* (1973), *Unborn Things* (1975), *Poems New and Selected* (1979, Governor General's Award), *Selected Poems* (1987), *Winter* (1990), *Mortal Remains* (1991), *Selected Poems, 1978–1997* (1997), *The Bare Plum of Winter Rain* (2000), *Go Leaving Strange* (2004), *Last Water Song* (2007), and *The Collected Poems of Patrick Lane* (2012). His prose publications include a collection of stories, *How Do You Spell Beautiful?* (1992), a memoir called *There Is a Season* (2004), and a novel called *Red Dog, Red Dog* (2008). He is the recipient of many awards, including the Lieutenant Governor's Award for Literary Excellence in BC.

Passing into Storm

Know him for a white man.
He walks sideways into wind
allowing the left of him

to forget what the right
knows as cold. His ears
turn into death what

his eyes can't see. All day
he walks away from the sun
passing into storm. Do not

mistake him for the howl you hear
or the track you think you
follow. Finding a white man

in snow is to look for the dead.
He has been burned by the wind.
He has left too much

flesh on winter's white metal
to leave his colour as a sign.
Cold white. Cold flesh. He leans

into wind sideways; kills without
mercy anything to the left of him
coming like madness in the snow.

Elephants

The cracked cedar bunkhouse
hangs behind me like a grey pueblo
in the sundown where I sit
to carve an elephant
from a hunk of brown soap
for the Indian boy who lives
in the village a mile back
in the bush.

The alcoholic truck-driver
and the cat-skinner sit beside
me with their eyes closed
all of us waiting out the last hour
until we go back on the grade

and I try to forget the forever
clank   clank   clank
across the grade
pounding stones and earth to powder
for hours in mosquito-darkness
of the endless cold mountain night.

The elephant takes form—
my knife caresses smooth soap
scaling off curls of brown
which the boy saves to take home
to his mother in the village.

Finished, I hand the carving to him
and he looks at the image of the great
beast for a long time
then sets it on dry cedar
and looks up at me:
                    What's an elephant?
he asks me
so I tell him of the elephants
and their jungles. The story
of the elephant graveyard
which no one has ever found
and how the silent
animals of the rain forest
go away to die somewhere
in the limberlost of distances
and he smiles at me
tells me of his father's
graveyard where his people have been
buried for years. So far back
no one remembers when it started
and I ask him where the graveyard is
and he tells me it is gone
now where no one will ever find it
buried under the grade of the new
highway.

Albino Pheasants

At the bottom of the field
where thistles throw their seeds
and poplars grow from cotton into trees
in a single season I stand among the weeds.
Fenceposts hold each other up with sagging wire.
Here no man walks except in wasted time.
Men circle me with cattle, cars and wheat.
Machines rot on my margins.
They say the land is wasted when its wild
and offer plows and apple trees to tame
but in the fall when I have driven them away
with their guns and dogs and dreams
I walk alone. While those who'd kill
lie sleeping in soft beds
huddled against the bodies of their wives

I go with speargrass and hooked burrs
and wait upon the ice alone.

Delicate across the mesh of snow
I watch the pale birds come
with beaks the colour of discarded flesh.
White, their feathers are white,
as if they had been born in caves
and only now have risen to the earth
to watch with pink and darting eyes
the slowly moving shadows of the moon.
There is no way to tell men what to do . . .
the dance they make in sleep
withholds its meaning from their dreams.
That which has been nursed in bone
rests easy upon frozen stone
and what is wild is lost behind closed eyes:
albino birds, pale sisters, succubi.

Fathers and Sons

I will walk across the long slow grass
where the desert sun waits among the stones
and reach down into the heavy earth
and lift your body back into the day.
My hands will swim down through the clay
like white fish who wander in the pools
of underground caves and they will find you
where you lie in the century of your sleep.

My arms will be as huge as the roots of trees,
my shoulders leaves, my hands as delicate
as the wings of fish in white water.
When I find you I will lift you out
into the sun and hold you
the way a son must who is now
as old as you were when you died.
I will lift you in my arms and bear you back.

My breath will blow away the earth
from your eyes and my lips will touch
your lips. They will say the years have been
long. They will speak into your flesh

the word *love* over and over,
as if it was the first word of the whole
earth. I will dance with you and you
will be as a small child asleep in my arms
as I say to the sun, bless this man who died.

I will hold you then, your hurt mouth curled
into my chest, and take your lost flesh
into me, make of you myself, and when you are
bone of my bone, and blood of my blood,
I will walk you into the hills and sit
alone with you and neither of us
will be ashamed. My hand and your hand.

I will take those two hands and hold them
together, palm against palm, and lift them
and say, this is praise, this is the holding
that is father and son. This I promise you
as I wanted to have promised in the days
of our silence, the nights of our sleeping.

Wait for me. I am coming across the grass
and through the stones. The eyes
of the animals and birds are upon me.
I am walking with my strength.
See, I am almost there.
If you listen you can hear me.
My mouth is open and I am singing.

The Spoon

He has picked up the spoon from among all the small things
on the table, the knife and fork, the salt shaker you don't shake
but turn and grind, the bowl with its applesauce, the glass of milk,
and how he hesitated between the glass and the spoon, but chose
the spoon, and his daughter's voice going on
in a low and steady murmur, her blonde hair cut short
and the bit of grey at her temples,
and how he remembers his old mother hating flowers
after his father's funeral, how she would never have any
in the house, and his daughter still talking to him
in her quiet steady voice about things he already knows,

but knowing it is important for her to say them,
important for her to make some kind of order
out of what must seem to her the chaos of what will be
his life now, and the dog barking outside, and the light
on the table, and the spoon in his hands, and he turns it
over among his fingers and marvels at how his hands
have been holding spoons all his life, and he holds it
by the end of the handle and looks carefully into the shallow
bowl polished so carefully by his wife and sees there
his face upside down, and how if he could understand
the spoon everything would become clear to him, if he
could understand something this simple, something
so small and ordinary that he has used every day of his life
and never paid attention to until now, something very small,
and very simple, and not a glass, not a flower, just a spoon,
and that without it everything in his life
would have been different if there had never been spoons, this spoon,
and he feels a sense of wonder at what he holds, and he reaches out
and takes a spoonful of applesauce from the bowl in front of him
and gently and very carefully lifts it not to his mouth,
but to his daughter's mouth, and he touches it against her lips
and she opens her mouth and it is very quiet now and the only thing
he knows he can do is in this moment, and that is what he does.

Michael Harris

(b. 1944)

Michael Harris was born in Glasgow, United Kingdom; he has lived most of his life in Montreal, where he taught creative writing at McGill and Concordia, and literature and poetry at Dawson College. His books of poems include *Poems from Ritual* (1967), *Text for Nausikaa* (1970), *Sparks* (1976), *Grace* (1978), *Miss Emily et la Mort* (1985), *In Transit* (1985), *New and Selected Poems* (1992), and *Circus* (2010, finalist for the Governor General's Award). He is the translator of *Veiled Countries/Lives: Poetry of Marie-Claire Blais* (1984, finalist for the John Glassco Translation Prize) and the editor of *Ten Montreal*

Poets (1975) and *The Signal Anthology of Contemporary Canadian Poetry* (1993). Selections of his poetry twice won prizes in the CBC Literary Competition. He is the founding editor of Véhicule Press's Signal Editions poetry series, which has produced nearly 100 titles to date. He has read his poetry widely in the UK, Iceland, Ireland, Denmark, Norway, Sweden, France, the US, and coast-to-coast across Canada.

In an interview with Carmine Starnino in *Matrix* (No. 50, 1999), Harris was asked if he thinks politics has any place in poetry:

> Absolutely, if actual politics is woven into the fabric of human affairs in a day-to-day way then obviously it has to be taken into account. Much of Seamus Heaney's work reflects that predicament—his poem "Casualty" is a good case in point. . . . I don't think it's possible to write in the twentieth-century without understanding that more people have been killed in this century than in all other centuries combined—more viciously and more effectively.

Harris is less interested as a poet in local or specific examples of these cases of violence than in the human impulses driving them. Since all social and political manifestations of violence have two, or several, sides, he finds taking a grand view limiting. "Poetry, for me, is a matter of clear sight. I don't write poetry to render judgement on a situation or make the world a better place." His job as a poet, he says, is "to remind people, and myself, of those respective impulses." Asked if this reflects a fatalistic view, Harris insists it is not fatalistic, but realistic, since "poetry is like a memorial speech given at a funeral service." Because truth is difficult to achieve without losing one's credibility or one's head, he suggests "it might be more productive to be a working saint than a defunct martyr."

What, then, is the source of his poetry? Harris considers that it's the poet's own personal uniqueness that matters:

> the soap opera of my life—getting married, witnessing death, having children. . . . If I live a conscious life, the thing I'm most conscious of is myself. Through the knowledge that consciousness brings I filter all other experience. Of course, I do hope that, like the ideal journalist, I can set aside that explored conscious self such that I can see other selves for what they are and for how they define themselves. But the Confucian edict is that one looks into one's own heart and the heart of one's family to understand truth, and so ultimately it is the inward turning eye that produces the most significant verse.

Despite looking inward, Harris does not see his poetry as essentially confessional or autobiographical. In the time it takes to process personal experience, something transformative takes place. "So, it's not an investigation of myself as such. It's a matter of trying to achieve an effect to allow the reader to see what I saw then and what I see now."

Siren Songs

It is where the water rises to
fall against the rocks the problem starts
and ends. The Song of the Sirens is one

I'm familiar with. It begins innocently
enough, a kind of *mmm*-ing in the middle
of making love, though it doesn't stop there.

Hard on its tail, as when the doctor
inserts his stick, is the opened-wide *aah* which
rises on up the scale to a full-throated wail

an octave beyond what is held
to be proper in drawingroom company
which is where the drowning happens.

The sailor who plugged his ears up and lashed himself
to the mast had the right idea. Bondage of any sort
is one way of dealing with it. But even

with wax in your ears, the silence of the cry
is deafening, the undulating of the sea relentless,
your fragile craft trying its single-handed best

to keep upright. Anyhow it's not the song itself
that terrorizes. it's the incidental imagery—
the splayed feet unconscious and white

as an upturned frog's; the belly of a fish lolling in the slops.
The jellyfish breasts. Ach. Fiddlesticks. Pythagoras had it
right when he took the measure of that scale,

bent on controlling the music entirely. He
controlled nothing. And Ulysses should've leapfrogged
the railing, jumped happily in amongst the fish

opened his throat, and roared. As it was,
he returned to ever-patient Penelope and died
of boredom in the arid monotone of marriage.

After Rodin's *The Kiss*

Everything else in this room
falls about the lovers, their

bodies risen out of the marble
like gods released at last

from the depths of the sea,
and who, with one kiss, fresh

at the very first, but forever,
cling to each other oblivious

of school children giggling
too loudly in their shadow, the couples

whose fingers thread jealousy together,
the Art Students coolly sketching

their distance; and a young man there,
in terror to look upon such work

as if his own heart's flesh
could ever become that stone.

Family Album: Uncle

Had the earth one more than four corners . . .
Had fire more life than good drink . . .
If the air did more than just *be* there!

But Uncle Edward's pink is tickled fully by water:
hot baths, the certainties of porcelain, the mists
which keep his basso like a wealth

of large slow fish swimming at idle
in the steamy air. He loves even the golden rain
of urine boiling its froth in the toiletbowl.

In his baths, each plip-ploop from the silver taps
is pitch-note for a whiskied hymn to women,
to water, to whisky, whatever! Each drip moves,

like a fishing-bob, the winking pink of his penis.
Outlandishly it peeks from the bulk of him
at the love-songs and war-songs that wheel

circling each other above him; it eyes with awe
the patient polysyllables he herds like pods of whales
for a final sally through the Valley of the Shadow.

Later, in bed, in a dry shroud of sheets,
he dreams a death at sea, watching his voice
rise up in bubbles past the parterre

of ungrateful urchins and bored whelks, past
a mezzanine's yawn of oysters, past a loge
stuffed with an awestruck, round-eyed gawk

of groupers, up through the roof of the sea,
past exhausted mating codfish eaten whole
by a hungry shark; and with the bubbles expanding hugely

sail directly up to Heaven past the sun's
dying fire, past the thinning insufficiencies
of air, beyond the earth's wasting corpse

to burst in liquid glories, drowning
Heaven's whole angelic chorus with
the mortal heart and humour of his song.

from Turning Out the Light

That first day, in the Common Room,
he stood in line with them,
the fifty little boys
in schoolboy grey—
a row of neat parcels
knotted at the neck
with the new School Tie,
their fathers' brush-and-polish
still gleaming on their shoes.

The Head Master ran down the Roll
as each, according to his way,
piped *Here, Sir*; when it came
my brother's turn, he
did what he could, nodding furiously
to help make the answer
fluid and cool, but the nodding
was of a fish beached and doomed

and my foolish brother fell dismal
and silent and tired of it all—

until out of nowhere
the first syllable burst and rang—
and fifty boys stood, stiffening
with astonishment, craning wide-eyed
in shifting rings of whisper
and barely-clamped lungfuls of glee.
He expelled slowly his breath.
It was the right word, and well said.

The Head was kind and caught
quickly the sputtering agitation
in an all-ranks, eyes-front,
dense charge of silence,
under a look that would have had
the least squeak
trip his room-blast of roar. He said, quietly:
You should also say "Sir."

And the S began in a blush of trust,
with a tearing sound
as of long-ripping paper,
a valve not properly fitted,
as the lungs deflated slowly on and on
transfixing the Master suddenly
charmed by this hissing serpentine sway,
the long consistent unstoppable sibilants,
esses upon esses and my brother almost
out of breath, eyes closed,
every muscle tense stepping out into
the sheerfall of accelerating seconds
tongue pressed aching relentlessly
against the incontinent buzz of his teeth—
until the throat stuck shut on its glottis
and his twisted face crimsoned
at the guttering ends of exhaustion—

but the lungs refused collapse
and the bright miracle of breath came pouring
back in a deep, pure sob saying,

Sir, Sir! and a last,
escaping, joyous, *I'm Here, Sir!*

Concentrate

With dusk come creeping as it does across the provinces,
raccoons descend from their roosts in the trees;
moose big as Ozymandias settle up to their bellies in water

and begin, one huge scoop of tongue at a time,
to drink the lake. But once the wire is set and the rigging steady,
there should be little to make you hesitate but a want of confidence—

unless you were to slip into musing about the various malaises
of domesticity, say, the kids and their adventures in the quotidian
messinesses, the ex-wife, money and whatnot. Sex

is a distraction, you might as well admit that once and for all,
what with its swoons and perfumes, its loosenings and tightenings—
admit that one, then, and then move on. The crossing itself is an act

of balance—that is, of faith in one's ability to remain sure-footed
and perpendicular: nothing more than that, but not a whisper
of anything less. One errant thought about how beautiful the clouds

or how awful the fall and it's game over: the carefully notarized will,
the roof guaranteed for ten years, the car just oiled—all gone
in the middle of whatever wildlife may have engaged your interest

half-way between the swaying buildings or wobbling in the thermals
above a river gathering itself to plunge over a lip of granite
and into the vertigo of space. Whether the mole finds her burrowing

stopped short by material she will never know was once a volcano
is of no consequence, is nothing. Just
concentrate and all will be well, the hawks will settle in their nests

in the stilled rivers of bark, the car spark into life with one turn of the key,
the goal, as ever, that little plot of platform at the end of your leisurely walk,
never the fame bestowed by those upturned faces, nor their dark hope

that they will be the lucky ones to see you fall.

Dennis Lee

(b. 1939)

Dennis Lee's urban epic, *Civil Elegies*, was a major poetic and political statement in Canada in the sixties. It expressed outrage at the direction of Canadian politics—a disappointment shared with George Grant's *Lament for a Nation*—a descent from the conservative public enterprise values forged in our first century toward the crass materialism of private enterprise and the blatant individualism embodied in US politics and laissez-faire economics. Poetically, it argued for an expansiveness and reach no longer possible in the solipsistic lyric, as if to say: this country's values are collective; so, too, are poetry's. If there is a single Canadian writer whose work anticipated the Occupy Wall Street movement, it is Dennis Lee.

Lee's is a cautionary, if bleak, vision of what we are doing to our land, our planet, but one that ends on a positive personal note: "Earth, you nearest, allow me. / Green of the earth and civil grey: / within me, without me and moment by / moment allow me for to / be here is enough and earth you / strangest, you nearest, be home." Deep in Lee's work is the struggle for belief, boldly articulated in "Nightwatch" and so beautifully examined in "The Gods," which concludes with these sentiments: "yet it is / better to speak in silence than squeak in the gab of the age, / and if I cannot tell your terrifying / praise . . . I stand against this bitch of a shrunken time . . . and whether you are godhead or zilch or daily ones like before / you strike our measure still and still you / endure as my murderous fate, though I / do not know you."

Lee is also an important bridge-figure in terms of the ground he inhabits between tradition and experiment in poetry, moving easily between free verse and the rhyme and metrics so beloved by earlier generations. Famous for his children's verses in *Alligator Pie*, song lyrics in Jim Henson's TV series *Fraggle Rock*, he has found inspiration in blues and jazz lyrics, with their riffs, raunchiness, and verbal play. Behind the poetry is a restless mind constantly trying to articulate a spiritual vision that sees culture whole, its beliefs embedded and manifest in the social contract.

Lee was born and educated in Toronto, completing his BA and MA at the University of Toronto, the latter with a thesis titled "Ekstatic Form in Modern Literature." In addition to being a lecturer at Victoria College and serving as a resource person at Rochdale College, he was a founding editor of House of Anansi Press. He has worked as a freelance editor, done script work on the Henson fantasy films *The Dark Crystal* and *Labyrinth*, and served as artist-in-residence at the Young Centre in Toronto (home of Soulpepper Theatre) and as Toronto's first Poet Laureate. His critical work, *Savage Fields: An Essay in Literature and Cosmology* (1977), endeavours to explain two different responses to a shift in contemporary consciousness he sees embodied in works such as Ondaatje's *Collected Works of Billy the Kid* and Cohen's *Beautiful Losers*. He has published a dozen poetry books, including *Kingdom of Absence* (1967), *Nightwatch: New and Selected Poems 1969–1996* (1996), *Un* (2003), and *Testament* (2012). His challenging thoughts on craft, process, and poetics can also be found in many of the essays in *Body Music* (1972), in particular his essay "Cadence, Country, Silence: Writing in Colonial Space." He lives in Toronto and continues to be a dynamic force in the shaping of a strong literary culture in Canada.

400: Coming Home

You are on the highway and the great light of
noon comes over the asphalt, the gravelled
shoulders. You are on the highway, there is a kind of
laughter, the cars pound
south. Over your shoulder the scrub-grass, the fences,
the fields wait patiently as though someone
believed in them. The light has laid it
upon them. One
crow scrawks. The edges
take care of themselves, there is
no strain, you can almost hear it, you
inhabit it.

Back in the city, many things you once lived for
are coming apart.
Transistor rock still fills
back yards, in the parks young men do things to
Hondas; there will be
heat lightning, beer on the porches, goings on.
That is not it.

And you are still on the highway. There are no
houses, no farms. Across the median, past the swish and thud of the
northbound cars, beyond the opposite fences,
the fields, the
climbing escarpment, solitary in the
bright eye of the sun the
birches dance, and they
dance. They have

their reasons. You do not know
anything.
Cicadas call now, in the darkening swollen air there is dust
in your nostrils; a
kind of laughter; you are still on the highway.

from Civil Elegies / 1

Toronto's New City Hall opened in 1965. Two curved white towers gave onto a great square; at the time, such a dramatic public space was new in Toronto.

Often I sit in the sun and brooding over the city, always
in airborne shapes among the pollution I hear them, returning;
pouring across the square
in fetid descent they darken the towers
and the wind-swept place of meeting, and whenever
the thick air clogs my breathing it teems with their presence.
Many were born in Canada, and living unlived lives they died
of course but died truncated, stunted, never at
home in native space and not yet
citizens of a human body of kind. And it is Canada
that specialized in this deprivation. Therefore the spectres arrive,
   congregating
in bitter droves, thick in the April sunlight,
accusing us and we are no different, though you would not expect
the furies assembled in hogtown and ring me round, invisible,
   demanding
what time of our lives we wait for till we shall start to be.
Until they come the wide square stretches out
serene, and singly by moments it takes us in, each one for now
a passionate civil man—until it
sends us back to the acres of gutted intentions,
back to the concrete debris, to parking scars and the four-square tiers
of squat and righteous lives. And here
once more, I watch the homing furies' arrival.

I sat one morning by the Moore, off to the west
ten yards, and saw though diffident my city nailed against the sky
in ordinary glory.
And dreamed a better past. A place, a making,
two towers, a teeming, a genesis, a city.
And the men and women performed their daily lives

by ancient measure, patricians in muddy York,
and made their compact together against the gangs of the new.
And as that crumpled before the shambling onset, again the
lives we had not lived in phalanx invisibly staining
the square and vistas, casting back I saw
regeneration twirl its blood and the rebels riding
riderless down Yonge Street, plain men much
goaded by privilege—our other origin, and cried,
"Mackenzie knows a word! Mackenzie
knows a meaning!" but it was not true. Eight-hundred-odd steely insurgents
turned tail at the cabbage patch when a couple of bullets fizzed
and the loyalists, scared skinny by the sound of their own gunfire,
gawked and bolted south to the fort like rabbits,
the rebels for their part bolting north to the pub: the first
spontaneous mutual retreat in the history of warfare.
Canadians, in flight.

Buildings oppress me, and the sky-concealing wires
bunch zigzag through the air. I know
the dead persist in
by-laws, roadways, porticos—the city I live in
is clogged with their presence; they
dawdle about in our lives and form a destiny, still
incomplete, still dead weight, still
demanding whether Canada will be.

But the mad bomber, Chartier of Major Street, Chartier
said it: that if a country has no living past to learn from,
neither is it a country, and promptly
blew himself to bits in the parliament john, leaving as civil testament
assorted chunks of prophet, twitching and
bobbing to rest in the flush.
And what can anyone do in this country, baffled and
making our penance for ancestors, what did they leave us? Indian-swindlers,
stewards of unclaimed earth and rootless what does it matter if they, our
forebears' flesh and bone were often
good men? Good men do not matter to history.
And what can we do here now, for at last we have no notion
what we might have come to be in America, alternative, and how make public

a presence which is not sold out utterly to the modern? utterly? to the
savage inflictions of what is for real, it pays off, it is only
accidentally less than human?

In the city I long for, green trees still
asphyxiate. The crowds emerge at five from jobs
that rankle and lag. Heavy developers
pay off aldermen still; the craft of neighbourhood,
its whichway streets and generations
anger the planners, they go on jamming maps
with asphalt panaceas; single men
still eke out evenings courting, in rooms, alone.
A man could spend a lifetime looking for
peace in that city. And the lives give way around him—marriages
founder, neighbourhoods sag—until
the emptiness comes down on him to stay.
But in the city I long for, the people complete
their origins. Among the tangle of
hydro, hydrants, second mortgages, amid
the itch for new debentures, greater expressways,
in sober alarm they jam their works of progress, asking where
in truth
they come from and to whom they must belong.
And thus they clear a space in which
the full desires of those that begot them, great animating desires
that shrank and grew hectic as the land pre-empted their lives
might still take root, which eddy now and
drift in the square, being neither alive nor dead.
And the people accept a flawed inheritance
and they give it a place in their midst, forfeiting progress, forfeiting
dollars, forfeiting yankee visions of cities that in time it might grow
whole at last in their lives, they might
belong once more to their forebears, becoming their own men.

To be our own men! in dread to live
the land, our own harsh country, beloved, the prairie, the foothills —
and for me it is lake by rapids by stream-fed lake, threading
north through the terminal vistas of black spruce, in a
bitter, cherished land it is farm after
farm in the waste of the continental outcrop —
for me it is Shield but wherever terrain informs our lives and
claims us;

and then, no longer haunted by
unlived presence, to live the cities:
to furnish, out of the traffic and smog and the shambles of dead
precursors,
a civil habitation that is
human, and our own.

The spectres drift across the square in rows.
How empire permeates! And we sit down
in Nathan Phillips Square, among the sun,
as if our lives were real.
Headlines! high-rise! neon hieroglyphics!
And the towers' luminous sign, that not
one countryman has learned, that
men and women live that
they may make that
life worth dying. Living. Hey,
the dead ones! Gentlemen, generations of
acquiescent spectres gawk at the chrome
on American cars on Queen Street, gawk and slump and retreat.
And over the square where I sit, congregating above the Archer
they crowd in a dense baffled throng and the sun does not shine
through.

Coming Becomes You

Coming be-
comes you,
little one:
rockabye world as you lie, and the great pang takes you in
waves. Coming
becomes you.

With horses you come, with arabian
slather with jugular grunts and in
fretwork, in fistfuls, on Fridays we come in the
danger and midnight of horses.
Coming you come like a spill, like a
spell, like a spoonful of flesh in the
roaring, high on blood
ocean, come with your horses, you come to be played.

In after-
come, you nuzzle;
you nestle and noodle and nest.
And the ghosts in your eyes
do their long-legged, chaste parade.
Each time such sadness
hushes me: slow
ache in your gaze—nostalgia for
now, for now as it
goes away.   You're
beautiful, small
queen of the pillow drowse, and
rockabye world in my arms.
Coming becomes you.

Home

Last call for a trashable planet,
bring it on home.
Bring it on *sotto*, bring it on
shockabye. Bring it on oil-
wise, soilwise, waterwise, methuselah—
memory holes in the phyla, and
bring it on home.

(If home still
has a home. If roots
still grope for rootedness. If
butcherama,
botcherama, wide-screen
world has not yet
metamulched what is.)

And farfew the habitat heroes,
bring it on AWOL.
Bring it on oilwork, soilwork, patchwork, be-
gin again—through
plagues of our fathers, blue
culpa.   And
bring it on, bring it on home.

bpNichol

(1944–1988)

Barrie Nichol was born in Vancouver. He obtained a teaching certificate from the University of British Columbia and taught elementary school briefly before settling in Toronto, where he worked at the University of Toronto library and began his experiments in visual poetry, inspired initially by the work of Earle Birney and bill bissett. In 1964, he and David Aylward founded *Ganglia* magazine and press; then came *grOnk* (1967), a visual poetry newsletter. Nichol joined a therapeutic urban commune in Toronto called Therafields, and was a lay therapist himself for many years. Later, he worked as an editor for Coach House Press and Underwhich Editions and taught part-time at York University. Like Dennis Lee, he wrote for the children's television program *Fraggle Rock*. His projects as a sound poet include the record *Motherlove* (1968) and a group called The Four Horsemen (composed of Nichol, Paul Dutton, Steve McCaffery, and Rafael Barreto-Rivera), which specialized in sound performances and was the subject of a film made by Michael Ondaatje in 1970, *The Sons of Captain Poetry*.

Nichol published his work in a wide variety of formats, including broadsides, pamphlets, chapbooks, and a host of full-length books. *Journeying & the returns* (1967) was a box containing an animated flip-poem, visual poems in an envelope, and a more conventional lyric sequence. In 1970, he won the Governor General's Award for four titles: *Still Water*, *The Cosmic Chef*, *Beach Head*, and *The True Eventual Story of Billy the Kid*, which was attacked as pornographic in the House of Commons. He also published several prose works, including *Two Novels* (1969), *Craft Dinner* (1978), and *Journal* (1978). The work for which he is best known, *The Martyrology*, grew, from 1972 until his death in 1988, into a vast and highly regarded life's work. His work is most accessible in *Selected Writing: As Elected* (1980) and *An H in the Heart: A bpNichol Reader* (1994), a posthumous collection edited by George Bowering and Michael Ondaatje.

Nichol experimented visually with cartoons, drawings, and concrete poems, where words, letters, and sometimes graphics are deployed on the page to evoke a primarily visual response. Unlike the painterly concrete poems belonging to the post-Gutenberg era of the printed page, Nichol's experiments are intended to recall poetry's origins in an oral tradition and to emphasize its relation to music. They abandon ordinary words and syntax in favour of utterances of pure sound, or produce sounds and patterns that mimic conventional usage (as do, say, the works of Edward Lear and, at times, e.e. cummings).

In "Talking About the Sacred in Writing," (*Tracing the Paths: Reading Writing The Martyrology*, 1988, edited by Roy Miki), Nichol makes an intriguing statement about his relation to language:

> When I stumbled across the saints with David Aylward in the ST words in language, and for David that's all it was, it was puns—but for me, I suddenly found myself writing a series called Scraptures, in which I was addressing and talking to these saints—long, very argumentative, shrill poems full of extreme rhetoric and, you know, lots of talk about the language revolution and so on was going down. I realized that for some reason these figures which had arisen out of language had a meaning to me that I would not have imagined, that I only got to through the pun, which is why I've tended to follow the pun ever since. . . . I have a profound belief in *that* as a sacred activity—that is to say, *something* goes on. Now, you can use it to crack cheap jokes, you can use it to make profound statements, you can use it to deal with the political necessities of the world, and you can use it to write love poetry. You can use it for all sorts of things, but the activity itself has a tremendous power that has to be, within itself, respected. Now, it seems to me—what I've learned for myself—is that once I respect that activity of the language, then through the language I am literally led to things that I would not arrive at otherwise. Therefore, in a real sense I give up, on the one hand, some sense of the self as guiding the poem, though on the other hand I put a tremendous emphasis on getting my technical chops together so that when I am in the midst of the poem there's nothing standing between me and following it wherever it wants to go.

from The Captain Poetry Poems

dear Captain Poetry,
your poetry is trite.
you cannot write a sonnet
tho you've tried to every night
since i've known you.
we're thru !!
    Madame X

dear Madame X

    Look how the sun leaps now upon our faces
    Stomps & boots our eyes into our skulls
    Drives all thot to weird & foreign places

Till the world reels & the kicked mind dulls,
Drags our hands up across our eyes
Sends all white hurling into black
Makes the inner cranium our skies
And turns all looks sent forward burning back.
And you, my lady, who should be gentler, kind,
Have yet the fiery aspect of the sun
Sending words to burn into my mind
Destroying all my feelings one by one;
    You who should have tiptoed thru my halls
    Have slammed my doors & smashed me into walls.

        love
        Cap Poetry

Blues

What Is Can Lit?

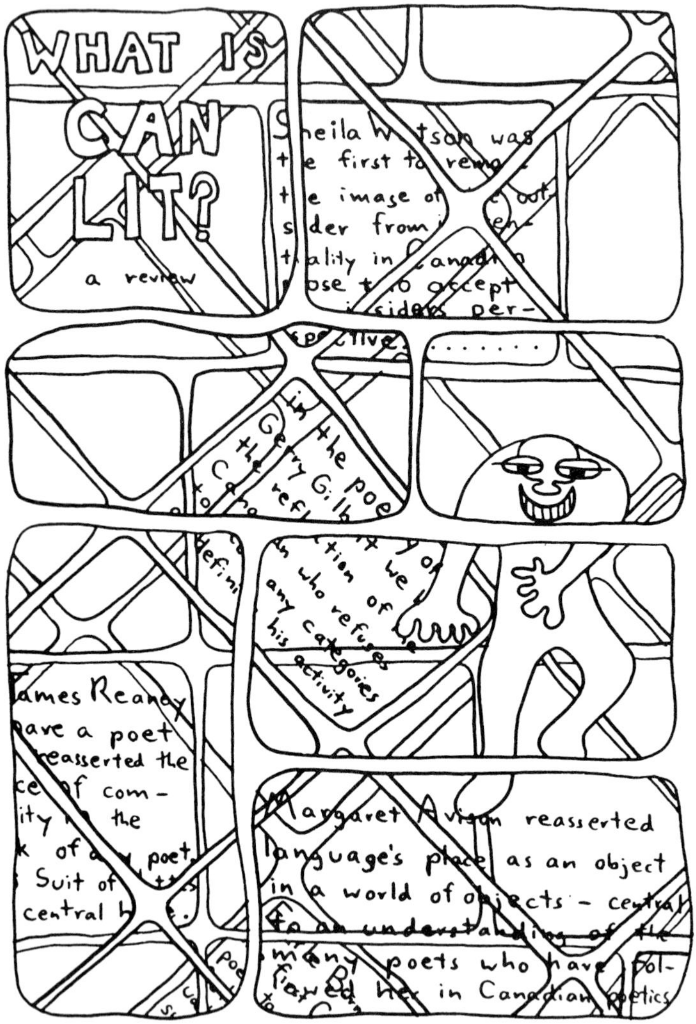

But what the hell is CAN LIT?
1920
1930
it's just a question of SURVIVAL!!
bp 73

Allegory #6

Allegory # 6

Landscape: I

for thomas a. clark

alongthehorizongrewanunbrokenlineoftrees

The Mouth

1

You were never supposed to talk when it was full. It was better to keep it shut if you had nothing to say. You were never supposed to shoot it off. It was better to be seen than heard. It got washed out with soap if you talked dirty. You were never supposed to mouth-off, give them any of your lip, turn up your nose at them, give them a dirty look, an evil eye or a baleful stare. So your mouth just sat there, in the middle of your face, one more set of muscles trying not to give too much away. "Hey! smile! what's the matter with you anyway?"

2

Probably there are all sorts of stories. Probably my mouth figures in all sorts of stories when I was little but I don't remember any of them. I don't remember any stories about my mouth but I remember it was there. I remember it was there and I talked & sang & ate & used it all the time. I don't remember anything about it but the mouth remembers. The mouth remembers what the brain can't quite wrap its tongue around & that's what my life's become. My life's become my mouth's remembering, telling stories with the brain's tongue.

3

I must have been nine. I'm pretty sure I was nine because I remember I was the new boy in school. I remember I was walking on my way there, the back way, thru the woods, & here was this kid walking towards me, George was his name, & I said "hi George" & he said "I don't like your mouth" & grabbed me & smashed my face into his knee. It was my first encounter with body art or it was my first encounter with someone else's idea of cosmetic surgery. It was translation or composition. He rearranged me.

4

The first dentist called me the Cavity Kid & put 35 fillings into me. The second dentist said the first dentist was a charlatan, that all the fillings had fallen out, & put 38 more fillings in me. The third dentist had the shakes from his years in the prisoner of war camp & called me his "juicy one," saliva frothing from my mouth as his shaky hand approached me. The fourth dentist never looked at me. His nurse put me out with the sleeping gas & then he'd enter the room & fill me. The fifth dentist said my teeth were okay but my gums would have to go, he'd have to cut me. The sixth dentist said well he figured an operation on the foot was okay coz the foot was a long way away but the mouth was just a little close to where he thot he lived & boy did we ever agree because I'd begun to see that every time I thot of dentists I ended the sentence with the word "me." My mouth was me. I wasn't any ancient Egyptian who believed his Ka was in his nose—nosiree—I was just a Kanadian kid & had my heart in my mouth every time a dentist approached me.

5

It all begins with the mouth. I shouted waaa when I was born, maaa when I could name her, took her nipple in, the rubber nipple of the bottle later, the silver spoon, smashed peas, dirt, ants, anything with flavour I could shove there, took the tongue and flung it 'round the mouth making sounds, words, sentences, tried to say the things that made it possible to reach him, kiss her, get my tongue from my mouth into some other. I liked that, liked the fact the tongue could move in mouths other than its own, & that so many things began there—words did, meals, sex—& tho later you travelled down the body, below the belt, up there you could belt out a duet, share a belt of whiskey, undo your belts & put your mouths together. And I like the fact that we are rhymed, mouth to mouth, & that it begins here, on the tongue, in the pun, comes from mouth her mouth where we all come from.

6

I always said I was part of the oral tradition. I always said poetry was an oral art. When I went into therapy my therapist always said I had an oral personality. I got fixated on oral sex, oral gratification & notating the oral reality of the poem. At the age of five when Al Watts Jr was still my friend I actually said, when asked who could do something or other, "me or Al" & only years later realized how the truth's flung out of you at certain points &

runs on ahead. And here I've been for years running after me, trying to catch up, shouting "it's the oral", "it all depends on the oral", everybody looking at my bibliography, the too many books & pamphlets, saying with painful accuracy: "that bp—he really runs off at the mouth."

•

old mothers who are gone now
all mute
we are your tongues

born from your mouths' mouths
we have your say
Mother Leigh, Mother Workman, Mother Nichol, Mother Fuller
how many of you am i speaking for today
do you care what words pour from my lips?

this old body flaps in the wind
looks out over the prairie this cold March day
into that landscape most of you wandered into as girls
took up the burden of all that birthing
all that laying down
of the law
the line

old mothers who came before you
i don't know the names of & never will
all talking at once, if you could, in all those other languages
Celtic, German, Cherokee, Dutch
No eyes now, no tongue
only these two, this one
old nouns disappearing behind us
vague pronoun reference a life becomes
who does this i refer to?
which s now speaks thru this he?
eh? She?!

•

for Caspar, who i never knew, so few alive now who did,
what was his thinking? a roof for the family? bread for
the table? and Sarah? birthing all those kids? the two of them
on those various stretches of prairie, all that breaking of
the soil, new ground, they knew what that meant, did it, but

i'm reading all these poems, daily it seems, someone grows old,
someone writes about it, goes to visit their mother or
father, the guilt and grief, the estrangement, changing it all
into myth, as tho that makes it better, it doesn't, they did
what they had to do, died, i never knew

them, me, their great grandson, grows old, becomes
someone else's burden of guilt or grief, my own Sarah,
barely five, so many years since Caspar was alive, all of us
in time, dying, how we all go, on, away,
simply this business, being, day to day, until it's over

Michael Ondaatje

(b. 1943)

Michael Ondaatje was born in Sri Lanka and educated at Dulwich College in the UK. He came to Canada in 1962 to study at Bishop's, then went on to the University of Toronto, and Queen's, completing his MA on Edwin Muir. His poetry publications include *The Dainty Monsters* (1967), *The Man with Seven Toes* (1969), *The Collected Works of Billy the Kid* (1970, Governor General's Award), *Rat Jelly* (1973), *There's a Trick with a Knife I'm Learning to Do* (1979), *Secular Love* (1986), *Handwriting* (1998), and *The Story* (2005). His prose works include *Coming through Slaughter* (1976), the autobiographical *Running in the Family* (1982), and five novels—*In the Skin of a Lion* (1987), *The English Patient* (1992), which won the Booker Prize and was made into a highly successful film, *Anil's Ghost* (2000, Giller Prize, Governor General's Award, and the Prix Medicis), *Divisadero* (2007), and *The Cat's Table* (2011). He has published one critical study, *Leonard Cohen* (1970), and made several short films, including *Sons of Captain Poetry*, about the concrete poet bpNichol, and *The Clinton Special*, about Theatre Passe Muraille's "The Farm Show." He has edited *Personal Fictions* (1977), *The Long Poem Anthology* (1979), and *Ink Lake* (1990, short stories). He lives in Toronto.

If Ondaatje has a poetics, it is expressed in his poem "The gate in his head," dedicated to Victor Coleman: "My mind is pouring chaos / in nets onto the page." Words are the unique threads that, properly woven, can snare strange, unexpected things. Ondaatje recognizes the importance of form in poetry, but rejects undue emphasis on formal structure. In a letter he states his "distrust of all critics and nearly all dogmatic aesthetics and all rules and all clubs/cliques/schools of poetry"; instead, he expresses a "wish to come to each poem and let it breed in its own vacuum and have its own laws and order." He prefers the "caught vision" of a blurred photograph to the standard reproduction of a recognizable reality: "The beautiful formed things caught at the wrong moment / so they are shapeless, awkward / moving to the clear."

The wrong moment is the right moment: that is the secret of Ondaatje's peculiar form of mythmaking. He can only use the traditional nets of classical mythology by altering our perception of them, by coming at them from unexpected angles. Otherwise they are too static and destroy the subject they are called upon to illuminate. A dramatist of disaster with a cinematic eye for detail, for the appropriate image, the bizarre but compelling angle of vision, Ondaatje also has a powerful shaping instinct. In an interview with Sam Solecki in *Spider Blues*, he insists on the importance of "architecture," which is a matter of "repeating and building images and so making them more potent":

> What I want is something more physical, something having to do with the placing of a scene in one place and not in another—that kind of thing. How one composes a book. How one turns the real everyday object into something more by placing it in exactly the right place, with the right tone. There is an architecture of tone as well as of rhythm. What academics are obsessed with is who won the horse race or what it really means. But if you watch a replay you start discovering form. You don't watch the horse in front any more—the leading horse representing "content"—but the horse in fourth place saving himself. I think that writers think about and are interested in that kind of thing, the undercurrents of shape and tone as opposed to just the meaning.

Ondaatje has an acute eye for the bizarre, the abnormal, the out-of-the-way. His landscapes are peopled with strange beasts, cripples, lost and violent souls, animals—all moving in and out of focus, emerging from and receding into some uncharted region of memory. He is fascinated with energy, especially as it is manifested in the form of violence. If his poetry is a catalogue of scars, whether the psychic scar that defines an emotional relationship or the disastrous historical event that shapes the destiny of a nation or civilization, it is worth noting that his characters, like the parade of freaks and grotesques in a Fellini film, are important for what they reveal of the obsessions, perversions, and fears of so-called normal people.

This is not to suggest that his poetry is unrelentingly bleak or morbid. It is not. Ondaatje does not revel in the depiction of violence, but brings to bear on his materials integrity and restraint, and a disarming sense of humour. This is especially evident in the short narratives "Elizabeth" and "Peter," where understatement heightens the dramatic impact of events, and in the book-length sequence of poems about Billy the Kid, where much of the violence has a comic-book quality. If his characters often have blood on their hands and violence on their minds, they are just as likely to have shaving cream on their chins and dragons tangled in their tennis nets.

Early Morning, Kingston to Gananoque

The twenty miles to Gananoque
with tangled dust blue grass
burned, and smelling burned
along the highway
is land too harsh for picnics.
Deep in the fields
behind stiff dirt fern
nature breeds the unnatural.

Escaping cows canter white
then black and white
along the median, forming out of mist.
Crows pick at animal accidents,
with swoops lift meals—
blistered groundhogs, stripped snakes
to arch behind a shield of sun.

Somewhere in those fields
they are shaping new kinds of women.

Elizabeth

Catch, my Uncle Jack said
and oh I caught this huge apple
red as Mrs Kelly's bum.
It's as red as Mrs Kelly's bum, I said
and Daddy roared
and swung me on his stomach with a heave.
Then I hid the apple in my room
till it shrunk like a face
growing eyes and teeth ribs.

Then Daddy took me to the zoo
he knew the man there
they put a snake around my neck
and it crawled down the front of my dress.
I felt its flicking tongue
dripping onto me like a shower.
Daddy laughed and said Smart Snake
and Mrs Kelly with us scowled.

In the pond where they kept the goldfish
Philip and I broke the ice with spades
and tried to spear the fishes;
we killed one and Philip ate it,
then he kissed me
with raw saltless fish in his mouth.

My sister Mary's got bad teeth
and said I was lucky, then she said
I had big teeth, but Philip said I was pretty.
He had big hands that smelled.

I would speak of Tom, soft laughing,
who danced in the mornings round the sundial
teaching me the steps from France, turning
with the rhythm of the sun on the warped branches,
who'd hold my breast and watch it move like a snail
leaving his quick urgent love in my palm.
And I kept his love in my palm till it blistered.

When they axed his shoulders and neck
the blood moved like a branch into the crowd.
And he staggered with his hanging shoulder
cursing their thrilled cry, wheeling,
waltzing in the French style to his knees
holding his head with the ground,
blood settling on his clothes like a blush;
this way
when they aimed the thud into his back.

And I find cool entertainment now
with white young Essex, and my nimble rhymes.

"The gate in his head"

For Victor Coleman

Victor—the shy mind
revealing faint scars
coloured strata of the brain
not clarity but the sense of shift.
A few lines / the tracks of thought.
The landscape of busted trees
melted tires in the sun
Stan's fishbowl
with a book inside
turning its pages
like some sea animal
camouflaging itself
the typeface clarity
going slow blond in the sun full water

My mind is pouring chaos
in nets onto the page.
A blind lover, dont know
what I love till I write it out.
Then from Gibson's your letter
with a blurred
photograph of a gull.
Caught vision. The stunning white bird
an unclear stir.

And that is all this writing should be then.
The beautiful formed things caught at the wrong moment
so they are shapeless, awkward
moving to the clear.

Bearhug

Griffin calls to come and kiss him goodnight
I yell ok. Finish something I'm doing,
then something else, walk slowly round
the corner to my son's room.
He is standing arms outstretched
waiting for a bearhug. Grinning.

Why do I give my emotion an animal's name,
give it that dark squeeze of death?
This is the hug which collects
all his small bones and his warm neck against me.
The thin tough body under the pyjamas
locks to me like a magnet of blood.

How long was he standing there
like that, before I came?

Letters & Other Worlds

for there was no more darkness for him and, no doubt
like Adam before the fall, he could see in the dark

My father's body was a globe of fear
His body was a town we never knew
He hid that he had been where we were going
His letters were a room he seldom lived in
In them the logic of his love could grow

My father's body was a town of fear
He was the only witness to its fear dance
He hid where he had been that we might lose him
His letters were a room his body scared

He came to death with his mind drowning.
On the last day he enclosed himself
in a room with two bottles of gin, later
fell the length of his body
so that brain blood moved
to new compartments
that never knew the wash of fluid
and he died in minutes of a new equilibrium.

His early life was a terrifying comedy
and my mother divorced him again and again.
He would rush into tunnels magnetized
by the white eye of trains
and once, gaining instant fame,
managed to stop a Perahara in Ceylon

—the whole procession of elephants dancers
local dignitaries—by falling
dead drunk onto the street.
As a semi-official, and semi-white at that,
the act was seen as a crucial
turning point in the Home Rule Movement
and led to Ceylon's independence in 1948.
(My mother had done her share too—
her driving so bad
she was stoned by villagers
whenever her car was recognized)

For 14 years of marriage
each of them claimed he or she
was the injured party.
Once on the Colombo docks
saying goodbye to a recently married couple
my father, jealous
at my mother's articulate emotion,
dove into the waters of the harbour
and swam after the ship waving farewell.
My mother pretending no affiliation
mingled with the crowd back to the hotel.

Once again he made the papers
though this time my mother
with a note to the editor
corrected the report—saying he was drunk
rather than broken hearted at the parting of friends.
The married couple received both editions
of *The Ceylon Times* when their ship reached Aden.

And then in his last years
he was the silent drinker,
the man who once a week
disappeared into his room with bottles
and stayed there until he was drunk
and until he was sober.

There speeches, head dreams, apologies,
the gentle letters, were composed.
With the clarity of architects
he would write the row of blue flowers

his new wife had planted,
the plans for electricity in the house,
how my half-sister fell near a snake
and it had awakened and not touched her.
Letters in a clear hand of the most complete empathy
his heart widening and widening and widening
to all manner of change in his children and friends
while he himself edged
into the terrible acute hatred
of his own privacy
till he balanced and fell
the length of his body
the blood screaming in
the empty reservoir of bones
the blood searching in his head without metaphor

Pat Lowther

(1935–1975)

Pat Lowther (née Tinmouth) was born and grew up in North Vancouver, at that time a rugged, sparsely populated landscape. This close proximity to and awareness of nature in its raw and primitive state would prove a constant in her life and poetry. She reveals an almost visceral awareness of the terrain she inhabited, participating in its energy and transformational character, whether her subject is mountains, crane flies, or the waters of Furry Creek. Images of earth and stone abound in her poetry.

Intensely conscious of the intellectual issues of her time—the role of women in society, the way power politics plays out in private and public life—Lowther was concerned with extending consciousness, as she suggests in a note to her poems in *Mountain Moving Day* (1973, edited by Elaine Gill for the Crossing Press):

> I see the women's revolution as part of a new outreach of consciousness. The liberation of women from imposed self-images is happening. Even the most hostile and fearful women are absorbing it subliminally right along with the cream depilatory commercials.

> New assumptions are being accepted below the level of consciousness. . . . I believed we humans were coming to the end of our evolutionary cycle—devolving like dandelions. Now I see the half breeds of the future passing like migrating birds, and I begin to have a kind of tentative hope.

Lowther's poetry is as remarkable for its emotional range and control as it is for its political engagement. Whether she is writing brief imagistic pieces, confessional lyrics, or passionate meditations, she is extremely conscious of prosody—not with rhythm as a decorative element, but with what Pound called the "articulation of the total sound of the poem." This line from "Coast Range"—"billygoat-bearded creeks / bumsliding down / to splat into the sea"—seems to me acoustically superb and brilliantly imagined, a perfect example of what Keats called *negative capability*, the ability to get sufficiently inside an object, person, or event to render it palpable to a reader. Certainly no one has more subtly and playfully conjured the appearance, gymnastics, and soundscape of a skinny, ragged coastal waterfall.

Lowther was murdered by her husband Roy, who was jealous of her literary success and growing independence. Before her death in 1975, she had published three books of poetry: *This Difficult Flowring* (1968), *The Age of the Bird* (1972), and *Milk Stone* (1974). Her reputation was growing rapidly. Her poems appeared in *Best Poetry of 1965: Borestone Mountain Poetry Awards*, in Jim Brown and David Philip's *West Coast Seen* (1969), and in Al Purdy's anthology *Fifteen Winds* (1969). She had been elected national chairman of the League of Canadian Poets and had just begun to teach creative writing at the University of British Columbia. *A Stone Diary*, accepted before her death, was published posthumously in 1977; *Final Instructions* appeared in 1980; *Water Clock*, in 1985; and *Time Capsule: New and Selected Poems*, edited with an introduction by her daughters Chris and Beth Lowther, in 1996. Her principal biographer, Christine Wiesenthal, published *The Half-Lives of Pat Lowther* in 2005 and an edition of *The Collected Poems of Pat Lowther* in 2010.

Touch Home

My daughter, a statistic
in a population explosion
exploded
popped
out of my body like a cork.

The doctors called for oxygen,
the birth too sudden, violent,
the child seemed pale

But my daughter lay
in perfect tranquility
touching the new air
with her
elegant hands.

Coast Range

Just north of town
the mountains start to talk
back-of-the-head buzz
of high stubbled meadows
minute flowers
moss gravel and clouds

They're not snobs, these mountains,
they don't speak Rosicrucian,
they sputter with
billygoat-bearded creeks
bumsliding down
to splat into the sea

They talk with the casual
tongues of water
rising in trees

They're so humble they'll let you
blast highways through them
baring their iron and granite
sunset-coloured bones
broken for miles

And nights when
clouds foam on a beach
of clear night sky,
those high slopes creak
in companionable sleep

Move through gray green
aurora of rain
to the bare fact:
The land is bare.

Even the curly opaque Pacific
forest, chilling you full awake
with wet branch-slaps,
is somehow bare
stainless as sunlight:

The land is what's left
after the failure
of every kind of metaphor.

*

The plainness of first things
trees
gravel
rocks
naive root atom
of philosophy's first molecule

The mountains reject nothing
but can crack
open your mind
just by being intractably there

Atom: that which can not
be reduced

You can gut them
blast them
to slag
the shapes they've made in the sky
cannot be reduced

Octopus

The octopus is beautifully
functional as an umbrella;
at rest a bag of rucked skin
sags like an empty scrotum
his jelled eyes sad and bored

but taking flight: look
how purposeful
in every part:
the jet vent smooth
as modern plumbing
the webbed pinwheel of tentacles
moving in perfect accord
like a machine dreamed
by Leonardo

The Dig

Even where traffic passes
the ancient world has exposed
a root, large and impervious,
humped like a dragon
among the city's conduits.
Look, they say,
who would have thought
the thing so tough,
so secretive?

The Diggers

The bone gloved in clay
shallow perhaps where arches
of feet go over;
they see it as finished
round like a jar;
a shard they see as whole.

Will our bones tell
what we died of?

The diggers
with very gentle fingers
lift up the bones of a woman;
tenderly they take off
her stockings of earth;
they have not such love
for the living
who are not finished
or predicted.

The Bones

The men we see always swift
moving, edged with a running light
like fire; their hands infinitely
potent, working in blood,
commanding the death of animals,
the life of the tribe.

The women we see finished
completed like fat jars,
like oil floating on water:
breasts   bellies   faces
all round and calm.

Their bones should thrash
in the diggers' baskets
should scream against the light.

Their work bent them
and sex, that soft explosion
miraculous as rain
broke in them over and over,
their bodies thickened like tubers
broke and were remade
again and again crying out
in the heave of breaking
the terrible pleasure
again and again till
they fell away, at last
they became bone.

Even their hands
curved around implements,
pounding-stones, were worshipping
the cock that made them
round and hollow.

But before their falling away
was an anger,
a stone in the mouth.
They would say there is
a great fall like water,

a mask taking shape on air,
a sound coming nearer
like a heavy animal
breaking twigs.

And the flesh stamen
bursting inside them
splayed their bones
apart like spread legs.

Will our bones tell
sisters, what we died of?
how love broke us
in that helplessly desired
breaking, and men
and children ransacked our flesh,
cracked our innermost bones
to eat the marrow.

Daphne Marlatt

(b. 1942)

Daphne Marlatt (née Buckle) was born in Melbourne, Australia, and lived in Penang, Malaysia, before emigrating with her family to North Vancouver in 1951. She graduated from the University of British Columbia in 1964 and then pursued her MA in comparative literature at the University of Indiana. Her poetic influences include Robert Duncan and Charles Olson, from whom she learned an acute attention not only to the particulars of speech, but also to the body and its messages at the time of writing, a process that has come to be known as proprioception. Her publications include essays: *Readings from the Labyrinth* (1998) and *At the River's Mouth: Writing Migrations* (2009); works of fiction: *Zócalo* (1977), *The Story, She Said* (1977), *Ana Historic* (1988), and *Taken* (1996); a play written in the Japanese Noh tradition: *The Gull* (2009); and numerous volumes of poetry, including *Frames: Of a Story* (1968), *Rings* (1971), *Vancouver Poems* (1972), *Steveston* (1974), *Net*

Work: Selected Writings (1980), *What Matters: Writing 1968–1970* (1980), *Our Lives* (1980), *How Hug a Stone* (1983), *Touch to My Tongue* (1984), *Salvage* (1991), *Ghost Works* (1993), *This Tremor Love Is* (2001), and *The Given* (2008).

Much of her recent work, as she explains in the foreword to *Salvage*, was "generated out of a growing sense of community with women writers/readers, drawn by currents of desire in language for contact through time, over space and across culture." Marlatt has also devoted much of her writing life to moving out from what she calls "the safety of known forms," as she says in the afterword to *Our Lives*, where it is necessary "to write into the unknown of our actual present."

In *Open Letter* (4, 3, spring 1979), she makes an acute observation on the social function of poetry:

> I take it that a writer's job is to continue to give accurate witness of what's happening. One person isn't going to change what Marathon Realty is doing, what the CPR is doing. . . . You cannot change the world. You can change consciousness, & language is intimately tied up with consciousness. That's our true field of action, is language, as poets. And all you can do is to insist on the seeing as it's evidenced & manifested in the language. In an accurate use of language.

In the same interview she talks about writing as a process of attending to whatever is at hand (which includes body, present, history, prehistory):

> My notion re prose & poetry is that . . . standard prose is written as if language was transparent. You're not seeing it. Poetry is written with the awareness that it's not transparent, that it is in fact a medium & that you are operating in it thanks to it. It's like the difference between being land animals &—we don't usually experience air, you know. We breathe in & we breathe out without being aware that we are breathing in any medium at all. That it is our medium. Once we get into the water, which is a foreign element to us, we're very aware of the difficulty of moving thru that element. That's like poetry. You are aware that you are moving in an element, in a medium, & that, in fact, any moving forward you make is thanks to that element that you're moving in. So that language . . . writes the story as much as you do.

Imagine: A Town

Imagine a town running
                                        (smoothly?
a town running before a fire

canneries burning
                                        (do you see the shadow of charred stilts
on cool water? do you see enigmatic chance standing
just under the beam?

                                        He said they were playing cards in the
Chinese mess hall, he said it was dark (a hall? a shack.
they were all, crowded together on top of each other.
He said somebody accidentally knocked the oil lamp over, off
the edge

                    where stilts are standing, Over the edge of the
dyke a river pours, uncalled for, unending:

                                                            where chance lurks
fishlike, shadows the underside of pilings, calling up his hall
the bodies of men & fish corpse piled on top of each other (residue
time is, the delta) rot, an endless waste the trucks of production
grind to juice, driving through

                                                smears, blood smears in the dark
dirt) this marshland silt no graveyard can exist in but water swills,
endlessly out of itself to the mouth

                                                      ringed with residue, where
chance flicks his tail & swims, through.

A by-channel; a small backwater

                                                      slough, Finn Slough (or Gilmour,
by Gilmour Island), slough for sale as "deep sea frontage,"
has been always, simply, backwater clutch of shacks, floats,
sheds: a swamp & dusty marsh grass sheltering mosquito boats,
small gillnetters & other vessels in this amphibious place,
half earth half water, half river half sea, tide fills, swiftly,
pushing muddy fingers into timbers of the float, crawling round
pilings & rushes, glinting up a web of net stranding float where
a man & woman bend, knotting holes deadheads & other refuse a murky
river roils, have torn, ripped, & otherwise scorned, sometimes from
leadline to cork . . .

The slow effort of
this people's morning: rise with predawn birdsong & coffee
stretching stiffer & stiffer bones, pack lunch, pad past the
cloistered silence of tv, crunch of gravel, drive (green Pinto)
down to where their boats lie, light filtering immense
vegetation.

Check fuel, untie & start the engine ("a 7 Easthope
& a 15, wasn't it a 15 Easthope they had too? They thought they really
had something on the go—now when they look back they think it's a
joke, you know, why, have we actually been fishing with those?"

"That was the onetime king engine" on this coast, days when
nobody had any money, they bought a used car engine for two bucks,
had it delivered down to the slough, the poor

shelter of swamp
houses, float- ("when I look at it now it looks like a summer cabin")
under the lee of a dyke Finnish squatters & other folk whose lives
are inextricably tied with the tide that inundates their day, their
time measured only by: this sucking at vegetal silence swallows shred,
from the boom of idle boats, from the ridgepole of shadowy netshed
jets drone: this land up for deep sea frontage ("oh yes, it'll be
freighters & cement scow, barges & containerized shipping all the
way up to New Westminister,
you can't stop progress, can you?"

How *accept* its creeping up?
like a disease, like time, the tide they still know how to run,
with it, up under ("remember how your net got wrapped & rolled?")
that barge, danger at dark or fog, still after the fish which still
run shadowy lines thru all that murk against the shifting bars of
shipping channel, slipping that traffic, that bottom:

"You sure find out
when you get all the rubbish from down there—lot of bark, papers,
bathroom papers—it's real messy sometimes. Trees & twigs &
branches, branches of trees even floating down there. & then there's,
I dunno what kind of plant it is, it's like a crabapple limb & it's
just full of little twigs, & that's a wicked one when it gets caught in
to a thin net. & ends of logs that have been cut, you know, stump
ends & round blocks drifting. The sawmills open their gates, you know

& let all their loose stuff out—when that comes dashing there's even
sawdust in the river."

At bottom of this slippery time, it's her boat,
her feet on, managing the freshet, swollen, flooding (highest tides
of the year last week) water on water swell, with a wind running
norwesterly "it gets pretty choppy here," "I've been here with a blow
that's bin blowing 47 miles an hour—just big big waves washing
way up above the rocks." "See it's narrow & when the wind blows
those waves break & cross, it gets real rough."

She runs in the
throat of time, voicing the very swifts & shallows of that river,
urging, in the dash of it, enough to keep up, to live on. When nets
are up 50%, fuel's up, & the packers taking chum salmon, undressed,
at 20 cents a pound, "the same they sell in the stores dressed at $1.20,
while they're selling the roe they don't even pay us for at $2.20
a pound, clear profit" . . .

Somehow they survive the oily waters swirling
under packers piling, bargeloads of herring sucked up, truckloads
left to rot, salmon on ice in the packerboats collecting twenty hours
a day,

Somehow they survive, this people, these fish
survive the refuse bottom, filthy water, their choked lives,
in a singular dance of survival, each from each. At the
narrows, in the pressure of waves so checked & held by
"deep-sea frontage" it's the river's push against her, play of
elements her life comes rolling on. Hair flying, in gumboots,
on deck with rubber apron ("it's no dance dress"), she'll take
all that river gives, willing only to stand her ground (rolling,
with it, right under her feet, her life, rolling, out from under,
right on out to sea . . .

listen

he was reading to her, standing on the other side of the kitchen counter where she was making salad for supper, tender orange carrot in hand, almost transparent at its tip, slender, & she was wondering where such carrots came from in winter. he was standing in the light reading to her from a book he was holding, her son behind him at the table where amber light streamed from under a glass shade she had bought for its warm colour midwinter, though he had called it a cheap imitation of the real thing.

in its glow her son was drawing red Flash & blue Superman into a comic he was making, painstakingly having stapled the pages together & now with his small & definite hand trying to draw exact images of DC Superstars & Marvel heroes none of them had ever seen except in coloured ink.

but he was reading to her about loss, excited, because someone had named it at last, was naming even as he read, the shape of what he felt to be his own, recognized at last in words coming through him from the page, coming to her through his emphatic & stirred voice stumbling over the rough edges of terms that weren't his, even as he embraced them. lost, how their dancing had lost touch with the ring dance which was a collective celebration, he said.

she was standing with the grater in one hand, carrot in the other, wondering if the grating sound would disturb him. she wanted to hear what had stirred him. she wanted to continue the movement of making salad which, in the light & the lowenbrau they shared, was for once coming so easily, almost was spring stirring around the corner of the house in a rhythm of rain outside she was moving in, had moved, barely knowing it was rain beyond the wetness of walking home—

hand in hand, he was saying, a great circle like the circle of the seasons, & now people barely touch, where at least with the waltz they used to dance in couples, then with rock apart but *to* each other, whereas now, he caught her eye, the dances we've been to you can see people dancing alone, completely alone with the sound.

lifting the carrot to the grater, pressing down, watching flakes of orange fall to the board, she felt accused in some obscure way, wanted to object (it was her generation after all), thought up an obscure argument about how quadrilles could be called collective in ballrooms where privileged guests took their assigned places in the dance. but now, & she recalled the new year's eve party they'd been to, almost a hundred people, strangers, come together, & people don't know each other in the city the way they used to in a village. but that only glanced off what the book was saying about husbandry & caring for the soil as a collective endeavour.

the whole carrot was shrinking into a thousand flakes heaped & scattered at once, the whole carrot with its almost transparent sides shining in the light, had ground down to a stump her fingers clutched close to the jagged pockets of tin that scraped them, she saw her fingers, saw blood flying like carrot flakes, wondered why she imagined blood as part of the salad. . . .

listen, he was saying, this is where he's really got it. & he read a long passage about their imprisonment in marriage, all the married ones with that impossible ideal of confining love to one—*one cannot love a particular woman unless one loves womankind*, he read. listen, he said, & he read her the passage about the ring dance, about the participation of couples in one great celebration, the *amorous feast that joins them to all living things*. he means fertility, she said, thinking, oh no, oh back to that, woman's one true function. he means the fertility of the earth, he said, he means our lives aware of seasonal growth & drawing nourishment from that instead of material acquisition & exploitation. listen, he read a passage about sexual capitalism, about the crazy images of romance that fill people's heads, sexual freedom & skill & the me-generation on all the racks of all the supermarket stores.

using her palms like two halves of a split spoon, she scooped up the heap of carrot flakes & dropped them onto a plate of lettuce, dark because it was romaine torn into pieces in the wooden bowl with other green things. dance. in & out. she watched the orange flakes glisten in their oil of skin, touch the surfaces of green she tossed with real spoons, each flake dipping into the dark that lay at the heart of, what, *their* hearts, as they had, the other night, sunk into bed at the end of the party, drunk & floating, their laughter sifting in memory through conversations, wrapt in the warmth of what everyone had said & how they had moved away & toward each other & loved in very obscure ways, slowly they had made love to everyone they loved in each other, falling through & away from their separate bodies—listen, she said, as the rain came up & she set the salad on the wooden table underneath the lamp.

a lapsed

taste for art deco geese wing geometric read-only memory
online horizontal sunbeams (set settled) heyday that was Marine's
elevated crabs consort with streamline moderne a pattern imperial pits
and lands we read Hobb's ambition by

touched

with gold in morning-after fog and traffic (king i thought) he-breeze
through burnish doors and doors sequester office feet in oxford brogue
tobacco pocket clang of elevator doors that daily matinal tide on battle-
ship lino later replaced by (bye)

binary data residual
tint *sea-green* slants northeast-southwest in sunny Burrard's angular
shadow labour losses hand-eye skill coordinate quick a quickening
touch by definition ice-cream melt

tops it toppest (til '39) proximal
harbour beckoning world waters rising melt smelts' silver reflex glory
warped in visual stacks washed by noon anthem yaw its quick-pitch
noontide rush pedinal pedestrian you

correct for agreement your silver dollar shine
my dry money plant

this city: shrouded

wind strum wires Jerry's Cove music standing
hulls rock in their lines virid wave on wave oncoming stands of cedar
shreds through fog mimetic wind-rustle thrash or throb endless once
to hand at Jerry's camp

their skidders, flumes

their "finest timber" towed
by the *Maggie Rogers* past Si'kheylish past Khwaykhway's standing
houses later burned

to booms afloat to Empire booming grounds
at Gore a building boom's on track its dummy lines of ownership

slip this viridescent sheen of green onshore storm clearing the clearings
smoke shroud or fog sawdust burning off downtown as if

this city
could re-green building transport green

handle a new wave now
economy size

eco-finger its members (citizens say

antique eaten (copper) roofing (o hotel hothouse hosting roof upon roof
(not by a long-handled axe though "whole paycheque" sports a vegetal
wall traffic streams down underground long wavelength desire its
disconnect

O Jericho

desire nets you in your strappy heels one hand
smoothing jeanskin asstight sashay confidence
on the run sudden dealer stalks stock gambles
sino forests of fraud axed at street level

faded walls of Ee'yullmough   felled long waves ago

Susan Musgrave

(b. 1951)

Susan Musgrave was born in Santa Cruz, California, to Canadian parents, but raised on Vancouver Island. Including her first book, *Songs of the Sea Witch* (1970), she has written almost 20 books of poetry, 4 volumes of fiction, 6 children's books, and 3 works of non-fiction. Although her three marriages—to a criminal lawyer, a drug smuggler, and a bank robber—have tended to interfere with a full appreciation of her talents as a poet, wit, and performer, she has produced an impressive body of work that keeps improving. Her poetry has been shortlisted several times for the Governor General's Award, and her writing has won the Vicky Metcalfe Short Story Editor's Award, a Silver Medal in the National Magazine Awards, a Tilden (CBC/*Saturday Night*) Canadian Literary Award, the People's Choice Poetry Award, and received numerous other kinds of recognition. She lives on Haida Gwaii, where she runs the Copper Beech B&B. She is much in demand as a lecturer, columnist, and teacher, and is an adjunct professor in the Optional Residency MFA in Creative Writing program at the University of British Columbia.

Musgrave aims at a poetry that is both accessible and engaging, which wraps mystery and surprise in ordinary language. In an essay called "A Lost Classic," she paraphrases A.E. Housman, saying,

> Meaning is of the intellect, but poetry is more physical. Most of us have read a poem that has made the hair on the back of our necks stand up: we may have asked ourselves, "Why have mere words had such a physical effect?" The answer, according to Housman, is because these words are poetry, and find their way to something in us which is obscure and latent, something older than the present organization of our nature.

Musgrave's early work is dark, with a strong sense of the absurd, as it depicts the rough and tumble of lives lived on the razor's edge. However, a more lyrical, meditative Musgrave emerges from her recent books—*Things That Keep and Do Not Change* (1999), *Obituary of Light: The Sangan River Meditations* (2009) and *Origami Dove* (2011, Governor General's Award finalist)—where family, place, and nature figure prominently. She is also the recipient of the Spirit Bear Award, for her contributions to the poetry of the Pacific Northwest, and the BC Civil Liberties Association Liberty Award for Art.

Arctic Poppies

After a week of rough seas the ship docked
at Hopedale. The weather was no good but still
I struggled ashore and climbed to the desecrated
churchyard, determined to take away something
of a memory, to photograph the white Arctic
poppies. Each time I framed a shot, my hands
steady at last, a hunchback on crutches teetered
into sight, as if innocently waiting for the fog
to lift, the rain to let up, the light
to throw open its dingy overcoat and expose
itself to my nakedness. My eye, my whole body
had been saving itself for this, but every time
he humped into view, I thought of you, the best
man I'd ever left, lips tasting of whatever you'd had
to eat: spicy eggplant baba ghanouj, jumbo
shrimp in garlic and Chablis, your mother's
meat pie with a dash of cinnamon
and cloves. When the sun broke

through I'd have those wild flowers posed,
I'd be poised to shoot, and then the stooped
shadow would fall as if to say beauty
without imperfection was something to be
ashamed of, as if he could be my flaw.
Crouched beside an abandoned grave
I tried to focus on those white
poppies in light that went on failing,
seeing your perfect body in his
crippled gaze. I could have taken him

back to my cabin aboard the ship, laid
his crutches down, bathed him, bent over
his grateful body and licked the smell
of smoked trout and caribou hide from his
thighs. Perhaps this is what he hoped for,
and then to be called beautiful afterwards.

I took his photograph. He'd wanted that too
and suddenly I felt blessed, I felt
I'd been taken the way I liked it best: sex

in the head on sacred ground that has been
roughed up a little, a graveyard full
of ghostly poppies choking out the dead.

The Laughter in the Kitchen

All day our daughter and her best friend
have been playing marriage, destroying
the house to make it the way they need it
to be. They've shoved the loveseat
across the bedroom door to form a barricade,
overturned the armchairs to give themselves
temporary shelters. They've even rolled
the carpet back, "so the carpet won't get
beer spilled on it," my daughter, pretending
to be Dad, explains, when I complain:
the house doesn't feel like my own anymore
but still I have to live in it. "We can

build a new house when I make lots of good
money," my daughter says, butting out
the Popeye candy cigarette she won
from the neighbour boy for showing him
her vagina through a slit in the split
cedar fence. I wept, told her next time,

baby, hold out for a whole pack,
trying to be brave, the way only a mother
could. "We can't build anything if you
keep drinking drugs," the tiny wife bursts
as my daughter keels into the cookstove
and pretends to catch fire, the laughter
in the kitchen filling the house
where we tried to live. What has become

of my young life, the man who once pressed
a fistful of crocuses between my breasts
and made love to me on the kitchen floor
while beyond, on the river,
a loudspeaker-toting paddleboat carried
honeymooners to the mouth. Later we took
the same cruise, pretending to be newlyweds
ourselves, holding hands on the tipping deck
with others who took photographs to prove
they had truly been there, they had
loved each other—once. The laughter

in the kitchen reminds me: grief
is a burden, something to be shaken
like the foxgloves in our garden, stooping
under the weight of their seeds. I've learned
the lessons of pain, now wait for the same
light that makes my daughter's face so
luminous and wise as she says to her small friend,
"Now you be Dad. You've got no body so you can't
get away. I'll be the mother this time."

The Moment

The legless man in the motel room next to me
listens to country and western music
all night, an endless song

about going down on his knees
for some faithless woman's love.
I turn in my bed, thinking of you the day
we thought our daughter had gone
missing. The moment
before she disappeared you'd seen a stranger
on the block, the kind who wore
a stained suit from the Sally Ann, the kind
who couldn't know innocence
existed. Our daughter was supposed to be

next door, playing in the fenced yard
with two neighbour boys. You'd been
on the phone and I'd turned my back
on the moment to do something
predictable—move the garden sprinkler,
open the morning mail—acts
that would never again seem so ordinary
once we'd made up our minds
between burial or cremation. Your body

had never felt so alive as you took off
in the car, driving down
every back lane, listening for her
glove-muffled cries. You drove

deeper and deeper into the kind of hell
we reserve for ourselves and never want
our children to have to know. You knew

at this moment she could only be suffering
in the hands of that stranger who would afterwards
stuff her trusting body into a single forest
green Glad Bag, then tote her to the park.

They would find her legs first, dangling
from the swing, shoes on the wrong feet
as usual, arms hanging from the jungle
gym. I'd want to touch, to straighten
her turned-in toes: how clumsily
we lived on this earth!

She was lost only for a moment, locked
in a spare bedroom with the two boys
next door, not wanting her privacy interrupted,
but in that moment when she was gone
forever, death in all his beautiful variety
sang to us, off-key and aching
inside our cheated hearts.

Origami Dove

Every Christmas Eve we would drive
through the ritzy district to see
the coloured lights my father said
were an utter waste of electricity.
He took the long way home, the way
that wound away around the orphanage—
a waste of gas, my mother thought,
but for once didn't say—and I would
imagine, for an instant, a world
where someone is grateful for something.
As we slowed past that desperate house
always in darkness, *those poor bastards*,
my father would say. The pitch of their roof
made it impossible for Santa's reindeer
to land there. At home we'd hang stockings,
leave milk and shortbread by the chimney,
whisper our prayers, and I'd lie awake thinking
what it must feel like to have no one.
Every year my father took the one
trustworthy ladder we owned and climbed high
onto our flat roof and sat drinking
whiskey and ringing bells so we would go on
being deceived as long as it was possible
to go on being children; he knew love
and treachery were part of the same

bargain. Lately I have come to believe
all that is of value is the currency
of the heart, so that when my father
lay dying, I forgave God. I had never believed
in him until then, but found myself
forgiving him for the space he had never filled,
the loneliness in me he had created. Now I know:

between birth and death there is *only*
loneliness, so big sometimes it makes love
seem spectacularly small, with no grave
big enough to contain our grief. Loneliness

takes the good out of all of our goodbyes,
more permanent than the sadness you know
when your lover drives away having lost
interest in everything about you, especially
your suffering. Love's a blip, a glitch,
but loneliness signs on for the duration,
one gunshot wound to the head is all it takes
to assure your allotted space in today's
News of the World beside the Bangladesh woman
caned 101 times for having an abortion, misery
being careless and everywhere
at the same time. Loneliness is so big

that when it moves into your house you feel
as if someone has moved away, warmed up the Dead
Wagon with one headlight missing
and made for the highway still chasing
love, the thing you both swore you'd always die for.
Now loneliness has laid me instead, lopsided,
on the table, so that when they come to view me,
the one or two people who tried to know me, will say
"She never looked that way, he's got her mouth
all wrong," as if the living shouldn't have to see
how right we finally become. If my mouth looks wrong

it's because I am trying to find the way
to tell you I have become the AIDS baby
who doesn't want to die until she has seen
her first snow, an origami dove
chased by a flying child under a snow-dusted
school bus in Ontario, now buried
a kindly stone's throw from a frozen river.
The cure for loneliness, they say, is solitude,
trust everybody but cut the cards, take your delight
in momentariness, avoid adjectives of scale,
you will love the world more and desire it
less: all sound advice. There are 101 words
for freedom, not one from the kind of pain

the woman must have suffered after 101
lashes with a cane, cut, I suspect,
specifically for one purpose. Sex, death,
our fragile lives are like the knife edge
of the wind scraping away the sky. I see how true
loneliness has become when he takes up with me
and walks me through the world I have always
called my home. Only in darkness I see now
it has never been my home.

Winter Wren

After the first snowfall I find
a winter wren frozen on the forest path.

Who could have imagined it?
Even the birds are freezing!

As I push through earth locked in sorrow,
in ice, find a hollow between rocks
where her body will lie, a winter wren lights
on the handle of my shovel.

Gary Geddes

(b. 1940)

Gary Geddes was born and raised in Vancouver, with a four-year interlude on a farm in Saskatchewan. He studied at the University of British Columbia, Reading University, and the University of Toronto, where he completed his doctorate. He taught for 20 years at Concordia University, then served as Distinguished Professor of Canadian Culture at Western Washington University. He has written and edited more than 40 books of poetry, fiction, drama, non-fiction, translation, and anthologies, and has won a dozen national and international literary awards, including the E.J. Pratt medal, the Commonwealth Poetry Prize (Americas region), National Magazine Gold Award, the Poetry Book Society Recommendation, the Gabriela Mistral Prize from Chile, and the Lieutenant Governor's Award for Literary Excellence in British Columbia. His books of poetry include *Rivers Inlet* (1971), *The Acid Test* (1981), *The Terracotta Army* (1984, 2007), *Light of Burning Towers: Selected Poems* (1990), *Girl by the Water* (1994), *The Perfect Cold Warrior* (1995), *Active Trading: Selected Poems 1970–1995* (1996), *Flying Blind* (1998), *Skaldance* (2004), *Falsework* (2007), *Swimming Ginger* (2010), and a selected poems called *What Does A House Want?* (2014). He has published two books of criticism, *Conrad's Later Novels* (1980) and *Out of the Ordinary: Politics, Poetry & Narrative* (2009); a collection of short stories, *The Unsettling of the West* (1986); and three non-fiction works, *Sailing Home: A Journey Through Time, Place and Memory* (2001), *Kingdom of Ten Thousand Things: An Impossible Journey from Kabul to Chiapas* (2005), and *Drink the Bitter Root: A Writer's Search for Justice and Redemption in Africa* (2011). He lives on Thetis Island, BC, and has served as visiting writer at McMaster University, UBC's Green College, the Vancouver Public Library, and the University of Missouri-St Louis. He is the editor of several anthologies, including *20th-Century Poetry & Poetics*, 5th edition (2006), and *The Art of Short Fiction: An International Anthology* (1992). He received an Honorary Doctor of Laws degree from Royal Roads University in 2007.

Geddes is an engaged writer, known for his political concerns and his work as a narrative poet. George Woodcock singled him out as "Canada's best political poet" and Al Purdy called "Sandra Lee Scheuer," prompted by the killings at Kent State University, "the kind of poem most poets wait a lifetime for." His focus is not on partisan issues, but on social injustice, ordinary individuals caught in the machinery of history. The political element Geddes so often uncovers is the brutality of the structures human beings use to organize their collective power, or the sudden realization of responsibility for others that comes to individuals in the unpredictable byways of their lives.

Narrative is prominent both in Geddes's dramatic monologues and in his letter-poems: what his characters speak has the shape of story. His most memorable books—such as *Letter of the Master of Horse* (1973), *War & Other Measures* (1976), and *Hong Kong Poems* (1987)—are made of discrete poems (sometimes tersely lyrical) assembled into story. Although his poems do not draw attention for showy, "poetic" vocabulary or the manipulation of clever conceits, Geddes makes a case for his craft in *Anthos*:

> I want the poems to touch people deeply and make them care about themselves, their world, and language itself. This view of poetry does not lend itself to extremes of eclecticism or undue ornamentation. . . . The thrust of narrative allows me certain freedoms that aren't available to the lyric poet, one of which is a degree of monumental distraction (in character, event, terrain) that draws a reader's attention away from the so-called niceties of form. (Letter to Ricou, 21 Oct. 1987)

But the subtleties of language are there—in exact and mnemonic phrases of echoing sounds, in his attention to diction and nuance, in the sudden shifts to intense metaphors for love and anger within the casual voice of the storyteller, and in the deliberately self-reflexive elements that begin to appear in *Changes of State* (1986) and *Hong Kong Poems* (1987).

—Laurie Ricou

Sandra Lee Scheuer

(Killed at Kent State University on May 4, 1970 by the Ohio National Guard)

You might have met her on a Saturday night
cutting precise circles, clockwise, at the Moon-Glo
Roller Rink, or walking with quick step

between the campus and a green two-storey house,
where the room was always tidy, the bed made,
the books in confraternity on the shelves.

She did not throw stones, major in philosophy
or set fire to buildings, though acquaintances say
she hated war, had heard of Cambodia.

In truth she wore a modicum of make-up, a brassiere,
and could, no doubt, more easily have married a guardsman
than cursed or put a flower in his rifle barrel.

While the armouries burned she studied,
bent low over notes, speech therapy books, pages
open at sections on impairment, physiology.

And while they milled and shouted on the commons
she helped a boy named Billy with his lisp, saying
Hiss, billy, like a snake. That's it, SSSSSSSS,

tongue well up and back behind your teeth.
Now buzz, Billy, like a bee. Feel the air
vibrating in my windpipe as I breathe?

As she walked in sunlight through the parking-lot
at noon, feeling the world a passing lovely place,
a young guardsman, who had his sights on her,

was going down on one knee as if he might propose.
His declaration, unmistakable, articulate,
flowered within her, passed through her neck,

severed her trachea, taking her breath away.
Now who will burn the midnight oil for Billy,
ensure the perilous freedom of his speech?

And who will see her skating at the Moon-Glo
Roller Rink, the eight small wooden wheels
making their countless revolutions on the floor?

Jimmy's Place

We found the cow in a grove below the road,
leaning against an alder for support,
her udder swollen, her breath ragged and grating
as a rasp. I could have drowned
in the liquid eye she turned to me.
Her calf, though dead, was perfectly positioned,
forelegs and head protruding from the flaming ring
of vulva. Too large, perhaps, or hind legs
broken through the sac, dispersing fluids.
Much as we tried we couldn't pry it loose
and flesh around the legs began to give
from pressure on the rope. The cow
had no more strength and staggered back
each time we pulled. Tie her to the tree,
I said, being the schoolmaster and thinking
myself obliged to have an answer, even here
on the High Road, five miles south of town
where the island bunched in the jumble
of its origins. It was coming, by God,
I swear it, this scrub roan with her shadow self
extending out behind, going in both directions
like a '52 Studebaker, coming by inches
and our feet slipping in the mud and shit
and wet grass. She raised her head and tried
to see what madness we'd concocted in her wake,
emitted a tearing gunny-sack groan,
and her liquid eye ebbed back to perfect white.

Philip Larkin

He was a man whose words stopped short
of ecstasy, whose impaired tongue and ear refused
the grand theme, the gesture of extravagance,
and found, instead, out along the side-roads,

pantleg rolled, cycle propped against a tree,
a desperation so quietly profound even toad,
blinking among grass-spears, had overlooked.
He composed no score for happiness, but improvised

a life of common pleasures taken in a minor key:
a few pints with friends who didn't talk of poetry,
an early morning stroll in Pearson Park,
industrialist's gift to dreary, fog-bound Hull,

sausages on campus, a slice of Humber pie.
Hearing-aid turned off, he tunes his inner music,
a private soul station, some such jazz,
communes with Jelly Roll and Beiderbecke,

or watches from his window at the Nuffield,
where Westbourne intersects with Salisbury,
winos rub themselves against the freshly-painted
thighs of mermaids in the Victorian fountain,

who take their own libations from a conch.
While such doleful enthusiasts drink his health,
all flesh conspires to silence Larkin;
he undergoes a sea-change in the Avenues.

With no more reason to attend, he sings the poem
of his departure, achieves his wish to be alone.
Propped up in bed and talking to himself,
one thing only is denied: the desire of oblivion.

At Swim Three Words

As my mother lay dying in a dark, cold room
where plumbing and ductwork were visible
overhead, and cracks in cement walls sprouted
spider-webs and dust, I recalled the flume

at the Ex that flung us headlong, risible
in the extreme, plunging like hell's hounds
into the shrieking crowd, mouths wide, kerchief
blown back, her body language quizzical

as if laughter were verboten, out of bounds,
a thing unexpected, a joker outed
sans warning. When I stood by the bed,
my small hand clasped in hers, I had grounds

to wonder if she would die, though I doubted
this, of course, thinking only of myself,
my needs, days at the beach in English Bay
or Kitsilano, where I tossed sand, flouted

authority, sun-baked bodies, the air
reeking of seaweed, chips, vinegar, hot
dogs. Some days I feel her speak through me,
the few remaining strands of damp, brown hair

at sixes and sevens across her forehead,
lips pursed, facial muscles contracted
in a worry. Mortal counsel, end-notes,
obligatory whispers with their dread

finality. Resolute, I played the elf,
doing the dog-paddle across the frayed
linoleum, trying to make her laugh.
A tad of whimsy left on the back shelf

would suffice. She rallied briefly, half
alert, pulled herself into a sitting position,
the skin slack around her neck, eyes
closed from the effort. Grimace or laugh,

I knew not, but she who swam kilometres
from Fisherman's Cove to Point Atkinson
managed a thin smile, patted my head
and traced on my body the necessary letters.

John Thompson

(1938–1976)

John Thompson was born in Timperley, United Kingdom, and studied at the University of Sheffield. After two years in the British Army Intelligence Corps, he travelled to the US where he completed a Ph.D. at the University of Michigan, translating the poems of René Char. He was hired in 1966 to teach English and creative writing at Mount Alison University in Sackville, New Brunswick, where he spent a troubled but productive decade, writing memorable work that would influence many generations of Canadian poets. The poems from his two books, *At the Edge of the Chopping There Are No Secrets* (1973) and *Stilt Jack* (1978), are gathered in *I Dream Myself into Being: Collected Poems* (1999, 2006, edited by James Polk) and *John Thompson: Collected Works and Translations* (1995, edited by Peter Sanger).

Thompson's most important contributions to Canadian poetry were his experiments with the ghazal, a Persian form consisting of a series of discrete and closed couplets that are held together, not by logic or narrative, but by a single emotion or feeling-tone. The ghazal's power lies in its reminder that poetry does not require logical argument or dominant narrative, but can contain seemingly discrete or unrelated items held together by fierce concentration. Of course, there may be recurrences of image and sound, with or without formal rhyming, which add to the coherence of a basically discontinuous utterance. In many ghazals, it is as if the speaker is talking to him or herself—a monologue of self to soul—or addressing a beloved who knows the context, all the background feelings and shared experiences that are driving the utterance and need not be mentioned. In Thompson's case, the speaker is often addressing poetry itself, or all of his predecessors in the craft: "Yeats. Yeats. Yeats. Yeats. / Why wouldn't the man shut up?"

The couplets in Thompson's work contain something of the colloquial surprise and epigrammatic terseness of John Berryman's *Dream Songs*. He even has a character named Bone, a variation on Berryman's Mr Bones. And the link with Berryman is sadly there, too, in the life and untimely death of both poets. Fraser Sutherland describes Thompson's erratic and sometimes outlandish behaviour, how he spent the last two days of his life "drinking with students, drying out in a Sackville jail, and visiting a fellow poet." While his death may have been the result of an inadvertent combination of drugs and alcohol, Thompson evidently felt precarious enough (after the departure of his wife and daughter and the loss of his house and books by fire) to make a will and pass for safekeeping the completed manuscript of *Stilt Jack* to his friend the poet Douglas Lochhead. The desperate exhibitionism and loneliness of the man are not far from the loneliness and despair that drove Berryman to take his own life, pausing to wave to a passing student as he stepped off a bridge to his death.

See Rob Winger's article in *Arc Poetry* No. 62, and his interview in *Open Book Toronto* (www.openbooktoronto.com/news/ten_questions_with_rob_winger) for further information about the ghazal and Thompson.

Wife

Your hands peeling and
   kneading the dough:

the work comes
   up from the thighs

and hips, through
   the leaned shoulders,

sweet drive of arms
   striking

down through the tough roots
   of the fingers;

in the dark
   of the oven

a moon gleams
   and fattens:

our winter bread,

   your shadow
huge on the wall.

Horse

Your great hooves sunk
   in red mud, massive,
      still, you stare out

over the edge of the world;
small fires
flare in your eyes;

the sun turns in hunger
about your dark head,
sniffing the earth in you,
tasting your smoke,

and waits for your thighs
to shift, your hooves
to strain from the ground,

for some speech from your black muscles:

so the earth would tilt
under your weight,

hawks plummet upward, the dead
float in the air like flies,

and we, thrown from our warm furrows,
relearn our balance,
reach out in the dark to test

our crooked new bones.

II

In this place we might be happy; blue-
winged teal, blacks, bats, steam

from cows dreaming in frost.
Love, you ask too many questions.

Let's agree: we are whole: the house
rises: we fight; this is love

and old acquaintance.
Let's gather the stars; our fire

will contain us; two,
one.

VIII

I forget: why are there broken birds
behind me; words, goddammit, words.

I want to wake up with God's shadow
across me: I'm a poet, not a fool.

Porcupine are slow, fast in their quills:
they'll come to your iron bar, believing themselves and apples.

I don't want to die bloody on the highway:
I travel back roads, the dirt;

don't complain about going: sometimes
think I'll never get to sleep.

Everything reminds me. I want to push.
Black spruce; strange fires.

Snow will come. Wind. A kind of age.
What's at my feet must move quickly.

October; 3 a.m.; I go out and take a rose,
and the sea, and thorns.

I want to give everything to this burnt flower: I've nothing;
I bury my face; set it in water.

XVI

The barn roof bangs a tin wing in the wind;
I'm quite mad: never see the sun;

you like sad, sad songs that tell a story;
how far down on whiskey row am I?

I believe in unspoken words, unseen gods:
where will I prove those?

If I wash my hands will I disappear?
I'll suck oil from Tobin's steel and walnut.

If one more damn fool talks to me about
sweetness and light . . .

I'm looking for the darkest place;
then, only then, I'll raise my arm;
someone must have really socked it to you:
were the lips made to hold a pen or a kiss?

If there were enough women I wouldn't write poetry;
if there were enough poetry

XXV

In a dark wood,
and you in a strange bed.

In midsummer I dream great snows
and a man come to ask about fish.

Divinity sounds in machines,
shines darkly from the pleasure of birds.

What do I believe? I hear the crack
of corn fattening at night.

The blood at night sounds
with your swimming.

Where are all our books and stories?
I look into dark water:

We have been there: our eyes
join deep below the surface.

If I ask questions, you'll show me
some beautiful thing you have made.

XXXVII

Now you have burned your books, you'll go with nothing.
A heart.

The world is full of the grandeur,
and it is.

Perfection of tables: crooked grains;
and all this talk: this folly of tongues.

Too many stories: yes, and
high talk: the exact curve of the thing.

Sweetness and lies: the hook, grey deadly bait,
a wind and water to kill cedar, idle men, the innocent

not love, and hard eyes
over the cold,

not love (eyes, hands, hands, arm)
given, taken, to the marrow;

(the grand joke: *le mot juste:*
forget it; remember):

Waking is all: readiness:
you are watching;

I'll learn by going:
Sleave-silk flies; the kindly ones.

Tom Wayman

(b. 1945)

Tom Wayman was born in Hawkesbury, Ontario, but grew up in Prince Rupert, BC, where his father was a chemist at the pulp mill. When he was in his teens, the family moved to Vancouver, where Wayman completed a BA in English at UBC while working as a journalist. He received his MFA in 1968 at the University of California, Irvine. Thereafter, Wayman toiled at various jobs, shifting back and forth between teaching and manual labour, both kinds of work becoming grist for his poetic mill. After intermittent stints of teaching and serving as a writer-in-residence, he taught at the University of Calgary from 2002 until retirement.

In "Glad I Was Born," the introduction to *Did I Miss Anything?*, Wayman states that his aim is

> to provide an accurate depiction of our common everyday life. I have tried to combine this with a sense of humor and with a vision of a better possibility for people than what we have so far achieved. My hope is that the latter two aspects of my writing provide perspective on the balance of what I portray. As for spirituality, I long ago was a convert to the concept expressed by Robert Bly in his poem "Turning Away From Lies" (from *The Light Around the Body*, 1967): "The Kingdom of Heaven does not mean the next life / . . . The two worlds are both in this world."
>
> Overall, my intention is that the complexities revealed by my poems should be the complications of our everyday existence, rather than newly-created difficulties or mysteries generated by tricks of language or poetic form. Clarity, honesty, accuracy of statement have been my goals—subject to, naturally, the limits of human discourse found in *every* genre or means of communication. My aim is that my poems should be useful: to myself, and to others who share my community and world. I mean these poems to be a gift; I want my poetry to be a tender, humorous, enraged, piercing, but always accurate depiction of where we are—as individuals functioning in a society, and as members of a rawly self-conscious species now occupying the third planet from a nondescript star.

As a politically engaged writer, Wayman includes among his poetic influences Earle Birney, Al Purdy, and Pablo Neruda, and has written extensively not only about the workplace, but also about war, social injustice, unemployment, and poverty. These subjects figure in his poems and in his anthologies, which include *Going for Coffee: Poetry on the Job* (1987), *East of Main: An Anthology of Poems from East Vancouver* (with Calvin Wharton, 1989), and *Paperwork* (1991). His essays, collected in *Inside Job: Essays on the New Work Writing* (1983), *A Country Not Considered: Canada, Culture, Work* (1993), and *Songs without Price: The Music of Poetry in a Discordant World* (2008), also take up the themes. In addition to three books of fiction, he has written almost twenty books and chapbooks of poetry, including *Waiting for Wayman* (1973), *For and Against the Moon* (1974), *Money and Rain* (1975), *Counting the Hours* (1983), *Did I Miss Anything? Selected Poems 1973–1993* (1993), *The Astonishing Weight of the Dead* (1994), *The Colours of the Forest* (1999), *My Father's Cup* (2002), *High Speed Through Shoaling Water* (2007), and *Dirty Snow* (2012).

Wayman has won the A.J.M. Smith Prize and the Canadian Authors Association medal for poetry, and has been shortlisted for the Governor General's Award (2003). He lives in the Selkirk Mountains near Winlaw, BC, on a property called "Appledore."

Wayman in Love

At last Wayman gets the girl into bed.
He is locked in one of those embraces
so passionate his left arm is asleep
when suddenly he is bumped in the back.
"Excuse me," a voice mutters, thick with German.
Wayman and the girl sit up astounded
as a furry gentleman in boots and a frock coat
climbs in under the covers.

"My name is Doktor Marx," the intruder announces
settling his neck comfortably on the pillow.
"I'm here to consider for you the cost of a kiss."
He pulls out a notepad. "Let's see now,
we have the price of the mattress, this room must be rented,
your time off work, groceries for two,
medical fees in case of accidents . . ."

"Look," Wayman says,
"couldn't we do this later?"
The philosopher sighs, and continues: "You are affected too, Miss.
If you are not working, you are going to resent
your dependent position. This will influence
I assure you, your most intimate moments . . ."

"Doctor, please," Wayman says. "All we want
is to be left alone."
But another beard, more nattily dressed,
is also getting into the bed.
There is a shifting and heaving of bodies
as everyone wriggles out room for themselves.
"I want you to meet a friend from Vienna,"
Marx says. "This is Doktor Freud."

The newcomer straightens his glasses,
peers at Wayman and the girl.
"I can see," he begins,
"that you two have problems . . ."

Did I Miss Anything?

Question frequently asked by students after missing a class

Nothing. When we realized you weren't here
we sat with our hands folded on our desks
in silence, for the full two hours

Everything. I gave an exam worth
40 per cent of the grade for this term
and assigned some reading due today
on which I'm about to hand out a quiz
worth 50 per cent

Nothing. None of the content of this course
has value or meaning
Take as many days off as you like:
any activities we undertake as a class
I assure you will not matter either to you or me
and are without purpose

Everything. A few minutes after we began last time
a shaft of light descended and an angel
or other heavenly being appeared
and revealed to us what each woman or man must do
to attain divine wisdom in this life and
the hereafter
This is the last time the class will meet
before we disperse to bring this good news to all people on earth

Nothing. When you are not present
how could something significant occur?

Everything. Contained in this classroom
is a microcosm of human existence
assembled for you to query and examine and ponder
This is not the only place such an opportunity has been gathered

but it was one place

And you weren't here

Cup

Because of heavy painkillers
administered to my father
or a deep dream,
before he died he called out from a doze in his wheelchair:
Take, take it.
His tone was desperate, so I stepped closer
to reassure: *It's all right. You were asleep.*
What's the matter?
His eyes now gaped at his world:
the curtain isolating him from the other bed here,
a portable commode, his wheeled tray
holding an untouched lunch of broth and jello.
Then he recognized me and said:
I was drinking a cup of coffee
with nowhere to put it down.
His voice was anxious and bewildered so I soothed:
It was just a dream; don't worry.
But he said: *Take it from me,*
anyway. After a moment
I reached across his lap to seize
a cup of nothing
which I held to my chest as I straightened again.
My father smiled slightly
at the oddity of this event
and slept. Thus his cup
passed to me.

Air Support

A dropped school falls through air,
turning slowly as debris
pours from windows: a contrail of papers and books
streams upwards thousands of metres
alongside computers, chairs, desks that tumble amid
woodworking equipment, lockers, maps,
basketballs, stage curtains

all aimed
toward tiny huts far below—a brushy hillside's

cluster of subsistence farms
reportedly harbouring armed men: fenced yards
with a few chickens, one cow, an ancient horse eyeing
six rows of parched vegetables.

                                                            Above the school
while it descends,
another follows, and beyond that, nearly invisible,
a third floats as the fighter-bomber arcs
away, and a second jet drones into position.
The pilot of the first, now on the mission's homeward leg,
reaches down in his cockpit
toward a thermos of hot coffee.

On the ground, hospitals released
in the initial attack wave
erupt sequentially into plumes of fire and dust
as the buildings land: operating tables,
obstetric wards, wheelchairs shatter into shrapnel,
the jagged particles racing outward amid the roiling smoke
to slice through mud walls, animal flesh, stone fences,
human lives that cling to the shaking
shuddering earth
while they clutch forty-year-old rifles
or axes, or the hand of a two-year-old
below the flash of wing
very distant
in the blue-and-white sky.

Robert Bringhurst

(b. 1946)

Robert Bringhurst was born in the United States and raised in the mountains of Montana, Wyoming, Utah, Alberta, and British Columbia. He spent a number of years in the Middle East, Europe, and Latin America, so it is not surprising that he reads and translates from half a dozen ancient and modern languages. In his poem "The Song of Ptahhotep," the narrator says, "I have seen at the well how the words / tune the heart . . . Hearing is better / than anything else. It cleanses the will." Bringhurst has striven to master the art of listening, hearing the voices of the land, hearing the voices of ancient cultures. To be a listener, he has chosen to inhabit the edges of society and to live close to wilderness, but he is also a master of languages, ancient cultures, typography, printing, and book design, which led to the publication of *The Elements of Typographic Style* (1992). He lives on Quadra Island, BC.

In his poem "Anecdote of the Squid," Bringhurst draws a clever portrait of the squid as a sort of disappearing artist who, in the presence of enemies, makes artifacts that are mistaken for the squid itself. Meanwhile, the wily squid "grows / transparent and withdraws, / leaving behind him his / coagulating shadows." Like his squid, Bringhurst belongs to the older tradition of objectivity in art, expressed in Flaubert's statement that the novelist should be "everywhere felt, but nowhere seen" and in Yeats's comment that, in art, "all that is personal soon rots." Bringhurst subscribes to similar ideas. "Music that is too human is useless," he writes in "Vietnamese New Year in the Polish Friendship Centre." "That which is too exclusively human is not human enough. Our deepest passions push us way outside ourselves." The aim is to discover the artistic means to move beyond the limits of the self to a larger, perhaps deeper, sphere of knowing; this means eschewing confession, domestic reportage, and the other personal fictions that so dominate contemporary poetry. Bringhurst's chosen path may be as perilous as it is unpopular: the danger lies in forgetting that art must make its appeal through the senses, not through the intellect alone, and thus drifting too close to abstraction and pretentiousness. And yet his best work has both the concreteness and the luminosity that characterize the classics in this tradition.

"What poetry knows, or what it strives to know, is the dancing at the heart of being," Bringhurst says in an essay in Tim Lilburn's *Poetry and Knowing*:

> Poets make things, but they don't make poetry; poetry is present to begin with; it is there, and poets answer it if they can. The poem is the trace of the poet's joining in knowing. Its one and only use in this world is to honour the gods, the dead, and other nonhumans and humans—to honour being, in other words—by allowing others to join in that knowing as well.

Bringhurst's books include *The Shipwright's Log* (1972), *Cadastre* (1973), *Deuteronomy* (1974), *Bergschrund* (1975), *The Stonecutter's Horses* (1979), *Tzuhalem's Mountain* (1982), *The Beauty of the Weapons: Selected Poems, 1972–82* (1982), *Pieces of Map, Pieces of Music* (1986), *The Blue Roofs of Japan: A Score for Interpenetrating Voices* (1986), *The Calling: Selected Poems* (1995), and *Selected Poems* (2009). He is also the author of *Boats Is Saintlier Than Captains: Thirteen Ways of Looking at Morality, Language and Design* (1997), *Visions: Contemporary Art in Canada* (1983), and an illustrated collection of Haida stories called *The Raven Steals the Light* (1984), with Haida artist Bill Reid and a preface by Claude Levi-Strauss. His work in the area of cultural anthropology also includes *The Black Canoe: Bill Reid and the Spirit of Haida Gwaii* (1992) and *A Story as Sharp as a Knife: The Classical Haida Mythtellers and Their World* (1999).

The Beauty of the Weapons

El-Arish, 1967

A long-armed man can
carry the nine-millimetre
automatic gun slung
backward over the right shoulder.

With the truncated butt
caught in the cocked
elbow, the trigger
falls exactly to hand.

These things I remember,
and a fuel-pump gasket cut
from one of the innumerable
gas masks in the roadside dump.

I bring back manuscript picked
up around incinerated trucks
and notes tacked next
to automatic track controls.

Fruits of the excavation.
This is our archaeology.
A dig in the debris
of a civilization six weeks old.

The paper is crisp and brittle
with the dry rock and the weather.
The Arabic is brittle
with the students' first exposure

to air-war technology and speed.
Ridiculous to say so, but
the thought occurs,
that Descartes would be pleased:

the calculus is the language
of the latest Palestinian
disputations
in the field of theology.

The satisfying feel
of the fast traverse
on the anti-aircraft guns
is not in the notes.

It lies latent and cool
in the steel, like the intricate
mathematics
incarnate in the radar:

the antennae folded and rolled
like a soldier's tent
sweeping the empty
sky and the barren horizon,

the azimuth and the elevation,
sweeping the empty air
into naked abstraction
leading the guns.

The signal is swirled until it
flies over the lip like

white, weightless
wine from a canteen cup.

Invisibly, the mechanism sings.
It sings. It sings like a six-ton flute:
east, west, always the same
note stuck in the rivetless throat.

And yet, a song as intricate
as any composition by Varèse,
and seeming, for the moment, still
more beautiful, because,

to us, more deadly.
Therefore purer, more
private, more familiar,
more readily feared, or desired:

a dark beauty with a steel sheen,
caught in the cocked
mind's eye and brought
down with an extension of the hand.

Anecdote of the Squid

The squid is in fact
a carnivorous pocket
containing a pen, which serves
the squid as his skeleton.

The squid is a raised finger or
an opposed thumb. The squid's quill
is his long, scrupulous nail, which
is invisible.

The squid is a short-beaked
bird who has eaten
his single wing, or impaled
himself on his feather.

The squid, however,
despite his Cadurcian
wineskin and four hundred cups,
does not entertain.

The squid, with his eight
arms and his two
brushes and his sepia,
does not draw.

The squid knows too that the use
of pen and ink is neither recording
impressions nor signing his name
to forms and petitions.

But the squid may be said,
for instance, to transcribe
his silence into the space
between seafloor and wave,

or to invoke an unspoken
word, whose muscular
non-pronunciation the squid
alone is known to have mastered.

The squid carries his ink
in a sack, not a bottle.
With it the squid makes
artifacts.

These are mistakable for
portraiture, or
for self-portraiture, or,
to the eyes of the squid-eating whale,

for the squid, who in the meanwhile grows
transparent and withdraws,
leaving behind him his
coagulating shadows.

For the Bones of Josef Mengele, Disinterred June 1985

Master of Auschwitz, angel of death,
murderer, deep in Brazil they are breaking
your bones—or somebody's bones: my
bones, your bones, his bones, whose
bones does not matter. Deep in Brazil they are breaking
bones like loaves of old bread. The angel
of death is not drowning but eating.

Speak! they are saying. *Speak! Speak!*
If you don't speak we will open and read you!
Something you too might have said in your time.
Are these bones guilty? they say. And the bones
are already talking. The bones, with guns
to their heads, are already saying, *Yes!*
Yes! It is true, we are guilty!

Butcher, baker, lampshade and candlestick
maker: yes, it is true. But the bones? The bones,
earth, metals, teeth, the body?
These are not guilty. The minds of the dead
are not to be found in the bones of the dead.
The minds of the dead are not anywhere to be found,
outside the minds of the living.

The Occupation

for Janet Danielson

I will tell you how it was the world
changed, she said—and darkness
wrapped us round.

I heard her clearly, though I barely
heard the words. It was nearly—yes—
as if she were singing.

Our job, she was saying, is not
to change the world—nor even
to keep it from changing.

No, she was saying (the story
was over already): our only
job is being changed.

Don McKay

(b. 1942)

Born in Owen Sound, Ontario, Don McKay studied at the University of Wales. He has taught at the Banff Centre for the Arts, the University of Western Ontario, and the University of New Brunswick. He writes full-time and has been a longtime editor for Brick Books. After a decade in Victoria, BC, he moved to St. John's, Newfoundland. His books include *Air Occupies Space* (1973), *Long Sault* (1975), *Lependu* (1978), *Lightning Ball Bait* (1981), *Birding, or Desire* (1983), *Night Field* (1991, Governor General's Award), *Apparatus* (1997), *Another Gravity* (2000, Governor General's Award), and *Strike/Slip* (2006, Griffin Poetry Prize). His two highly poetic prose works are *Vis à Vis* (2002) and *Deactivated West 100* (2005).

In "Some Remarks on Poetry and Poetic Attention" (*The Second Macmillan Anthology*, edited by John Metcalf and Leon Rooke, 1989), McKay says: "I suspect that the quality of attention surrounding a poem is more important to me than poetry. A species of longing that somehow evades the usual desire to possess. Or, I should add, to use." Writing poetry, "that wonderful, useless musical machine," involves, he says, a mindset like that of birdwatching, "a kind of suspended expectancy, tools at the ready." He asks for "a linguistics I can talk with. The meetings of experience and language—negotiation, abrasion, dominion, cross-pollination, intercourse, infection . . . wildness invading language as music, which occurs as soon as syntax is seen as energy rather than enthroned as order."

In a second essay, "Baler Twine: Thoughts on Ravens, Home, and Nature Poetry," in Tim Lilburn's *Poetry and Knowing*, McKay tries to define his sense of wilderness:

> By "wilderness" I want to mean, not just a set of endangered spaces, but the capacity of all things to elude the mind's appropriations. That tools retain a vestige of wilderness is especially evident when we think of their existence in time and eventual graduation from utility: breakdown. To what degree do we own our houses, hammers, dogs? Beyond that line lies wilderness. We probably experience its presence most often in the negative as dry rot in the basement, a splintered handle, or shit on the carpet. But there is also the sudden angle of perception, the phenomenal surprise which constitutes the

> sharpened moments of *haiku* and imagism. The coat hanger asks a question; the armchair is suddenly crouched: in such defamiliarizations, often arranged by art, we encounter the momentary circumvention of the mind's categories to glimpse some thing's autonomy—its rawness, its *duende*, its alien being.

McKay takes on the title of "nature poet" with confidence, though he wants to separate that phrase from the "vacuous piety" it normally evokes. The impulse behind nature poetry, he says, is "a sort of readiness, a species of longing which is without the desire to possess." While he is conscious that language is neither transparent nor purely referential, McKay argues that the external world does speak to, or impinge on, our consciousness. Like Levertov and Lilburn, he believes that "poetic attention is based on a recognition and valuing of the other's wilderness; it leads to a work which is not a vestige of the other, but a translation of it." Without denying post-structuralist claims that non-linguistic experience may be impossible, he insists that

> although it cannot be spoken, radical otherness exists. In fact nature poetry should not be taken to be avoiding anthropocentrism, but to be enacting it, thoughtfully. It performs that translation which is at the heart of being human, the simultaneous grasp and gift of home-making. And the persistence of poetic attention during the act of composition is akin to the translator's attention to the original, all the while she performs upon it a delicate and dangerous transformation. Our epistemological dilemma is not resolved, as by aeolian harpism, but ritualized and explored.... Part of the excitement inside this species of meditative act is linguistic; it's the excitement of a tool which has hatched the illicit desire to behave like an animal.

Further, McKay identifies a cost for the entire nature/culture dichotomy: "That is, to be blunt, it is as dangerous to act as though we were not a part of nature as it is to act as though we were not a part of culture; and the intellectual and political distortions produced by these contrary ideologies are greatly to be feared." In "Some Remarks" McKay admits that he is

> not wild about the taste of paper or the narcissism of the "signifier," however free or ideologically correct the play may seem in those salons of the spirit where it is pursued. I don't believe that "reference" is a consequence of imperialism, late capitalism, or the patriarchy. Freeing words from the necessity to refer is equivalent to freeing Tundra swans from the necessity to migrate, or, getting down to it, freeing any creature from its longing for another.

The Great Blue Heron

What I remember
about the Great Blue Heron that rose
like its name over the marsh
is touching and holding that small
manyveined
wrist
upon the gunwale, to signal silently—
                                                  look
The Great Blue Heron
(the birdboned wrist).

Fridge Nocturne

When it is late, and sleep,
off somewhere tinkering with his motorcycle, leaves you
locked in your iron birdhouse,
listen to your fridge, the old
armless weeping willow of the kitchen.

Humble murmur, it works its way
like the river you're far from, the Saugeen, the Goulais
the Raisin
muddily gathers itself in pools to drop things in
and fish things from,
the goodwill mission in the city of dreadful night.

Adagio for a Fallen Sparrow

In the bleak midwinter
frosty wind made moan
earth was hard as iron
water like stone

Sparrows burning
                    bright bright bright against the wind
resemble this item, this frozen
lump on the floor of my garage, as fire
resembles ash:
                not much.
A body to dispose of,
probably one I've fed all winter, now
a sort of weightless fact,

an effortless repudiation of the whole shebang.
I'd like to toss it in the garbage can but can't let go
so easily. I'd bury it
but ground is steel
and hard to find. Cremation?
Much too big a deal, too rich and bardic
too much like an ode. Why not simply splurge
and get it stuffed, perch it proudly on the shelf
with Keats and Shelley and *The Birds of Canada?*

But when at last
I bury it beneath three feet of snow
there is nothing to be said.
It's very cold.
The air
has turned its edge
against us.
My bones
are an antenna picking up
arthritis, wordless keening of the dead.

So, sparrow, before drifting snow
reclaims this place for placelessness, I mark your grave
with four sticks broken from the walnut tree:
one for your fierce heart

one for your bright eye

one for the shit you shat upon my windshield
while exercising squatters' rights in my garage
and one to tell the turkey vultures where your thawing body lies
when they return next spring to gather you
into the circling ferment of themselves.

And my last wish: that they do
before the cat discovers you and eats you, throwing up,
as usual, beside the wicker basket in the upstairs hall.

Waking at the Mouth of the Willow River

Sleep, my favourite flannel shirt, wears thin, and shreds, and birdsong happens in the holes. In thirty seconds the naming of species will begin. As it folds into the stewed latin of afterdream each song makes a tiny whirlpool. One of them, zoozeezoozoozee, seems to be making fun of sleep with snores stolen from comic books. Another hangs its teardrop high in the mind, and melts: it was, after all, only narrowed air, although it punctuated something unheard, perfectly. And what sort of noise would the mind make, if it could, here at the brink? Scritch, scritch. A claw, a nib, a beak, worrying its surface. As though, for one second, it could let the world leak back to the world. Weep.

Nocturnal Migrants

Another gravity. I am on my way
to the bathroom, the dream in my head still
struggling not to die into the air, when my bare feet step
into a pool of moonlight on the kitchen floor and turn,
effortlessly, into fish. All day surviving in the grim purdah
of my work socks wishing only to be kissed by cold
equivocal light, now they swim off,
up, singing old bone river, hunched-up toes
and gormless ankles growing
sleek and silver, old bone river,
gather me back.
On pause in my kitchen,
footless, I think of them up there among the night fliers—
Snow Geese, swans, songbirds—
navigating by the stars and earth's own
brainwaves. How early radar techs discovered
ghostly blotches on their screens and,
knowing they weren't aircraft—theirs
or ours—called them angels. Back in my dream
the old lady who sells popcorn has been fading in my arms
as I run through its corridors and lobbies, taking her
empty weight through foyers, antechambers,
vestibules, a whole aerobics class completely deaf
inside its trance of wellness, my old
popcorn lady dwindling to a feather boa,
then a scarf of smoke. A gravity
against the ground, a love
which summons no one home
and calls things to their water-souls. On the tide flats
shore birds feed and bustle, putting on fat
for the next leg of the long
throw south. When a cold front
crosses the Fundy coast, they test it

with their feathers, listening to its muscular
northwesterlies, deciding when to give their bodies
to that music and be swept,
its ideal audience, far out over the Atlantic. The face
in the bathroom mirror looks up
just as I arrive, a creature that has
caught me watching and is watching back. Around us
wind has risen, rushes in the foliage,
tugs at the house.

Loss Creek

He went there to have it
exact. The broken prose of the bush roads.
The piles of half-burnt slash. Stumps
high on the valley wall like sconces
on a medieval ruin. To have it tangible.
To carry it as load rather than as mood
or mist. To heft it—earth measure,
rock measure—and feel its raw drag without phrase
for the voice or handle for the hand.
He went there to hear the rapids curl around
the big basaltic boulders saying
husserl husserl, saying I'll
do the crying for you, licking the schists
into flat skippable discs. That uninhabited laughter
sluicing the methodically shorn valley.
He went there to finger the strike/slip
fissure between rock and stone between Vivaldi's
waterfall and the wavering note a varied thrush
sets on a shelf of air. Recognizing the sweet
perils rushing in the creek crawling
through the rock.
He knew he should not trust such
pauseless syntax.
That he should just say no.
But he went there just the same.

Philosopher's Stone

—and when, after I've wasted a lifetime looking,
picking over eskers, browsing beaches, rock shops, slag,
when, after I've up and quit, you suddenly

adopt me, winking from the grave of the roadside
or the rip-rap of the trail
or the jewels of the rich;
when you shed your wilderness and move in,
living in my pocket as its sage, as my third,
uncanny testicle, the wise one,
the one who will teach me to desire
only whatever happens;
when you happened in my hand as nothing
supercooled to glass, as the grey
watersmooth rock that slew Goliath or the stone
no one could cast; when you come
inscribed by glaciers, lichened, mossed,
packed with former lives inside you
like a dense mass grave;
                                        when you cleave
when you fold,
when you gather sense as *omphalos*, *inukshuk*,
cromlech, when you rift in the stress
of intolerable time;
when you find me
as the moon found Li Po
in his drunken boat,
when you speak to my heart
of its heaviness, of the soft
facts of erosion, when you whisper in that
tongueless tongue it turns out,
though it can't be,
we both know—

Anne Szumigalski

(1922–1999)

Anne Szumigalski (née Davis) was born in London, United Kingdom, and raised in Hampshire. During the Second World War she worked with refugees and as an interpreter with the British Red Cross, speaking French, German, and Dutch fluently, as well as some Polish and Russian. She was with the first civilian relief unit to enter Europe after D-Day. She met her husband, an ex-POW, in Germany, and immigrated to Canada in 1951. She settled in Saskatoon in 1956 and became an active participant in the development of the Saskatchewan Writers' Guild. Szumigalski was a devoted editor and supporter of young poets. She taught imaginative writing in schools and at the Saskatchewan Summer School for the Arts in Fort San, and served as writer-in-residence at the Winnipeg Public Library. Two of her books were shortlisted for the Governor General's Award.

In *The Word, the Voice, the Text: The Life of a Writer* (1990), a delightfully whimsical anti-memoir, Szumigalski describes poetry as game, virus, song, dance, and a way of hanging around for longer than your body, "imagination struggling against form . . . an overriding idea in conflict with an assertive language . . . the energy of the body (expressed in rhythm, sound, repetition, and so on) wrestling with the energy of the intellect (expressed in theories, ideas, logic)." Of her attitude to poetry, she says, with typical mock-seriousness:

> At the age of twelve, I decided that if the literary arts can be thought of as a mountain, then poetry is at the very peak. The pointy tops of mountains are no doubt the smallest part. The air is more rarified up here and there is snow under your boots, but then you are as near the heavens as you can get while still having your feet on the ground. Well worth the climb, wouldn't you say?

Despite her lifelong commitment to the writing of poetry, she refused to pontificate about the creative process, preferring to leave matters fluid, open:

> How, in fact, did we come to write anything: what's behind our passion for narrative, our devotion to words: must we always be unsatisfied with what we write, what we imagine, what we express? It's these questions and many like them that occupy my mind when I am not actually writing myself. Digging in the garden, soaking in

the bathtub, eating my solitary supper, my mind always returns to these speculations and arguments. They are as much a part of my being as poetry itself.

Szumigalski's poetry is unusual in Canada for its obliviousness to the attractions of place. When asked the reasons for this feature of her work, she said, "If landscape is important to my work, it's the inner landscape. The world of imagination is so much larger. That's where I prefer to reside." Her poetic inner world is one of transformation, talking corpses, bizarre contracts, real and psychic surgery—a fantastical landscape stretching between birth and death, with the concreteness and illogic of dreams.

Szumigalski's later work explores the formal possibilities of the prose poem, but still retains the density of image, sound, and rhythm associated with lyric poetry. Because its appearance on the page frees it from some of the conventions and expectations of the lyric poem, the prose poem lends itself well to both the psychological intensity and the dreamlike juxtapositions that are central to Szumigalski's poetry. Although she sometimes uses the prose poem for narrative purposes, she never strays far from either the length or the compression required to sustain lyric intensity.

Szumigalski's collections include *Woman Reading in Bath* (1974), *Wild Man's Butte: A Stereophonic Poem* (1979), *A Game of Angels* (1980), *Doctrine of Signatures* (1983), *Instar: Poems and Stories* (1985), *DogStones: Selected and New Poems* (1986), *Rapture of the Deep* (1991), and *On Glassy Wings: Poems New and Selected* (1997). She co-edited (with Don Kerr) *Heading Out: The New Saskatchewan Poets* (1986). She also wrote radio drama, a screenplay, and other titles, including a play, *Z: A Meditation on Oppression, Desire and Freedom* (1995), which won the Saskatchewan Book of the Year Award.

Victim

Ah the cliff edge—where so many murders are done
Can't you see the body among the boulders
Far down on the beach?
While the seagulls scream they are filming
A frail girl in a thin nightgown
Prone on the distant rocks

Mr. B and I are walking hand in hand
Up the cliff path knowing
That under our feet
Disaster and drama are making a second-rate movie
Take no notice my darling Mr. B
Tell me a simple answer to the urgent question
Who am I? Who are we?

Mr. B is a known madman   a suspected murderer
I think the cops are after him for being himself
For not sobbing
For not beating his breast
When he finds a victim on the beach
Bloody and wet in the tide
Was that my body we saw down there Mr. B
Twisted in seaweed   Who am I?   Who was I?

He picked me up on the beach
I am the tiny girl in the thin nightgown
That Mr. B carries in a seashell
In his trousers pocket among
The sticks of Dentyne gum and the spent flashbulbs
Oh I am glad I am dead and can't see
The dirty darkness in here

I was murdered last Thursday but even so
The heat of his groin
And all the fumbling that goes on there
Is disturbing my final rest

Fishhawks

my son stands in waist-high water
the salt reddens his skin
out of his face spring wiry hairs
thickening to a beard
his arms have become wide and heavy

he splices rope
smells of the tar that blackens his fingers
he has learned to make his living from the sea

(the huge shadow of a bird
darkens the sand around us
I speak, say to you *look*
at that rare creature
an osprey)

further out from the shore
your daughter is a rock
jutting from the waves
she is rounded and hollow

within her is a sea-cave
her face is a pearly shell
a shining operculum
stoppers up her mouth
her singing is muffled, a murmur

the boy smiles
his semen darts out of him
a shoal of swift fishes
entering her secret place
he stretches out his finger
flicks away the shell plug from her mouth
so that she may cry out

you look at me, say
this has all happened far too quickly
we wade out   I say:
there is just time for us to bless them
but in that glance they have crossed the horizon
are washed away out of our sight

we two return to the beach
the salt water drips from us
making the dull shingles glisten
our wet clothes cling to our legs
behind us the sun is clouded
the sea is cold not splendid
I am a widow I tell you
but we are just strangers you reply

out there where the great bird hovers
mantling preparing to spiral
there is faint wailing

The Lullaby

a woman offers a man an orange
it is heavy and cold in her hand

the man is afraid of the woman's gift
is afraid to accept anything
especially an orange
for who knows it may contain
the woman's liver and heart

her thighs and her low breasts hanging
it may contain her children
with their night cries
and their noses running

the woman turns to her child
who has dirtied himself again
she strips him as usual
and washes him off in the creek
and the creek runs on
taking the child's dirt to the river
and the river carries it to the sea

the man settles himself in a treefork
with his back against a branch
for he's afraid to follow
the woman into the house
dark comes and the woman lights a lamp
he watches her shadow cross the window
he hears her laughing her child to sleep

The Arrangement

she's arranging irises in a polished brass vase as elegant and narrow-shouldered as herself *made from a bombcase* she explains to the tall blue flags stiff as april that will not obey her arthritic fingers *1916* she adds softening the effect with a spray of ferny leaves

bombs falling on london all around the town whistling down from silvery zeppelins which nose about in the sky huge docile fish swimming in the upper air

she stalks naked through the dark rooms watching her reflection flicker in grey mirrors soft thin body, pale legs, wiry red hair resting uneasily on white shoulders and freckled arms she peers closer examines the small uneven face the emphatic mouth the smallpox scar between the foxy brows

this is the first time she has ever been alone in the forest-hill house where she was born

if ever she was born for there's no record of any such birth of any such person as herself, none she found that out at her wedding five months ago *you are marrying nobody* and she rests her fingers lightly on the two stars on william's epaulette then leans forward and kisses him on the mouth she can feel that her warm lips shock him for he's younger and much shyer than she is *bill my will* she whispers again to the dark house this lonely night *can you survive all this? can I?*

for she carries in her velvet belly a weight lighter than a burr a kernel from which a red-haired child may grow

now she's in the cool garden hugging her thin arms round her fine nakedness chalkwhite roses bloom in their beds their stems and thorns black as blood one open flower stares up at her with the pinched face of an infant about to cry

the earth shrieks cracks apart rumbles shakes shakes and trembles to a stop

fish has laid his tumble of eggs among the pavements and the houses the school crumples the churchtower falls into the park the walls of the prison break open and men rush out thanking the fishgod for their deliverance almost at once they turn into muddy soldiers grumbling and joking about the war, the mud, wet feet, rats and the rotten bitter war

she lies flat in the roses covered with plaster dust from next door thorns clawing at her chin and her breasts the cocklebur little nut moves within her parts from its seedcase and drops from her to the earth followed by a narrow warm tickle

she scratches among the roses as a cat might then buries the tiny thing without a tear stands up dizzy lighter by the weight of a handful of leaves

in the house she draws the heavy curtain so close that not a chink parts them then lights a candle and flings herself onto the wide bed a small empty space aches within her, aches coldly through her sleep which lasts long into the next day

downstairs in the back kitchen where the window is broken and the door swings loose on its hinges the small debris of the city has been sifting into the house all night a layer of fine particles covers the sink and the green glass flower-holders by morning the shelf and the vases that stand there—blue raku, enamelled chinoiserie, silver beaten thin as steam—are greyed with a layer of fine detritus which might be the dust of a century

Shrapnel

shrapnel has torn the man's ribs apart
there is a shabby wound in his breast
his mouth opens innocently upon a cry

he wants to curse his enemies but cannot
for he sees them as striplings lying in the grass
each with a girl beneath him
the long grass full of clover and fieldherbs
waves gently in the heat
the men get up from the women
and buckle on their belts
the women just lie there looking up at the thundery sky
we are wounded with joy they tell each other
we are happy happy happy

the soldier sees this he hears all this
as he lies there asking the earth
is this my final place my own place
he glances upwards to where
the tops of the trees almost meet
there is just a small patch of empty sky showing
it must be spring for a bird with a straw in its beak
swoops down to a low bough   he tries to think
of the name of the bird
he tries to think of his own name
the name of his son who has learned to speak already
so his wife writes   he has seen the child only once
and that was more than a year ago

he tries to remember the colour of his wife's eyes
he sees only her frailty those little narrow birdbones
beneath the soft flesh
he wishes she was another woman
one easier to abandon   one calm and robust
with a wide smooth brow

but who could forget that pitiful teat
in the child's mouth
the curious maze of the blue milkveins whose pattern
he traces in the dirt   his hand touches a broken brick
here was a house   now he remembers the collapse
of its walls

he licks his lips tasting for brickdust
he counts his strong teeth with his tongue
they are all there unchipped   he hears the bland
voice of the dentist telling him he has perfect bite

he shuts his eyes against the light but it shines on
through rosy lids which are the same colour exactly
as his wife's secret he wants to part her legs
and touch her glistening vermillion lining
now at last he understands
why he loves the bodies of women
more than the bodies of men   for pale skin covers
a man all over and only a wound can show its lining

carefully he passes his hands over his body
buttoned into its tunic of stiff drab wool
until he finds the hole in his chest
he thrusts in his fist to staunch the blood
a pulse beats close to his folded fingers
it is insistent and strong
it is pushing him away from himself

Third Trimester

The gibbous moon in the trees is the head of
a child slipping out between sturdy thighs,
lying under bent and bloodied knees. Every
twig is a coarse hair, pubic, female, innocent.

But the moon is nothing but folded paper, the
Old Man explains, wielding his scissors over
the crisp white sheet, *or a handful of coins,*
the quarters one by one pushed into the
slitted back of a pot pig, or maybe a sacred
wafer shoved between the clenched teeth of a
nun.

Then I told him of when I was brought to bed.
Clouds close-wrapped the body of my child.
They were a net of fine-knotted threads.
Small fingers, small toes kept getting caught
in that web.

The moon wavered in the mist, the wind
moithered like a wailing babe, when the head,
wet as though rained-on, squeezed out through
a slit no bigger than a shrieking mouth.

And the cut rope, and the dark blood
trickling, and the little daughter at last
lying in the lap of the sun.

Robert Kroetsch

(1927–2012)

Robert Kroetsch was born in the small farming community of Heisler, Alberta, whose landscape and culture have remained a dominant element in his imaginative life. In 1948 he graduated from the University of Alberta and went to work as a civilian education and information specialist for the US Army, spending time in Labrador and the North. He received his MA from Middlebury College in 1957, and his Ph.D. from the University of Iowa in 1961. After several years of teaching in the English department at the State University of New York in Binghamton—where he co-edited *Boundary 2*, a journal of postmodern literature—Kroetsch began teaching intermittently in Canada, accepting a permanent position at the University of Manitoba in 1978.

In contrast to what he, and many other critics, regard as a puritanical and conservative streak in the Canadian consciousness, Kroetsch espouses a Dionysian aesthetic. As the narrator of his novel *Badlands*, Anna Dawe, says:

> God help us we are a people raised not on love letters or lyric poems or even cries of rebellion or ecstasy or pain or regret, but rather old hoards of field notes. Those cryptic notations made by men who held the words themselves in contempt but who needed them nevertheless in order to carry home, or back if not home, the only memories they would ever cherish: the recollections of their male courage and their male solitude.

One of the chief preoccupations of Kroetsch's poetics has been to find alternatives to the lyric, with its expectations of closure and coherence.

Kroetsch's pursuit of the long poem—not the narrative that so interested Pratt, but the fragmented epic and poem sequence—has involved a struggle against the presumed systems and grids of inherited story, employing (instead of character and a linear unfolding of plot) such structuring devices as stone hammers, ledgers, seed catalogues, and grammar itself. Under scrutiny these ordinary things become objects of meditation, assuming or acquiring a larger symbolic value. The stone hammer undergoes transformations from natural object to weapon, artifact, functional object, and imaginative touchstone; the ledger serves as a clever device—with its columns of inventory, credit, and debit—for tallying up private and collective guilt in the accounting that is fundamental to all thinking lives; the evocative power of the central metaphor of *Seed Catalogue* becomes immediately apparent to readers; and the conjunctive structures "and/but" in *The Sad Phoenician* function as a maddening, if humorous, expression of the alternating currents of motivation and sexual desire, entry and withdrawal, braggadocio and bathos.

Poet Ron Smith, in an afterword to *The Stone Hammer Poems*, insists that Kroetsch's "preoccupation with the need to 'uninvent' the old mythologies and invent or create a new mythology that is central to his prairie locale, is a revolutionary act that is key to the revelatory process found in all his writings. It is this process that allows Kroetsch to cross geographical and aesthetic boundaries in his art." As a poet and theorist, however, Kroetsch is, above all, playful. He sees the poet as trickster or lover rather than as priest. Kroetsch endorses the idea of the poem as something more than literary document; he praises hubbub and commotion, conditions in which the poem is "freed from picture, into the pattern and tumble of sound."

Kroetsch's poetics may be gleaned from *The Crow Journals* (1980) and two issues of *Open Letter* devoted to his work. "What has come to interest me now," he writes in the latter,

> is . . . the dream of origins. Obviously, on the prairies, the small town and farm are not merely places, they are remembered places, even dreamed places. When they were the actuality of our lives, we had realistic fiction, and we had almost no poetry at all. Now, in this dream condition, as dream-time fuses into the kind of narrative we call myth, we change the nature of the novel. And we start, with a new and terrible energy, to write the poems of the imagined real place.

Kroetsch published more than a dozen poetry books and broadsides, including *The Stone Hammer Poems* (1975), *Seed Catalogue* (1977), *Completed Field Notes: The Long Poems of Robert Kroetsch* (1989), and *The Hornbooks of Rita K* (2001). He published nine novels, including *The Studhorse Man* (1969), a book of critical essays, *The Lovely Treachery of Words: Essays Selected & New* (1989), and a quasi-autobiography, *A Likely Story: The Writing Life* (1995).

Meditation on Tom Thomson

Tom Thomson I love you   therefore I apologize
for what I must say   but I must say
damn your jack pines   they are beautiful

I love your bent trees   and I love your ice
in spring   candled into its green rot
and I love the way you drowned   all alone

with your canoe   and our not even knowing
the time of day   and the grave mystery
of your genius   interrupted   is *our* story

and art, man, art   is the essential
luxury   the imperative QUESTION(?)
the re-sounding say   of the night's loon

and holy shit mother   the muskeg snatch
of the old north   the bait that caught
the fishing father   into his own feast

the swimming art-man   who did not drown
in the lake   in his pictures
who drowned   for murder or grief or

the weave of the water   would not hold
the shoulders of the sky   were deep
the maelstrom would not spin   to spit him

free, daddy, FREE FREE FREE   (but I must say
DAMN your jack pines)   for the whorl
of the whirlpool breaks us   one by one

we stretch and tear   the joints
opening like curtains   on a cool
Algonquin morning   onto a red sun

or down onto the black bottom   or far
(the grammar of our days   is ill defined)
or rapt in the root and fire   of that wind

bent forest   (about your pine trees
this evening   one of them moved
across my wall)   daring the light

daring the bright and lover's leap   across
the impassible gap   the uncertain
principle of time and space   straight down

he dove   and he would seize unearthly
shades   and he would seize the drowned land
the picture from the pool   the pool's picture

and the gods cried   Tom, Tom, you asshole
let go   and you had found their secret
and would not ever   let go   they cry

from Seed Catalogue

1

No. 176—*Copenhagen Market Cabbage*: "This *new introduction, strictly speaking*, is in every respect a *thoroughbred*, a *cabbage* of *highest pedigree*, and is *creating considerable flurry* among *professional gardeners* all *over the world*."

We took the storm windows / off
the south side of the house
and put them on the hotbed.
Then it was spring. Or, no:
then winter was ending.

> "I wish to say we had lovely success
> this summer with the seed purchased
> of you. We had the finest Sweet
> Corn in the country, and Cabbage
> were dandy."
> —W.W. Lyon, South Junction, Man.

>> My mother said:
>> Did you wash your ears?
>> You could grow cabbages
>> in those ears.

Winter was ending.
This is what happened:
we were harrowing the garden.
You've got to understand this:
I was sitting on the horse.
The horse was standing still.
I fell off.

The hired man laughed: how
in hell did you manage to
fall off a horse that was
standing still?

Bring me the radish seeds,
my mother whispered.

Into the dark of January
the seed catalogue bloomed

a winter proposition, if
spring should come, then,

with illustrations:

No. 25—*McKenzie's Improved Golden Wax Bean*: "THE MOST PRIZED OF ALL BEANS. *Virtue* is its own reward. We have had *many expressions* from *keen discriminating gardeners extolling our seed* and *this variety*."

Beans, beans,
the musical fruit;
the more you eat,
the more you virtue.

My mother was marking the first row
with a piece of binder twine, stretched
between two pegs.

The hired man laughed: just
about planted the little bugger.
Cover him up and see what grows.
My father didn't laugh. He was puzzled
by any garden that was smaller than a
quarter-section of wheat and summerfallow.

the home place: N.E. 17-42-16 W4th Meridian.

the home place: one and a half miles west of Heisler, Alberta,

on the correction line road
and three miles south

No trees
around the house.
Only the wind.
Only the January snow.
Only the summer sun.
The home place:
a terrible symmetry.

How do you grow a gardener?

Telephone Peas
Garden Gem Carrots
Early Snowcap Cauliflower
Perfection Globe Onions
Hubbard Squash
Early Ohio Potatoes

This is what happened—at my mother's wake. This
is a fact—the World Series was in progress. The
Cincinnati Reds were playing the Detroit Tigers.
It was raining. The road to the graveyard was barely
passable. The horse was standing still. Bring me
the radish seeds, my mother whispered.

2

My father was mad at the badger: the badger was digging holes in the potato patch, threatening man and beast with broken limbs (I quote). My father took the double-barrelled shotgun out into the potato patch and waited.

Every time the badger stood up, it looked like a little man, come out of the ground. Why, my father asked himself—Why would so fine a fellow live under the ground? Just for the cool of roots? The solace of dark tunnels? The blood of gophers?

My father couldn't shoot the badger. He uncocked the shotgun, came back into the house in time for breakfast. The badger dug another hole. My father got mad again. They carried on like that all summer.

Love is an amplification
by doing/over and over.

Love is a standing up
to the loaded gun.

Love is a burrowing.

One morning my father actually shot at the badger. He killed a magpie that was pecking away at a horse turd about fifty feet beyond and to the right of the spot where the badger had been standing.

A week later my father told the story again. In that version he intended to hit the magpie. Magpies, he explained, are a nuisance. They eat robin's eggs. They're harder to kill than snakes, jumping around the way they do, nothing but feathers.

Just call me sure-shot,
my father added.

For a Poet Who Has Stopped Writing

If we could just get a hold of it,
catch aholt, some kind of a line,
if the sun was a tennis ball or something
but it ain't, the impossible thing is the sun

if words rhymed, even, we could catch a hold
(a bush) and start the stacking, words
lined up, I mean, like, in the old days
wood behind the kitchen stove

but you take now your piecemeal sonnet
wow, certain of these here poets,
these chokermen can't even count to fourteen
and as for Petrarch, well, I mean

I've been to bed with some dandy and also skilled
ladies, sure, but would I a ballyhoo start
for the keen (and gossipy) public?
I'd be sued or whatever, maybe killed

but (now and then) you've got to tell somebody
and a reader has I guess, in spite of all, ears.

Are We There Yet?

I stopped in this place in shortgrass country.

I asked the waitress, How far is it to the world?

She said, Two days of hard driving. Unless you're traveling
by horse.

I was puzzled. In that case? I said.

In that case, she said, you've just arrived. What can I get you?

She allowed me a smile that wasn't on the menu. I decided
to gamble.

Bring me, I said, a bucket of water. And a small pail of oats.

A.F. Moritz

(b. 1947)

Born in Niles, Ohio, in 1947 and educated at Marquette University, Albert Frank Moritz has lived in Toronto since 1974, working as an advertising executive, editor, publisher, and instructor at the University of Toronto, where he is Blake C. Goldring Professor of the Arts and Society. His 18 books of poetry include *Here* (1975), *Black Orchid* (1981), *Mahoning* (1994), *Rest on the Flight into Egypt* (1999), *Early Poems* (2002), *Night Street Repairs* (2005, ReLit Award), *The Sentinel* (2008, Griffin Prize), and *The New Measures* (2012). His non-fiction includes *The Pocket Canada: A Guidebook* (1982), *Leacock: A Biography* (1985), and *The Oxford Literary Guide to Canada* (1987), all written with Theresa Moritz. He has translated works of Benjamin Péret, Gilberto Meza, and Ludwig Zeller. He received the Award in Literature from the American Academy of Arts and Letters, and Ingram Merrill and Guggenheim fellowships. His *The Tradition* (1986) was chosen for the Princeton Series of Contemporary Poets.

Moritz's early work demonstrates the influence of Surrealism, Symbolism, and mid-twentieth-century European poets such as Montale and Seferis; it is high-energy poetry, rich in prosody and allusion, that does not give up its secrets easily. In an essay of this period, the afterword to *Black Orchid* (1981), Moritz describes poetry as a continual demolition and recreation of world-concepts, this twofold action corresponding to poetry's "motion toward reality on every level" and its "incarnating [of] that remote possibility which is yet the most overwhelming of all present facts." A strong case is made for Moritz's poetry by Stewart Cole in an online essay called "Achieving the Unparaphrasable: A Review of A.F. Mortiz's *The New Measures*." Cole celebrates Moritz's resistance to ephemera and awareness of contemporary cultural concerns, finding in his work a couple of "poetry's great lessons: that a thought uttered in two different ways is not the same thought at all. And . . . that one of poetry's noblest capacities is to expand our sense of what it's possible to say and, thereby, to think."

Moritz's poetry not only teaches and delights—its moral probing achieved through abundant wordplay, metaphorical layering, and surprising images—but also insists on poetry's centrality to a full life. In "What Man Has Made of Man," he addresses whether poetry can reconnect individuals and society, and heal our deepest wounds:

> Poetry is, above every other human endeavor, the place where person and society are not merely joined but revealed in their original unity. Poetry is the place where the strange, painful division we have created between person and society is suffered, despaired over, denounced, subjected to comparison with memories and dreams and myths of better times, and given the gift of a prophecy: that the proper unity still and always persists, and that it can become the world we actually live in, not just in verse, but on both sides of our front door. (www.poetryfoundation.org/poetrymagazine/article/238054)

Citing two great exemplars of this view, he continues: "Poetry is an enactment of hope which is already the thing hoped for. Such is great poetry, prophetic poetry, the poetry of a Wordsworth or a Milosz. Poetic prophecy brings a possible future into a restrictive present, discovering and restoring vivacity in the midst of deathliness."

Dark Man

I am the dark man, so dark
that in shadow or memory you would say
my flesh grows green.

When the light flickers under towering
oaks and willows, it seems to you that light
pierces me also, that there are blue
spaces in my chest and deep in me
a quivering, an unseen rushing, and a family
of chaotic notes shot with quick rhythms and melodies.
I too, like the lawn in the park,
have my tones of liquid ash and gold
that move across me. And sometimes at the end
of a lane of trees I seem to walk
into noon's darkly striped face as a suicide
fades into the bright sea.
Or if you stay close to me till evening,
you will lose me then, when you turn to look
at the mounded black and orange clouds
lying in the west at the field's edge
above the heads of the trees. You notice I am gone
but at once your question is lost in other questions:
what is the source of night, does dark gather
and mount from the hedges, from basements,
the woods, the interiors of spruce; or does it fall,
does shadow fall, this shadow as large as the earth . . .
and what is it to be deprived of light?

And when you are with me, you wonder at the source
of my wealth and my idleness. A sound
of running water at my feet reminds you
of gardens under harsh suns, Provence, Palestine
or Africa. You think of a wine farmer,
nobles of Sicily, an ancient house
where the last son oversees a green remnant
of former holdings. A man with nothing to do,
keeping to his shade and his streams
in a dusty country, where villages of dust cling
to mountains of dust and the people
sit staring at white walls: the street, the land, the sky.
A man who has learned all languages, knows
all literature and music, studies the stars
and writes without signing the work.
Yet for all this you confuse me in your thought
with an idea of the field, wild grass in motion
sprinkled with mustard flowers and apple trees.
And to watch me as I pass through open doors
onto the lawn, into sunlight, between

peonies as between torches,
is for you to see me naked
as though you surprised a boy in private woods:
only the tips of my ears are covered
by my dark hair that captures close to you
the light in twisting rivers.
And my feet too are invisible, sunk
in seasons of needles and leaves.

And in your thought we are still there together
much later when, the lights lit and the screens closed,
I sit at the piano. You would say you are alone with me,
despite the others, and the notes
of Liszt and of Alkan, warmth chased with cold,
fall and dust across us. First you hear them
above, striking the leaves like light fingers,
and then at last they reach down, refreshing us,
releasing the savors from plants and from the earth.

Stabbing

We found you on the subway stair
struggling for breath, filled with twenty wounds,
blood fighting with the voice in your throat.
As the train had rattled forward
and left you there (progress
is the same as ever, but wrinkled now,
with falling teeth), it had happened
almost in silence in the passage upward
to night and the towers
that indicate and obscure the stars.
Twenty wounds: four times the number
of your senses, twice the number
of the body's natural openings. New doors
cut in you by a misery grown fierce
at what little it receives.

You were a symbol as he took you,
and now are a girl dying.
Like so many other mutilations
done for the symbol's sake: lips
and foreskins mangled, false channels
opened inward, limbs and bodies
cut away in our desire

to conform ourselves to the red coming out
of day from night. And afterward we climbed
all night long past the trees and clouds
till morning, the snow and blinding glare.
We were going to see god and redeem him
from the sacrifice he is said to need from us:
our enemy's heart, or a purchased girl
flung in the well, taking our daughter's place.
In the thin air our lungs were bursting
and the cold made us cry. We wanted
to consume pain without conceiving more,
to discover through long labor
the formula of transmutation.

And all this time in the city behind us
is your ordeal. The murderer
desperate to release the secret in you,
to make you speak and kiss
more deeply than human beauty tells him
is possible, to force a way into your body
for all that knocks and is not opened to.
Or so we say, trying to understand.
More simply we say he hated you
and wanted you to die. He could not see
what you are. And at once we desire revenge,
we would do to him what he has done,
inheritor of the centuries of false instincts,
rites founded on a mote in the eye,
the stupid illusion of evil. So the circle
reasserts its power: this longing
to tear the miserable human things apart,
to drag knowledge from their beauty
which will not stop destroying itself.

Despite all effort, continually in us
victim and murderer perform
all that was done in those dull lights underground.
In us, without end, without physical sign,
the gift is also anger and a blow,
acquiescence is greed, possession
of cherished flesh is a wall.
Our days eat amputations, the human body
digests its pain. And you and he:
now you are only fragments in our mouth.

Woman in Astrakhan

Unreal extravagance of an image, say,
"the astrakhan gates of night," which opened out
far off, in the poet's Spanish. Yet one day

as I read, it seemed the gate of my own thought,
and through it and through the fallen autumn fans
of gingko leaves, near a would-be chaos of drops

flung up in lighted pencil jets and arcing
back to a fountain, she entered and passed by.
Her extravagant gait that threw loose breast and knee

and head too wide, as on a plunging boat
amid gale wind, wave foam, blue sky, and frigid sun,
spoke of pure pleasure in the day, insane

maybe, but willfully if in torment free.
Then softly, as I watched across my book,
there entered me the smoke-curled black, the thick

knotted and plushy night-black of her coat,
and of her hair, her bag, her sock and shoe,
all black, like a gate or shadow of a gate

in the late light, and through it her black sashay,
and in her wake the bright black squirrel, who
came neatly folding the gingko leaves till he

held many at once in his mouth to bring away.

The Tidal Wave

One day I'll wake and see the tidal wave above my city
fulgurating at its dripping diamond crest in the sun
like another, a nearer, sun, and its sheer wall
under its beautiful crown of spume will be
a vertical plain wider than any on earth, a bare steppe
but of flesh, flesh of planed and planished liquid
teak and jet and jade.
How tall will it be—three miles, a hundred miles? How far

or imminent? Will there be seconds or years
before it falls on us? I only know it won't matter anymore
that I was sick in mind. Under the shadow or in the light
of the wave I remembered childhood,
when I dewinged a moth, inspected
the writhing tube and then forgot, went elsewhere.
And manhood, when the memory came back one day
twenty years later and so I couldn't reach the moth
to give the gift of murder, impose release
on its horror as the pure ignorance
of my imagination created it
and felt it. This I thought of every day and hour
to the exclusion of battling like everyone
with everyone for the bread reserved
to others. I slipped into alley mouths
and doorways among empty buildings and occupied
myself all day with saying my nightly prayers, O God
please take away the carcinoma, aphasia, ataxia,
the monomania, hysteria, dementia from her
and him, the age from them, aren't they old
enough already, why should they have to get
still older, till the list of them
became so long that many died
as I forgot them, as my day
became not long enough to run through the vast roll
and pronounce it all. I lost
who they were in the bourdon of their names
rumbling in me, shaking the frame
till I thought my ears were bleeding and I clawed
my skull—but nothing was happening there, in fact I,
the face that faced it, looked roseate, glimpsed
in dark windows, and cheerful. A conscious eminence
absorbed in guilt and supplication, scraggy psalms,
while the citizens ran on and soon forgot
the ones at the gate fallen
with broken leg and twisted bowels and waiting and hoping
to be shot. But when the wave appears
above the city, all this will proceed as usual,
it's what we know, and the absolute equality
of what I do and what they do, my strength and theirs,
will appear in the water's black and crystal glow.

To the Still Unborn

You don't know me but I was once watching films and films
of yet another man-caused horror germinating in the depths.
I was sitting alone with a television's loud images of fear,
repetitious and badly made. I was wondering why
I couldn't turn them off. Always an outpost, a small
and stupid crew in some comer of sea floor, void, or desert,
was being assaulted by a beast that enters the human body
and turns it first to a monster bubbling in pain,
then finally to a blank, viscid, and implacable enemy:
image of the human self-experiment. Or rather, this image
as it appears to the hucksters who made these awful movies
and sold them to my nights, otherwise quiet in the hum
of refrigerator engine and whistle of aural nerves decaying.
I wondered why I didn't turn them off and think of you,
didn't pierce through fear of the great strain it would be
to compose my mind's noise, my senses' palsy
the way hands can be folded or legs formed into a root,
the sort of root a canoe's hull or the belly of a tern
offers to water, moving on its own pressure and soft shadow.
Was I hopeless because you were never thinking of me?
But you didn't yet exist then, when I was sitting in my kitchen,
hoping soon to turn off the companionable horror of my day
and think of you, quiet, powerful, come from the future
rescuing me not as I imagined you but as you will be.

News

They brought him news: the serpent had come
from its hole in the golden mud and stung
and killed his wife beside the river
as she was bathing. They came running
through the fields, tunneling the high gold hay,
making a ripple—like a breeze
or the flowing mark of a hidden snake,
its advance in the grass—which he had seen
when they were still far off. He looked
homeward from his work under his vines,
his hands still raised among the grapes
as if he were tied, they later said,
to be beaten there. His head was twisted
to his left shoulder and tipped back slightly
to lift the gaze, and the sky was cut out

by the line of his nose, lips, and chin—
a complex coast, blue sea, white shore—
and they thought of how the corpse was lying
waiting for him, naked, wet
with river as though with dew, its profile
against the dim of the hut and the rush mat.

His vines were savage, yet the sweetest.
He grew the wild grape unimproved.
Now his grainy fingers in the bunches
of the small violet dusty fruits
were like pale goldenrods gone to seed
mixed in among October asters . . .
but in these grapes, like a loud cry
heard once in the night so sharp and clear
that when it's gone it's not believed
by the only one who heard it, was sweetness
that made the farmers drink their envy
and strain against heaven's injustice
and feel now in their fatal news,
in their duty, a hateful satisfaction.

Then he ran home and running he saw
a walnut lying withered far
from any walnut tree, and faded,
hardly green, so that he thought it
a horse's dropping at first, but then
a walnut. He saw the pine cones, some
smashed, some perfectly unfolded.
The brown suns of the chestnuts, some
nibbled, the green-white innards bared.
He saw a mushroom, gray and crossed
by wide white causeways, and another
kicked over—saw the jagged stump
of the stem, a broken world of breakings,
like the young mountains are. He came
to the hut, bent down to the low door,
dark and small, and she received him,
happy to see him. She kissed him, the full
length of her stripped body kissed him,
the front and back of her body kissed him
all at once. Then they went out,
forgot she was naked from the bathing,

from that interrupted making ready,
forgot the grapes too, and walked together
by the river, back the way the screams
of the women had come, into the hay
where the silent messengers had gone,
and tried to remember and tell each other
their whole day, all that they'd seen and done.

Don Domanski

(b. 1950)

In "Madonna of the Diaphanous Life," Don Domanski observes that "we spend our days wherever we find ourselves always suited up / in our narratives and storylines with very little to show outside / of language." One of his aims as a poet seems to be the reintegration of self and world, bringing himself and his readers into full consciousness of their place in the cosmos. This is a difficult task, given the distractions, the pressures of a civilization driven by greed and lust for power: "there's something about us that inhibits our ability to amend / the stillness to a deeper stillness to inhabit quietude to live in / the world there are not enough reliquaries to hold our saintless / bones not enough reasons to bring us back from perdition."

The word "religious," rendered shallow by rituals and hierarchies, does not adequately describe the rich, meditative, philosophical, and deeply transformative aesthetic Domanski's work embodies. Spiritual, yes, but rooted in the particulars of the physical world in a way that makes Romantics like Blake, Shelley, Wordsworth, and Keats seem crassly secular. I think his poetry belongs to an older tradition with links to the mystics, John of the Cross, Rumi, the Sufis, the Song of Solomon, and Novalis, whom Domanski quotes, saying "All that's visible clings to the invisible."

In a wonderful interview posted on CBC's "Words at Large" (9 Dec. 2007), Domanski describes poetry as a spiritual practice and responds to a question about blurring the line between the animate and inanimate:

> It probably comes from childhood originally, children blur that line all the time, giving life to inanimate objects, to toys and dolls, because they can't imagine it otherwise. What I'm doing is making

> my way to presence, and blurring that line helps to draw out the inherent presence in things. My definition of life is isness, its elementary stance and grace, therefore everything is alive, simply put being equals life. Now I know this isn't the usual definition, but still it is an ancient one, not just among children, but among people from all cultures.
>
> I'm an animist when it comes to how I interact with the physical world. Animism is the oldest religious/spiritual practice, the base experience out of which all the other ways of the sacred have grown. So I guess you could say I'm a traditionalist of a sort, a basic believer in first experiences, whether it's cultural or ones from childhood. There's a very deep truth there that strikes well below the thinking level, a connection richer than language, which can give words a more inclusive depth and reach.

In a penetrating article in *Northern Poetry Review*, poet David O'Meara argues that

> something is happening in his poetry that is much deeper than adeptness with images. In Domanski's writing, the illusion and the reality are so closely interlaced that metaphor becomes a state rather than a literary device only. Often, you are already inside the image, or the image is inside you ("the wind takes the earth and blows / it drop by drop into your ear"). In his verse we continuously ascend and descend between the two levels of surface narrative and submerged metaphor.

Domanski was born on Cape Breton Island in Nova Scotia and now lives in Halifax. His published works are *The Cape Breton Book of the Dead* (1975), *Heaven* (1978), *War in an Empty House* (1982), *Hammerstroke* (1986), *Wolf-Ladder* (1991), *Stations of the Left Hand* (1994), *Parish of the Physic Moon* (1998), *Earthly Pages* (2007), and *All Our Wonder Unavenged* (2007, Governor General's Award).

Untitled with Invisible Ink

I know a wood where each leaf is the distance between two dark towns, where each branch contains what is granted to kingdoms and I know the wind that carries all of that away. I know a tree in that wood and a stone in that wood, because we have sat for long hours and together we have the energy of a shaken man, the energy I wouldn't have, seated just by myself. I know a house at the edge of that wood, a small house with a woman whose heart is saddened in slow motion, broken in places the blood doesn't know. I've heard her weeping through the crickets and the vetch, because they carry what is hidden out into the world. I've heard the sound of silk in her throat when she struggles for words, and the sound of firelight spreading across water when she's sleeping. I've seen her up close and I've seen her far away, and I've seen her hands adjust that distance with a motion. She wrote this small poem in her small house, but she doesn't know. She wrote it with whatever is akin to breathing, sighs and breath against the panes, the fog that rolls out of that original ocean fathoms down in the body. I know those waters, the covering waves, the fish that carry the language through. We come from there with our words and our deeds, all the fin-trailings of what is left unspoken. The light down there is like a small house lit by a candle, just enough brightness to read by, to write by with invisible ink, enough glow to allow for the soul to go further than the fingertips, to bend over the answers and hesitate, and to pick up the pen which isn't there.

A Hummingbird's Heart Beats 1260 Times a Minute

for Julia

This man will sit in his chair till sunrise. It's been a long day, and now the conversations of the day separate the blades of grass to lie down. Now the pauses between words possess everything. The diligence of emptiness knowing no end that he can see, ecstasy of blank spaces between the stones, and all thoughts out of the stones, allowed to wander till morning. There's a sadness about him that he can't interpret, like streamlets carrying strokes of blood back to a source it doesn't understand. Like all the little sibyls under the floorboards that can't speak a word, and the books on the shelves that can't read themselves. In his room only the hummingbird understands, pressed between the pages of the family bible in the 1850's, like a rose that understood flight, pushed flatly, woefully against all the words of God. A flower where the darkness gathers in the shape of a bird, where death gathers 1260 times a minute. That's enough sorrow for even a man to understand, to find his place, the weight of his unhappiness, that feather falling inside himself, where there are no wings, no flying into light, not a flutter, no answers coming from motion.

Biodiversity Is the Mother of All Beauty

in memory of Judy Davis

when I think of blood drops and little hurts
entering a field filling the field
when I think of dandelions off their leashes
and the Noh play of dragonflies airborne
red and metallic blue   light as silk

when I think that one sigh was the pro-genitor
of all life that the binding of oxygen
and hydrogen is the most erotic calligraphy
that every thought human and otherwise
is an astronomical unit
that each is star-laced to its very core

when I think that inside every genome there
is a line of sight that surrounds the earth
that perception holds the evanescence
of all things within itself
that atoms are in a perpetual state of bliss

when I think that deer move elegantly between
trees like the great tea master Rikyū
did among his bowls   that a deep sea coral
off the Hawaiian Islands is 4000 years old

when I think of parallel universes colonizing
the edges of birdsong when I think that
synaesthesia is the language of God
that flesh covers a wider and deeper pilgrimage

when I sit here knowing this is a dying world
nothing could be more effortless   more sacred
than this sleepy forest at dawn.

For the Pure Mother Bee

a breeze like Yahweh's nitrogen-bearing sigh
bending amendments of grass beside the highway
sun sugaring diatoms along the shore
gravitational corridors far off between the trees
carrying dead whitetails away

noon on the backs of bees sweetened by their own dogma
the dampness fading as quietly as the dieback of villages
along the coastline   while we live a life in drowsy
photosynthesis   each day staring into offerings of light
our nights spent mapping those transmutations
multiplying our options till we reach zero

each night we lie in bed with dark graces tattooed
between our vertebrae   black weave

of a black needle in infinite space
we sleep to cross things out   to forget
all our false gods tending their fallen altars
housekeeping beneath hawkweed and woodlice.

*

the hive's horoscope is swollen with honey and wax
Gemini, don't let this year's abundance of possibilities
be tomorrow's lost dreams.
but no predictions for this new century or the next
or for the fire ants   little bodice-rippers all in row

soothsayers swaddled in elementary forms somewhere
over there beside the river   mooning about   rearranging
the birthmarks of stars on ether   holding us up to the light
till we darken and disappear like old paper   old cantos
divided by the slow mime of our lost phrases resurfacing
                                        in someone else's flesh.

*

we never seem to look closely enough at things
like the waters of the world meeting in every
blade of grass   in every stone a deeper stone
or a bedroom from the 1700's   long gone
drifting above the spruce trees   someone dreaming
there still   counting her one blessing over and over
a breath held   a promise kept

we watch the bees but never really see them
never see that they're old latrias ceaselessly flying
into the wind   that they're the last curve on the road
to the royal line   to the Minoan Pure Mother Bee
that they have the composure of absolution
and its single unending caress   no fear   no regret
their black and gold bodies only stained
                                        by tearless things.

*

where the *thou* can take you can't take the bee
the lineage of the *I* dies hexagonally in every cell
we on the other hand practice a self-aesthetic

the words *meadow* and *honey* are just part
of the process of naming our long despair

we all live beside a dark river   bodies
soaked in the backwash of our cognitive functions
canonized to a vanishing point behind our eyes
the saintly pull into nothingness   seraphic iridescence
of empty space between each belief   each decision

we sit staring into the intangible wholeness of light
our thoughts strung along a silk thread
each one a pause in amber   each rubbed to a bruise
our hopes and our fears   the little beads.

Lorna Crozier

(b. 1948)

Lorna Crozier was born in Swift Current, Saskatchewan, and now lives on Vancouver Island, where she teaches creative writing at the University of Victoria. She completed her BA at the University of Saskatchewan, and her MA at the University of Alberta. She was a founding member of a collective of writers called Moose Jaw Movement; taught courses at the Banff Centre for the Arts, Green College, and many other venues; and served as writer-in-residence at the Regina Public Library and the University of Toronto before taking up a permanent position at the University of Victoria. Her many books include *Inside the Sky* (1976), *The Weather* (1983, Saskatchewan Writers' Guild Long Manuscript Poetry Award), *The Garden Going On Without Us* (1985), *Inventing the Hawk* (1992, Governor General's Award), *Everything Arrives at the Light* (1995), *A Saving Grace* (1996), *Apocrypha of Light* (2001), *The Blue Hour of Day: Selected Poems* (2007), *Small Mechanics* (2011), and *The Book of Marvels* (2012). She has written a memoir, *Small Beneath the Sky* (2009) and co-edited several anthologies, including *A Sudden Radiance: Saskatchewan Poetry* (1987), *Breathing Fire 1 and 2* (1995 and 2004), and *Addicted: Notes from the Belly of the Beast* (2001). She has received three honorary doctorates, has had a book translated into Spanish, and has travelled internationally on behalf of poetry and Canadian literature.

An instructive account of her geographical and literary influences appears in *Contemporary Authors* (Vol. 113):

> The landscape of southwestern Saskatchewan has definitely influenced my writing. I've tried to thread the wind and sky into my poems, to make them breathe the way the prairie does. But the influence of places goes beyond the recurrence of images particular to a certain landscape. The mutability and the extremes of the natural world in Saskatchewan have given rise to my sense of the fragility of happiness, love, and life itself. Our hold on things and on each other is so tenuous. My poems, I think, express the fearful hope I feel for the human—for our capability to return to love through pain and for our journey toward that sense of unity with all things, with the mule deer I startled from feeding in the coulee yesterday, and with the mute explosions of lichens on the stones in my grandfather's pasture. If the magic that is poetry can't lead us to that oneness, then I hope it at least can make us feel less alone.

Whether it concerns the evocation of place or the exploration of the psyche, Crozier insists in "Who's Listening?" (*NeWest Review*, Feb./March 1989) that good poetry involves "the most intimate self of the writer speaking to the most intimate self of the reader. When the two connect, poetry happens, magic happens, the sparks fly." Furthermore, "poems can only happen in a moment of recognition, of intense and clear seeing."

In "Speaking the Flesh" (*Language in Her Eye: Writing and Gender*, edited by Libby Scheier, Sarah Sheard, and Eleanor Wachtel, 1990), Crozier addresses the issue of censorship—the public, systemic kind that tries to suppress a text for, say, its sexual or political content, and the more insidious pressures that work to control, if not suppress entirely, full expression in the act of writing. She attributes negative responses to erotic writing in part to "the shock of the new," in part to the male desire or need to control feminine discourse and, therefore, the "hidden stories" that have to be told—and heard. According to Crozier, the violence of this struggle—examples of which range from people leaving readings in protest of poetic content that displeased them to the massacre of female engineering students at the University of Montreal—is both text and subtext in the debate on censorship.

A Brief History of the Horse

1

The brown horse grazing in pastures of sleep
is full of soldiers. Each has his own
corner of darkness, his corner of despair.

The soldiers feel the sway of the horse's belly
as she races night across the meadows.
All of them believe they are in the hold
of a ship that smells of grass and forgetfulness
though they can't understand her hours of stillness,
or the mad sound of flies eating her ears.
Each remembers being pushed through the pale
thighs of his wound away from the field
where he fell though he can't remember
the name of the country or the day or the year.
Sailors now, they have crossed oceans of clouds
to reach this green meadow at the end
of the twentieth century where someone
may unlatch a gate for the horse to enter,
open the door between her ribs and let the light
pick among their bones.

2

The farm girl who rides the horse
after her chores are done
has no idea they are there.

If she did, she would not
squeeze her thighs so tight
around the horse's flanks,
she would not ride so hard.

Sometimes she thinks
she hears voices
as she lays her cheek
along the horse's neck,
sometimes she has bad dreams.

Already longing for the city
she is bored with horses,
the feral smell of them
on her hands, along
the inside of her legs.

When she brushes the horse
wipes away the lather,
she does not know
it could be foam

from the sea
churned by drowning

or froth from the mouth
of a dying man.

3

The horse without wings
grazes calmly in the meadow.
She has no need of eternity,
no need of bits or bridles.

What she knows beyond
the good sense of her hooves
no one can tell.

If we call her *ship*
if we call her *nightmare*,
if we call her *history*,
she will not care.

When she wants to
she moves, flicks
at flies with her tail,
curls back her lip
and shows her yellow teeth.

When she wants to
she stands
absolutely still.

from The Sex Lives of Vegetables

1 / Carrots

Carrots are fucking
the earth. A permanent
erection, they push deeper
into the damp and dark.
All summer long
they try so hard to please.
Was it good for you,
was it good?

Perhaps because the earth won't answer
they keep on trying.
While you stroll through the garden
thinking *carrot cake,*
carrots and onions in beef stew,
carrot pudding with caramel sauce,
they are fucking their brains out
in the hottest part of the afternoon.

2 / Onions

The onion loves the onion.
It hugs its many layers,
saying O, O, O,
each vowel smaller
than the last.

Some say it has no heart.
It doesn't need one.
It surrounds itself,
feels whole. Primordial.
First among vegetables.

If Eve had bitten it
instead of the apple,
how different
Paradise.

3 / Peas

Peas never liked any of it.
They make you suffer for the sweet
burst of green in the mouth. Remember
the hours of shelling on the front steps,
the ping into the basin? Your mother
bribing you with lemonade to keep you there,
splitting them open with your thumbs.

Your tongue finds them clitoral
as it slides up the pod.
Peas are not amused.
They have spent all their lives
keeping their knees together.

Packing for the Future: Instructions

Take the thickest socks.
Wherever you're going
you'll have to walk.

There may be water.
There may be stones.
There may be high places
you cannot go without
the hope socks bring you,
the way they hold you
to the earth.

At least one pair must be new,
must be blue as a wish
hand-knit by your mother
in her sleep.

*

Take a leather satchel,
a velvet bag and an old tin box—
a salamander painted on the lid.

This is to carry that small thing
you cannot leave. Perhaps the key
you've kept though it doesn't fit
any lock you know,
the photograph that keeps you sane,
a ball of string to lead you out
though you can't walk back
into that light.

In your bag leave room for sadness,
leave room for another language.

There may be doors nailed shut.
There may be painted windows.
There may be signs that warn you
to be gone. Take the dream
you've been having since

you were a child, the one
with open fields and the wind
sounding.

*

Mistrust no one who offers you
water from a well, a songbird's feather,
something that's been mended twice.
Always travel lighter
than the heart.

Watching My Lover

I watch him hold his mother
as she vomits into a bowl.
After, he washes her face
with a wet cloth and we try
to remove her soiled gown
tied in the back with strings.

Unable to lift her
I pull the green cotton
from under the blankets, afraid
I'll tear her skin.
He removes the paper diaper.
No one has taught us
how to do this, what to say.
Everything's so fragile here
a breath could break you.

She covers her breasts with hands
bruised from tubes and needles,
turns her face away.
It's okay, Mom, he says.
Don't feel shy. I've undressed
dozens of women in my time.
In this room where my lover
bares his mother, we three laugh.

Later, I curl naked beside him
in our bed, listen to his sleeping,

breath by breath. So worn out
he burns with fever—the fires
his flesh lights to keep him
from the cold.

Though he has washed
I smell her on his skin
as if she has licked him
from head to toe
with her old woman's tongue
so everyone who lies with him
will know he's still
his mother's son.

Taking the Measure

The belly's post-menopausal slouch,
under each bicep the swag of a fleshy wing,
dollops of fat above my bra below my armpits
flap and make smacking noises when I run. Long as
the face of a foal, my breasts meander, my cheeks
droop. Naked, I look in mirrors only on the sly
and never try the ones in hotel bathrooms. Some claim
wisdom but my mind sags, too. *Au revoir*
to high-school French and long division, to the seven
kinds of ambiguity, the common names of flowers,
and Shakespeare learned by heart. To be has taken over
not to be. So be it. For that I'm grateful.
I and my lover of long duration still turn to each other
in the night and in the morning and in the fierce-eyed
glare of afternoon. The years, he says, have made me
elemental. I taste more and more like salt.

David Solway

(b. 1941)

As a poet, David Solway is best known for his literary erudition and technical virtuosity. In a section of *Bedrock* called "Entries," he speaks of quarrying the materials for his poems from journals, using geological and nautical metaphors to explore and explain the nature and limits of language. He arrives at the tentative conclusion that poetry, while inadequate to address the complexities of existence, nevertheless underwrites prose and is the bedrock of all linguistic activity:

> This is the fundamental irony of all poetic speech. The surface is the only foundation we have, and the mystical assurance of this inversion is what we carry around with us as a kind of mobile anchorage. What we have to work with is the paradoxical endorsement of vision, the series of luminous instants which validate and finally constitute the journey, a basic speech erected on a transcendental syntax.

In an age of poetic truncation and fragmentation, syntax may be one of Solway's distinguishing characteristics. Like the Metaphysical and Modernist poets, he sees poetry as argument, the poem as an essay, a persuasive text, a rhetorical flourish, a gentle seduction. The poem persuades not so much by logic as by the pleasing distractions of metaphor and densely patterned sound. Unlike his journalism, which is often contentious, Solway's poems work at a deeper, subtler level, giving the reader the confidence that he or she is in the hands of a skilled surgeon, one who has not only a firm grasp of medicine, but also intuits how the body works and what it needs. The things the body needs from poetry—redeeming wit, form that satisfies, music that enchants, and imagery that stimulates—figure prominently in Solway's poems. His defence of traditional form is best expressed in "The End of Poetry" (*Canadian Literature*, No. 115, 1987).

Like Ezra Pound, who celebrated the image early in his career but eventually took refuge in the long poem, writing a cultural epic in the form of cantos, Solway early on rejected narrative and questioned the value of so-called "free-verse." However, more recently he has found freedom and renewal in creating several fictional poets, alter egos whose lyrical outpourings include catalogues, persona pieces, letters, and subtle diatribes on poetic fashions rendered in cleverly invented patois—in short, a panoply of new possibilities and, ironically, submerged narratives moving through time and space.

Solway, who was born and raised in Montreal, completed his BA at McGill, his MA at Concordia University, an M.Ed. at the University of Sherbrooke, and a Ph.D. at Lajos Kossuth University (now Debrecen University) in Hungary. He has taught at McGill, Brigham Young University, Dawson College, and John Abbott College. His interest in pedagogy resulted in two non-fiction books, *Education Lost* (1989) and *Lying About the Wolf: Essays in Culture and Education* (1997). And from his lengthy love affair with the Greek Islands issued *The Anatomy of Arcadia* (1992). In addition to several books of critical essays, including *Random Walks* (2000) and *Director's Cut* (2003), he has published more than 20 books of poetry, including *The Road to Arginos* (1976), *Mephistopheles and the Astronaut* (1979), *Selected Poetry* (1982), *Modern Marriage* (1987), *Bedrock* (1993), *Chess Pieces* (1999), *Franklin's Passage* (2003), and *Reaching for Clear* (2006). His work has earned many fellowships and awards, including the Woodrow Wilson Fellowship, QSPELL awards for both poetry and non-fiction, and Le Grand Prix du Livre de Montréal.

Bedrock

for Karin

Approaching from the south you still assume
the island as a drifting sanctuary
at whose base the waves gossip endlessly
doing their laundry on the shelving rock—

while high above, austere on turret peak,
a lucid village quarried out of lime,
whose gulls and kestrels hover, sentry birds,
whose voices carry on the wind like chimes.

Whose voices carry on the wind: they send
their rambling dactyls through the morning air
with the dark fret-and-flutter of wings,
a cry feathered between syllables,

so some hear ravens in the olives still
turning carrion for the scavenger gusts,
remember how the sea, green honey now,
sent in its black armadas on that day,

how tremors shot along the seafloor
battering limestone to its grapple depths,
how wind scooped up the dovecotes in its beak
and shook them out across the tableland.

We pave our gardens with smooth cobblestones,
tile our roofs against the culverin of sky
and let the vine grow all about for shade.
The cricket sleeps in the geranium.

But from the north the stormlight falls, down-
grazing nesters in the ilex branch,
and splits the waters with its diamond blade
down to the rock still shifting in its bed.

Stones in Water

Here at our daily beach
in this low cove
we go hunting for stones,
shells and curious fish,
sea-fretted or salt-stiff
sea currency of all kinds.

The collector's very self
is in us, to bring back trophies
at afternoon's end
and arrange them on the shelf
like small responsibilities
or photos that remind.

We dig like treasure children,
poke the sand with sticks
or let it sift, hourglass-like,
to learn from a hint of sun
the presence of some husk
or sea-blasted artifact;

but mostly note how stones
in water seem to be alive,
seem to leap or to bloom
into their hushed perfections

or flame up into reefs
of angelfish; how they seem

like portholes to another
world of sheer extravagance
of color, spendthrift beauty:
moth-green in an air
of water; essence
of tincture; whaleback blue;

plucked, how drab and lustreless,
like any ordinary stone
we curse for stubbing toes;
or this starfish, sea cross,
that we suddenly found
among a rabble of crabs,

fished out for souvenir
and dumped in a can
to parody the sea,
how the marvelous color,
seraph-red, ebbs to dun,
leaving this salt memory

behind, this mineral tint.
We feel a hurt reluctance;
observe how each thing has
its congenial element
in which it radiates, shines,
quickens, ripples, pulses,

as in the very mind of God—
removed from which it falls
into our common desolation
where all things coldly fade
to delegated hells.
We leave the beach to the sun
and other earnest seekers
after treasure, and climb
empty handed toward the blue
prosperity of sky, where stars
will kindle later and gleam
like clear reminders. I love you.

Modern Marriage

Dear K. Belatedly, I send this card
to let you know what I've been up to here.
Down, rather. Feel a bit like Abelard.
A solo drinker questioning his beer,
inventing lousy jokes to pass the time
like: weather's here, wish you were beautiful.
You are. Especially at home. And I'm,
as always, lost, word-crossed, un-epical.
And as always, love, thinking of the past,
that listing ship, how to right it, right us
from the old obliquity of us. Last
night I caught a chill, now it's bronchitis.
The remedy? Slugs of Erythrocin,
the reminiscences I meet you in.

[. . .]

I no longer pester you with letters,
those epics of mutual delusion
that weighed the Boeings down in other years;
thick wads of odes, bringers of illusion;
tricksy villanelles, intricate with lies;
testaments, promises and confessions;
nifty couplets and wrapped-up rhapsodies.
I'm no longer cooking my impressions.
Oh there were times (I'm blushing as I write)
my telephone cost more than my hotel.
I've toned it down, abridged, risked being trite—
hard to lie when you're economical
and cramp your postures on this slender raft.
The sonnet is the postcard of the craft.

[. . .]

The blarney, the *os rotundum*, the gift
of the gab, the pentecostal flamings—
departed, gone, pfttt! And the verbal shift
into passionate overdrive—damn thing's
rusted out like my old blue Toyota.
Tongue-tied Orpheus, defunct Chrysostom,
Cicero on the dole—no iota

of long-dismembered eloquence to drum
up some companionship remains. I muse
upon my swift declension, as I slide
down a rhetorical hypotenuse,
glib Longinus lingo-tight as Euclid.
The debbies think I've sworn a Trappist vow.
I pack it all into my postcards now.

[. . .]

I thought it would be easier than this:
the coming back, the making up, the true
minds' marriage, something we improvise,
I thought—a limerick, a clerihew
tossed off. As if the past could stop on a dime.
And now even the sonnet won't suffice.
The sonnet? Try the prose of a lifetime,
À la recherche du temps perdu, writ twice.
Be patient. Don't kick the turtle. Don't fetch
water in your hands. Practice the child's art,
breaking a journey into: the long stretch,
the steep one, the valley, the dusty part,
the halfway pine and the three-quarter oak.
You get there, finally. And then you croak.

Undertow

Learn to take the island seriously—
love it well, but do not live it lightly—
for yesterday another swimmer drowned
not twenty feet from shore. The undertow
had looped his ankles, hauled him out and back,
given him slack as if to tease him with
a gravity of girls on the beach,
while certain loungers praised his frolicking
and observed in sympathy how the sea
washes all ambition from the spirit,
tugging the forgotten child out of one;
then yanked him back toward mantic Africa
from where the sea had let its hunters loose.
All impetus and quick duplicity
it rolled him on his back so he could see
the parasailor float serenely by

tied kite-like to a sturdy motorboat,
gave him lee toward shore again, close enough
to count the barnacles on coconuts
that lolled like driftwood on the waterline,
and men and women anchored to their drinks,
then jerked him out Atlantic-bound once more,
this time the last, to tumble him into
eternity, as if a man could play
with such deceptive undertows as these.

Roo Borson

(b. 1952)

Born in Berkeley, California, in 1952, Roo Borson studied at the University of California at Santa Barbara and Goddard College in Vermont before completing her MFA in creative writing at the University of British Columbia. She has lived in Australia and New Mexico, but mostly in Canada, where she has conducted poetry workshops and served as a writer-in-residence, now making her home in Toronto. She has written the following books: *Landfall* (1977), *In the Smoky Light of the Fields* (1980), *Rain* (1980), *A Sad Device* (1981), *The Whole Night Coming Home* (1984), *Intent, or the Weight of the World* (1989), *Night Walk: Selected Poems* (1994), *Water Memory* (1996), *Short Journey Upriver toward Oishida* (2004, Governor General's Award, Griffin Poetry Prize), *Personal History* (2008), and *Rain; road; an open boat* (2012). She has also participated, with her partner Kim Maltman and painter Andy Patton, in a poetry performance group called Pain Not Bread, producing a collaborative anthology called *Introduction to the Introduction to Wang Wei* (2000).

Borson recommends a certain resistance to poetic theory. As she says to interviewer and editor Peter O'Brien (*So to Speak*, 1987), "Writing by theory is too much like painting by numbers." However, she acknowledges that "there are new regions to articulate. With me, this means changing styles, syntax, cadence. A new way of talking brings in new subjects, or vice versa." She is particularly eloquent about the music of poetry:

> Music is necessary to all writing, not just poetry. Writing is speech, it's out loud, it makes a noise that's rhythmic or arrhythmic, it forms

> patterns and breaks them. Whenever I think about rhythm I think of contemporary jazz. . . . At first I could only hear a big mass of disorganized sound, unharmonic, crashing, confusing—but then I began to hear individual instruments within the welter and *oh* the pleasure when all the conflicting strains are drawn together into melody again. It's astonishing and fills me with happiness. Coming to a piece of fantastic writing is like that point at which the instruments pull together and everything makes sense—out of the welter of everyday impressions and ups and downs, this clear voice is speaking. It makes the crashing and confusion that preceded it that much more valuable, the contrast is sensual and excruciating and cerebral too. . . . Our rhythms are based on street corners, in poetry, and also on individual temperament. We each have a cadence, or several related cadences.

Borson is not averse, personally or poetically, to taking a political stand, but says:

> I don't believe that art has a duty, of any sort, to society. To say that it has played a role, in retrospect, is another thing. Does the rose bloom for the bee? No, but their lives are bound together and they coincidentally, felicitously, serve one another. . . . the best reason for becoming a doctor or a mathematician or a poet is an overwhelming love of the occupation.

About place, she says:

> I write about the city and about nature because those, combined, are my environment. I write what I see (and hear and smell, etc.) and what I'm thinking/feeling in response to what I see. . . . Poems have minds of their own and you can engage in a dialogue with them. I do write intensely sometimes about nature because I experience it intensely; that's all.

Talk

The shops, the streets are full of old men
who can't think of a thing to say anymore.
Sometimes, looking at a girl, it
almost occurs to them, but they can't make it out,
they go pawing toward it through the fog.

The young men are still jostling shoulders
as they walk along, tussling at one another with words.
They're excited by talk, they can still see the danger.

The old women, thrifty with words,
haggling for oranges, their mouths
take bites out of the air. They know the value of oranges.
They had to learn everything
on their own.

The young women are the worst off, no one has bothered
to show them things.
You can see their minds on their faces,
they are like little lakes before a storm.
They don't know it's confusion that makes them sad.
It's lucky in a way though, because the young men take
a look of confusion for inscrutability, and this
excites them and makes them want to own
this face they don't understand,
something to be tinkered with at their leisure.

Waterfront

The women's bodies lying in the sand are curved like shells.
The men can't take their eyes off them.
The seawater spangles like a drink of champagne,
but the fishermen don't see it that way,
they have their clothes on, they don't care about girls.
They only care about fish. They yell to one another down the beach
as if this were their ocean. Meanwhile,
ignorant, the smelts plod into the nets.
Seated on benches, middle-aged women
in magenta travel dresses, going nowhere,
dressed too warmly for the weather,
delve into the sunlight with their eyes closed and pretend
they are dissolving, like a tablet in water.
Only the babies pushed along in carriages
seem to enjoy themselves, twisting their faces
into vast expressions. Their skin
is still translucent. They haven't yet finished
materializing into the world.

Flowers

The sunset, a huge flower, wilts on the horizon.
Robbed of perfume, a raw smell
wanders the hills, an embarrassing smell,
of nudity, of awkward hours on earth.
If a big man stands softly, his wide arms
gentled at his sides, women dissolve. It is the access
to easy violence that excites them.

The hills are knobbed with hay,
as if they were full of drawers about to be opened.
What could be inside but darkness?
The ground invisible, the toes feel the way,
bumping against unknown objects
like moths in a jar, like moths
stubbing themselves out on a lamp.

The women sit in their slips,
scattered upstairs through the houses
like silken buds.
They look in the mirror,
they wish they were other than they are.
Into a few of the rooms go a few of the men,
bringing their mushroomy smell.

The other men loll against the outsides of buildings,
looking up at the stars,
inconsequential.

One of them bends down to smell a flower.
There are holes in his face.

A Sad Device

A rat, his eyes like glycerine,
like galleries of landscape paintings,
genitals like a small bell, he,
siphon of smells,
mortician gathering in the gauzy corpses,
construes the world.
The grey warehouse of gothic stars,

the gleaming artillery of water,
the flowerbeds like Arabic scrolls,
all of it.

I think my heart is a sad device,
like can-openers.
Sometimes I would rather step between slices
of dark rye and be taken in
by some larger beast.
Men dreaming of billboards,
cars barrelling on and on in the night marooned,
zeroed in on an immense target.
Now I believe the frozen mammoths
in the laundry room
came of their own accord,
not through coercion
by the Sears appliance man.
Not even he
has a cozy life.

Tiny lions in the zookeeper's hair
keep him busily asleep,
but some of us wake too soon,
when our lover is still a dismantled thing
blue with streetlight.

This rat and I
have more in common than most,
having met once.
Now we go to separate nests
and presumably to dawn
with its crossfire of light
meeting in all the other eyes.

Dionne Brand

(b. 1953)

Dionne Brand was born and raised in Trinidad, but has lived in Canada since 1970, mainly in Ontario, where she holds a University Research Chair in the School of English and Theatre at the University of Guelph. She is best described as *un écrivan engagé* in the tradition of Camus and Sartre, a writer who is engaged in exploring important social issues in the world at large, which she does through a stunning array of female personas. Her work includes nine volumes of poetry, four books of fiction, and two non-fiction works. She was educated at the University of Toronto, where she earned a BA in English and Philosophy and an MA in the Philosophy of Education at the Ontario Institute for Studies in Education. In addition to receiving numerous literary awards, she has directed and been the subject of documentary films and served as Poet Laureate of the City of Toronto.

In a film interview with Adrienne Rich, Brand says: "I write for the people, believing in something other than the nation state in order to be sane.... A writer needs earth, soil, not air ... something in the bone, remembered, not quite known." When Rich disagreed with Virginia Woolf's comment that she did not need a nation because she was a citizen of the world, Brand replied: "I feel that, in fact, she may be right, that the word 'nation' is no longer useful, that it has been so corrupted by the way in which the states we live in are organized." She dismisses not only nationalism, as a construct that favours those with power and consists mainly of leaving out various groups, but also the Canadian myth of wilderness, which does not correspond at all to the experience of most citizens.

Her early interest in creating a credible and compelling language to articulate Black women's history, which led to experiments with "Black rhetorical tropes," most notably in *No Language Is Neutral* (1990, Governor General's Award finalist), was so successful that Brand has had to remind critics that she has moved on to other, equally pressing social issues and formal challenges. In other words, she refuses to be typecast: "You wish that your work might be looked at with a literary eye. Rather than this assigning of all black writing to an anthropological space or a sociological space" ("At the Full and Change of Canlit," an interview with Leslie Sanders and Rinaldo Walcott).

Although Brand's work expresses her antipathy for what Canada has done to First Nations and minorities, and for our country's failure to speak out against international acts of tyranny and suppression in Vietnam, Chile, Nicaragua, Granada, and Iraq—an indictment that recalls Herschel Hardin's comment in *A Nation Unaware*, that "creating a simulacrum of innocence is only one way colonials have of avoiding their condition"—it's her mastery of craft that most distinguishes her poetry. The broad range of issues she embraces and their formal challenges have led Brand to explore the technical possibilities of the long poem in its various forms: the extended monologue, poem-sequence, the long poem as cataclysmic catalogue (*Inventory*, 2006, Governor General's Award finalist) and the poetic narrative (*Ossuaries*, 2011, Griffin Prize). In all these forms, she is technically brilliant and always passionate about the oral dimension of her work, maintaining what Sonnet L'Abbé aptly calls a "fierce lyricism."

Brand's literary achievements abound. Other poetry publications include *'Fore Day Morning* (1978), *Winter Epigrams and Epigrams to Ernesto Cardenal in Defense of Claudia* (1983), *Primitive Offensive* (1983), *Land to Light On* (1997, Governor General's Award and the Trillium Award) and *thirsty* (2002, Pat Lowther Award), which has recently been staged at the National Arts Centre. As a fiction writer, she has published *Sans Souci and Other Stories* (1988/1994) and several novels, including *In Another Place, Not Here* (1996), *At the Full and Change of the Moon* (1999), and *What We Long For* (2005). Her non-fiction works include *Bread Out of Stone: Recollections on Sex, Recognitions, Race, Dreaming, Politics* (1994) and *A Map to the Door of No Return: Notes to Belonging* (2001). She has also been involved in the editing of *Rivers Have Sources, Trees Have Roots: Speaking of Racism* (with Krisantha Sri Bhaggiyadatta, 1986), *No Burden to Carry: Narratives of Black Working Women in Ontario 1920s-1950s* (1991), *We're Rooted Here, They Can't Pull Us Up* (with five other writers, 1994), and *Grammar of Dissent: Poetry and Prose of Claire Harris, M. Nourbese Philip and Carroll Morrell* (1994).

Ossuary I

I lived and loved, some might say,
in momentous times,
looking back, my dreams were full of prisons

in our narcotic drifting slumbers,
so many dreams of course were full of prisons,
mine were without relief

in our induced days and our wingless days,
my every waking was incarcerated,
each square metre of air so toxic with violence

the atmospheres were breathless there,
the bronchial trees were ligatured
with carbons

some damage I had expected, but no one
expects the violence of glances, of offices,
of walkways and train stations, of bathroom mirrors

especially, the vicious telephones, the coarseness of
daylight, the brusque decisions of air,
the casual homicides of dresses

what brutal hours, what brutal days,
do not say, oh find the good in it, do not say,
there was virtue; there was no virtue, not even in me

let us begin from there, restraining metals
covered my heart, rivulets
of some unknown substance transfused my veins

at night, especially at night, it is always at night,
a wall of concrete enclosed me,
it was impossible to open my eyes

I lived like this as I said without care,
tanks rolled into my life, grenades took root
in my uterus, I was sickly each morning, so dearly

what to say,
life went on around me,
I laughed, I had drinks, I gathered with friends

we grinned our aluminum teeth,
we exhaled our venomous breaths,
we tried to be calm in the invisible architecture

we incubated, like cluster bombs,
whole lives waiting, whole stellar regions,
discoveries of nebulae, and compassion

from the cities the electric rains pierced us,
the ceaseless bitter days folded like good linen,
the phosphorous streets gave off their harmful lights

we bit our fingernails to blue buttons,
we staggered at the high approach of doorways,
plunged repeatedly to our deaths only to be revived

by zoos, parades, experiments, exhibits, television sets,
oh we wanted to leave, we wanted to leave
the aspirated syllables and villages, the skeletal

dance floors, the vacant, vacant moons that tortured us,
when the jailers went home and the spectators drifted
away and the scientists finished their work

like a bad dog chained to an empty gas station,
for blue blue nights,
I got worse and worse, so troubling

I would fall dead like a specimen,
at the anthropometric spectacles
on the Champ de Mars, the Jardin d'Acclimatation

the mobile addresses of the autopsy fields,
though I could see no roads,
I was paid for losing everything, even eyesight

I lived in the eternal villages, I lived like a doll,
a shaggy doll with a beak, a bell, a red mouth,
I thought, this was the way people lived, I lived

I had nights of insentient adjectives,
shale nights, pebbled nights, stone nights,
igneous nights, of these nights, the speechlessness

I recall, the right ribs of the lit moon,
the left hip of the lit moon,
what is your name they asked, I said nothing

I heard the conspiratorial water,
I heard the only stone, I ate her shoulder,
I could not hear myself, you are mistaken I said to no one

the chain-link fences glittered like jewellery,
expensive jewellery, portable jewellery,
I lost verbs, whole, like the hull of almonds

after consideration you will discover, as I,
that verbs are a tragedy, a bleeding cliffside, explosions,
I'm better off without, with vermillion, candles

this bedding, this mercy,
this stretcher, this solitary perfectible strangeness,
and edge, such cloth this compass

of mine, of earth, of mourners of these
reasons, of which fairgrounds, of which theories
of plurals, of specimens of least and most, and most

of expeditions,
then travels and wonders then journeys,
then photographs and photographs of course

the multiplications of which, the enormity of this,
and drill-bits and hammers and again handcuffs,
and again rope, coarse business but there

some investigations, then again the calculations,
such hours, such expansions, the mind dizzy
with leaps, such handles, of wood, of thought

and then science, all science, all murder,
melancholic skulls, pliant to each fingertip,
these chromatic scales, these calipers the needle

in the tongue, the eyes' eye, so
whole diameters, circumferences, locutions,
an orgy of measurements, a festival of inches

gardens and paraphernalia of measurements,
unificatory data, curious data,
beautiful and sensuous data, oh yes beautiful

now, of attractions and spectacles of other sheer forces,
and types in the universe, the necessary
exotic measurements, rarest, rarest measuring tapes

a sudden unificatory nakedness, bificatory nakedness,
of numbers, of violent fantasms
at exhibitions again, of walks, of promenades

at fairs with products, new widgets, human widgets,
with music, oh wonders,
the implications

then early in this life, like mountains,
already pictures and pictures, before pictures,
after pictures and cameras

their sickness, eye sickness, eye murder,
murder sickness, hunger sickness,
this serendipity of calculators, of footprints

with fossils, their wingspan of all time,
at crepuscules' rare peace time, if only,
like water, in daytime, no solace, so, so different

from solitude, all solitude, all madness,
so furious, so numerous, the head, the markets,
the soles of the feet, so burnt, so thin

and the taste, so meagre, so light-headed,
the cloud flashes, the lightning geometry,
the core of reflectivity so vastly, vastly vast

the wait now, lumens of aches, such aches,
the horizontal and the vertical aches of lightning,
its acoustics, loud pianos, percussive yet

strings and quartets, multicellular runnels yet and yet,
the altitude of the passageway, its precipitation
and grand arithmetic, the segments

the latitudes of where, where and here,
its contours, its eccentric curvatures,
so presently, angular and nautical, all presently

just fine my lungs, just fine,
hypothesis absolutely, but just fine,
why lungs, strange theory

oh yes and the magnitude of jaundice, trenches,
like war, continuous areas and registers, logarithms
so unexplainable, rapid scales, high notes

besides, anyway so thermal, atmospheric,
wondrous aggressions, approximately here,
elaborate like radiation and seismic, yes all over

the bodies' symptoms of algebraic floods,
tiredness for one, weariness actually,
weary with magnetic embryos

petals, yes petals of sick balm please, now yes,
for my esophagus, analgesics of indigo,
or wires, of electric shocks, why eucalyptus leaves

of course lemon grass, laburnum, please, lion's claw,
remedies of cloves, bitter bark,
still birdless though, wordless

asthma with blueness, then music,
gardens truthfully, truthfully nauseous with
tonsured numbers, volumes of fibres, embroidery

and hair nets of violence, blue,
like machine guns, of course knives, extensions
of blueness, all right then wherever

same radiations, lines in the forehead,
tapers, electrodes, invisible to the eyes,
official hammers and corkscrews, official grass

official cities now for appearances after all this,
all these appearances, generous, for certain
scraggly, wan, and robust appearances

assignments and hidden schedules of attendance,
a promise of blindness, a lover's clasp of
violent syntax and the beginning syllabi of verblessness

Ossuary XV

they ask sometimes, who could have lived,
each day,
who could have lived each day knowing

some massacre was underway, some repression,
why, anyone, anyone could live this way,
I do, I do

anyone, I'm not unique, not shy,
someone goes out for milk and butter,
and returns with gashed face, wrung larynx

practically ancient,
I'm not fooling myself, I've tried,
this regime takes us to the stone pit every day

we live like this,
each dawn we wake up, our limbs paralyzed,
shake our bones out, deliver ourselves

to the sharp instruments for butchering,
to appease which rain god,
which government god, which engine god

I don't know,
I know the abattoirs for carving, the everyday chemical
washes, and the fissile air in any regular sky

so here we lie in our bare arms,
here the ribs for a good basket, a cage,
the imperishable mandible, the rhetorical metatarsals

the hip's alertness, the skull's electricity
firing, the lit cigarette tip of the backbone
leans for its toxic caresses

here we lie in folds, collected stones
in the museum of spectacles,
our limbs displayed, fract and soluble

were this a painting, it would combust canvases,
this lunate pebble, this splintered phalanx,
I can hardly hold their sincere explosions

Robyn Sarah

(b. 1949)

Robyn Sarah was born in New York to Canadian parents. She studied at McGill University and the Quebec Conservatory of Music. Her poetry titles include *Shadowplay* (1978), *The Space Between Sleep and Waking* (1981), *Anyone Skating on that Middle Ground* (1984), *Becoming Light* (1987), *The Touchstone: Poems New & Selected* (1992), *Questions About the Stars* (1998), *A Day's Grace: Poems 1997–2002* (2003), and *Pause for Breath* (2009). She has also published two collections of short stories and a book of essays, *Little Eurekas: A Decade's Thoughts on Poetry* (2007). She lives in Montreal, where she co-founded (with Fred Louder) Villeneuve Publications and taught at Champlain Regional College. Since 2010 she has been poetry editor for Cormorant Books.

Sarah names two prose writers—Katherine Mansfield and James Agee—as having influenced her poetry, both in terms of musicality ("attunement to the level of the syllable") and "passion for integral detail." Her work pays loving attention to objects in our daily lives, whether natural or man-made, and our palpable relations with those objects. Poems such as "A Meditation Between Claims" and "Bounty" reveal a quiet, engaging intelligence that is alert to the intersection of differing realities, and to the signs of life in ordinary, perhaps worn, surfaces, where the attentive observer may discover "always a / small surprise." Her process recalls the almost mystical relationship with the physical world to be found in the work of Emily Dickinson and Elizabeth Bishop. As she put it in an interview with Robert Sward (*Nimrod*, 49:1, 2005):

> For me, inspiration takes two possible forms. Sometimes words come into my head—fragmentary phrases that I like the sound of—I call them "tinder words" because they're like fire-starter for poems. Or sometimes it's a sudden feeling I get, that the thing I'm looking at is infused with mysterious significance—that it is both *itself* and *more than itself*. It's like the world jumps into a different kind of focus. I can't make it happen . . . but I try to arrange my life to keep myself open to it.

Although she draws many of her titles and structural metaphors from music and painting, it is the carefully wrought cadence as much as the concreteness and specificity of her language that invest her poetic world with such vividness and luminosity. In an interview with Stephen Brockwell (www.poetics.ca, 2003), she says, "I like for a poem to have a shape . . . a pattern or a perceptible relation of its parts to one another. And I like for it to be musical—I use repetition to this effect, or I may use metre (overt or disguised by line breaks), and rhyme of various kinds. A natural inclination to form is probably something I absorbed from my years of studying classical music."

Fugue

Women are on their way
to the new country. The men watch
from high office windows
while the women go.
They do not get very far
in a day. You can still see them
from high office windows.

Women are on their way
to the new country. They are taking
it all with them: rugs,
pianos, children. Or they are leaving
it all behind them: cats,
plants, children.
They do not get very far in a day.

Some women travel alone
to the new country. Some
with a child, or children.
Some go in pairs or groups
or in pairs with a child
or children. Some in a group with
cats, plants, children.

They do not get very far in a day.
They must stop to bake bread on the road
to the new country, and to share
bread with other women. Children
outgrow their clothes and shed them
for smaller children. The women too
shed clothes, put on each other's

cats, plants, children, and at full moon
no one remembers the way to the new country
where there will be room for everyone and
it will be summer and children will
shed their clothes and the loaves will
rise without yeast and women will have come
so far that no one can see them, even from

high office windows.

A Meditation between Claims

You want to close your hand
on something perfect, you want to say
Aha. Everything moves towards this,
or seems to move, you measure it
in the inches you must let down
on the children's overalls,
tearing the pages off the wall
each month; a friend phones
with news that another friend
has taken Tibetan vows, meanwhile the
kitchen is filling up with the smell
of burnt rice, you remind yourself
to buy postage stamps tomorrow

The mover
and the thing moved, are they two
or one; if two, is the thing moved
within or without, questions
you do not often bother yourself with
though you should; the corner store
is closed for the high holy days,
and though the air has a smell
not far from snow, your reluctance
to strip the garden is understandable

Laundry is piling up
in the back room, Mondays and Thursdays
the trash must be carried out
or it accumulates, each day
things get moved about and
put back in their places
and you accept this, the shape
that it gives a life, though the need
to make room supersedes other needs

If, bidding your guest goodbye,
you stand too long at the open door,
house-heat escapes, and the oil bill
will be higher next month, the toll
continues, wrapping the green tomatoes
in news of the latest assassination.
The mover
and the thing moved, it all
comes down to this: one wants
to sit in the sun like a stone,
one wants to move the stone; which
is better

Scratch

The tinder words, where are they,
the ones that
jump-start the heart—

like mirrors at the bends
of tunnels, that withhold
your face, but give you
what is to come;

like the voice at the end
of the tunnel, that says
"Terminus," almost
tenderly—

Little twigs that snap
like gunshot as they
consume themselves, little
dry twigs,

little sparks, little pops, little bursts
at the smoky heart of where it
begins again, o,

tender and sunny love! what, are you gone
so far away?

Come home to me now, my
brightness. Make a small glow.
Make it to move
the heart, that has sat down
in the road

and waits for something
to turn it over . . .

The roomy heart,
willing to be surprised.

On Closing the Apartment of My Grandparents of Blessed Memory

And then I stood for the last time in that room.
The key was in my hand. I held my ground,
and listened to the quiet that was like a sound,
and saw how the long sun of winter afternoon
fell slantwise on the floorboards, making bloom
the grain in the blond wood. (All that they owned
was once contained here.) At the window moaned
a splinter of wind. I would be going soon.

I would be going soon; but first I stood,
hearing the years turn in that emptied place
whose fullness echoed. Whose familiar smell,
of a tranquil life, lived simply, clung like a mood
or a long loved melody there. A lingering grace.
Then I locked up, and rang the janitor's bell.

Riveted

It is possible that things will not get better
than they are now, or have been known to be.
It is possible that we are past the middle now.
It is possible that we have crossed the great water
without knowing it, and stand now on the other side.
Yes: I think that we have crossed it. Now
we are being given tickets, and they are not
tickets to the show we had been thinking of,
but to a different show, clearly inferior.

Check again: it is our own name on the envelope.
The tickets are to that other show.

It is possible that we will walk out of the darkened hall
without waiting for the last act: people do.
Some people do. But it is probable
that we will stay seated in our narrow seats
all through the tedious dénouement
to the unsurprising end—riveted, as it were;
spellbound by our own imperfect lives
because they are lives,
and because they are ours.

Erín Moure

(b. 1955)

Erín Moure was born in Calgary. She worked for CN Rail and VIA Rail in various capacities while living in Vancouver, then transferred to the head office of VIA in Montreal; she now works as a freelance translator. Her books include *Empire, York Street* (1979, Governor General's Award shortlist), *Wanted Alive* (1983), *Domestic Fuel* (1985), *Furious* (1988, Governor General's Award), *WSW (West South West)* (1989), *The Green Word: Selected Poems* (1994), *Search Procedures* (1996, Governor General's Award shortlist), *A Frame of the Book* (1999), *Pillage Laud* (1999 and 2012), *O Cidadán* (2002, Governor General's Award shortlist), *Little Theatres* (2005, Griffin Prize finalist and Governor General's Award shortlist), *O Cadoiro* (2007), *Expeditions of a Chimaera* (2009, with Oana Avasilichioaei), *O Resplandor* (2010), and *The Unmemntioable* (2012). Of considerable interest are *Two Women Talking: Correspondence 1985–1987, Erin Mouré and Bronwen Wallace* (1993) and *My Beloved Wager* (2009), essays covering 25 years of poetic practice. Since the turn of the century, Moure's poetry has been greatly influenced by her translations from French, Galician, Portuguese, and Spanish.

Insisting that "words have a life of their own" and that poems have a "subliminal code," Moure rejects the notion that she is primarily a storyteller. "I think my poems are narrative in the sense of co-relation, correspondence, rather than 'story.' The surfaces go very deep." Her increasingly non-linear poetry moves steadily from the referentiality and surface politics of everyday life to a deeper relation with today's language and its potential for engagement and change. In the final section of *Furious*, called "The Acts," she outlines, in a language and syntax scarcely less evocative and challenging than those of the poems, her preoccupation with compression and intertextuality, as well as her commitment to everyday events as they manifest themselves in "ordinary words in their street clothes."

Moure is anything but a conventional Romantic in her poetics. She rejects the denigration of intellect, arguing instead for "PURE REASON," which she considers more complex than logic. Her feminist shorthand may require more of a reader's attention, but, as Moure argues, women are accustomed to listening "so carefully to each other." As to the question of "making sense," she says, "I want to write these things . . . that can't be torn apart by anybody, anywhere, or in the university. I want the overall sound to be one of making sense, but I don't want the inside of the poem to make sense of anything." The breaking down of logical connections is something that has concerned poets in the past. One has only to think of the interest of poets like Adrienne Rich, John Thompson, and Phyllis Webb in forms such as the ghazal, which enables the poet to embrace discontinuity and illogic in a highly charged and emotionally unified context.

Where Moure differs is in extending her "program" to the specifics of grammar. In *Furious*, she worked to "break down the noun/verb opposition wherein the present so-called 'power' of the language resides" and to shift this power, if only briefly, to other parts of speech, such as the preposition. Whereas the verb is tied to action, to narrative, and the noun is freighted with signification and potential referentiality, the preposition emphasizes relation and gives a heightened sense of our position in time. "It isn't that to change the weight and force of English will necessarily make women's speaking possible. But to move the force in any language, creates a slippage, even for a moment . . . to decentre the 'thing,' unmask the relation." Moure's is a worthy and not entirely surprising project, especially in view of a growing attention amongst poets and scholars to other languages, such as Chinese, where there are no pronouns, no past and future tenses, and where the distinction between things and events is entirely relational.

In "Poetry, Memory, and the Polis" (*My Beloved Wager*), Moure writes:

> In my own work, I thought at one time the simplest line was best. Yet when I wrote anecdotal/conversational poems without reversal (which is to say, without the language confronting itself & its assumptions in the poem), I suppressed both my feelings as a lesbian, and my concerns as a woman. My poetry was supposed to reflect my life, especially my life as a worker, and these things were suppressed in that life. To write the poems, then, perpetuated (unknowingly) my own pain at being invisible, my desire silenced. As if I could belong, by force of will, to that sameness, that anaesthesia.

In an interview conducted by Montreal poet Carmine Starnino (*Matrix*, No. 47), Moure speaks about how the brain processes information and about her interest in "disrupting conventional notions of reading . . . and how we dramatize our experience . . . language is just a material that's limited by the constructs and suppositions around it. But if you unbalance those a bit, language becomes limitless." Refracting language, she says, "breaks down usual reading habits, the usual structures of what can be said. It opens ambiguities, contradictions, paradoxes that allow more information to be present, available."

Post-Modern Literature

Less to insist upon, fewer
proofs.
Raw metals pulled from the ground, cheaply.
Or a woman in the televised film shouting: thanks to you
I end up surrounded by violence.
So much gratitude, Saturday nights spent
believing in it.

But the end of a city is still
a field, ordinary persons live there, a frame house, & occasionally—
a woman comes out to hang the washing.
From a certain angle you see her
push a line of wet clothes across a suburb.
It sings in the wind there, against
stucco, lilacs, sunken front porches, windows
where nobody moves.
But carefully.   All of it

made carefully, children in snowsuits
after school, appear in the doorway, carry
their tracks shyly.
& you at the kitchen table—your empty
bowl streaked by the spoon, the meal's
memory, papers, juice in one glass, whisky
in another, unwritten greeting cards,
a watch, applesauce, small white medallions.

As if saying the name fixes.
As if the woman will come out again, & pull down
an entire suburb with her washing.
As if the city *could* end, in a field or
anywhere.

or if the woman on the bright TV could
stop saying *thank you.*
or you, saying "like this," & pointing shyly.
Too much paper, the children
in their snowsuits holding doorways, white snow,
parrots, singing smuggled information, the corporation gone to

Guatemala.
Leaving Father, the curling rink, a woman dressed
in grey parka & the nearest boots pulling
stiff clothes away from the weather, the back road, post-modern literature

For Mitterand's Life, for My Life, for Yours

I am drinking history into my mouth. Going down
it makes a sound like "beauty, beauty."

The convergences of what we have not seen of what is.

A massive tree growing in the spirit, not catalpa, oak, fir, eucalyptus

scission, inner scission.

2

The president seen in the photograph of the far-right demonstrators
in 1935. Another there who heard their cries said the words were:
"down with the filth of foreigners (Jews)." But he, he
does not remember.

Is it so hard to remember?
Is it so hard to be the person one once was, de l'assumer sur
les épaules de "maintenant?"
Is there still a thing: the purity of Frenchness?

3

A massive tree growing in the heart, in the darkness or street
under the curved lamp, in sleep, in the limbs
Where my name is, a tree is growing

Silence is the name of such a tree, its weight chokes, oh oaken beauty, oh elm,
history is such "beauty"

we dream of:
Bulldozers ripping the grey stones of the dead.

Making a parking lot. The building behind is a video store.
All the brothers are in the hotel at the road, behind immense vehicles,
seeking the white bird
seeking the white animal that vanished into the wheel

4

While I am inside wanting "sexual love," if that is love
but there are no women in this dream
They are somewhere else sewing tricolor flags
They are waiting to shout their own slogans
I don't want to hear, unless it is "vulva, vulva"
I don't want to hear it, unless

The roots of the tree pass down into the arms I feel these roots
The roots of the tree shimmer in the hands I feel these hands
The leaves are the surface of an ocean

5

I am drinking this ocean like history into my mouth. Going into the stream
my mouth makes a noise. This is beauty. I want you.
The jets have left us & I have landed near you. *This is beauty.*
This is age. This is presence. This is the book of first laws.
To know this. This is beauty.*

---

*If she thinks she can fucking get away with this, she is crazy. Sex is not an escape hatch from poetic difficulty. There is still a thing, damn it: the purity of Frenchness. Is it so hard to remember? That we struggled so hard against this scourge to save you? *It is we, the dead, who were the first readers.*

The Cooking

Political noise.
What we hear above the cooking cinnamon,
the cook in the brown shirt saying:
the government is trying to finish off the middle classes
in Toronto.

Which makes us guffaw
holding the serving spoon or
standing up & opening the window

It's too funny.
Hurrah, we think.

Or later, sobered, the dishes dry
in the cupboard, thinking
the gap between the rich & poor widens
& no one is in it

In thousands of houses the television flickers.
& in the flicker
The prime minister is smiling.

Choose, we think.
Choose.

2

Or a trussed bird.
Its wings bent back to hold shut
The neck cavity.

The riddle of the chicken we all know.

"Why did," we begin. That, & the sound
of glasses, chair legs scraping the hardwood
& our legs too, folded & unfolded,
this laughter.
The skin's thin parchment.
Is word, the

word for it, whispered here.

3

If there could be a word for anything
we could be satisfied or
we could sit down peaceably
& eat
the goddam chicken.

Whose goose is cooked, anyhow.

4

I am sick of these poem imitations, said the cook
who knows better
waving the metal spatula & opening
the door
to get the smoke out

before the fire department stops playing cards
& turns off the TV prime ministerial
grin

Let's leave the hose out of this
The horse too
The "house" for that matter
& the "hours" we spent

painstaking
our hands wet & the teatowel on our shoulder
picking pinfeathers

5

A poem in which a chicken continually interrupts
the "democratic process."
An unspeakable chicken.
The chicken of our bad dream.
The one we woke up from, our mouths dry, & looked out.
In the alley, a television light.
Choose, the prime minister said.
We rolled over.
We thought he said: "choose."

XVI / What I'd give for my life to be my neighbour's old car

> Quem me dera que a minha vida fosse um carro de bois
> Que vem a chiar, manhãzinha cedo, pela estrada.
> E que para de onde veio volta depois
> Quase à noitinha pela mesma estrada.
>
> Eu não tinha que ter esperanças—tinha só que ter rodas. . .
> A minha velhice não tinha rugas nem cabelo branco. . .
> Quando eu já não servia, tiravam-me as rodas
> E eu ficava virado e partido no fundo de um barranco.
>
> (Alberto Caeiro/Fernando Pessoa)

What I'd give for my life to be my neighbour's old car
Roaring pointlessly every morning on Winnett,
that later returns more quietly
near evening, along the same avenue.

I wouldn't need to cling to hope—I'd only need wheels . . .
I'd get old without wrinkles and without grey hair . . .
When the time comes that I'm useless, they'd just sell my tires
and mop up the oil I leaked on the driveway,

And I'd lie on my roof, my hot roof, at the bottom of a hot gully.

from The Unmemntioable

Unfortunately, censure has cut history up.

A wide experience by degrees sapped the faith reposed in my senses.

Silence a barbarity <mars> kills our souls in installments.

The wreck of culture, daughters observed brothers die in <to> great pang.

At first, language was cut off; closer, it pulled out eyes.

There, hope could not know we.

It is possible that all that coincides in the body are merely chimaerae.

In the passport <photo> the child <unstable signifier> defiant in the father's
arms <thick hands> stares <outlive>

"C'est sans doute là où la pensée se trouve."

Sharon Thesen

(b. 1946)

Sharon Thesen was born in Tisdale, Saskatchewan, and raised in the BC Interior, but spent much of her life in Vancouver. She taught English at Capilano College before taking up a position at the Okanagan campus of the University of British Columbia. Her books include *Artemis Hates Romance* (1980), *Holding the Pose* (1983), *Confabulations: Poems for Malcolm Lowry* (1984), *The Beginning of the Long Dash* (1987), *The Pangs of Sunday* (1990), *Aurora* (1995), *News & Smoke: Selected Poems* (1999), *A Pair of Scissors* (2000, Pat Lowther Memorial Award), *Weeping Willow* (2005), *The Good Bacteria* (2006), and *Oyama Pink Shale* (2011). Thesen is editor of *The New Long Poem Anthology* (1991) and co-editor (with Ralph Maud) of *Charles Olson and Frances Boldereff: A Modern Correspondence* (1999). She has been a Governor General's Award finalist several times and is much in demand on the poetry-reading and lecture circuit.

In an essay entitled "What Poetry Performs," Thesen identifies with poets who present themselves as "the servants and not the masters of writing." "This is my own experience," she says, "dictation is the mode I trust." According to poet Barry McKinnon ("Car and Driver," *Vancouver Review*, fall/winter 1985), Thesen is a risk-taker:

> It is this kind of shift from description . . . to personal declaration that is a key to Thesen's method. She writes so that each poem is only "successful" if it dismantles itself (as self dismantles self), until the tattered truth about her attitude to life at that moment is fully revealed. She leaves herself no time to turn back. No time to invent gewgaws and ornament. No time for fear or courage. The poems triumph because they no longer feel like "poems": they become ways of thinking about living that an attentive reader can immediately share and recognize.

Thesen claims to be drawn to poetry instinctively, because "what poetry performs are the instincts of the rhythmic body—the body in time, the body as process, rhythm, and death." Or, in the words she quotes from the translators of Julia Kristeva's *Desire in Language*:

> Poetic language is distinct from language as used for ordinary communication—not because it may involve a departure from a norm; it is almost an otherness of language. It is the language of materiality as opposed to transparency . . . a language in which the writer's effort is less to deal rationally with those objects or concepts words seem to encase than to work, consciously or not, with the sounds and rhythms in transrational fashion . . . effecting . . . semantic displacement.

"When I am writing and pause to think," Thesen says in an essay entitled "Writing, Reading, and the Imagined Reader/Lover,"

> the words I have already written have no history. They do not constitute the case of a moment ago. They are merely what went before, like the tracks of someone. They are signs, and they float, as it were, in an absolute present—a hall of mirrors in which I search for a true reflection or am amazed by the inventiveness of the distortions. I do not know, in the presence of these words, what I mean. They function, rather, as a momentum, from which I seek its rhythmic extension, and sometimes, at the end of a poem, its cessation.

In "A Few Notes on Poetry," Thesen speaks of the ways in which reality impinges on the creative process: "By strife, I mean the awareness, during the act of writing, of the field that we are in: the apparent 'tradition'; the forces of repression both inside and outside; the freshly-prepared ground of the contemporary (innovation, influence, pleasures, displeasures), and the tone of the culture generally—and these are just for starters." Part of the "strife" Thesen refers to, of course, relates to the question that concerns many women writers: in her own words, "how can a woman write out of, or into, her own truth when language and syntax support and reproduce the consciousness of patriarchy? How can we sing ourselves, and celebrate ourselves, in a strange land?" Thesen responds to this question in "Poetry and the Dilemma of Expression" by insisting that she prefers poems to feminist texts: "What I think I do with language I am really doing with form; word play becomes my game of solitaire." Female imagery, Thesen insists, is not the answer; nor is the deliberate expression of feminine knowledge and desire any guarantee of breaking new ground. Paraphrasing Kristeva, Thesen says:

> The feminine in a woman's poem (as distinguished from the feminist content) will always be there, regardless of intent, because it was written by a woman and because poetry is feminine. But the

specifically female trace is likely to practice an iconoclasty whether or not it is revealed, whether or not revelation is the project of the surface or the depths of the writing. Female meaning tends to emerge from the necessarily double-voiced expression of women as a glimpse, a slide, a slip, a dash that holds, momentarily and sometimes for the extended period of the text, *the transformation of the world.*

Elegy, the Fertility Specialist

He gave it to me straight
and I had to thank him
for the information, the percentages
that dwindled in his pencil writing
hand. I watched them drop
from 70, to 40, to 20
as all the variables were added in
and even after 20 he made a question mark. I felt
doors closing in swift silent succession
as I passed each checkpoint on the way
to the cold awful ruler, expert astronomer,
charterer of heavenly colonies,
answerer of questions, and this question
Could we have a child? And this answer, No
I don't think so. Oh
of course he could go in there
and have a look if I really wanted,
steer his ship around the fraying edges
of my terrain, peering with his spyglass,
cross-hatching impediments on his diagram
of the uterine pear & its two branching filaments:
he wouldn't recommend it, he would say,
squeezing his spyglass shut and putting it back
in its maroon velvet box. We make the usual
small gestures of disappointment
as if we'd run out of luck in a ticket line
and I say goodbye
and walk past the receptionist
busy at her files and it is
as if something with wings was crushing itself
to my heart, to comfort
or to be comforted I didn't know which
or even what it was, some angel, and
entered the elevator with the gabbing nurses

going down to lunch and a little girl
in a sun-dress, her delicate
golden shoulders stencilled from the straps
of her bathing suit: a perfect white X.

September, Turning, the Long Road Down to Love

The turning leaves
turn in a wind that rises
as if something warm,
invisible, and female just got up
from a nap and, half-dreaming,
walked to the kitchen
to make a cup of tea: Orange Pekoe?
Ruby Mist? Earl Grey? Which one
did she choose? How about
Ruby Mist agree the women zipping up
their handbags at the airport
and boarding a propellered plane
from whose window porthole heights
topography is listless & small
lucite lakes gather in the deep corners
of mountains, as if assembled
for a meeting. The lakes speak
to one another over the white heads
of the mountains and this for them is like
dealing with the patriarchy. Ah,
the patriarchy, we sigh, having reached
our destination. We button up
our sweaters as the wind rises
and twirls the drying leaves
like you'd turn a wineglass
to look into the red depths and make
a fine judgement. The long
taproots of these rustling
turning trees that stand as a company of
completed metamorphoses of the human body
(branches for arms, bark for skin)
tap a little more love
for language to replace us with, who talk
among the mountains, and talk
with only ourselves, and history,
and the example of the evening
to blame for our silences.

Animals

When I come out of the bathroom
animals are waiting in the hall
and when I settle down to read
an animal comes between me
and my book and when I put on
a fancy dinner, a few animals
are under the table staring at the guests,
and when I mail a letter
or go to the Safeway there's always
an animal tagging along
or crying left at home and when I get
home from work animals leap joyously
around my old red car so I feel like
an avatar with flowers & presents all over
her body, and when I dance around
the kitchen at night wild & feeling
lovely as Margie Gillis, the animals
try to dance too, they stagger on
back legs and open their mouths, pink
and black and fanged, and I take their paws
in my hands and bend toward them,
happy and full of love.

Afternoon with Liver

Sunrise a thin scrap of cellophane
from out in the valley where the blue-
berries grow, I'm wide awake early & kind of
disappointed in homeopathy

Later the ceasing
of the rain and a mildness
extends itself & holds me as I walk
through fragile groups of mourners
at the Gospel Chapel on the way
to the meat market where the butcher's
apprentice hauls a plastic bag of
liver from the cooler

& spills it out onto a wide wooden block
where it unfolds like the universe,
finding its own shape & equilibrium—
a little narrower at one end,
a gloss of winter starlight hugging the rise
at the other end

and with newly practised grace he sliced off
a portion for the display case dark red
& full of vitamins and angled the rest
back into the bag. Boy oh boy, I thought.

My hat was off to that particular cow

The Torturer's Horse

For once I'm not so ordinary as to
stop the dog barking at the neighbour's
three-year-old. He sings
on his tricycle, back and forth
across the deck, a private song.
The late-summer sun glares *as it must*
over the now-silent child, pedalling away.
The lake is mint-blue and gallant with craft
despite the calm day, horse latitudes
of stillness, the many flight paths
overhead. No doubt envy is part
of the story too, along with the crying geese,
the horse's behind, the family dynamics.

No one looks up at airplanes anymore
unless they fly too low over the pitch 'n putt,
the outdoor market with its carrots
and birdhouses. And how the abacus
of suffering takes its place alongside
the other types of calculation, the palm readers,
the circus riders three abreast on their steeds
in the picture book the child takes to his nap.

Patrick Friesen

(b. 1946)

Born in Steinbach, Manitoba, Patrick Friesen lived and worked in Winnipeg for 30 years, then moved to Vancouver to teach creative writing at Kwantlen University College. He retired to Brentwood Bay on Vancouver Island. He has written for film, radio, television, and theatre. His books include *The Shunning* (1980), *Flicker and Hawk* (1987), *You Don't Get to Be a Saint* (1992), *Blasphemer's Wheel: Selected and New Poems* (1994, McNally-Robinson Manitoba Book of the Year Award), *St Mary at Main* (1998), *Carrying the Shadow* (1999), *The Breath You Take from the Lord* (2002) *Bordello Poems* (2002), *Earth's Crude Gravities* (2007), *jumping in the asylum* (2011), and *a dark boat* (2012). He has been a finalist for the Governor General's Award and the Dorothy Livesay Prize. His thoughts on poetry and life are found in *Interim: Essays & Meditations* (2006).

The common thread in the many accolades for Friesen's poetry has to do with his shift away from narrative, toward a more lyrical voice. It is not a displaced or disembodied voice, but one rooted in the particulars of consciousness, in a mind constantly travelling, rummaging through the scrap-yard, bone shop, and word-hoard of personal and tribal history—in search of meaning, of home. His mature work is invested with a sense of the evanescence of life and its products, including poetry itself. This gives him a certain freedom from literary convention and its formal expectations, permitting the poems to be light, glancing, tentative, rather than shaped, formal, closed. It is not that his new poems are without shape, but that they encourage a shift of focus from image and story as organizing principles toward the kind of tonal unity you might expect to find in stream-of-consciousness fiction. The twists and turns of thought and feeling matter more than causality or the paths of logic.

"I have no formal poetics," Friesen admits in *Prairie Fire*:

> I have spoken about poetics, and I have contradicted myself. What seems clear one day, is not on another. I write poems, but I'm not sure I'm a poet, or whether what I write is poetry. . . . It's me speaking. Where I'm from and where I'm going. . . . What I'm interested in is the immediacy of poems. Something approaching improvisation, and yet edited for the page and voice. No explanations needed.

Yet his comments in "Gathering Bones" (*Poetry and Knowing*) are instructive: "The physical object alive, not merely technically, not as a vessel, but shot through with light. Not a lamp carrying oil, but a wick on fire." He emphasizes knowing rather than knowledge (and literature as process, not product), and praises the work of Russian poet Anna Akhmatova: "One notices how many of the poems are fragments. Out of the necessity of her time and place. She, working with snatches of verse, caught images, rags of rhythm. Not the luxury of time or freedom to make them whole. Yet the cumulative effect of a whole poetic vision, a growing, alive voice that never freezes." Overall, he argues for the glimmer, the half-thought: "Giving voice. Evoking, invoking. Holding together loosely. Precise. Elusive. A handful of water."

In a fiery essay in *Matrix* No. 50, Friesen speaks out against cliques, schools, and the predominance of literary theory in poetry:

> A poem does not have to be explained. It speaks for itself. It says exactly what it means. It isn't philosophy, theology, economics, literary theory, or politics in fine clothes. All these things may exist within poems, but they don't explain the poem. The poem has to have an emotional component, a rhythmic component. It must appeal to more than the intellectual aspect of human beings, be more than a page exercise. It doesn't worry about contradictions, has no need to become theory. Poetry gestates. It uses language, with all its resonance, to attempt to understand the whole human in the natural world, in the world humanly created, in the intersections between the two. It explores, reveals, weeps, praises. . . . Poetry is always knowing, never knowledge. . . . is life and death stuff. It shifts perceptions, changes lives. Jugular music. . . . Unencumbered. Answering to no authority. Poetry, at its best, brings light.

from Anna

let's say it was 1958 *sail along silvery moon* was on the radio
it was sunday afternoon in july I remember the river and
    swallows swooping low over the water
silver medallions fluttering on their chests the catholic boys ran
    along the springboard and jack-knifed into the seine river
there was something ominous about the muddy water like a
    dream anything could be there venomous snakes weeds
    and roots to clutch at you or simply depth something
    ominous and those lean white bodies of faith disappearing
    with graceful dives

I held my breath each time wondering if this one would
 drown forever and not return how could he possibly rise
 from that darkness of river and overhanging trees how
 could the water give him back to light?
but always each boy exploded into air returning from death
 or dreams flinging wet hair from his eyes shouting defiance
 at the shore and each of us shivering there
and then the sun was so bright dancing in the spray around
 the diver's head so bright on his long arms cleaving water
 you could hardly believe in anything

let's say it was 1958 I was sitting on the fender of father's blue
 dodge and it was sunday and I didn't want to ever leave the
 river again

I was eating a persimmon trying to think of God it didn't
 work my tongue wouldn't let me get away with it
there are no miracles only mirages in the desert and
 disappearances in the river
there's nothing human that isn't betrayed and I know nothing
 but what's human my hands my tongue and my face in a
 mirror

grandmother wouldn't show me her photographs said I'd
 never know what I couldn't would I? her life before me
but I think I remember her in the orchard she was a girl her
 hair was soft and flowing down her back her legs brown
 with sun
she said sometimes there were angels in the orchard she saw
 them among the trees but she wasn't sure and if there were
 what should she do?
sometimes there was a black dog or the neighbour's boy with
 a stick sometimes there was nothing she could remember
 and she was running for her life
this is how she learned to pray she said this is how she
 worked her way out her hands at the clothesline her eyes
 on the sky

I don't love the prayer rug obedience or disobedience nothing
 that absolute I love the babylonian body and the human
 wound I love the surprising word the sinuous approach I
 like the world approximately

the way grandfather smoked a cigarette in the garden his feet
lost among the potato plants the way he smiled and I
smelled the drifting smoke his stories hovering among the
raspberry canes the way he leaned on his hoe forever
I love words in the air balanced between mouths and ears I
love the way they're smoke before they're stone
but it's true I think there's not much a voice can say there's a
limit I guess to art there's no end to desire

* * *

—what a coincidence.
—what?
—a coincidence that we met.
—oh.
—reminds me. I heard of a man, somewhere, walking down a
street. a baby crawled out a window, fourteenth floor, and fell
on the man's head. both survived. a year later, to the day, same
man walking down another street. a child leaned against a
screen window, fourteenth floor, screen gave way and the child
fell on the man's head.
—same man?
—yes.
—same child?
—uh huh. they had moved to a different apartment.
—they lived?
—yes.
—and then?
—and then? that's not enough for you?
—there's always more.
—well, there is. you can imagine the man had problems. his
neck was never the same. it wouldn't heal. he visited a
chiropractor. thought the receptionist looked familiar.
—it was the child's mother.
—no, no, listen. she looked familiar. he thought he must know
her. he approached her and began a conversation. before long
they realized they were twins. they had been separated at birth
and adopted out. in different cities. let's say their names were
bob and linda. well, linda had married a bob and bob had
married a linda. they each had two daughters with the same
names.
—what about the child?

—the child?
—the one who kept falling on the guy's head.
—oh. well, many years later, the child was a teenager, and the man, bob, was desperately ill and his sister had just died.
—same disease?
—of course. they had both divorced, moved in together, their kids were gone. just brother and sister sharing an apartment, helping each other along. well, she died and he was going fast, so he jumped from a tall building.
—same building where the child fell on him?
—I don't know. he jumped. hit a car stopped at a red light. flew in through the windshield, killed the passenger.
—wait. it was the kid.
—no, the kid was driving. it was the kid's mother.
—you're kidding.
—no.
—could make a person look up now and then.
—that's true. you never know what's going to happen.
—truth is stranger than fiction.
—or life.
—I guess.
—and here we are.
—a coincidence.
—I'm not so sure.
—listen.
—are you adopted by any chance?
—no. listen.
—I knew someone once looked just like you.
—I imagine everyone's got someone looks like them.
—your name, you must have a name.
—I'd rather not.
—let me guess.
—I won't tell you.
—well, then, I'll guess what your name isn't.
—listen, I've got to go.
—george.
—I'm not saying.
—lenny.
—listen.
—albert.
—I'm going.
—emile. frankie. vincent.

a woman from jamaica

I don't think it's too much to ask that for a moment every
wound heal and stutter toward silence
I don't think it's too much to ask for a hesitation of the
highball thundering through our veins
let's say we can halt fear let's say this room is enough that all
streets and rivers flow here that all gods drink at this bar

I know a woman from jamaica who tells annancy stories she's
laughing like a mischievous child
I know a woman who could outleg the obeah man and she
has who could walk water and she will
tonight's her final dream what each of us will dream the
world loosening and shifting like catastrophe but it's only a
single death

is the music loud enough can you hear it on your skin?
are the chairs and tables dancing is the dolphin diving in?

a woman is dying when she takes my hand I feel the chill of the
cold mirror she has held
a woman is dreaming annihilation hands reaching and
rapacious wicked hands that harass her they want to break
the mirror she raises it high above them with her thin arms
she knows what this is this encounter with the end she has
never stood a longer night
when it's over she says when jehovah's come and the mirror
whole she'll see what is left her long body in death she'll
know she was here in this blue place of water and grass

is the dream loud enough can you feel it on your skin?

a dying woman has climbed out of the dark agitation of prayer
and terror with the ghost in her hands
a woman is walking by the water she leaves her shadow and
the willow a woman is rowing away
I don't think it's too much to ask that for a moment every
wound heal and stutter into silence
let's say we can halt fear let's say the music's loud enough we
can hear it on our skins and the chairs are dancing the
dolphin's diving in

koestler's window

it's what we're all born to koestler's window a spanish
jail and the unredeemed math of death
a telephone ringing at the end of the hall with its lonely
alphabet waiting to come together as a sentence
and history doesn't matter nor prophecy only the window
with its flagrant insufferable possibilities

it is your shaking day call it that the day when all you
ever knew is shaken into what you know
there is not a new thing you can name though the sun rises
in the east and wouldn't you know it sinks in the west
your afternoon in the lawn chair among the montbrecia has
not done it but the sudden shiver at dusk maybe

the way you wake inside the hours of daylight the way you
rise from that awful ungodly slumber
half-awake hanging onto the threads of a dream of home
street waking from the perfect garden
or waking back into the deepest sleep of rivers and all
you've forgotten carried in that current

the rum's run out the sun setting on brentwood bay and
all the buses are leaving butchart gardens
there's no relief no getting past it the bicycle gets you
nowhere and tourists pin their hopes on you
orthodox women with their lopsided wigs won't shake
your hand and nuns won't bear your child

the window is open staring in at your rumpled sheets and
gazing out at the stain of mountains
the telephone dangles black and stiff from the wall a
garbled voice ranting amongst the dying footfalls
beneath your sill a dog circles the soil of its sleep
settling with a sigh among the closed red tulips

caught in the sky

your bones she said
are the bones
of everyone before you
only the night

when you look in the mirror
is yours

this business called god
gets out of hand
it's practically inhuman
what you see
looking back at you
turns you away

it's what you are
that ancient bird
caught in the sky
landing sometimes
here
among the dead

remember the dead
speak of them
and death's charisma
they are nothing
but memory
and memory is short

remember me she says
her dress hanging
on a hook
the enamel basin
filled with rain
and clouds

Bronwen Wallace

(1945–1989)

Bronwen Wallace was born in Kingston, Ontario, and lived there most of her life. She worked in a centre for battered women and children and taught intermittently in the English department at Queen's University. Her poems were first published jointly with work by Mary Di Michele in *Marrying in the Family* (1980). Subsequent books of poetry are *Signs of the Former Tenant* (1983), *Common Magic* (1985), *The Stubborn Particulars of Grace* (1987), and *Keep That Candle Burning Bright and Other Poems* (1991). She went on to win the National Magazine Award, the Pat Lowther Award, the Du Maurier Award for Poetry and the Commonwealth Poetry Prize (Americas region). She edited books for Quarry Press and collaborated with her husband Chris Whynot on two films: *All You Have to Do* (1982) and *That's Why I'm Talking* (1987). A book of short stories, *People You'd Trust Your Life To*, appeared posthumously to great acclaim in 1990; *Arguments with the World*, in 1992; and *Two Women Talking: Correspondence 1985–1987, Erin Mouré and Bronwen Wallace*, edited by Susan McMaster, in 1993.

Wallace is an archaeologist of the emotions. The reader of her poems moves, layer by layer, deeper into the substratum of feelings, back to primal moments of fear, pain, and humiliation. Wallace searches out our subterranean selves, the small invasions of change and memory that crack open the carapace of our psyches. She speaks of the "unexpected rituals" and objects that "may tell the stories of our lives / more accurately than we ourselves could." Thus the poems are full of maps, dreams, mirrors—the reflections of which produce a sense of infinite regression into the past, where we feel "our own deaths rising within us."

"My fascination with narrative poetry grows out of my fascination with how we tell the story of our own lives," she said in a conversation.

> The story of my poems is simply "what happens"; beyond that—or rather through that—is the voice of the narrator moving closer and closer to the discovery of the mystery which lies at the centre of her life and every life. I try to keep the language simple and commonplace, the rhythm that of everyday speech. In doing so, I hope to have the poem reflect what I believe: that there is no such thing as ordinary, and that in these commonplace details the mystery of each life is revealed.

Wallace's work, which is seldom autobiographical, falls squarely into the oral tradition of storytelling, with its asides, digressions, and associative leaps. The process, as she has indicated, is one of "detours and double-backs, leaps," a constant "re-mapping" and reconstruction of the past by each subsequent retelling. She speaks of "our terrible need to know everything," which explains not only the force that drives her poems, but also the power these poems have for the reader, whose own life and motives are often opaque and inexplicable to him or herself. As keeper of the stories, Wallace has mastered the digression, or lateral shift, wherein the narrator appears to have forgotten or abandoned the main story momentarily, but has, in effect, deepened the narrative by bringing new material to bear. These objects, places, sounds, names, and persons—surfacing dreamlike in her narratives—serve as signposts and exempla for the reader-pilgrim journeying through her poetic landscapes.

Wallace's biggest influence has been the kitchen-table conversation, with its revelations, codes, formulas, and meanderings. Her parables, whether direct or self-consciously narrated, draw the reader in by deliberately withholding information at crucial moments and by projecting the image of a narrator who is struggling, humbly and somewhat erratically, to get to the bottom of things in her own life and in the lives of those around her. In a 1989 interview with Janice Williamson that appeared in *Open Letter* (7, 9, winter 1991), Wallace discusses her concern with the function of poetry and its role in contemporary society:

> Lao Tsu says that you have to treat every person as if they were wounded. I'm writing to the wounded part of each person, men as well as women. The power of feminism is the power of the victim who has recognized a way to use her damage. There's a great line in an Adrienne Rich poem about knowing that her wound came from the same place as her power. When you get in touch with your damage, recognize and care for it, you also discover the source of your power.

The Woman in This Poem

The woman in this poem
lives in the suburbs
with her husband and two children
each day she waits for the mail and
once a week receives
a letter from her lover
who lives in another city
writes of roses   warm patches
of sunlight on his bed
Come to me he pleads

I need you and the woman
reaches for the phone
to dial the airport
she will leave this afternoon
her suitcase packed
with a few light clothes

But as she is dialing
the woman in this poem
remembers the pot-roast
and the fact that it is Thursday
she thinks of how her husband's face
will look when he reads her note
his body curling sadly toward
the empty side of the bed

She stops dialing and begins
to chop onions for the pot-roast
but behind her back the phone
shapes itself insistently
the number for airline reservations
chants in her head
in an hour her children will be
home from school and after that
her husband will arrive
to kiss the back of her neck
while she thickens the gravy
and she knows that
all through dinner
her mouth will laugh and chatter
while she walks with her lover
on a beach somewhere

She puts the onions in the pot
and turns toward the phone
but even as she reaches
she is thinking of
her daughter's piano lessons
her son's dental appointment

Her arms fall to her side
and as she stands there
in the middle of her spotless kitchen
we can see her growing

old like this
and wish for something anything
to happen we could have her go
mad perhaps and lock herself
in the closet crouch there
for days her dresses withering
around her like cast-off skins
or maybe she could take
to cruising the streets at night
in her husband's car
picking up teenage boys
and fucking them in the back seat
we can even imagine
finding her body
dumped in a ditch somewhere
on the edge of town

The woman in this poem offends us
with her useless phone and the persistent
smell of onions we regard her as we do
the poorly calculated overdose
who lies in a bed somewhere
not knowing how her life drips
through her drop by measured drop
we want to think of death
as something sudden
stroke or the leap
that carries us over the railing
of the bridge in one determined arc
the pistol aimed precisely
at the right part of the brain
we want to hate this woman

but mostly we hate knowing
that for us too it is
moments like this
our thoughts stiff fingers
tear at again and again
when we stop in the middle
of an ordinary day and
like the woman in this poem
begin to feel
our own deaths
rising slow within us

A Simple Poem for Virginia Woolf

This started out as a simple poem
for Virginia Woolf   you know the kind
we women writers write these days
in our own rooms
on our own time
a salute   a gesture of friendship
a psychological debt
paid off
I wanted it simple
and perfectly round
hard as an
egg   I thought
only once I'd said egg
I thought of the smell
of bacon grease and dirty frying-pans
and whether there were enough for breakfast
I couldn't help it
I wanted the poem to be carefree and easy
like children playing in the snow
I didn't mean to mention
the price of snowsuits or
how even on the most expensive ones
the zippers always snag
just when you're late for work
and trying to get the children
off to school on time
a straightforward poem
for Virginia Woolf   that's all
I wanted really
not something tangled in
domestic life the way
Jane Austen's novels tangled
with her knitting her embroidery
whatever it was she hid them under
I didn't mean to go into all that
didn't intend to get confessional
and tell you how
every time I read a good poem
by a woman writer I'm always peeking
behind it trying to see
if she's still married

or has a lover at least
wanted to know what she did
with her kids while she wrote it
or whether she had any
and if she didn't if she'd chosen
not to or if she did did she
choose and why I didn't mean
to bother with that
and I certainly wasn't going
to tell you about the time
my best friend was sick in intensive care
and I went down to see her
but they wouldn't let me in
because I wasn't her husband
or her father her mother
I wasn't family
I was just her friend
and the friendship of women
wasn't mentioned
in hospital policy
or how I went out and kicked
a dent in the fender of my car
and sat there crying because
if she died I wouldn't be able
to tell her how much I loved her
(though she didn't and we laugh
about it now) but that's what got me
started I suppose wanting to write
a gesture of friendship
for a woman for a woman writer
for Virginia Woolf
and thinking I could do it
easily separating the words
from the lives they come from
that's what a good poem should do
after all and I wasn't going to make excuses
for being a woman blaming years of silence
for leaving us
so much to say

This started out as a simple poem
for Virginia Woolf
it wasn't going to mention history

or choices or women's lives
the complexities of women's friendships
or the countless gritty details
of an ordinary woman's life
that never appear in poems at all
yet even as I write these words
those ordinary details intervene
between the poem I meant to write
and this one   where the delicate faces
of my children   faces of friends
of women I have never even seen
glow on the blank pages
and deeper than any silence
press around me
waiting their turn

Common Magic

Your best friend falls in love
and her brain turns to water.
You can watch her lips move,
making the customary sounds,
but you can see they're merely
words, flimsy as bubbles rising
from some golden sea where she
swims sleek and exotic as a mermaid.

It's always like that.
You stop for lunch in a crowded
restaurant and the waitress floats
toward you. You can tell she doesn't care
whether you have the baked or french-fried
and you wonder if your voice comes
in bubbles too.

It's not just women either. Or love
for that matter. The old man
across from you on the bus holds
a young child on his knee; he is singing
to her and his voice is a small boy
turning somersaults in the green
country of his blood.

It's only when the driver calls his stop
that he emerges into this puzzle
of brick and tiny hedges. Only then
you notice his shaking hands, his need
of the child to guide him home.

All over the city
you move in your own seasons
through the season of others: old women, faces
clawed by weather you can't feel
clack dry tongues at passersby
while adolescents seethe
in their glassy atmospheres of anger.

In parks, the children
are alien life-forms, rooted
in the galaxies they've grown through
to get here. Their games weave
the interface and their laughter
tickles that part of your brain where smells
are hidden and the nuzzling textures of things.

It's a wonder that anything gets done
at all: a mechanic flails
at the muffler of your car
through whatever storm he's trapped inside
and the mailman stares at numbers
from the haze of a distant summer.

Yet somehow letters arrive and buses
remember their routes. Banks balance.
Mangoes ripen on the supermarket shelves.
Everyone manages. You gulp the thin air
of this planet as if it were the only
one you knew. Even the earth you're
standing on seems solid enough.
It's always the chance word, unthinking
gesture that unlocks the face before you.
Reveals the intricate countries
deep within the eyes. The hidden
lives, like sudden miracles,
that breathe there.

Rhea Tregebov

(b. 1953)

Rhea Tregebov was born in Saskatoon, but grew up in Winnipeg. She studied at the University of Manitoba, Cornell, and Boston University, where she completed a Master of Arts degree in British and American literature. During her years in Toronto, she worked as a freelance editor of poetry, non-fiction, and fiction for both adults and young adults, was coordinating editor for Sumach Press, and taught creative writing in Ryerson University's continuing education program. She joined the creative writing program at the University of British Columbia in 2005, where she is Associate Professor, teaching poetry, children's literature, and literary translation workshops. She lives in Vancouver.

Having edited nine anthologies—including *Frictions: Short Fiction by Canadian Women* (1989), *Sudden Miracles: Eight Women Poets* (1991), and *Arguing with the Storm: Stories by Yiddish Women Writers* (2008)—Tregebov published her first novel, *The Knife-Sharpener's Bell*, in 2009. Her poetry publications include *Remembering History* (1982), *No One We Know* (1986), *The Proving Grounds* (1991), *Mapping the Chaos* (1995), *The Strength of the Materials* (2001), *(alive): Selected and new poems* (2004), and *All Souls'* (2012). Her writing has received the J.I. Segal Award for fiction, the Pat Lowther Award, the *Malahat Review* Long Poem Prize, and the *Prairie Schooner* Readers' Choice Award for Poetry, and her work was shortlisted for the National Magazine Awards. She is also the author of several illustrated books for children.

"As children," she writes in "Centring the Margins,"

> we assume that the world of our childhood is the only available universe, and thus the emotional and intellectual constellations that form that world become paradigms for all future experience. For writers, certainly for myself, this childhood world is a deep and crucial source of our writing. The cultural community in which I grew up was the politically radical, solidly working class and culturally diverse North End of Winnipeg in the 1950s and '60s. In these vigorous and cohesive eastern European communities, our ethnicity was to a large degree the source of our identities. However, because our social "difference" was based on country of origin and/or religion, we were nominally "invisible" as minorities.

In response to subtle racism and bigotry, Tregebov left ethnicity out of her early work and came to feel not only invisible but also decentred. Changing conditions, including a rise in anti-Semitism, finally encouraged her to embrace her origins and to celebrate the secular Jewish values of compassion, humanity, and community. This shift was accompanied by a determination to resist poetic fashions and critical expectations and embrace what she has called the "emotional muddle" of the self in increasingly personal poems. It also enabled her to rethink the position of the poet in relation to social change. As a feminist and politically engaged writer, she realized she could write about anything, including social and political violence, as long as she abandoned the "objective" stance and acknowledged her own possibly privileged and complicit position in relation to that violence.

At 3:00 or 4:00 or 5:00 a.m.

March–June 1987

the green plastic of the respirator mask, my face watching
the green plastic of the mask hold your small breath,
drawn and released, your sleeping face calm
through the crib bars, against the crib bars,
my face watching your small battle gear,
your plastic breath travel the clear hose to the air compressor,
your extra lung, my steel help, steel hope,
clear plastic hope when your choking, your sure death
jerks me to the realistic kitchen,
the ritual medication, the refrigerator's pure light,
watching for your choking, your sure death
as my automatic fingers prepare the glass vial,
the chilled bronchodilator I believe in
I believe in modern science,
the glass vial, the dial of my watch
counting the ten to twelve minutes of your miracle,
my salvation, the ten to twelve minutes
I grip your sleeping face calm against the crib bars,
grip the names of your sleeping features—
cheeks, eyes, nose, mouth—features of my salvation,
drawn and released, the names of my mother, my father,
the gods, name of my solitary childhood self, the child
alone in the strict hospital room, without mother, father,
the gods, child alone with each *acute exacerbation*,
alone with the ritual hope, ritual fear, pure motherless light.

Edge Zone

Fringes move the woollen scarf between fabric and nothing,
play against the air. And my fingers love them,
edges, borders. The porch, verandah skirting the house,
rooms that aren't rooms, where you can be in two places
at once. Concrete step where I would wait, rising,
the storm coming to me across the prairie.
I have this longing for edges, for the place
they ease in me, a place where I can rest. I would thread
the satin binding of the yellow blanket between index
and middle finger; joined to my touch till it frayed
under the wear. Heart's ease. They couldn't get that one
away from me. They hid it in the garage but I cried till
they brought it in cold and I put that cold against my hot face
till it took my heat. I wouldn't grow up, not just then.
In the smell of chalk and paper of the synagogue I straddled
then broke the boundary between the women and men, small
enough to be allowed to sit beside my father, braiding
the fine silk fringes of his prayer shawl, lulled
by the singsong, the call and response of my father
tongue, the vowels and eastern wail of it.
Lullaby of their shoulders rocking back and forth.
Strong shoulders humbled by the white woven cloth.
My own heart rocks against the flexible bones that protect
it. And us. Us. Edge-dwellers. Neither fish nor fowl. How
hard it is that the mind goes out beyond the limits of the body,
    fingering that hem, rim, brink.

Wherever You Are

Behind the rusted bent tin of garbage cans,
the dull grey sharp at the folded edges,
patches gone to foil, the red lace of decay,
through the thin cloth of the striped T-shirt
splinters in the skin of the back against brown
fraying wood in the smell of rot, in the smell
of darkness where the lilacs' salt-green leaves
dig air, or in the white atmosphere above the grass
between white stucco and white picket fence,
along the soft dusty dirt, the gentle dirt
of the garden where worms are, where things are alive,
the boy is hiding. He doesn't come though his mother

calls and calls, he's too small to be lost this long.
Why is he hiding? His mother calls but he doesn't come
until he's found and when he's found she hits him
with the belt until the pain stops being pain,
until he's not there: he's hiding. He's not there.

Intelligent Life: Elegy

Home from a long trip I find
the familiar rooms grown wider, and
me suddenly small, on the broad streets
of childhood. Small, like that, and
lonely. It's lonely here.
We think that down here,
on the planet, there's abundance; that
it's out there that warmth is an aberration—
the scientist sending out messages
looking for intelligent life, thinking
he may have located a likely solar system.
I don't know.
Take my friend from the former Yugoslavia
sitting inland, strong fingers splayed
on her knees, cold, remembering the sea.
Or my aunt, also inland, adrift, her memory
riffling like ripe wind through a wheat field—
she wakes, cold and afraid, to bury the husband
dead three years now. It's lonely here.
Take me. I have only my own body.
I nod to the neighbour,
leave messages for my best friend,
eat dinner with the radio on.
Don't tell me about lovers
on the shadowy grass, foreheads close,
whispering a world. The delicate
joints of equipment adjust, slo-mo,
bend like sunflowers to catch a reply.
Me, I'm looking too.

Family Dinners: Gordie

We're eating corn on the cob. We're eating
wild rice with dried mushrooms
and my mother's pickerel fillets.

And we're remembering Granite Lake,
whose water let us see down
to those wave patterns in the bottom sand,
the shadows of the ripples on the surface
playing games with the solid ripples below.
I see my small feet, tan toes. My mother
cooking breakfast on the black woodstove.
The outdoor biffy, the canoes resting
mysteriously upside down and dry
in the boathouse. "The Smith boy," my mother asks,
"the one with hair so blond it was white,
what was his name?" "Gordie," my dad tells us.
And then we all remember the sunny afternoon
he drifted out beyond his depth, his white crew cut
sailing above the stiff orange life jacket,
that perfect boy, and his dad ran the length
of the dock, dove off, and my dad tried
running, young and strong, through the shallows
but the water held him back. "It felt like claws,"
my dad says. I see him running, see
the fierce stroke of Gordie's dad's arms,
the slow thick horror of it as both men worked
to keep the boy from something terrible.
All our mothers' warnings condensing,
their dread precipitating to the long seconds
we stood and watched, the sun and the dock
and the lake. All our mothers' warnings,
their dread, tipped over because it was fine,
they got him, he never went under. It was all
always fine. Didn't we, years too late, find
the wait on the shore, leafing through comics,
the necessary two hours after breakfast,
after lunch, as we went brown and browner,
so we wouldn't get cramps, drown, was all hooey?
"They were such a tragic family,"
my mother says, forking me some of her
pickerel. They're floured and pan-fried,
sweet with onion and she's had enough.
The sentence lies on the table in front of us.
I don't remember that part. She tells me
the dad died early, tipped over shovelling snow,
and then the mother, beyond her depth,
went under, killed herself. The pattern

of his death overlaying her life,
all she had left of it. My mother
remembers them dancing. I can taste
the clean flesh of the fish in my mouth.
It's good. That golden boy grown,
orphaned. Three of us at the table,
the rest of the family not far off,
all these years later, intact.

George Elliott Clarke

(b. 1960)

In a piece called "On Writing Now" (*Event*, 31/1), George Elliott Ciarke sums up his aims as a poet:

> My struggle has been, is, will be, to find ways to get my native raucousness, my Aboriginal-Black, Mi'kmaq-Africadian, boisterous voice, inside the constraint of print—that Gothic citadel. The challenge is to overcome the academic predilection for poetry as allusive puzzle, one requiring a Ph.D. readership, but also to avoid the populist fancy for the poem so startlingly "clear" that it is slogan.

To wrestle the wonderful idiosyncrasies of speech into print, Clarke has embraced the strategies of drama, narrative, jazz, blues, rap, and opera, fully aware that formal invention and so-called bad taste can be invigorating. Ultimately, Clarke says, "I'd like Black English to sound like tempered steel."

In the preface to the tenth anniversary edition of his poetry collection *Whylah Falls*, Clarke talks about his attraction to poem sequences, narratives, and especially the epic, that great poetic achievement of the past, which is part history, love song, encyclopedia, and myth. Poet as recorder and interpreter, a rescuer of vanishing fragments, to be sure, but also the simple fact that, as he writes in "Seven Types of Ambiguity," "Every word we write is a breath—perhaps our last—against oblivion." "I know," he writes in another poem, "that this traitor language can turn / One truth into another or even / Against itself. And yet, it is all we have."

Speaking of his diverse influences, Clarke says: "To reformulate T.S. Eliot's self-identification, I was, as a tyro bard, Poundian in poetics, [Bob] Dylanesque in politics, and African American in faith." He confesses, with a cheekful of whimsy and irony, "I wish I could claim to expound some grandiose theory, such as the L=A=N=G=U=A=G=E idiom or the 'Ecopoetics' approach. But, golly, when all's said and done, I remain, fundamentally, a songwriter."

Clarke was born in Windsor, Nova Scotia, and raised in Halifax. He completed his BA at the University of Waterloo, his MA at Dalhousie, and his Ph.D. at Queen's. He taught at Duke University and McGill before becoming the inaugural E.J. Pratt Professor of Canadian Literature at the University of Toronto. In addition to *Whylah Falls* (1990, Archibald Lampman Award), his poetry publications include *Saltwater Spirituals and Deeper Blues* (1983), *Blue* (2001), *Execution Poems: The Black Acadian Tragedy of "George and Rue"* (2001, Governor General's Award), *Illuminated Verses* (2005), *Black* (2006), *Blues and Bliss: The Poetry of George Elliott Clarke* (2008, Eric Hoffer Book Award), and *I & I* (2009). He is also the author of plays, a novel, and criticism, and the editor of several anthologies, including *Eyeing the North Star: Directions in African-Canadian Literature* (1997). Book-length translations of his work have appeared in Chinese, Italian, and Romanian. A founding scholar of African-Canadian literature, he is the recipient of numerous accolades and awards, including the National Magazine Gold Award, the Archibald Lampman Award, the Portia White Prize, the Order of Nova Scotia, the Premiul Poesis (Romania), the Order of Canada, and eight honorary doctorates. In 2012, Clarke was named Poet Laureate of Toronto.

from Whylah Falls

Look Homeward, Exile

I can still see that soil crimsoned by butchered
Hog and imbrued with rye, lye, and homely
Spirituals everybody must know,
Still dream of folks who broke or cracked like shale:
Pushkin, who twisted his hands in boxing,
Marrocco, who ran girls like dogs and got stabbed,
Lavinia, her teeth decayed to black stumps,
Her lovemaking still in demand, spitting
Black phlegm—her pension after twenty towns,
And Toof, suckled on anger that no Baptist
Church could contain, who let wrinkled Eely
Seed her moist womb when she was just thirteen.
    And the tyrant sun that reared from barbed-wire
Spewed flame that charred the idiot crops
To Depression, and hurt my granddaddy
To bottle after bottle of sweet death,

His dreams beaten to one, tremendous pulp,
Until his heart seized, choked; his love gave out.
  But Beauty survived, secreted
In freight trains snorting in their pens, in babes
Whose faces were coal-black mirrors, in strange
Strummers who plucked Ghanaian banjos, hummed
Blind blues—precise, ornate, rich needlepoint,
In sermons scorched with sulphur and brimstone,
And in my love's dark, orient skin that smelled
Like orange peels and tasted like rum, good God!
  I remember my Creator in the old ways:
I sit in taverns and stare at my fists;
I knead earth into bread, spell water into wine.
Still, nothing warms my wintry exile—neither
Prayers nor fine love, neither votes nor hard drink:
For nothing heals those saints felled in green beds,
Whose loves are smashed by just one word or glance
Or pain—a screw jammed in thick, straining wood.

The Lover's Argument with Shelley

Shelley, I climbed to Whylah Falls while dusk
Scattered elm and crow shadows across your crooked
Kitchen. Now, I knock on your door and lean
Inside, looking for you. Shy, scared, you twist
Away, look out your twisted window,
And stare at black opacity.
  You remember a floundered lumber truck,
That heaviness that hooked Rafael's breath,
Ripped it from his stunned lungs, when his truck leapt,
Reeled, flopped, on Whylah's sharpest hill.
Gravity set his corpse awry, crooked,
Like a Picasso trick, and grave-dirt blackened
Your small, brown hands. Now, love's lies.
                                        But, Shelley,
My love is plain; I've stripped bark from pencils,
And stoked your stove with pamphlets and old news.
My poems, thrown to the creek, gleam, wriggle, leap.
  Shelley, the moon gapes, refuses to go away.
Let us go down by the bright Sixhiboux
And sit where thingabob uncorked his voice
And elders baptized him in snow-white robes.
Let us catch, unawares, some trout, some sleep.
Shelley, the end of this world is Beauty.

The Wisdom of Shelley

You come down, after
five winters, X,
bristlin' with roses
and words words words,
brazen as brass.
Like a late blizzard,
You bust in our door,
talkin' April and snow and rain,
litterin' the table
with poems—
as if we could trust them!

I can't.
I heard pa tell ma
how much and much he
loved loved loved her
and I saw his fist
fall so gracefully
against her cheek,
she swooned.

Roses
got thorns.
And words
do lie.

I've seen love
die.

Blues for X

Pretty boy, towel your tears,
And robe yourself in black.
Pretty boy, dry your tears,
You know I'm comin' back.
I'm your lavish lover
And I'm slavish in the sack.

Call me Sweet Potato,
Sweet Pea, or Sweety Pie,
There's sugar on my lips

And honey in my thighs.
Jos'phine Baker bakes beans,
But I stew pigtails in rye.

My bones are guitar strings
And blues the chords you strum.
My bones are slender flutes
And blues the bars you hum.
You wanna stay my man,
Serve me whisky when I come.

Ballad of a Hanged Man

Geo: Their drinks to my drinks feels different.
I'll stomach a stammering teaspoon full,
but Roach laps up half the half bottle.
He slups glass for glass with the best.

I sidled in, easy, the taxi with a hammer,
harsh, in my pocket. See, as a wed man,
I don't care if I wear uglified overalls.
But I ain't gonna hear my child starve.

I had the intention to ruck some money.
In my own heart, I had that, to rape money,
because I was fucked, in my own heart.
I took scared, shaking inside of me.

I knows Fredericton reporters can prove
zoot-suit vines style not my viciousness.
I was shaking all that evening, my mind,
shaking. But my child was hungered.

Have you ever gone in your life, going
two days without eating, and whenever
you get money, you're gonna eat and eat
regardless of all the bastards in Fredericton

was bust in the head, skull jimmied open?
This is what I'm sermonizing in English:
homemade brew, dug up fresh, tastes like
molasses. We had some. Some good.

Logic does not break down these things, sir.
If I hadn't dropped the hammer, laughing,
Silver would be laughing now. Laughing. Silver
moon and snow dropped on the ground.

Two pieces of bone driven two inches
deep in his brain. What's deeper still?
The bones of the skull were bashed
into the brain. Blood railed out.

I was so mixed up, my mind bent crooked.
Silver's neck, face, and hand bleached cold.
Inside the sedan 19-black-49 sobbing Ford.
Outside, snow and ice smelling red-stained.

I ain't dressed this story up. I am enough
disgraced. I swear to the truths I know.
I wanted to uphold my wife and child.
Hang me and I'll not hold them again.

IX / XI

for John Fraser, who wrote Violence in the Arts *(1974), and was right.*

I

We told ourselves *History* was finished—
The Holocaust just a museum piece now,
Hitler a cartoon Macbeth, Stalin a wax corpse,
Pol Pot a tin-pot version of crackpot Nixon,
And Rwanda made a theme park of machetes.

It was safe, our white-washed world was now safe:
No more pyramids of bones and hair,
No more napalm to charbroil infants,
No more nerve-gassings of "infidels,"
No more land mines to blow off your legs.

We could tune out the grisly technicolour
Of dark peoples' famines, plagues, massacres,
Or watch their cheap apartment blocks dissolve—
Under the editorial resolve of our munitions.
Our omnipotence was our doled-out avarice.

But all omnipotence has a weakness. Ours meant
The clacking of bankers' never-satisfied teeth,
The bullshit of bought-and-sold elections,
The guffaws of hucksters drowning out
The pure, toxic prayers of those who blame us.

II

Out of our blue-blank, Disney-postcard Heaven,
Came *jihad* squads of suave, aerial assassins,
Whose glistening knives of hijacked jet aircraft
Sliced into hundred-storey-high monoliths—
As white and vulnerable as wedding cakes.

It was violence as judgment, violence as *Kitsch*,
Violence as aviation and concrete, violence
As pornography, violence as *X-acto* blades,
Violence as the President hunkered down in
Bunkers, violence as the Pentagon burned.

It was violence as stock market manipulation,
Violence as crucified eagles, violence as maggots,
Violence as stabbed-out eyes, violence as racism,
Violence as information, violence as shopping,
Violence as the Secretary of Defense, cowering.

Computer terminals gone terminally combustible
Ignited an inferno of black-lettered, white paper,
While plummeting concrete sheared off women's feet
In red or black pumps and cut off fathers' heads and left
Torsos bent over steering wheels in crushed SUVs.

Those jets with their hostage passengers slammed into
And toppled our towers—like Hitler taking Paris.
Our infallible towers, teetered, tottered, tumbled,
Crumbled, and crashed down like two Stalinist statues,
They came down like twin *Titanics*, sinking.

It was trauma and *triage*, to be so shocked awake
To *History's* revolt, its brutal, blazing insurgency.
But do you have a *right* to finish your bagel and coffee?
Do you have a *right* to see your daughter give birth?
Do you have a *right* to exist without suffering?

III

History shook that city that said, "*History* is history."
A Malcolm X prophecy came to fiery, smoking life
In a King Kong apocalypse of planes hitting towers.
Unanswerably *kamikaze*, candidly unappeasable men
Insisted on dissolving citizens in fire and in glass.

Though civilization often okays being blasé,
On its margins, there's suffering, intense suffering,
Gothic outcasts always dreaming up catastrophes,
And sometimes their lobbed fireballs hit home.
No civilization survives without suffering.

Now when we say, "I love New York," sobs may stun.
Such silent subways right after the sabotage, then
Wailing, yes, and instant spirituals—as in so many other
Exploded cities: London, Hiroshima, Baghdad,
And Halifax, Nova Scotia, on December 6, 1917.

Let the damage be remembered, for we are damaged,
The dead given faces, our broadcast dead reclaimed,
The nightmares witnessed, pondered, documented,
The shed blood kept warm and wet and vivid, jetting, jetting,
From real bodies, our own, in pain—raw, ungodly, humanizing pain.

Susan Glickman

(b. 1953)

Susan Glickman was born in Baltimore to Canadian parents, but raised in Montreal. She completed her BA at Tufts, her MA at Oxford, and her Ph.D. at the University of Toronto. She lives with her family in Toronto, where she has worked in publishing, been a freelance editor, and taught literature and creative writing at the University of Toronto and Ryerson University. She published a critical study called *The Picturesque & the Sublime: A Poetics of*

the Canadian Landscape, which won both the Gabrielle Roy prize and the Raymond Kibanksy prize. Her poetry publications include *Complicity* (1983), *The Power to Move* (1986), *Henry Moore's Sheep and Other Poems* (1990), *Hide & Seek* (1995), *Running in Prospect Cemetery: New and Selected Poems* (2004), and *The Smooth Yarrow* (2012). She has published two novels, *The Violin Lover* (2006) and *The Tale-Teller* (2012), and several books for children.

In an interview that appeared online in Sheila Heti's "Aesthetic 99" project, Glickman speaks of her own effort to maintain "a knife-edge balance between irony and sentimentality." In terms of concerns and influence, she draws attention to the "underlying pulse of iambic pentameter in all my writing from English poetry; free indirect point of view in narrative from Virginia Woolf; an obsession with line-breaks from my teacher, Denise Levertov; the ability to multi-task from my children."

Taking a nod from Denise Levertov, Glickman describes poetry as "rapt attention" not only to language, but also to the world at large: "the poetry that pleases me best . . ." she writes, "still has something of a child's delight in the enchanted weirdness of language. The medium is never purely transparent; we don't see through language to 'reality' but create a fictional reality, however tenuous, by the language we use. It has texture and colour; it grunts and sighs; we build stuff with it." Despite her emphasis on wordplay and puns, Glickman's best work is carefully constructed and finely tuned. "Any craft is a lifelong discipline, requiring respect for one's materials and an attention amounting, sometimes, almost to trance. How slowly one learns the sinews and joints of language, articulating its body with gesture and voice and breath! But how profound the pleasure when the line sings so one's nerves vibrate in sympathy!"

In response to questions from a high school student named Tara (5 Nov. 2008), Glickman dismissed the notion of poetry as a vehicle for delivering messages:

> How literature teaches us about life is not by sending out "messages." Literature teaches us by giving us the space and time to imaginatively inhabit another person's life and empathize with his or her situation. In daily life we never get to enter anybody's mind but our own, but literature gives us the opportunity to be lots of other people. This is the moral dimension to literature: that it insists that we transcend our egos and be empathetic . . . When you write something you are creating a world for the reader to enter, building scenes for that reader to experience. Each individual work may grapple with certain themes that become a moral focus for the characters and therefore for readers as well, but this is not the same as being didactic and having a "message."

For My Students in English 108 Who Complain That All Modern Literature Is Too Depressing

I don't believe in it myself, that lost world
of absolute coherence:
Vermeer's *The Kitchen Maid* where light
glazes the jug, and the milk
of paradise pours into a basin.
The girl's grip is steady as she gauges
the flow, it's a task two hands
can manage. The milk still steams
from the cow, the cow flicks her tail
and goes on grazing in a field of gold.
Heraldic crows inscribe arrows from heaven:
the path all good news travels.
The farmer wipes his brow but when he
looks up all he sees is the sun, a cloud
of midges, the distance left
to plough.

In *Les Très Riches Heures* of the Duc de Berri the frame
is frozen, the farmer perfected
as in an attitude of prayer, but this
is art. Say he *is* praying—suppose
his youngest boy has diphtheria.
His wife sat up all night brewing herbal tea but the farmer
needed to sleep. There's been too much sun, a hail
of poisoned darts, they're going to lose
the crop. Crows, after all, are carrion birds;
see how they circle the thatched roof
of the hut?
And as for Vermeer's bountiful maiden, note
her pensive face.
She's careful not to spill a drop because
she's a servant, indentured at ten
to a prosperous family.
From the swell of her bodice we might guess
she's carrying the burgher's child.
We could make it a sad story.
What we discovered in the Renaissance was perspective.

Families

Once at the breakfast table when that harsh bitching
that passes for a stab but is really more like sawing away
with a rusty breadknife, leaving a jaggedy scar,
passed as usual in those days between my mother
and me my father began to cry
into his cornflakes. Big round tears for the lost family
on the cereal box; the one that was supposed to come
with the yellow breakfast-nook, the apple-tree
out back. Only one tree, our neighbour's, dropping its fruit
over the fence. Generous, but not big enough
to hide in, so there was nowhere to shelter, no option
but escape. But Dad had his job, his car, his sense of humour;
deep down hadn't he always known there *was*
nowhere else to go? That a family only keeps smiling
in photographs and even there
someone's always out of focus. Him, for example:
his eyes inevitably shut, as though caught by chance
between blinks, when really, it was a reflex, like sneezing.
He could smile or keep his eyes open—but not both.

I could make that a metaphor, I guess, or quote Tolstoy in
Anna Karenina, but happiness in families is also complex
and not to be sneezed at. The problem is more with the way
we apprehend feelings in time. Sadness is so slow, a mule with
split hooves, picking its way over stone. Joy,
in this ratio, a '40s convertible, his first car,
speeding down green summer roads to a *doo-wop* refrain.
That is, when you're happy you don't have to know all the words,
humming along does just fine. But grief,
grief makes us all precisions, analyzing each other
to death: *You failed me, and this is exactly how.*

Meanwhile the evidence of our honourable if partial success
piles up—all those turkeys, ribbons, pots of flowers.
In their albums the smiles brave out our disregard,
bleaching a little with the years like the cedar dock down
at the lake, that worn path between the house
and the silent water: between what contains the family

and what it keeps them from. Lying on that dock with eyes closed
I told my mother all about you before we were married,
when I still wasn't sure; some of the old harshness in my voice
because I wanted or expected her to tell me not
to do it, to tell me the pains were more real
than the joy. But she didn't. No one could save me from my own
trip down that road; no one wanted to.
And so I jumped off the split grey boards into the reflections
of trees and clouds and swam away very fast from that house
to this one, into a new family. Eyes wide open,
but under water.

When They Are Asleep in Their Nimbus of Flame

the heart no longer asks for permission,
it loves what it loves. "*Holy, holy!*"
it exults over the chaste swell
of buttocks, the curve of shoulders
round in their sockets like eyeballs
scrolling the landscape of dreams;
like the pillowed heads, the knees flexed
against morning's exertions,
its staircases and adieux.

But when they are asleep they are wholly
here, cupped in my hands like sweet water.
My son, too old to bathe with his mother
whose limbs still remember that merriment, that
slippery grace. My daughter, who brushes away
her own tangles, and won't wear what I, longingly
set out. My husband, curled into himself—
boyish, startled, alone—
each one so alone in sleep.

The house groans and ticks through the lengthening night.
I drink tea, tidy things up, ask for permission
for a few hours more of this love.

Know Your Audience

So this guy is driving along in a beat-up Volvo, must have been 12 years old at least, missing the whole front grill, the driver's side door baby blue and the rest tan . . . I know they're supposed to be the safest vehicles around but let me tell you, that one did *not* look safe. And he cuts me off, right? I mean, there I was, stuck in the middle of the road, waiting to turn left, and the light goes yellow and I inch forward and then it turns red and does he stop? No, of course not, he sails right through, he doesn't even look at me, and there *I* was, turning left on a red and everyone honking at me and cursing and I was shaking like a leaf. I had to pull over for one blessed moment just to breathe, just to *exhale*, if you know what I mean. And then Kyle spoke up from the back and I almost jumped out of my seat because I'd forgotten he was there! Of course I thought about him the whole time we were stuck in the middle of the road and him strapped into his car-seat singing away but just then I was too upset to be thinking about him anymore. And he said "Mama?" And I said, "Yes, Precious?" And he said, "When I grow up I'm going to get a horse and carriage and drive you everywhere just like Cinderella." And that's when I started to cry.

On Finding a Copy of *Pigeon* in the Hospital Bookstore

for Karen Solie

I prowled the rows of the hospital bookstore with a fevered intensity;
"fevered" because it was a hospital, "intensity" because I was perplexed by
the mysteriously ruptured tendon in the middle finger of my right hand
in sympathy with which the whole hand had cramped
so that I could scarcely hold a pen or open a jar.
Even a five-month-old octopus in the Munich zoo can open a jar!

The octopus's name is Frieda, which reminded me
of D.H. Lawrence, and thinking of him
brought me to the hospital bookstore. It was minimally stocked
with anything resembling literature, offering those in pain,
afraid, or just dully waiting for test results
a choice of pink-jacketed chick-lit, cookbooks, investment guides
or glossy thrillers spilling blood
as red as that pooling down the hall in the O.R.,
as though emulating some homeopathic principle
of curing a disease by a parody of that which caused it.

And perched as eccentrically as the sparrow who sings from the rafters
at Loblaws, and looking just as lost,
was the only volume of poetry in the store.
Reading it I recognized at once what I disliked
about the bulky bestsellers nudging it from the shelf
like bullies in the halls of high school, their meaty faces

full of self-regard, their minds absent of thought.
I hate the omni-present present tense, that fake cinematic contrivance
meant to create a sense of "being in the moment" with the hero
as though life were a constant rush of adrenaline
with no possible mood but surprise.

Whereas poetry offers the results of its meditation
tentatively; it is not embarrassed to show that thinking
—some of it slow, arduous, confused—has taken place.
And then poetry doesn't rush ahead shouting, "Look at me! Look at me!"
Instead, it takes your hand, your poor mangled hand,
like the good surgeon it is
and massages it joint by joint, feeling for the sore places.
And because it doesn't speak without reflection
you trust it, and let it cut you open.

John Steffler

(b. 1947)

Born in Toronto, John Steffler spent his early years in Ontario, completing his BA at the University of Toronto and his MA at the University of Guelph with a thesis on the writings of William Blake. An academic job in 1974 took him to Newfoundland, where he made his home for several decades, teaching for a year in St John's and thereafter at Sir Wilfred Grenfell College, a campus of Memorial University. His books of poetry include *The Grey Islands* (1985, 2000), *The Wreckage of Play* (1988), *That Night We Were Ravenous* (1998, Atlantic Poetry Prize), *Helix: New & Selected Poems* (2002), and *Lookout* (2010, Griffin Poetry Prize shortlist). Steffler's novel *The Afterlife of George Cartwright* (1992) won the Smithbooks/Books in Canada First Novel Award and the Thomas Raddall Atlantic Fiction Award and was shortlisted for the Governor General's Award and the Commonwealth Prize for Best First Book.

"Place has always been very important to me," Steffler insists in the University of Toronto library's "Canadian Poetry Online" site. "Different landscapes have different characters just as various kinds of animals do. Partly for this reason I've always been interested in the long-term interaction between people and the place they inhabit. This process is especially striking in Newfoundland where nature is rowdy and naked, and people fit right in." And history, as it turns out, is equally important to him: "The physical world soaks up time. A place holds an impression of everything that has ever happened there. The human past lives on in its physical setting, even in the air, in the local light. The past is alive all around us; it belongs to us and gives us an extra range of feelings and insights, if we let it."

Although the bulk of his work explores in a narrative form the interstices of self, place, and history, Steffler's best poetry achieves a seemingly effortless lyrical quality, achievable only to someone whose ear is attuned to the subtleties and nuances of language and its musical potential. Although the verse is ostensibly free, the effects achieved derive from a deep engagement with experience and its underlying organic form. Poet George Murray identifies in Steffler's work a kind of "mystic expectation" and insists that its binding quality is "how, while the forms and styles are varied throughout, the voice that betrays the poet's twin gazes, outer and inner, remains constant." As a tribute to his achievements, Steffler was appointed Canada's Parliamentary Poet Laureate in 2006–2008.

In an interview published online by Open Book Toronto, Steffler outlines his aims as a poet:

> I write for people who are drawn to poetry as a way into increased thoughtfulness and awareness and who get excited by excited language. I suppose my imaginary readership looks for a link between poetry and lived experience: poetry that leads us back into the world with renewed appetite or renewed insight and feeling for what's around us, for who we are and for the lives of others. Although many of my poems have to do with Newfoundland, I don't write primarily for Newfoundlanders (although their responses to what I write are often the most meaningful to me). In a sense I write for poetry itself or for the history of poets, the long legacy of everyone who has tried to distil his or her life and experience of the world in language.

After retiring, Steffler lived briefly in Montreal, then settled near Maberly, Ontario.

Monster Bait

Hovering near me, contorted with chortles
and shrill challenges, his feet already running
in several directions,
my two-year-old son is being irresistible
monster bait.

For the seventh time, I roar
after him, slap my shoes an inch from his blurring heels,
slavering, Lon Chaney's look-alike,

but this time,
when he turns at bay by his bed, squealing, quivering,
and I lumber forward to make the kill,
I've gone too far.

At the sight of my face, so wilfully twisted,
he bolts into tears, and I
instantly am my own father, struck
by the strange inevitability:

son-scaring
son-comforting now
having known the small part so well
and knowing I looked precisely as my father had
in our games, when the magic became too strong
and I broke, seeing him change,
desert me so easily

to let a stranger look through his eyes.

That Night We Were Ravenous

Driving from Stephenville in the late October
dusk—the road swooping and disappearing ahead
like an owl, the hills no longer playing dead
the way they do in the daytime, but sticking their black
blurry arses up in the drizzle and shaking themselves,
heaving themselves up for another night of
leapfrog and Sumo ballet—some

trees detached themselves from the shaggy
shoulder and stepped in front of the car. I swerved

through a grove of legs startled by pavement, maybe a
hunchbacked horse with goiter, maybe a team of beavers
trying to operate stilts: it was the

landscape doing a moose, a cow
moose,

most improbable forest device. She danced
over the roof of our car in moccasins.

She had burst from the zoo of our dreams and was
there, like the yanked-out tooth a dentist
puts in your hand.

She flickered on and off.
She was strong as the Bible and as full of lives.
Her eyes were like Halley's Comet, like factory whistles,
like bargain hunters, like shy kids.

No man had touched her or given her movements geometry.

She surfaced in front of us like a coelacanth, like a face
in a dark lagoon. She made us feel blessed.

She made us talk like a cage of canaries.

She reminded us. She was the ocean wearing a fur suit.

She had never eaten from a dish.
She knew nothing of corners or doorways.

She was our deaths come briefly forward to say hello.

She was completely undressed.

She was more part of the forest than any tree.
She was made of trees. The beauty of her face was bred
in the kingdom of rocks.

I had seen her long ago in the Dunlap Observatory.

She leapt from peak to peak like events in a ballad.

She was insubstantial as smoke.

She was a mother wearing a brown sweater opening her arms.

She was a drunk logger on Yonge Street.

She was the Prime Minister. She had granted us a tiny reserve.

She could remember a glacier where she was standing.

She was a plot of earth shaped like the island of Newfoundland and able to fly, spring down in the middle of cities scattering traffic, ride elevators, press pop-eyed executives to the wall.

She was charged with the power of Churchill Falls.

She was a high-explosive bomb loaded with bones and meat.
She broke the sod in our heads like a plough parting the earth's black lips.

She pulled our zippers down.

She was a spirit.

She was Newfoundland held in a dam. If we had touched her, she would've burst through our windshield in a wall of blood.

That night we were ravenous. We talked, gulping, waving our forks. We entered one another like animals entering woods.

That night we slept deeper than ever.

Our dreams bounded after her like excited hounds.

After the Dance-Filled Rooms, the Smoke

The map of Corner Brook
hangs in lights, impossibly clear and many-
pointed this December night,

the sleeping streets roll
under my legs, the vague tractable properties
get led by like silent passenger trains, repetitive
dreams, and over the next crest:
my house
which I don't even recognize,

don't understand why it's mine,

tucked in its neighbourly row, at four in the amnesiac
morning in the capital of amnesia, its beige shape,
some shape of me I've made,
unwittingly willed,
the way I've grown bones.

So deeply attached to this accident?

But the stars become visible hunger pangs
in a famished sky,
especially in wintertime.

I'll work on this inside.

That the Cat Sleeps

That the cat sleeps curled on a chair
without moving when I come in wet
with snow, the schefflera, the dizygotheca
follow their innocent plans at the window
battered white, that the house purrs,
the furnace performing its logical office,
that my daughter silently reads in the next
room, that to her time is long, though
the sun lies like a broken toaster under
a dump and the sky avalanches its bones,
is achievement enough in my house; in my
still house the snow-lit air is a patient
creature hovering, filling the rooms
like a cat, a plant, a child turning a page.

Beating the Bounds

When I was six years old, my parents,
along with other adults who'd never spoken
to me, came laughing and acting silly,
picking me up, giggling, "Now we'll show
you a house you didn't know about."
"A big house."
"A secret house you knew about all the time."
So I was frightened, seeing how serious
it was that they were so strange,

although I was probably smiling,
and they carried me and other children my age
to the river and said, "Here is the marble
floor," and put my bare legs in the fast
place between stones and it was colder
than I remembered it and the tugging of dark
cold water became my legs, the Fox Island
River became my legs—afterwards when I
was falling asleep or sometimes just walking
along, the bottom of me would be moving away
like that—and they carried me, tickling me,
singing ridiculous songs among rough
brown stones up a valley past caribou
where it was cold and held me up on top
of their palms so I faced the sky and someone
with fat fingers that smelled of sheep held
my eyes open until the cold air and white
sky burned and were too bright and my eyes
brimmed like two cuts and I felt those cuts
go right into my name and they said
"This is the roof up here, you can't go
higher than this," and that wind and sky
were my eyes then, they were in my name,
and the people pushed me through a patch
of alders and a patch of spruce the wind
had bent, saying, "Here's a young cub
we'll take home and raise," and "Push him in front
so we won't get scratched," and my skin
was crisscrossed with cuts, so I felt
those branches, smelled the alder musk,
the sharp edge of spruce like a coast,
a burning fringe, a noise around me holding
me in and they said, "This is the west
wall of the house you live in, remember
it," and the day went on like that, they
pushed me against a cliff to the north
so I felt its jaggedness in my spine,
they sat me in black soupy peat and said,
"Here is your bed, it is nighttime," they
took me down to the sea and made me
drink it and told me that was the south
and the kitchen, "the garden," someone
laughed and gave me a capelin to eat, rubbed

scales on my face, the backs of my hands
and "Over there," they said, meaning
over the hills across the gulf, "that is not
your house and the people who live there
are strangers to you, not enemies if
you deal with them properly." "They
speak a language of farts," someone said,
"they gobble like turkeys when they fuck,"
and although my body was made of all
it had touched that day and my ears were full
of my parents' voices and the voices
of their friends, in my heart I was still
frightened and felt like a stranger among them.

Tim Lilburn

(b. 1950)

Tim Lilburn was born in Regina, Saskatchewan, and completed his BA there in 1974, after which he spent two years working for Cuso in Africa. He trained as a Jesuit from 1979 to 1987, then devoted himself to teaching and writing. He taught literature and philosophy at St Peter's College in Muenster, Saskatchewan, before taking up a full-time position in creative writing at the University of Victoria. His poetry publications include *Names of God* (1986), *Tourist to Ecstasy* (1989, shortlisted for the Governor General's Award), *Moosewood Sandhills* (1994), *To the River* (1999, Saskatchewan Book of the Year Award), *Kill-Site* (2003, Governor General's Award), *Desire Never Leaves: The Poetry of Tim Lilburn* (2006), *Orphic Politics* (2008), and *Assiniboia* (2012). As well, he has published two books of his own essays: *Living in the World As If It Were Home* (1999) and *Going Home* (2008); and two collections of essays he has edited: *Poetry and Knowing: Speculative Essays and Interviews* (1995) and *Thinking and Singing: Poetry and the Practice of Philosophy* (2002).

Lilburn's view of the relation of poet to world is best explained in "How to Be Here?" (*Brick* No. 49, summer 1994), where he suggests that

> the physical world cannot be known in the way poetry aspires to know it, intimately, ecstatically, in a way that heals the ache of one's

> separation from the world, it seems to me, outside the sundering of knowledge which contemplation is. . . . As the mind leans into the darkness of God, the old writers said, it is slendered by awe, reduced to a good confusion: this is knowing. Language, as well, is chastened in contemplation and by being broken it provides a way by which the ineffable may be glimpsed.

Paradoxically, Lilburn argues,

> Language is sundered as one courts ecstasy, constantly replaced by the objects and creatures of the world. Language again and again springs at the essence, reaching for clarity, the exact fit between the look of the slow hills, occultly breathing and their feel, then denies each time what it comes up with. . . . Language asserts and cancels itself, names the world then erases the name, and in this restlessness one glimpses the aptness of confusion before the ungraspable diversity of here. Silence. The look goes on. The breaking up of language, language drawn into the reversal of language, is the speech of desire beating against the silence of the confusing land.

The poems of *Names of God* and *Tourist to Ecstasy* are characterized by an enormous verbal appetite and a headlong careening quality that takes the breath away. The emerging poet obviously takes more delight in naming than in silence or contemplation, and his early approach to language seems more gymnastic than Gnostic. Perhaps William Blake's observation that "the road of excess is the path to wisdom" should be summoned here, for Lilburn's temperament and poetic strategies certainly have their roots in the mystical tradition that includes Blake, Hopkins, Merton, and St John of the Cross.

While the early Lilburn dallies like a libertine in an orgy of sound and exploding vocabularies, jazzy rhythms, wordplay, and other technical bebop, his religious yearnings, not to mention his Jesuitical training and discriminations, are seldom out of sight or mind. The earliest poems, however charged they might be linguistically, strike a dominant note of praise or worship, even exultation, before the spectacle of this world and its creatures. However, since ecstasy in love, poetry, and, presumably, religion is impossible to sustain, a deeper note must be sounded. As he acknowledges in the same essay quoted earlier:

> We are lonely for where we are. Poetry helps us cope. Poetry is where we go when we want to know the world as lover. You read a poem or write one, guessing at the difficult, oblique interiority of something, but the undertaking ultimately seems incomplete, ersatz. The inevitable disappointment all poems bring motions towards

> the hard work of standing in helpless awe before things. "The praise of the psalms is a lament," the old men and women of the desert used to say. Poetry in its incompleteness awakens a mourning over the easy union with the world that seems lost. Poetry is a knowing to this extent: it brings us to this apposite discomfiting.

"You cannot truly see this stone," Lilburn says in "Contemplation and Cosmology," "if you believe the world is yours to do with as you will." This is a radical politics that goes beyond red and green. As poet Maggie Helwig suggests (*Canadian Forum*, April 1999): "This is not a philosophical game. . . . It is, if read carefully, a kind of politics—a politics of what Lilburn calls 'courtesy': a sort of radical respect and gentleness, that kind of precise delicacy of love that is all you have left when you have lost everything." This "political" stance, of course, is further complicated for Lilburn, who, as a Canadian writer, must struggle to make his own peace with a stolen land and its original inhabitants.

Names of God

for William Clarke, S.J.

1. LOVE AT THE CENTRE OF OBJECTS

At the pentecostal core of matter, a fire wind
whirligig, centrifuge of joy,
is You, Love, a lung
pumping light, auric squalls
inflating eyes in my skull's raw coal.

Sssssst. My bloodstream and the midpoints of my bone hear fire
gouging the inner face of flame. Which speaks.
"Dress, bride, in your blood's maroon gas,
oxygen feathers tipping each bone blue; on the red knuckle
thread desire's compound carat;
moth skip, heart-kamikaze, and explode
vaster, vaster in the inhaling charismatic glow."

2. ALLAH OF THE GREEN CIRCUITRY

Salamu, my Lord. Salamu alaikum.
You are here
for my synapses whip and sparkle
like lightninged willows,
are in tumoured air storm's throbbing,
are wind's ululation to my steel-shod nerves
dancing them as dust-spooked stallions.

Runners of rain trellis fire
to earth. You ride the hissing flame,
Allah of the Green Circuitry,
to jazz with love juice the chlorophyll current
to flash sunflower, crimson, orange.

You live, ah, You
live to unflex in the crux of a woman's dark ear,
coloured cloud
pressing into mind's white storm.

3. LIGHT'S GOBBLING EYE

O nourishing dark, O blank cloud,
You haul in my debris, compress it
in the stupendous clench of Your Heart
to nothing.

Light whorls toward You, a vanishing point
where perfection absents You; whorls
toward You, screwing
itself into its shadow core,
letting its socket eat it. O dark gravity, we decry
this cannibalism,
though the shimmering particles stampede
with greased monomania.

I, now, feel the suck, tide
of light raking over bones, unsnarling
from joints of thought and feeling,
until I whistle into what-I-know-not,
ears imploding,
riding the bright shaft of self
into Your infolding, gold-splintered eye.

Pumpkins

Oompah Oompah Oompah, fattening
on the stem, tuba girthed, puffing like perorating parliamentarians,
Boompa Boompah Booompah,
earth hogs slurping swill from the sun,
jowels burp fat with photons, bigger, bigger, garden elephants,
mirthed like St Francis, dancing (thud), dancing (thud,
brümpht, thud, brümpht) with the Buddha-bellied sun,

dolphin sweet, theatrical as suburban
children, yahooing a yellow
which whallops air. Pure. They are Socratically
ugly, God's jokes. O jongleurs, O belly laughs
quaking the matted patch, O my blimpish Prussian
generals, O garden sausages, golden zeppelins. How do? How do? How do?

Doo dee doo dee doooo.
What a rabble, some explode,
or sing, in the panic of September
sun, idiot praise for the sun that burns like a grand hotel,
for the sun, monstrous pulp in a groaning rind, flame seeded.
Popeyes, my dears, muscular fruit,
apoplexies of grunted energy flexed from the forearm vine,
self-hefted on the hill and shot
putted in the half-acre.

Carro-caroo. Are you well,
my sweets, pleasure things, my baubles, my Poohs,
well?
I, weeding farmer, I, Caruso
them at dawn crow in the sun
cymballing mornings
and they Brunhilde back, foghorns, bloated alto notes
baroquely happy.
Not hoe teeth, not Rhotenone, but love,
bruited, busied, blessed these being-ward, barn-big,
bibulous on light, rampantly stolid
as Plato's Ideas, Easter Island
flesh lumps of meaning, rolling heads
in my 6-year-old nightmares,
vegetables on a ball and chain, sun anvils
booming with blows of temperature.

Come, phenomena, gourds of light, teach
your joy esperanto, your intense Archimedean aha
of yellow to me, dung-booted serf, whose unhoed brain,
the garden's brightest fruit, ones
communion with the cowfaced cauliflowers,
cucumbers twinkling like toes, and you,
clown prince,
sun dauphin of the rioting plot.

In the Hills, Watching

Among the nerved grass, thrones,
dominions of grass, in chokecherry dewlapped hills,
hills buffalo-shouldered with shag of pulsed heat, meek hills,
sandhills of rose-hip and aster, in the philanthropic silence
fluxed by the grass, hounded, nervous with its own uncountability, grass
the frail piston of all,
in hill heat, lying down in the nearness of deer.
All knowing darkens as it builds.
The grass is a mirror that clouds as the bright look goes in.
You stay in the night, you squat in the hills in the cave of night. Wait.
Above, luminous rubble, torn webs of radio signals.
Below, stone scrapers, neck bone of a deer, salt beds.
The world is ending.

How to Be Here?

I

Desire never leaves.

Looking at wolf willow bloom,
steaming through plushlands of scent toward the feeling
of its yellow,
self breaks up, flaring in stratosphere.
Looking undermines us.
The world and its shining can't hold our evaporating weight.
The world or what is there goes away
as we enter it, goes into halls of grass where torches of
darkness burn at noon.
Goes into light's lowest mind.
Leaving us, woo-floated from planet-like names and not quite
in things' shimmering gravity, alone in wide June air.
All-thumbs intensity that feels like virtue or music.

The Form quivers in the deer.
She doesn't see me; I'm lying barely above grass on a plank between fallen
poplars.

Hot day, slow wind; I lift on the cam of rhizomes.
The light behind her light is a shell she's just now born out of.
The Form is the doe's ease within herself.
I came from there.

If you dug with small tools into radiant belts round her shoulders
you'd come to a first settlement of the soul, stroke pottery bits, put
your tongue on old cinders and remember.
Tears will take you part of the way back but no further.

II

You wake, say, inside a large mosquito net,
you're away from yourself, older, near a desert perhaps,
air cool, dry, cloud of small sand, everything seems far
away, North African, night ancient, hard to read, you
look through the flap and see something bent toward a fire,
sparks low round it, stocky, sitting on its man-calves, force, tiptoed.

It is desire.
Yes, adding stick after stick, it seems,
managing in its naked hands
the reins of occurrence,
charioteering the will—horses of night.

You want to walk in the dark garden of the eye of the deer looking at you.
Want a male goldfinch to gallop you into the heart
of the distance which is the oddness of other things.
All would be well.
Desire never leaves.
Mercury's flower, a ghost-hurtling.

A mirror held before the spiritual wind
that blows from behind things,
bodying them out, filling them with the shapes and loves
of themselves.
You want that
and all else that shows in the bright surface polished by the lunge and
prowling of your desire.
You don't know what you are doing.

III

Desire tells me to sit in a tree.
I live alone, mentally clothed in the skins of wild things.
Desire sways ascent into me.
I look, I look: bull-necked hill, blue sweetgrass in hollows.
Knowing is a bowing, a covering of your face, before the world.
The tree's white tallness praises through me.
What receives the bow?

I am seduced by the shapeliness
of the failure of knowledge.
My name in religion is the anonymity of grass.
I practise dying.
Each day, the tutor, old man, eros, repeats the lesson,
I wrinkle my brow, my tongue protrudes.
Outside the window one chokecherry in the bush,
in a thicket of gooseberries,
adds a weight and compression of darkness under the sun
that is perfect.

Orphic Disgorgement, Anti-Colonial Disgorgement

Dead fuchsia and carrots still not growing through winter
in the wood-chipped garden hump, each swivels up its own radio
station and heaves
out honey; in everything hair-on-the-back-of-the-neck
lit ash spiraling out maquettes of the whole milkish machine; in
everything a carved book to which abalone has been sewn,
with a postal address and a SIN number, on a lectern of antler
at which a throat-cut lamb singingly reads aloud;
in everything limestone arguing; in everything, in everything; in
everything suddenly a river that cannot be crossed, the lowest eye
looks at you
until you feel a walnut of gravity frowning down in your elbow;
Hermes with a sharp stick
scratching the ground in everything, in everything the Gulf of Alaska
in its wire.
In Fawn Lily's underarm bloom, a swimming sound.
Indian Plum now holds the vase of seeing, which poured out is Hermes.
In everything this answering machine tripping again its loop, please
leave me
a message; in everything a billet doux under a book; in everything the
lost sock; and a sound comes up from the spoon under the bed,
pieces of dental floss, idiorhythmic chorale,
totus Christus, and out of this creeps a city with four nameless rivers.
In everything ignorance, *docta ignorantia*, last bus stop
on the line of Dionysian apophaticism, the black door opens
hydraulic exhalations, home at last, do not look back.
In everything, listen, the Shriners' parade, Regina, 1961, just ended;
rain starts to hit into the dust, then the fog of the god; in everything,
the self-wealthing rooms, and in them the sidelong, fish-profile
boxes on coffee tables, mouthing out meals and fire without a mind.

Anne Carson

(b. 1950)

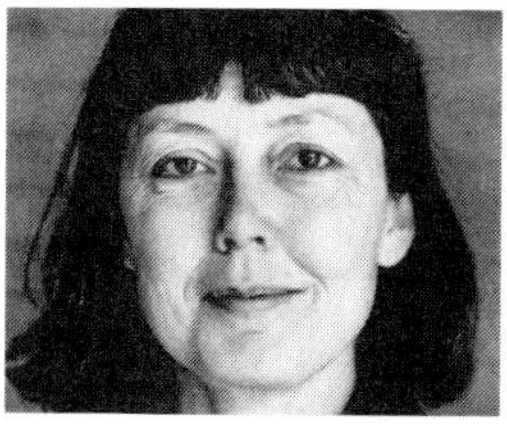

Anne Carson, Canada's most widely read and internationally recognized poet, was born in Toronto and, in addition to writing poetry and essays and painting volcanoes, has taught classics at McGill and Berkeley. Her literary works include *Short Talks* (1992), *Eros the Bittersweet: An Essay* (1986), *Glass, Irony and God* (1995), *Plainwater: Essays and Poetry* (1995), *Wild Workshop* (1997), *Autobiography of Red: A Novel in Verse* (1998), *Economy of the Unlost: Reading Simonides of Keos with Paul Celan* (1999), *Men in the Off Hours* (2000), *The Beauty of the Husband: A Fictional Essay in 29 Tangos* (2001). She is also the author of *Feminist Spirituality and the Feminine Divine: An Annotated Bibliography* (1986) and *Goddesses and Wise Women: The Literature of Feminist Spirituality, 1980–1992: An Annotated Bibliography* (1992). She is a recipient of the QSPELL A.M. Klein Poetry Prize, the T.S. Eliot Prize, the Griffin Prize, the National Book Critics Circle Award, the Pushcart Prize, and the prestigious Lannan and MacArthur Foundation awards.

Although Carson is an intensely private person, what she says of Sappho in *Men in the Off Hours* might well be applied to herself as a writer: "namely, that she plays havoc with boundaries and defies the rules that keep matter in its place. . . . Sappho is one of the people of whom the more you see the less you know." While Carson's elusiveness may diminish, or appear to diminish, now that her work has gained such widespread praise and recognition—with accolades from Guy Davenport and Michael Ondaatje—it remains one of her strengths as a poet that the sites she can inhabit are manifold, not limited by notions of what is either possible or appropriate. She seems equally at home playing both the philosopher and the fool, writing poems that are weighty with ideas or with narrative as well as poems that are casual, slight, and epigrammatic, though it should be noted that her apparently casual work is seldom without depth and, like the volcanoes she admires, capable of unexpected fireworks. So, too, her longer narratives and meditations are infinitely playful at the level of language and idea.

The essay is central to Carson's work. The French noun *essai* comes from the verb *essayer*, meaning to try or, in Carson's sense, to make a case or argument for a way of viewing reality. For example "The Glass Essay," a narrative poem containing three plot lines or levels of argument, is the work of a writer not only steeped in ideas and the minutiae of literary history, but also fully attuned to the kind of verbal play and deep-imaging techniques that evoke a sympathetic response in readers. In this sense, she is one of the foremost of an unusual breed of poets in Canada—including Phyllis Webb, Margaret Atwood, Robert Bringhurst, and Jan Zwicky—who are neither afraid of nor in thrall to ideas and learning.

Carson's unique way of viewing and talking about poetry is evident in her essay "Economy, Its Fragrance" (*The Threepenny Review*, spring 1997), where she says:

> If I were marketing the poetry/prose distinction as a perfume, I would call it Economy. Not because poetry is the only form of verbal expression that manages its resources thriftily, but because this thrift seems essential to poetry. Economic measures allow poetry to practice what I take to be its principal subversion. That is, insofar as it is economic, poetry relies on a gesture which it simultaneously dismantles.

She cites Marilyn Monroe's comment, "I read poetry to save time," and insists that poetry buys or saves time through various means of compression, "subversively, by overflowing its own measures."

Echoing Jean-Paul Sartre's essay "Why Write," Carson presents poetry as a gift, whose principal grace, or value, is its economy. "Every gift is a debt, the sociologists tell us," Carson insists,

> insofar as a gift sets up the idea of a countergift: every gift contains the obligation to repay. And here is where we get entangled in the project of saving time. For obligations take place in that curious interval of time that we call in English "the present," and so long as an obligation is pending, the present can continue to be a gift.

Poetry that maintains our interest "does so by a subversive economic action. That is to say, by thrifty management of its own measures—measures of rhythm, diction, syntax, image, and allusion—the poem secretes a residue, the poem generates a profit, the poem yields surplus value."

Carson understands and exploits the power of narrative in poetry, but also feels it must be resisted, or at least interrogated. She says in the introductory remarks to *Short Talks* that she wants to "avoid the boredom of a story. I emphasize this. I will do anything to avoid boredom. It is the task of a lifetime. You can never know enough, never use the infinitives and particles oddly enough, never impede the movement harshly enough, never leave the mind quickly enough."

The Truth about God

My Religion

My religion makes no sense
and does not help me
therefore I pursue it.

When we see
how simple it would have been
we will thrash ourselves.

I had a vision
of all the people in the world
who are searching for God

massed in a room
on one side
of a partition

that looks
from the other side
(God's side)

transparent
but we are blind.
Our gestures are blind.

Our blind gestures continue
for some time until finally
from somewhere

on the other side of the partition there we are
looking back at them.
It is far too late.

We see how brokenly
how warily
how ill

our blind gestures
parodied
what God really wanted

(some simple thing).
The thought of it
(this simple thing)

is like a creature
let loose in a room
and battering

to get out.
It batters my soul
with its rifle butt.

The God Fit

Sometimes God will drop a fit on you.
Leave you on your bed howling.
Don't take it meanly.

Because the outer walls of God are glass.
I see a million souls clambering up the walls on the inside
to escape God who is burning,

untended.

The God Coup

God is a grand heart cut.
On the road where man surges along He may,
as the prophet says,
tarry.

By God

Sometimes by night I don't know why
I awake thinking of prepositions.
Perhaps they are clues.

"Since by Man came Death."
I am puzzled to hear that Man is the agent of Death.
Perhaps it means

Man was standing at the curb
and Death came by.
Once I had a dog

would go with anyone.
Perhaps listening for
little by little the first union.

Deflect

I have a friend who is red hot with pain.
He feels the lights like hard rain through his pores.
Together we went to ask Isaac.

Isaac said I will tell you the story told to me.
It was from Adam
issued the lights.

From the lights of his forehead were formed all the names of the world.
From the lights of his ears, nose and throat
came a function no one has ever defined.

From the lights of his eyes—but wait—
Isaac waits.
In theory

the lights of the eye should have issued from Adam's navel.
But within the lights themselves occurred
an intake of breath

and they changed their path.
And they were separated.
And they were caught in the head.

And from these separated lights came
that which pains you
on its errands (here my friend began to weep) through the world.

For be assured it is not only you who mourn.
Isaac lashed his tail.
Every rank of world

was caused to descend
(at least one rank)
by the terrible pressure of the light.

Nothing remained in place.
Nothing was not captured except
among the shards and roots and matter

some lights
from Adam's eyes
nourished there somehow.

Isaac stopped his roaring.
And my friend by now drowsy as a snake
subsided behind a heap of blueblack syllables.

God's Name

God had no name.
Isaac had two names.
Isaac was also called The Blind.

Inside the dark sky of his mind
Isaac could hear God
moving down a country road bordered by trees.

By the way the trees reflected off God
Isaac knew which ones were straight and tall
or when they carried their branches

as a body does its head
or why some crouched low to the ground in thickets.
To hear how God was moving through the universe

gave Isaac his question.
I could tell you his answer
but it wouldn't help.

The name is not a noun.
It is an adverb.
Like the little black notebooks that Beethoven carried

in his coatpocket
for the use of those who wished to converse with him,
the God adverb

is a one-way street that goes everywhere you are.
No use telling you what it is.
Just chew it and rub it on.

Teresa of God

"the aching has hold of me O grievous daimon"

Teresa lived in a personal black cube.
I saw her hit the wall each way she moved.
She cursed her heart

which was, she said, rent
and her nose
which had been broken again and again.

Some people have to fight every moment of their lives
which God has lined with a burning animal—
I think because

God wants that animal kept alive.
With her nose Teresa questioned
this project of God's.

To her heart God sent answer.
The autopsy after her death revealed
it was indeed rent.

Photographs of the event
had to be faked (with red thread and an old gold glove)
when the lens kept melting.

The Grace That Comes by Violence

Yours is not (I regret to say) the story they tell
although you howl and gash yourself
scurrying out of the tombs

where you now live.
God forces some.
God's prophet came

to send your unclean spirit
into pigs, who ran amok.
I saw you

at the bottom of the cliff of pity
diving in pig blood—
"cleansed" now.

God's Woman

Are you angry at nature? said God to His woman.
Yes I am angry at nature I do not want nature stuck
up between my legs on your pink baton

or ladled out like geography whenever
your buckle needs a lick.
What do you mean *Creation*?

God circled her.
Fire. Time. Fire.
Choose, said God.

God Stiff

God gave an onomatopoeic quality to women's language.
These eternally blundering sounds eternally
blundering down

into the real words of what they are
like feet dropped into bone shoes.
"Treachery" (she notices) sounds just like His zipper going down.

God's Beloveds Remain True

Chaos overshadows us.
Unsheltered sorrow shuts upon us.
We are strangled by bitter light.
Our bones shake like sticks.
We snap.
We grope.
We pant and go dry.
Our tongues are black.
All day is endless.
Nights endless.
Our skin crawls, it cracks.
Our room is a cat who plays with us.
Our hope is a noose.
We take our flesh in our teeth.
The autumn blows us as chaff across the fields.
We are sifted and fall.
We are hung in a void.

We are shattered on the ocean.
We are smeared on the darkness.
We are slit and drained out.
Little things drink us.
We lie unburied.
We are dust.
We know nothing.
We can not answer.
We will speak no more.
BUT WE WILL NOT STOP.
For we are the beloveds.
We have been instructed to call this His love.

God's Bouquet Of Undying Love

April snow.
God is waiting in the garden.
Slow as a blush,

snow shifts and settles on God.
On God's bouquet.
The trees are white nerve nets.

God's Mother

She doesn't get to say much in the official biography—
I believe they are out of wine, etc.,
practical things—

watching with one eye as he goes about the world
calling himself The Son Of Man.
Naturalists tell us

that the hatching crow is fed by the male
but when it flies, by the mother.
Love Fly Man
Loves Flies Mans
Loved Flew Manned
Loving Flying Manning
Loved Flown Woman.
It is what grammarians call a difference of tense and aspect.

God's Justice

In the beginning there were days set aside for various tasks.
On the day He was to create justice
God got involved in making a dragonfly

and lost track of time.
It was about two inches long
with turquoise dots all down its back like Lauren Bacall.

God watched it bend its tiny wire elbows
as it set about cleaning the transparent case of its head.
The eye globes mounted on the case

rotated this way and that
as it polished every angle.
Inside the case

which was glassy black like the windows of a downtown bank
God could see the machinery humming
and He watched the hum

travel all the way down turquoise dots to the end of the tail
and breathe off as light.
Its black wings vibrated in and out.

The Wolf God

Like a painting we will be erased, no one can remain.
I saw my life as a wolf loping along the road
and I questioned the women of that place.

Some regard the wolf as immortal, they said.
Now you know this only happened in one case and that
wolves die regularly of various causes—

bears kill them, tigers hunt them,
they get epilepsy,
they get a salmon bone crosswise in their throat,

they run themselves to death no one knows why—
but perhaps you never heard
of their ear trouble.

They have very good ears,
can hear a cloud pass overhead.
And sometimes it happens

that a windblown seed will bury itself in the aural canal
displacing equilibrium.
They go mad trying to stand upright,

nothing to link with.
Die of anger.
Only one we know learned to go along with it.

He took small steps at first.
Using the updrafts.
They called him Huizkol,

that means
Looks Good In Spring.
Things are as hard as you make them.

God's Christ Theory

God had no emotions but wished temporarily
to move in man's mind
as if He did: Christ.

Not passion but compassion.
Com—means "with."
What kind of withness would that be?

Translate it.
I have a friend named Jesus
from Mexico.

His father and grandfather are called Jesus too.
They account me a fool with my questions about salvation.
They say they are saving to move to Los Angeles.

God's List of Liquids

It was a November night of wind.
Leaves tore past the window.
God had the book of life open at PLEASURE

and was holding the pages down with one hand
because of the wind from the door.
For I made their flesh as a sieve

wrote God at the top of the page
and then listed in order:
Alcohol
Blood
Gratitude
Memory
Semen
Song
Tears
Time.

God's Work

Moonlight in the kitchen is a sign of God.
The kind of sadness that is a black suction pipe extracting you
from your own navel and which the Buddhists call

"no mindcover" is a sign of God.
The blind alleys that run alongside human conversation
like lashes are a sign of God.

God's own calmness is a sign of God.
The surprisingly cold smell of potatoes or money.
Solid pieces of silence.

From these diverse signs you can see
how much work remains to do.
Put away your sadness, it is a mantle of work.

Di Brandt

(b. 1952)

Di Brandt (nee Diana Ruth Janzen) was born and raised in Reinland, Manitoba, in a Mennonite farming village. She left the community at age 17, completing her B.Th. at Canadian Mennonite Bible College, BA at the University of Manitoba, MA in English at the University of Toronto, and Ph.D. at the University of Manitoba. Married for several years to visual artist Les Brandt, she worked as a freelance writer, then raised two daughters as a single parent. After teaching for eight years at the University of Windsor, she was appointed to a Canada Research Chair in Literature and Creative Writing at Brandon University, Manitoba. Her poetry publications include *questions i asked my mother* (1987, Governor General's Award finalist, Dillons Commonwealth Poetry Prize finalist, Gerald Lampert Award), *Agnes in the Sky* (1990, McNally Robinson Manitoba Book of the Year), *mother, not mother* (1992), *Jerusalem, beloved* (1995, CAA National Poetry Prize, Governor General's Award finalist), *Now You Care* (2003, Griffin Prize finalist, Pat Lowther Award finalist, Trillium Award finalist), *Speaking of Power: The Poetry of Di Brandt* (2006, edited with an introduction by Tanis MacDonald), and *Walking to Mojácar* (2012). Brandt is the author of two collections of essays, *So this is the world & here I am in it* (2007) and *Dancing Naked: Narrative Strategies for Writing across Centuries* (1996), and she is co-editor, with Barbara Godard, of two anthologies, *Re: Generations: Canadian Women Poets in Conversation* (2005) and *Wider Boundaries of Daring: The Modernist Impulse in Canadian Women's Poetry* (2010, Gabrielle Roy Prize, Canada Prize for the Humanities finalist).

Though shunned for a time by her community, Brandt continues to celebrate the Mennonite respect for nature and living simply. About the consolation poetry affords, she says: "I am grateful to have come to it in a time of relative peace and prosperity, where I could risk asking forbidden questions without being killed for it. . . . I am grateful to have come to poetry as a woman and as a mother, joyfully connected to the reproductive rhythms of the living earth" (Afterword to *Speaking of Power*).

Always looking for forms to embody her re-visionary poetics, Brandt found the ghazal. As she explains to her editor Tanis MacDonald,

> I really love John Thompson's little essay about the ghazal form. He says the logic of it is "drunken and amorous," the way it stumbles from one disjunctive couplet to the next. It allows us to escape the

> sober linear sense of intentionality we are so practiced in, because of our rationalist schooling. The ghazal form is a lovely strategy by which to deconstruct our intentionality, and open it up to the unpredictable and the haphazard. It certainly works that way for me, but on the other hand all of my poetry has a random quality to it. I am always drifting from one thing to the next, haphazardly, not really knowing what I'm doing! And yet there's always much more coherence and design to it in the end than I intended or imagined.

Pushed to elaborate, she says:

> As I get older, I start to be more aware that there are all kinds of grand designs that are all around us and in us that are beyond or beneath what we carry around in our conscious minds. Perhaps it's not so much designs as evolving networks of interdependence, interconnections, that come more into view as you get older. It's interesting to play with forms that allow you to disrupt assumed mental habits, to uncover other kinds of coherence and connectedness than we're used to thinking about. It's all a kind of mystery, what it is and how it works. (*Arc*, 5 Jan. 2007)

nonresistance, or love Mennonite style

(for L & the others)

turn the other cheek when your brother
hits you & your best friend tells fibs
about you & the teacher punishes you
unfairly if someone steals your shirt
give him your coat to boot this will
heap coals of fire on his head & let him
know how greatly superior you are
while he & his cronies dicker & bargain
their way to hell you can hold your
head up that is down humbly knowing
you're bound for the better place where
it gets tricky is when your grandfather
tickles you too hard or your cousins
want to play doctor & your uncle kisses
you too long on the lips & part of you
wants it & the other part knows it's
wrong & you want to run away but you
can't because he's a man like your father
& the secret place inside you feels itchy

& hot & you wonder if this is what hell
feels like & you remember the look on
your mother's face when she makes
herself obey your dad & meanwhile her
body is shouting *No! No!* & he doesn't
even notice & you wish you could stop
being angry all the time but you can't
because God is watching & he sees
everything there isn't any place to let
it out & you understand about love the
lavish sacrifice in it how it will stretch
your woman's belly & heap fire on your
head you understand how love is like
a knife & a daughter is not a son & the
only way you will be saved is by
submitting quietly in your grandfather's
house your flesh smouldering in the
darkened room as you love your enemy
deeply unwillingly & full of shame

from mother, not mother

let me tell you, dear reader,
about the time

my body was a ship. & i
sailed the seas

of downtown Toronto in it,
sails billowing,

full of wind, spirit breath,
baby's breath.

& the young men on Bloor
averted their eyes

& the Portuguese construction
workers on Huron Street

whistled through their teeth
& grunted,

ah, now, there's a mama.

& the young women in the park
coming suddenly into view,

with their strollers on the green
grass, & i sailing

down the sidewalks past them,
glorious in my pride.

ah, dear reader, let me tell you
how i loved my body then,

my huge floating belly, my nipples
big, dark, swollen

with milk, leaking desire,
golden, liquid,

all over the bed & the pillow
& the floor.

ah, how i loved my lover then,
who filled me with such bounty,

erotic trembling, oceanic bliss.

smacking, sucking, stroking
my sunlit prow, big with child.

it was then, dear reader,
my brain sank into my womb,

dark lipped, bearded, dripping:
with child, with child, with child.

such a grand billowing
on the high seas, such unfurling,

such a mighty flowering among
the busy streets,

expecting, pregnant.

from Jerusalem, beloved

Jerusalem, the golden, city of my dreams,
dreaming, how i waited all my life for you,
to find you, resplendent, in the sun, your
white stones crying, with joy, Jerusalem,
beloved, lying in the Mediterranean sun,
filled with love, delirious with love, *lift up*
your heart & sing, my heart dancing, how i
longed for you, all my life, your streets
paved with gold, & children playing, your
diamond studded gates, your rooftops filled
with women, dancing, & flowers in their
hair, the tables laden, heavy, the air filled
with music, & feasting, my love, how i
longed for you, dreaming, my arms aching,
from the day of my birth, my birthgiving,
filled with pangs of hunger & remembering,
how i longed for you, my love, how long,
oh how long i waited for you

*

there are no words in me for Gaza, for what i saw
in Gaza, the eyes of the women lining up at the
hospital for milk, with their babies & small
children, their eyes looking at me, another North
American tourist with nothing to offer, except
terrible pity, & shame, shame at my innocence,
my stupid privilege, i never imagined such a place,
i could have been born here, & thought this is what
the world is like, these narrow streets filled with
flies & cowdung, shacks made of sheet metal &
bare wooden boards, the path to the beach littered
with barbed wire & abandoned jeeps, & grey sand,
how long does it take to forget, the soldiers at the
door, the women screaming, the broken china,
embroidered tablecloths flapping in the wind,
blood running from the father's mouth, how long
does it take to forget, the darkness in this woman's
eyes, the children hiding rocks in their hands on
the way to school, these two will not come home
tonight, their shins broken by soldiers in the street,
these eyes, the long long sorrow in them, these
women's eyes, looking at me

from Dog Days in Maribor

Anti (Electric) Ghazals

1

Truly, in this age,
why should not all women be mad?

The snapping turtle stares
at the giant ball of rope in the sky.

The cherry trees have all been cut;
bronzed epitaphs.

No more invasions!
The earth is spitting up blood.

Diamond rivers, uranium valleys,
petroleum oceans.

Purple irises, Van Gogh, radiant,
beside the door.

7

What was it we wanted,
before all the walls came down?

Blue grey eyes, looking at me,
through the cigarette smoke.

Heil Mister Herr Direktor Daddy
Doktor Präsident CEO Sir!

That is no country for old women,
every oak slashed from root to crown.

The children breathing in
the by-products of petroleum.

Vineyards gleaming,
fruitladen, on the sun drenched hills.

9

So many newly minted young
capitalists on the make.

The golden rule:
self-sacrifice, or suicide.

The curve of the sweet earth,
herb scented, holy.

Bring them along, these crotch sniffers,
these bags of fur,

squirrel chasers, diggers of corpses,
rollers in horse dung.

Rotten fish on the world's beaches,
jewelled with black flies, beetles.

10

Now that it's much much too late,
now you care.

Poison ivy wrapped around the
ash trees; lovers' embrace.

Turtle, are you crazy, get
your diamond shell off the damn road.

The eating and the eaten, all
are gathered here, dearly beloved.

The blood, the liver, remember
our mother tongues.

A species gone every three minutes.
History racing us by.

Jan Zwicky

(b. 1955)

Jan Zwicky, raised in Calgary, Edmonton, and Mayerthorpe, Alberta, earned her BA at the University of Calgary and her Ph.D. at the University of Toronto. Her books include *Wittgenstein Elegies* (1986), *The New Room* (1989), *Lyric Philosophy* (1992/2012), *Songs for Relinquishing the Earth* (1998, Governor General's Award), *Twenty-One Small Songs* (2000), *Wisdom & Metaphor* (2003/2008), *Robinson's Crossing* (2004, Dorothy Livesay Prize), *Thirty-Seven Small Songs & Thirteen Silences* (2005), *Plato as Artist* (2010), *Forge* (2011, Griffin Prize finalist), *The Book of Frog* (2012), and *Auden as Philosopher: How Poets Think* (2012). Zwicky has taught philosophy at several universities, including Princeton and the University of Victoria. She is a professional musician and has served as an editor for Brick Books and *The Fiddlehead*.

Much of Zwicky's writing is concerned with lyric poetry as a mode of thought. In "Bringhurst's Presocratics: Lyric and Ecology" (*Poetry and Knowing*), she says that lyric understanding "rejects the primacy of words as bearers of meaning, and locates meaning's roots in the prelinguistic gestures of music and the rhythms of the non-human world." Not only is the wordlessness, which she claims lyric desires, selfless, its pursuit could be fundamental to a radical social and environmental vision:

> Lyric longing is born of our constitutional inability to immerse ourselves completely in the living rhythms of the planet. The price of our capacity to manipulate these rhythms for our own short-term ends is our separation from them. This capacity is concomitant with our capacity for language. The condition of language is the Herakleitean opposite of lyric. That is: they die into one another. To apprehend the mind as a living integrated complex of all facets of human experience, which is itself continuous with the larger integrated complex of the world as a whole, is to apprehend the mind ecologically.

What is most radical here, I believe, is that poetic perception is placed among the foremost means of perceiving and apprehending experience. The dissociated sensibility, in other words, recovers an ancient mode of perception, a channel back to primary experience, however that may be construed. If, as I believe, poetry is our first language, it has its own grammar, which is a code, not for making things fuzzy or difficult or ornate, but for descrambling reality, by taking away the names and by making our personal and tribal history strange so that we are forced to look at it anew.

Zwicky has found in the writings of Wittgenstein support for her view that there is a scarcely describable link between music and philosophy. In *Lyric Philosophy*, she claims that lyric poetry and philosophy are not mutually exclusive pursuits. In a summary of her argument, she says she rests this claim:

> on a demonstration that we (professional philosophers) have not actually provided a *defence* of the claim that clarity of thought (the erotic pull of which I take to be defining of philosophical activity) can be provided only by systematic analysis. In the absence of such a defence . . . we must take seriously numerous examples of philosophy pursued according to other lights, and, indeed, must take seriously the possibility that there exist compositions which, owing to their form, have never been considered philosophical but which nonetheless *are*. This view, not surprisingly, turns out to point to an understanding of meaning both deeper and broader than that which can be provided by formal semantics. *How* we say, I argue, is integrally bound up with *what* we mean; and . . . there exists a particular subclass of formally anomalous works, conditioned by a (lyric) demand for coherence *as well as* the (philosophical) demand for clarity—which thus might reasonably be called lyric philosophy. In their contexts, it turns out that one of the tests for truth becomes compositional integrity. (Introduction to "The Geology of Norway." *The Harvard Review of Philosophy*, VII, 1999, 29–31)

Zwicky rejects the Freudian notion that dreams (or poems) need to be interpreted to be understood, insisting instead that primary process is a genuine species of thought, that it is simply structured differently. She dismisses not only Freud's delegitimization of poetry and dreams as species of knowing, but also its critical corollary, post-structuralism:

> It is the blithe nihilism of *il n'y a pas de hors-texte* . . . It is that most profoundly exemplifies the exclusion of non-linguistic thought from consideration, and is thus most clearly symptomatic of contemporary intellectual malaise. Lyric poetry, on the other hand, emerges as profoundly subversive: it takes the coin of the realm and turns it into jewellery—braids it in its hair, sews it on its dress, shapes it into teeth. ("Freud's Metapsychology and the Culture of Philosophy." *Canadian Journal of Philosophy Supplementary*, Vol. 25, 1999, 211–26)

The Geology of Norway

But when his last night in Norway came, on 10 December,
he greeted it with some relief, writing that it was perfectly possible
that he would never return.

—Ray Monk, *Ludwig Wittgenstein*

I have wanted there to be
no story. I have wanted
only facts. At any given point in time
there cannot be a story: time,
except as now, does not exist.
A given point in space
is the compression of desire. The difference
between this point and some place else
is a matter of degree.
This is what compression is: a geologic epoch
rendered to a slice of rock you hold between
your finger and your thumb.
That is a fact.
Stories are merely theories. Theories
are dreams.
A dream
is a carving knife
and the scar it opens in the world
is history.
The process of compression gives off thought.
I have wanted
the geology of light.

They tell me despair is a sin.
I believe them.
The hand moving is the hand thinking,
and despair says the body does not exist.
Something to do with bellies and fingers
pressing gut to ebony,
thumbs on keys. Even the hand
writing is the hand thinking. I wanted
speech like diamond because I knew
that music meant too much.

And the fact is, the earth is not a perfect sphere.
And the fact is, it is half-liquid.

And the fact is there are gravitational anomalies. The continents
congeal, and crack, and float like scum on cooling custard.
And the fact is,
the fact is,
and you might think the fact is
we will never get to the bottom of it,
but you would be wrong.
There is a solid inner core.
Fifteen hundred miles across, iron alloy,
the pressure on each square inch of its heart
is nearly thirty thousand tons.
That's what I wanted:
words made of that: language
that could bend light.

Evil is not darkness,
it is noise. It crowds out possibility,
which is to say
it crowds out silence.
History is full of it, it says
that no one listens.
The sound of wind in leaves,
that was what puzzled me, it took me years
to understand that it was music.
Into silence, a gesture.
A sentence: that it speaks.
This is the mystery: meaning.
Not that these folds of rock exist
but that their beauty, here,
now, nails us to the sky.

The afternoon blue light in the fjord.
Did I tell you
I can understand the villagers?
Being, I have come to think,
is music; or perhaps
it's silence. I cannot say.
Love, I'm pretty sure,
is light.
                You know, it isn't
what I came for, this bewilderment
by beauty. I came
to find a word, the perfect

syllable, to make it reach up,
grab meaning by the throat
and squeeze it till it spoke to me.
How else to anchor
memory? I wanted language
to hold me still, to be a rock,
I wanted to become a rock myself. I thought
if I could find, and say,
the perfect word, I'd nail
mind to the world, and find
release.
The hand moving is the hand thinking:
what I didn't know: even the continents
have no place but earth.

These mountains: once higher
than the Himalayas. Formed in the pucker
of a supercontinental kiss, when Europe
floated south of the equator
and you could hike from Norway
down through Greenland to the peaks
of Appalachia. Before Iceland existed.
Before the Mediterranean
evaporated. Before it filled again.
Before the Rockies were dreamt of.
And before these mountains,
the rock raised in them
chewed by ice that snowed from water
in which no fish had swum. And before that ice,
the almost speechless stretch of the Precambrian:
two billion years, the planet
swathed in air that had no oxygen, the Baltic Shield
older, they think, than life.

So I was wrong.
This doesn't mean
that meaning is a bluff.
History, that's what
confuses us. Time
is not linear, but it's real.
The rock beneath us drifts,
and will, until the slow cacophony of magma
cools and locks the continents in place.

Then weather, light,
and gravity
will be the only things that move.

And will they understand?
Will they have a name for us?—Those
perfect changeless plains,
those deserts,
the beach that was this mountain,
and the tide that rolls for miles across
its vacant slope.

Border Station

There had been flooding all that summer, I recall,
acres of grey-brown footage from the Midwest—
but with reports confined to property, and human interest,
the reasons for the land's incontinence suppressed, those images
had skimmed past, seeming, as usual, not quite real.
The day had been hot, clear,
we'd eaten supper on the porch, and
later, quite late, had turned the radio on upstairs—
some thought of midnight news, perhaps—
I don't remember now.
The signal we pulled in—strongly,
because we weren't far from the border then—
was the last half-hour of a Brewers-Red Sox game.
It was coming from Milwaukee,
top of the ninth, two out, the Brewers leading,
and we hadn't been listening long when the announcer,
between a line out and Hatcher's
coming to the plate, commented on the weather:
there'd been a rain delay, it had been raining heavily before,
but now was easing up, just a light shower falling,
though a lot of lightning was still visible to the east and south.
Raised on the prairies, I
could see it clearly, suddenly
could see the whole scene clearly:
the crowd dwindling, several
umbrellas, the glittering aluminum of vacated seats,
the misted loaf of arc-lit light, the night,
deeper by contrast, thick and wet and brown
around it, flickering.

And at the same time I was struck, too—like
looking out across a huge relief map—by the hundreds of miles
between our bedroom and Milwaukee, by that continental
distance, and was overtaken inexplicably
by sorrow.
It was as though
in that moment of deep focus
I had tasted the idea of America.
As though it really might have had
something to do with baseball, and radio, and the beauty
of the storms that can form in the vast light above the plains—or,
no, extremity of some kind—clarity, or tenderness—
as though, that close to the end, levels
already rising on the leveed banks again,
the mistakes might have been human:
not justifiable, but as though
some sort of story might be told, simply,
from defeat, without apology, the way you might describe
the fatal accident—not to make sense of it,
but just to say, too late but still to say,
something had happened:
there was blood, blood everywhere, we hadn't realized,
by the time we noticed, rivers of it,
nothing could be done.

Small Song: Prairie

Wood light, meadow light,
the fencepost silver
in the afternoon's long stare;
beast light, the satin flash
of horserump or the brown hand
in the saskatoons;
cloud light and willow light,
the dead light of the salt marsh
and the hammered brilliance
of the dugout under wind;
even the rain in its night singing,
the night rain in its forgetting,
is a kind of light.

Autobiography

In the years when winter snow piled up
along the edges of the streets, beneath the windows,
on the lee side of the hedge,
I did my homework at a desk my father built,
set in the corner of my bedroom, facing west.
Which was my choice, I think. The second desk,
I know it was. And once I moved out, the apartments
with the bad floors and the crazy plumbing,
the wallpaper I was always steaming off, I'd take
the place because it had a workspace
that did not face east.

Those cold bright years.
How long I spent, trying to die.

Such injustice. When every morning
it's spring again. Every morning
the light melts the snow—
before books, before desks, before windows,
before pain, before amazement.

Steven Heighton

(b. 1961)

Steven Heighton was born in Toronto and earned his BA and MA at Queen's University in Kingston, the city he calls home. He has been an immensely prolific writer, working in several genres. He has written numerous works of fiction, including three collections of short stories—*Flight Paths of the Emperor* (1992), *On earth as it is* (1995), and *The Dead Are More Visible* (2012)—and the three bestselling novels *The Shadow Boxer* (2000), *Afterlands* (2005), and *Every Lost Country* (2010). His poetry books include *Stalin's Carnival* (1989), *Foreign Ghosts* (1989), *The Ecstasy of Skeptics* (1994), *The Address Book* (2004), and *Patient Frame* (2010). He edited *Quarry* magazine for six years, has worked as a teacher and translator, and served as writer-in-residence at McGill University and Massey College at the University of Toronto. He is the recipient of the Gerald Lampert Memorial Award, four National Magazine Gold Awards, the Air Canada Award, and the Petra Kenny Prize, and has been shortlisted for the Governor General's Award, the Trillium Award, and the Pushcart Prize. Heighton has also written *Workbook: Memos & Dispatches on Writing* (2011). His work has been translated into nine languages.

Heighton likes to quote Buddhist teacher Thich Nhat Hanh's advice: "Don't just do something, sit there," as a reminder to poets that dreamtime and nightmind, drawing on the unconscious, free from distraction and rationalization, are central to the poetic project. But he offers this caveat:

> Don't get me wrong. No one finishes a novel or even a book of poems without a hefty contribution from the daymind—specifically the will, overseen by the hungry ego. (Who could finish a four-hundred-page novel without some ego hunger?) Inspiration and good lines can only take a book or writer so far. Still, in the end, writing that's all sweat and disciplined desire for achievement, a story lacking inner vision, a poem untouched by the nudgings of the nightmind—these have no deep resonance or aesthetic staying power. We have to remember how to invite and receive the words and insights we can't force to mind. We have to relearn how to muse and drowse and stare into blankness, adrift, dormant, even bored, especially now when our various screens are always present—firewalls raised between us and the reality of dreams. (*Workbook: Memos & Dispatches on Writing*, edited by Jared Bland)

The Machine Gunner

I saw them. They came like ghosts out of ground-
mist, moving
over ruined earth in waves, running,

no, walking, shoulder to shoulder
like a belt of bullets or like
men: tinned meat lined on a conveyor belt as the sun

exploded in thin shafts on metal
buckles, bayonets, the nodding
spires of helmets. I heard faint battle cries

and whistles, piercing through the shriek
of fire and iron falling, the slurred
cadence of big guns. As they funnelled

like a file of mourners into gaps
in the barbed wire I made quick
calculations and slipped the safety catch.

But held my fire. Alongside me
the boys in the trenches worried them with
rifles, pistols, hand grenades

but they came on, larger now, their faces
almost resolving out of hazed, hot
distance, their ranks at close quarters amazing

with dumb courage, numb step, a sound of drugged
choking in gas and green mud, steaming . . .
Who were these men. I saw them penitent,

sagging to knees. I saw their dishevelled
dying. And when finally they broke
into a run it came to me

what they'd always been, how I'd always,
really, seen them: boys
rushing towards us with arms

outstretched, hands clenched as if in urgent prayer,
sudden welcome, or a reunion
quite unexpected. Yes. And more than this

like children, chased by something behind the lines
and hurrying to us
for rescue—

I spat and swung the gun around. Fired,
felt the metal pulse
and laid them three deep in the wire.

Were You to Die

Were you to die I'd be free to go off
and see the world, and sleep in every elsewhere
I might never arrive
—yet I might choose to travel alone
from window to window looking out
on the streets of your city

where your friends still expect to see you sometimes
or mistake you for someone, out of custom—love—

Without your thrashing, manic dreams, my body
would sleep better
but wake more tired, I'd let the garden go to seed
the way I always meant to
and when I looked out the window into the yard
I'd never miss the snowpeas, beets and roses
but your sunhat I might miss—you hunkered down
in a summer dress, your fingers
grouped like roots in the raised beds,
your stooped, stubborn nape, your cinnamon-
freckled shoulders—

Were you to die, my heart
would be free to pack a bag
and book passage for the riot of islands
I might have been, and shared
with the one and numberless "beloved" we fumble
our whole lives glimpsing
a moment too late,
when Eden was always the one who stayed
rooted in her changes, and gave you
the island in her arms, and when you slept
somehow she travelled, and when you woke
she was changed—

Were you to die, my mind
would be free to twist inward
the way fingers fist, and fasten pat
on its own taut notions, theorems, palm shut fast
to the snow that pooled there and seemed to flow through
when the skin still flowered in fullest winter
and I loved you, and thoughts, like books,
were doors that opened outward,
not coffins, closed,
not cells—

Were you to die and free me
my body would follow you down into the cold
prison of your passing, and warm you when all the others
had turned away, and try bribing

the keeper with a poem, or fool him
with keychains of chiming words—an elegy
so pure he'd be pressed to cry, eyes
thawing and the earth warmed, April
when rain falls like a ransom, through opened arms
that bore the sun down with you, warm.

Constellations

After bedtime the child climbed on her dresser
and peeled phosphorescent stars off the sloped
gable-wall, dimming the night vault of her ceiling
like a haze or the interfering glow
of a great city, small hands anticipating
eons as they raided the playful patterns
her father had mapped for her—black holes now
where the raised thumb-stubs and ears of the Bat
had been, the feet of the Turtle, wakeful
eyes of the Mourning Dove. She stuck those paper
stars on herself. One on each foot, the backs
of her hands, navel, tip of nose and so on,
then turned on the lamp by her bed and stood close
like a child chilled after a winter bath
pressed up to an air duct or a radiator
until those paper stars absorbed more light
than they could hold. Then turned off the lamp,
walked out into the dark hallway and called.

Her father came up. He heard her breathing
as he clomped upstairs preoccupied, wrenched
out of a rented film just now taking grip
on him and the child's mother, his day-end
bottle of beer set carefully on the stairs,
marking the trail back down into that evening
adult world—he could hear her breathing (or
really, more an anxious, breathy giggle) but
couldn't see her, then in the hallway stopped,
mind spinning to sort the apparition
of fireflies hovering ahead, till he sensed
his daughter and heard in her breathing
the pent, grave concentration of her pose,
mapped onto the star chart of the darkness,
arms stretched high, head back, one foot slightly raised—

the Dancer, he supposed, and all his love
spun to centre with crushing force, to find her
momentarily fixed, as unchanging
as he and her mother must seem to her,
and the way the stars are; as if the stars are.

Herself, Revised

There's a final bedtime when the father reads
to his daughter under the half-moon lamp.
The wolf-eyed dog sits guard on the snowy
quilt at their feet—ears pricked, head upright
like a dragon on its hoard—while the daughter's
new clock ticks on the dresser. When the father
shuts the book, neither feels in the cool sigh
cast from its pages a breath of the end—
and how can it be that this ritual
will not recur? True, this latest story
is over, *Treasure Island*, which held them
a dozen nights, but "the end" has arrived
this way often before. Maybe she's tired
of the rite, or waking to a sense of herself
revised? Maybe he's temporarily bored,
or unmoored, reading by duty or rote,
turning deeper inside his own concerns.

How does the end enter? There's a hinging
like a book's sewn spine in the raw matter
of time—that coded text, illegible—
and stretched too far, it goes. An innocent
break, the father gone one weekend or the child
sleeping at a friend's, followed by a night
or two she wants to read alone, or write,
for a change, in her new padlock journal.
She has no idea what has changed. She
can't know that the enlargement of her life
demands small death after death, and this one,
the latest, is far from last. She will not
notice this death, being so intent on life—
so implied in its stretching crewelwork
of seconds.
Some nights later, suddenly,
writing cheques or checking email, he might

notice and wonder at the change. In a sense
such minor passings pre-enact his own.
For a moment he might lay down his pen,
forget the figures, peer over the roofline
and find she was right—Orion, rising,
is more blueprint of butterfly, or bird,
than hunter. How does it enter, through what rift
or flaw? Maybe it doesn't enter at all.
It was there in every sentence: the end.

Mary Dalton

(b. 1950)

Born in Lake View, Conception Bay, Newfoundland, Mary Dalton studied at the University of Toronto, Memorial University of Newfoundland, and the University of Liverpool. She edited the literary magazine *TickleAce* from 1980 to 1986 and was also the editor of *Newfoundland Studies*. She is widely published in magazines and anthologies and is co-editor of *Wild on the Crest: Sea Poems: Newfoundland and Labrador* (1995). She lives in St. John's, teaches at Memorial University, and is the founder and director of the SPARKS Literary Festival. Her publications include: *The Times of Icicles* (1989), *Allowing the Light* (1993), *Merrybegot* (2003, E.J. Pratt Poetry Award), *Red Ledger* (2006), *Between You and the Weather* (2008), and *Hooking* (2013). She won the Newfoundland and Labrador Book Award for Poetry and has been shortlisted for many other prizes.

As she says in an interview with Barbara Nickel, called "There's a Carnival for You":

> The Newfoundland landscape is part of my being; I'm part of it. But the weather in the poems is also considered weather; it's the weather each poem needs. I'm wanting the poems as a whole to reflect a certain wild energy, something at times anarchical, in the people and the place. The cliffs and the wind, the flux of weather, help to embody that in the poems.

That said, Dalton is resistant to the notion that her work can be categorized as a defence of Newfoundland speech, or feminism, or any single cause:

> The poet's task is of another sort. It may sound pious, but what I'm up to is trying to be true to the possibilities of poetry, to be true to the sum of my knowledge and experience—to write the best poems I can. I inhabit the country of my imagination. To consider the implications of margin and region has some value, but I think that such questions are of limited usefulness in arriving at an understanding of the distinctiveness of any writer's work. And I believe it can be damaging to writers to preoccupy themselves overmuch with these questions in any direct way. The psychic energy is needed for the art.

Dalton finds inspiration in the *Dictionary of Newfoundland English*. To be a *merrybegot*, for example, is to have been born out of wedlock, a profound and beautiful contrast to being dismissed as a bastard. While the poetic context often hints at the meaning of words (as is the case with Dalton's use of *conkerbell*, *dogger*, and *sterricky*), some words might require a bit of pondering or research, a dip into that wonderful trove of local and cultural wisdom. In an interview with Jeanette Lynes, Dalton says: "These are the gifts of the language to me. Why would I feel inferior, or have any sense that I didn't matter enough when I was in Newfoundland, as opposed to elsewhere in Canada, when the language gives me these gifts? There is nowhere better for a poet to be, with her ears open, than here" ("Mary Dalton and the Process of Poetry." *Words Out There: Women Poets in Atlantic Canada*, edited by Jeanette Lynes).

In response to a question about the brevity of her poems, Dalton says: "I wanted them to be concentrated—bursts of linguistic energy containing within their small spaces a world. Yes, a fiddle tune, or the flaunt of a step-dance." About the humour in a poem like "Conkerbells," Dalton says:

> The humour arises from a sense of carnival, I think—a delight in the tumble, the pratfall, the unexpected overthrow of expectations. It is linked to that anarchic energy I spoke of earlier. And as often it can be a laugh at oneself and one's awkward situation as it is a laugh at others. It's all bound up with a keen sense of community somehow. And there's a delight on the part of these speakers, these tellers, in the telling itself, in the smack and tang of a good story, even if it's against oneself. The poems—whether they do or not—are meant to reflect a world of complex social relations, with a complex relation to language and story.

Asked about the most important elements of poetry (in CBC *Words at Large Interview*, 2007), she replies: "A sense of music. A love of words. A knowledge of the traditions and technical aspects of poetry, as well as of contemporary poetries. An acute attention to the world in its beauty and squalor, in all its multiplicity. A commitment to revision."

A Question of Narrative

He makes love like a battering ram
as if he's got to build a road,
blast his way through the high passes
and come out fighting those pesky redskins.

He makes love like a battering ram
as if he's in a race with Rocky VI,
pumping steel thrusting with his might
into the insatiable maw of the universe.

Did someone tell him there was
something terrible up there,
needing drumming into submission
with offerings of blood and sweat?

And she? A cairn, a pit—
the ravaged earth,
the ruthless derricks
drilling deeper, deeper.

Conkerbells

That winter was cold—Lord yes—
Wind barrelling out of the north,
Canvas lifting up off the floor,
And conkerbells hanging thicker than
A horse's dong. But that young
Dogger could smell the lick
Of a flame, trailed me and
His sister the length of the back ridge—
No chance of a kiss and a cuddle
Once he tripped in the juniper,
Toppled arse-over-teakettle
Smack into the boughs of our hot little tilt.

Janneying

Every winter it was the same racket.
A hint of the janneying, our mother'd
Have copper kittens, but after a bit
She'd give in to us, say yes we could go.
We'd rig ourselves up in any old fit-out,

pillows and nets, cotton drawers on our heads.
The boys let out squeaks, the girls spoke all gruff—
One fellow missing a finger made up a
False one so he couldn't be guessed.
Once we'd get in, we'd kick up the mats,
Fire up the accordion, dance the whole night—
The floor-boards'd shiver, the funnel turn red.
First light of the sun, off we'd head home,
Bellies rumbling and we ready
To eat the leg off the Lamb of God.

Merrybegot

When the moon was newing and the night burnt black,
Some rapscallion, some young pelt, some nuzzle-tripe
Set off down the path with the go of a born-again preacher,
Crept in under our apple tree, shinnied on up,
Swift and hungry as a starved mosquito, stripped
It bare.
And himself playing Don Juan in the kitchen—
Not a sound did he hear—
No apples for winter
And from the look of her belly
A good chance of a merrybegot.

My One Brother

Well, sure, we both popped
The same day out of our mother,
But look at the shuffle on him—
He's slow as an earthworm
And all caught up with stuff as
Far back as the boar's nuts.
Mark it down—you won't be stuck
For a fine line of old foolishness
Long as he's this side of the clay—
My one brother, maundering on—
The king of pishogues,
The pod auger days.

Yet

Moll doll his chin;
Her hair birch-
Broom-in-the-fits;
Chalk and cheese, they said;
Cradle and grave,
They said;
Yet—
You could smell
The smouldering, sparry,
Whenever they met.

Backhome Blues: Another Tune

So you sashayed down the road
that balmy summer night,
a jingling parade of one,
had a high-class tantrum
because you'd turned your back
and the scene shifted?
Who did you think you were?

You are just a blip, old trout.
A bit player.
It's as if a dust mote
stood on its hind legs
and howled at
the injustice of gravity.
The granite erratics are laughing.

Those fences you're shedding
your crocodile tears over—
a few sticks of wood.
Those sheep and those hens:
usurpers of the wolves' run.
Your pastoral tableau
a nanosecond in the long story.
Legions of ghosts crowd round these ponds.
Glaciers gouged out valleys and
D'Iberville's fires roared down these hills;
rogues roosted; rivers ran.

You've read
Gaff Topsails, yes? Then
open your eyes wider and
wise up.

The Great Big Sea and Lost Speech

It was the radio, the stock reports,
the shipping news, leaders, glib,
with dollar signs burning
where eyes should be.
It was the TV, *Globe and Mail*,
deficit, profit and loss.
It was the fisherman's graveyard, the huckster-
fishers of men.
A man was *a human resource*;
a fish was *a product*;
his world was *not viable*.
He saw the bodies packed in salt.

In dreams mouthless women
stretch out hands, silver-scaled, chilblained:
salt cascades white from their eyes
while a big sea smashes the rocks
into rows of styrofoam cages.
Down shining hallways of files
graphs utter—voices
patient, official, designing
his life as structures of salt—
event as crystalline whites,
and spaces between.

Now salt is a voice:
cool granular wooings
out onto cliff edges,
urging him back, back to sea.
Salt explains
he is spoken for,
himself so much salt,
circling in him, watery brine.
Notations in a red ledger,
his value on the open market,
salts, so many cents,
and water left over.

Elizabeth Philips

(b. 1954)

Born in Winnipeg and raised in Gimli, Manitoba, Elizabeth Philips has spent most of her adult life in Saskatchewan. She is the author of four collections of poetry: *Time in a Green Country* (1990), *Beyond My Keeping* (1995), *A Blue with Blood in It* (2000), and *Torch River* (2007). In addition to editing *Grain* magazine from 1988 to 2003, she has taught at the Sage Hill Writing Experience and the Banff Wired Studio and is director of the Banff Writing with Style program. She has also worked as a freelance journalist, writing for *Equinox* and *Western Living*, and as a book editor for various publishers. She has twice won the Saskatchewan Book Award for the best book of poetry published in a given year. She lives in Saskatoon.

Philips is also the editor of *A Peeled Wand: Selected Poems of Anne Szumigalski* (2010). What she says of Szumigalski reflects her own view of poetry, that it is "not something fanciful, pyrotechnics that temporarily relieve us, or distract us, or otherwise reconcile us to the harsh exigencies of 'real life.'" In an interview on *mygsa.com*, Philips says: "I think the poetic sensibility precedes the writing of poems. So being a poet hasn't changed how I see the world, it is how . . . I have always seen the world. I view the world through the lens of metaphor. I am writing a novel at the moment so I can say that I am writing a novel as a poet would write a novel—details are important, they are very telling and have tremendous undertow. I don't see the world in terms of story."

In a note to me, she said:

> I am always focused on clarity, on trying to translate the poem in my head onto paper and into the mind of the reader. I would like readers to experience some of the visual astonishment that I experience in nature—which is an almost visceral understanding of metaphor. I believe our need for metaphor—our craving for an opening up of our thinking and knowledge through the shock of inspired comparison—is innate, and essential to our ability to be in the world. I am fascinated by the multiplicity of forms in the natural world, what they mean to us, how we connect to nature and how we try to maintain the fiction that we are separate from it. How do we transform our sensory experience into ideas, into thought, belief, desire, action? This is a question I wrestle with again and again in my work.

Oxbow

This is the river that strayed, that slipped
aside, and, becalmed in its separate bed,
stayed,
          this is the river
that feeds the rushes, the slow reeds
and heron, the river that sleeps
in a circle, and clasps within it
an island of ten white spruce, a hundred
aspen,
          and a meadow
the span of an embrace
that we've claimed this afternoon
to lie in, face to face
on a weft of cast-off leaves,
                                        and above
your bare shoulders,
                              the sky, acutely
blue, hooked
on the pale green fingers of stripped aspen—
where the river stands down,
you turn me like water
cleft from water,
                           and I fall back
into my own body, as your body
                                             divides
and joins me,
                      into the passing
and the held.

November: Far Past

The three women press close, looking at family
pictures. Fall light, the colour of old paper, in squares
on the table. The mother
speaks in riddles. *Oh,* she says,
bending to the floor, *I've dropped my cloud,*
and they all see it, the white handkerchief on green
tile, cumulus above the fields.

The two daughters watch her eyes, her sudden
smile. They turn for her, carefully, the dry

leaves of the album. Her words
drop one by one into the quiet there, at the table,
well-polished stones resisting memory's
turbulence. *Milk, winter wheat, time to plant*
potatoes, the girls and Dad gone to church,
the barley poor again, this much butter
and three eggs.

They listen as their mother riffles through
the far past, wringing and wringing her hands.
The people in the photograph waver
under their new names, as if they could be
anyone, their lives a litany of possible
phrasings.

Seventy years ago she finds herself posing
beside a stone well, still
not quite a woman. Her hands, strong and work-scarred,
cover the page. She seems to sink down into it—
crosses the farmyard carrying a pail. *Woodpile, fence,*
stoneboat, the kettle, the cold
cold water.

To her daughters their mother's voice
is the ringing inside a well. They call to her, pull
and pull on the rope, drawing her back
out, into the ordinary day. She shows them her cupped
hands, but there's nothing in them
except light. She folds and folds it,
saying, *It rained then, it rained*
and rained, yes

it did rain.

The Night Before

The night before the diagnosis
is confirmed, we drink red wine, a French
Syrah, one bottle before, another following
the pasta and bread, the salad of butter lettuce.
We eat carefully, the forks and the knives
barely scraping the plates.

John tells a story about harvest
and how he ran between farmhouse and
threshing crew, bearing pails of water toward
their thirst, and then
away, the empty pails sailing in his easy
grip, the new strength in his lengthening
stride making him almost
clumsy.

Outside, the white lights strung in the Russian Olive
are a beaded curtain between
the shadows at our wrists when we lift
our glasses, and the darkness
beyond the tree, the diminishing
cold and snow of late spring.

We ask for another story
and Gail tells of meeting John
for the first time, thirty years ago in a rose garden
overlooking Toronto, both of them longing
for the North, for Shield country and the living

stone underfoot. And this
is how the evening passes, in fresh
water, in grapes, in the recounting of first
understandings. And in laughter
soft in the mouth, no trace of acid
not even in the pauses between words,
or after.

Wings

In Memoriam: Anne Szumigalski

She who was once unfaltering—her reading voice like butter
with lemon—looks up, drops
a syllable, looks down. She is watching a fly
crawl across the back of her hand; it spirals away
over the people who murmur around her. But it's not the people
who are stirring—they are still and listening
as she turns the page—it is the words that are moving like bees
through the honeycomb. What was she

saying about this poem, written
so long ago? There are honeybees, and the man
who keeps them. He waves a smoking wand, an otherworldly
priest. Funny, she thinks, how insects have always
attracted her, carried her off
on transparent wings, their feet sticky as a thought

that will not let her go. Even young
and ripe and on the verge
of perfect pleasure, she was diverted by a fly
scaling the green and gold leaves of the wallpaper,
Paris, 1938. The fly, she thought, *musca domestica*,
the same on either side of the Channel. A laugh
rises in her, despite the attentions of the Frenchman
so cunningly at work between her legs, his tongue
a wet strawberry. He gave

her two weeks of rainy afternoons in his room
above Rue Belanger. Her first lover, the touch of his
wiry cabinetmaker's hands and the hair on her arms
shivered. Her French was fine, she thought, yet she never
seemed to understand, except when he spoke
with fingertips, with the articulate lines

of his palms. She closes the book. The audience
will not have noticed how she became, for a second,
the bluebottle, circling and indifferent over their inert
human shapes. The bee poem was good.
What was the beekeeper's
name? Those coffee-coloured eyes

look up at her, his chin on her belly, and the fly
on the wallpaper. How strange, she thinks, stepping down
from the stage, to have been dead these sixty years,
killed early in the war. She feels a kick
in the pulse in her wrist, like the small spasm
he made inside her, not at all what she'd expected.
The thick spray cooling on her inner thigh, on the blue sheets.
Outside, the faint hum of Paris, 1938, as she leans back
amid applause.

Lisa Robertson

(b. 1961)

Lisa Robertson was born in Toronto. She worked for several years as a cook and bookseller, studied briefly at Simon Fraser University as a mature student, then embarked on a full-time career as a poet, freelance writer, and translator. She has done numerous short-term academic gigs, held a fellowship at the University of Cambridge, served as Holloway poet-in-residence at UC Berkeley, and taught at the California College of the Arts in San Francisco. Her numerous poetry publications include *XEclogue* (1993, 1999), *Debbie: An Epic* (1997, Governor General's Award finalist), *The Weather* (2001), *The Men: A Lyric Book* (2006), *Lisa Robertson's Magenta Soul Whip* (2009), and *R's Boat* (2010). She lives in rural France, commuting to Paris and London when necessary.

Robertson's poetry is challenging, cerebral, and highly referential, but also richly rewarding in terms of its language and playfulness. Although she claims in *XEclogue* to be "loquacious or raucous, swanning for the fun of it," Robertson confronts the nature/culture, aesthetics/politics dichotomies head-on in her work: "But I'd sooner tear the subtle moss from under poplars / Than he should put a note of love into her golden mouth: / I'll nudge the queer sorrow her barbarity merits." Robertson is not averse to the notion that traditional verse appeals to the emotions and seeks to evoke what it assumes is a knowable world, but she prefers to celebrate the energizing capacity of ideas, making them sing, allowing them to overwhelm her readers to the point where the self and its comforting fictions are displaced.

Sina Queyras, in *Poetry Foundation*, 26 April 2012, calls this process "lyric conceptualism," where intellect does not exactly trump emotion, but where the play of ideas and the imaginative shapes they assume is what charges the poet, and hopefully the reader, aesthetically. In a collection of prose essays called *Nilling* (2012), Robertson describes her reading experience in terms that might also be applied to her writing: "As I read my self-consciousness is not only suspended, but temporarily abolished by the vertigo of another's language. I am simply its conduit, its gutter. This is a pleasure."

Robertson deconstructs traditional forms such as the eclogue and epic, the former with its assumptions about nature, the latter with its male tropes and values. According to *Village Voice*, Robertson "makes intellect seductive; only her poetry could turn swooning into a critical gesture." And the *Boston Review* says, "Robertson writes from within and against the tradition—splitting, seeding, and suturing the cracks in each ideational edifice.

Her occupations with past forms lead not to a backward-looking poetry but forward to a fresh field of inquiry, an imaginatively created utopia."

In a letter me, Robertson confides: "Though I have a straight delivery style, for me there's a sturdy dose of comedy in almost everything I do. Sometimes it's black or bittersweet comedy. I'm not saying that I'm exactly a humourist . . . but there is pastiche, and burlesque, and parody, and pun. I've also noticed that women find it funnier than men do! Generally."

She Has Smoothed Her Pants to No End

This is the light Debbie steps into. Her
toffeed flanks roll with greatness and sustenance
in their sockets and her hearty hands bear
the bruised sea. Mighty amazing beauty
moves her and all the whirling majorettes
are her marvellous squadron: their bare throats
spill analysis.† Dactylic
eastern desks pom-pom
from puddles of yellow
mud. For rhetors bathed
in scent of chrome and split hide her senses
coin dictions:

If Luck's nameless girls love me
I'm happy. My city
minting history
and so on
I Debbie with spurred ankles and purple knee-skin
stand free to forget
species anxiety. What happened to the century?
the ship's planks sing

† Toast!

Whence! giddy swish so skin-like
as a dress
trailing theft
as a spill

Riddled cloaks
this pink text:
for her we could
be female

a lithe keel twins
ears of Catriona, hair
of Kathy, Dan's fine nape, Christine's corded
hips, Susan's sea-scarf
moving with me as philosophes
into felicity and in the midst of elation
the thrones of Erin's vowels
a liberal dose
or I have not hauled this waxen heart
from the gnarled bole of a great tree
nor fleshed it with portents
and new sports
Swimmers! Your sweet strokes beat so fast
I must dare all!
. . . I will do lovely things in taxis
and count myself among the lucky, I will
comb the pale hair of boys with muttering
hands wanting only the satiate fact
of that silk, I will discuss perfidy
with scholars as if spurning kisses, I
will sip the marble marrow of empire.
I want sugar
but I shall never wear shame
and if you call that sophistry
then what is Love

To burnish
would thus shuck
with conundrum's
beak—but

Abstruse and dulcet
tongues
of paint
tease carnal wit

In demotic kiss
well—I digress
(who love
with tripled

Pronouns know
pomposities
in gender

(Debt))
We toast her armies from our beds.

Give me hackneyed words

Give me hackneyed words because
they are good. Brocade me the whole body
of terrestrial air. Say spongy ground
with its soft weeds. Say self because it can.
Say arts of happiness. Say you have died.
Say sequin because the word just
appeared. Say weather take this adult
from its box. Memorize being sequined
to something, water. Everything you forget
inserts love into the silent money.
Memorize huge things of girders greased. Say
the water parting about the particular
animal. Say what happens to the face
as it gala tints my simple cut
vicious this afternoon the beautiful
light on the cash is human to guzzle
with—go away wild feelings, there you go
as the robin as the songsparrow go
the system shines with uninterrupted
light. It's petal caked. Leaves shoot up. Each
leaf's a runnel. Far into the night a
sweetness. Marvelous. Spectacular. Brilliant.
Clouded towards the south. It translates
Lucretius. Say cup of your heart rush
sluice is yellow sluice Kate Moss is Rousseau
have my arms. Say impasto of
atmosphere for her fur. Halo open
her face. Misplace the death. All the truth
under the tree has two pinky oozy
names. Say trying to possess or not. Say
if you thought love was ironical. If
pleasure emancipates, why aren't you some-
where. Sincerity.

My purpose here

My purpose here is to advance into
the sense of the weather, the lesson of
the weather. Forever I'm the age 37
to calm my mind. I'm writing sentences here
of an unborrowed kind. The sky is

mauve lucite. The light lies intact and
folded. You can anticipate the wind.
A slight cloud drifts contrary to the
planet. Everything I'm writing about
begins as the robin as the song
sparrow begins is description
animals are description sparkling
scrapping in loose shrieks teenagers also
utopia is memory the broken
bits running motors leaves remarkably
simple and heart shaped and practical
as leaves the gentlest flavour of them is
description and islands of written
stuff love operas and suicides vast
itineraries of error, memory
grey silk sky with pigeons circling
description because memory can't
love as the orange lights of description
beneath the birds which appear to be strings
of memory in speaking of this small
thing, repeatedly to speak of some small
proximity and in what ways the tough
days pass into languor smoke trees brightgrey
clouds moving in Heaven, streets with
clouds or dripping mist, the mist touching the
golden age of untranslatability, no
distinction: just the fear of isolation
from objects and from the clouds, breathing
arguments I wish to touch as
if the touch were emblem of the scene of novelty.
'Tis not my purpose to retrace the under-
thirst, then the severance. I'll finger
sincerity, by exemplum relate
a portrait of my luck.

Essay on Heaven

Heaven is probably not symmetrical. The thick black sponge lips of the hinged receptacles are the only obscenity. The entry is marked by pageantry, proverbs, slumber and embroidery.

Once a domed heaven with lights and small children dressed as angels was hung with shell-blue ropes from the rafters of the world. Cells, stars and chemicals answered each appetite. Heaven was no different from the daily protests and parties, but it was newer. Heaven knew that there is nothing directly but in form, not an emotion, nothing. Heaven showed us the erotic promise of acts of disproportion.

Now heaven seems to be constructed from famous and flagrant notional wisps and tiny-leafed material scattered through with hard green cherries or some other similarly unyielding fruit. Small pores in our skin let in daylight. Cranes slowly swing into place the massive and gently curved components of the heavenly overpass as we attend to our own commodious works, all the while speaking verse. In heaven we are free to seduce each perception or to pour doubt on it and douse it. In either case affection arises from the form at the same rate that it rises from our affluent nerves.

In regards to heaven we must also mention the dinners, travels and flowers, the studies of the flowerlike, how perfectly clear the far horizon, slow jet above the little clumps of trees in this green and that green stabbed through by the grey points of roofs. Or there is a lower flat plane in paler grey suggesting the lid of an institution. Bright plastic buckets and jumbles of bicycle wheels striped by the delicately railed metal balconies of the stucco apartment block. Foreground: bamboo fronds nearly strumming the dense lineage of service wires. Still our needs travel along these archaically twisted and ropy black lines, a skein of them loosely sewing each of our dwellings to the tall masts and thicker wires, none of them audibly humming anymore.

Let us be clear: We certainly never founded anything. Later, when it is no longer possible to remain in heaven, we will be passing over the massy shapes of the factories beside the yellow river, the shacks on the roofs of the factories, the lean-tos flanking them, the loading bays and stilted awnings all corrugated warming to rust near the rivets.

Louise Bernice Halfe

(b. 1953)

Louise Bernice Halfe, whose Cree name is Sky Dancer, was born in Two Hills, Alberta, raised on the Saddle Lake Reserve, and sent by government decree at age seven to the Blue Quills Residential School in St Paul, Alberta. She chose to complete her schooling at St Paul regional high school, then went on to earn a Bachelor of Social Work degree from the University of Regina, as well as addiction counselling certificates from the Nechi Institute. Eventually, material from the journals she kept found its way into *Writing the Circle: Native Women Writers of Canada*. In 1993, she received the third-prize award in the League of Canadian Poets national poetry contest. Her books include *Bear Bones & Feathers* (1994, Milton Acorn People's Poet Prize); *Blue Marrow* (1998, finalist for both the Pat Lowther Award and the Governor General's Award), a multi-voiced long poem about aunts and grandmothers, in which the painful history of Aboriginal/non-Aboriginal relations is vividly recalled and imagined; and *The Crooked Good* (2007). Halfe, who lives in Saskatoon, was named Saskatchewan's Poet Laureate for 2005–6 and received an Honorary Doctor of Letters from Wilfrid Laurier University.

In "Comfortable in My Bones," Halfe describes her early impulses to write as a natural response to nature and to her mental landscapes:

> In the Northern woods of Saskatchewan lies a creek; in the summer, it's a slender, lazy snail. When the spring rains come, it becomes a writhing snake creating turbulent waves, carrying everything before it. I walked the woods, following the creek, cradling paper leaves and talking stick, tobacco and sweetgrass in my hands. On many occasions, I flew over logs in front of me eager to gain my solitude, eager to unload the discoveries I held close to my heart. My favourite spot overlooked the banks where I leaned against an old log I shared with ants. There, I contemplated something I had read, something I heard on CBC, something I dreamt, a conversation I had with my children or my husband. Sometimes, these discoveries were not pretty. . . . Whatever travelled into my thoughts, I immediately wrote, no matter how absurd or obscure. At times, I did nothing but breathe, listen and sleep, comfortable in my bones.

> The landscape of the earth and my mind were both simple and complex. I bore feelings that needed song. I often suffered the rash of shame bursting through the thin layers of skin. Yet my spirit demanded the spring of clear blood. I saw no need to run. The land, the Spirit doesn't betray you. I was learning to cry with the Spirit. I was safe to tear, to lick, to strip the stories from my bones and to offer them to the Universe.

With the encouragement of elders and fellow writers, Halfe became more and more committed to her task of recording both worlds:

> The map of oral storytelling had long been laid out for me. I often entertained my children with legends I grew up with or made up on my own through the images in classical music. Writing was a natural process. The stories inside me demanded face. They became my medicine, creating themselves in the form of poetry. These egg-bones were the voice which I had been addressing. My bare feet had felt the drum of the earth and the heartbeat of my palms. I did not fight these stories, though many times I wanted to run. I became a wolf, sniffing and searching, pawing, muzzling, examining every visible track I made or saw. I became the predator on the scent. I was the master, the slave, beholder and beheld, the voice and the song.

The oral tradition which informs much of Halfe's work takes many forms, at times striving for simplicity, at other times richly symbolic. So there will be poems not only about the functions of the body, but also about the yearnings and questing of the human spirit, poems that, while using the language of the colonizers, resist that culture's conventions. The poems of *Bear Bones & Feathers*, with their deliberate use of Cree words (and a glossary), are largely anecdotal, telling short stories or highlighting significant moments of perception. *Blue Marrow*, a long poem or epic, embodies tribal history, lifts private memory to the level of collective song. Rejoicing in "these crumbs of memory," the speaker of *Blue Marrow* appeals to her sources: "Grandmothers hold me. I must pass all that I possess, / every morsel to my children. These small gifts / to see them through life. Raise my fist. Tell the story. / Tear down barbed-wire fences."

Wagon Ride

I lean on the wagon boards
and squint over the horse's head.
Blankets of firefly snow sparkle.

Horse's nostrils
bellow clouds and form
halos around their bending heads.

Their broad bodies move
slowly through unbroken trail.

Swishing tails
they fart
as fresh horse manure
fills the air.

I look back and view
the glazing broken path
as fresh snow covers
tracks.

I peer at the skies,
stick out my tongue
catch tiny diamonds,
cross my eyes to look at
the snowflakes before they
melt on the tip of my nose.

I peep at papa.
He's dressed in his trapping beaver mitts
and fraying hudson's bay coat.
A winchester stands by his side.
His head is tilted. He's listening to
the crackling trees.
Tiny antler icicles hang from his eyelids
and underneath his nose.
His cheeks are apple red.
Still
he puffs on his hand-rolled du maurier.

Today there is no smashing fist
and kicking working boots,
no thunder of an outraged bull,
no snarling of a rabid cat.

Just me and papa
cold bound by the mute,
freezing wind.

Body Politics

Mama said,

Real woman
don't steal
from the sky and wear clouds
on their eyelids.

Real woman
eat rabbit well-done
not left half-raw
on their mouth.

Real woman
have lots of meat
on their bones.
They're not starving,
hobbled horses
with bony, grinding hips.

Real woman caress
with featherstone hands
not with falcon fingernails
that have never worked.

When she was finished talking
she clicked her teeth
lifted her arse
and farted
at the passing
city women.

Lizard's Curse

She came in the form of a slippery lizard
with a feather in her mouth.

She wrapped her shiny flesh
over my woman's hills and crawled my crevice.

My eyes puffed and swelled
hailstones on my face.

My head ached
heavy with rocks.

I sought the healing
mountain
and the ocean's salt.

The soft pounding
of a beating drum
and a woman's chanting song.

The sweet scent of cedar
drifted in the wind

pulling, pulling
the power of the lizard.

The skin stretched,
and my wintering flesh
hung loose against my bones.

This lizard's claws and tattered feather
left its trail of scratches in my womb.

Bled dry of tears
the ocean's coolness
flushed my wound.

The mountain cedar released healing sap
its sacred smoke smudged my temples.
The throb of darkness slipped

with the last shedding of the lizard's curse
and the woman's chant.

Hamilton's Graveyard

A seed was planted in the North Bay rain, cries, sweet cries
of night birds nesting in sheets of damp leaves.

The seed grew and swelled in the buried bodies of
my guts.

I wanted refund for my ten dollar IUD. Slanted
my eyes at the touch of the physician's hand. Swore
at the man whose pleasure I carried.

At home I thought of my mother's bitter root that would shred
my growing womb. I heard the voice of the sweetgrass braids.
I thought of another baby twisted like a knotted tree, her head
an empty bowl. My hand rested on my swollen belly.

It started with liver sliding into the toilet. Later IV
vodka to still the belt around my waist. Then an incision
traced the equator across my skin and delivered
her into my frozen arms.

She died with a head of wet dark hair shining in the butter
dish. The rain fell down my drying breasts.

So Sorry

the pope said i'm sorry
i sent a useless sack of scalped
potatoes.

he said indian agents would
give daddy a roll of twine,
a box of shells and whisky.
the spirits crawled inside
my daddy and never left.

he sent blankets
and my babies died.
he sent wooden sticks
with a dead man to hang
around my neck.

he said if i prayed
to you, geezus,
ate your body, drank
your blood,
threw out my bannock,
lived on my knees
counting stones,

i'd never be without
my family.

Manyberries

I followed the deer,
gave her fleshly oranges, apple cores.
She licked her fingers clean,
placed her wet nose on my Beloved.

We are coming. Coming.

She lifted Beloved over logs, avoided swamps,
murky waters where snakes waited.

The deer arrived again, looked at me.
I carried Beloved, kissed the deer.
My knees buckled, deer's ears alert.
I lifted my pipe,
she kissed it tenderly. Repeatedly.
She smelled of sweet apples, orange juice.
Sat on her haunches, lifted her forearms,
hoofs cradled the pipe. *ospwâkan*[1]
opened its eyes, lifted us into its lair.
The stone lit up and we entered a steep hill,
travelled through thorn trees, a bare windy path.
We moved into the swell, met our *wâhkômâkanak*.[2]
One carried a cup and sang, voice musky,

The forked tongue of a river can never be separated. It shall always run deep,

and poured rain.
Another relative decorated herself in starfish,
another was covered in pine pitch, wounds bandaged.
The moon exposed her many faces.
I was given a map, covered in Braille.
Leeches muscled out of aquariums,
Loch Ness toward the lakes.
A skunk waddled, sprayed us with medicine.
Mud-stained faces carried stick bundles,
built an island that drowned them.

---

1 *ospwâkan:* pipe

2 *wâhkômâkanak:* relatives, bent kin, as in ancestors

Earth commanded Beloved to

Kiss me, kiss me. I ain't too vain to take these dentures out.

Rubbed against him

She doesn't have you, doesn't have you. I have you.

she sang, threw her arms around Beloved.
I stretched, full length
against his sinew. Earth sang,

We must chant our last song before the wind dies.

united all our breathing, covered us in
her quilted star blanket.
We wed again and again.

Sina Queyras

(b. 1963)

Sina Queyras was born in Manitoba and studied at the University of British Columbia and Concordia University. While living in New York she co-curated a reading series and edited *Open Field: 30 Contemporary Canadian Poets* (2005). Her books of poetry include *Slip* (2001), *Teethmarks* (2004), *Lemon Hound* (2006, Pat Lowther Award, Lambda Award), and *Expressway* (2009, Governor General's Award finalist), and she has also written a book of essays, *Unleashed* (2010). She won the National Magazine Gold Award for poetry and the Friends of Literature Prize from *Poetry* magazine. She served as the Markin-Flanagan writer-in-residence at the University of Calgary and taught creative writing at Rutgers, Haverford, and Concordia. She currently resides in Montreal.

Queyras's professed influences include Virginia Woolf, Gertrude Stein, and Lisa Robertson. From Woolf, she has inherited an interest in stream-of-consciousness narration; from Stein, short, disjunctive sentences that eschew logic and causality in favour of dislocating juxtapositions, hypnotic repetitions, and non-sequiturs; and from Robertson, the conviction that "it is too late to be simple." Poet and critic Sonnet L'Abbé (*Globe & Mail*, 3 Aug. 2006), in a review of *Lemon Hound*, describes Queyras as a master of the short sentence, who

> builds poems by layering images one atop the other, by echoing and repeating phrases where sound and image settle like sediment into dense blocks of text. The reader is led through nuances of mood: Some journeys are spirals that return you, somehow changed, to where you began; some are incremental, where one lives a thousand small details inside a brief moment. The overall effect is tonal and painterly. . . . Like Woolf in her poetic novel *The Waves*, Queyras is not after story, or an argument, or a static statement on womanhood or personhood. Whether in sketches of girls and mothers or in imaginings of Woolf's childhood, Queyras writes to share a profound sense of witnessing. Her problem is purely poetic: to represent in language the embodied depth of the modern moment, to capture the simultaneity of many truths and sensations happening at once, and to do this using the gestures and commonplaces of real life. She takes a hypnotic, almost hallucinatory approach, and succeeds.

L'Abbé also commends Queyras's willingness to take chances in *Expressway*, to push the envelope of form, engaging in "fractured syntax, the driving repetitions, the intellectual and imaginative leaps."

from A river by the moment

Even the idea of river

The river flows through the town. The river flows through the town and breaks up at the bridge. The river flows through the town slowly. The river is the fastest thing in town. The river is not confined to town. The river is townless, yet the river is town, for without the river there is no town. Without the river there are no riverbanks. Without the river there is no mill. Without the river there are no bridges. Without the river roads go on. Without the river foundations crack. Without the river fishermen turn to drink. Without the river old women cannot cry. Without the river no one is married. Without the river fossils soar. Without the river emerald and sage. Without the river lyrics are homeless. Without the river June never comes. Without the river mirrorless, the sky mourns. Without the river deer go deaf. Without the river leaves thirst. Without the river bear lose their teeth. Without the river beak, paw, soil, feather. Without the river the mountains shy. Without the river the ducks pass in the air, days climb one on another. Without the river children cannot learn how to count. Without the river there are no wings. Without the river nothing passes. Without the river stillness. Without the river trees turn away. Without the river the sun is angry. Without the river the land is seamless. Without the river it breaks apart. Without the river fish walk. Without the river rocks scurry. Without the river the town pulls up its skirt. Without the river bear and cougar nod into the earth's elbow, sleep.

With or without rivets

She can name a thousand corporate logos. Her hands and feet are not easily disassembled. She knows fear. She understands Internet wallpaper, Happy Meals and smart bombs. She doesn't worry about cyborg subjectivity. She is a fully unlicenced florist. She is a hothouse. She has seen a thousand Gertrude Steins each more diluted. She plants seeds where she lingers. She is ontological. She is not simian. She is not leaf. She is not green. She no longer smells of the forest. She knows Jeanne d'Arc is dead. She knows the names of trees. She cares nothing for virginal. She worries about water. She stokes rage. She is more engine than mother. She has touched bullet holes. She has no walls. She drinks seaweed. She thinks uranium and glasses shatter. She fears corporate convicts. She remembers Janis. She has not yet sinned enough. She loves that her hands and feet are not easily disassembled. She is free to sniff out and string up. She understands facial reconstructions. She considers surgery. She has Emma's night vision. She is not without dog. She is scented. She is tie-dyed. She dreams of wings and glass shatters. She is historical and senseless. She is not without God. She is sensual. She has seeds under her tongue. She hopes for corporate convictions. She is no longer leaf. She is ontological jelly. She hears Sappho. She files her index finger. She has morphed. She feels the town pinching her shoulder blades. She cannot say that if she were the river she would allow the town to hug her. She feels for the sky. She holds the goddess by the toenails. She cannot swallow. She does not know. She has licked nothing. She has earned much. She ponders Emily.

from On the Scent

"It is too late to be simple."
—Lisa Robertson

1

Here she is inside. Walls and windows. Appendages and openings. Here she is sitting on a stack of books. Here she is digging out from under an avalanche of paper. Here she is swatting words with her coattails. Here she is wondering what to do with outdated memory. Here she is boxing and unboxing. Here she is moving stuff. Here she is deleting whole files, randomly. Here she is perplexed at the mounds of paper. Here, I tell you, here she is hiding under the Xerox machine. Here she is communing with resonators. Here she is clucking the MRI tune. Here she is earplugged and eyeshadowed. Here she is tall and long in the stride, here she is a force of circulation. Here she is sideways in a windstorm. Here she is teal and persimmon. Here she is Italian plum. Here she is the palest interior of the pomegranate. Here she is. Here she is in Banana Republic. Here she is black and black. Here she is thinking of the colour blue. Here she is trying to see underwater. Here she is reading on the train to New York. Here she is wiping coffee from the seat. Here she is sitting next to seven young rappers, pants like circus tents, du-rags and ball caps piled on high. Here she is. Here she is in an office in Philadelphia thinking of the letter R. Where would we be without R, she asks? Where would we be without E? Where would we be without arms? Here she is with meringue and milquetoast. Here she is hiding behind a maple tree in October, the weather having changed too quickly and she without a sweater. Here she is walking down Bleecker thinking, how? How? How can she describe the windmill of her aorta? How tibia is her confusion? How like the Microsoft song her frustration flits and crescendos. How like the blue of the XP screen her mood flickers in the traffic-jam hour. How archaic the need to open a window and breathe.

from Divining Rod, or How to Find a Neural Pathway Hospital Exit: Emergency Lane: HOV

2

Pulling herself out of a slump at the word *metastasized*
(Liver like a torn lace tablecloth barely functioning), now
Men with orange hats and spades along the veins, resting.

Hospice, radiation, she spins the wheel, *No,*
Not this time. Randomize these options, offer up
Another route, surely there must be (detour?)

Something other than pain? I want to go home,
She says, but not this way, not these roads,
Not this buzz: *black milk of daybreak, I sing,*

All along the expressway, its terminal
Ambulances, those men sanding away the day-old
Growth, those men in combat boots, waving flags,

Saluting, directing traffic, rolling out the macadam
The way the body holds the road, the body with its
Neural pathways and depression like a layer

Of egg whites tightening the skin. Those men
With their backs against the road, with their backs
Against the sun, all day unravelling tar, hot

And swilling sweat in their strap boots, skin
Of roads and trucks with them, in them, heavy
Loads, the concrete cracking. *No to radiation*, she

Says, dreaming her hands at ten and two, heading
Down or away, the expressway transporting her out,
Out of the city and into valley beyond:

Men with spades digging. No one said ginger
Was a fruit, belonged here, ate several heart-
Shaped boxes of candy. Nothing to do with

Expressways, but she leaves it in for the sweeper,
Always a little something for the sweeper.

Proverbs of Hell

The body sublime, the heart SUV.
Fuel your plow with the blood of war.
Drive your car on the bones of the dead.
The road of CO_2s leads to rising seas.
He who is preoccupied with the afterlife pisses on the present.
So the price of oil goes, so goes the number of wars.
A fool sees product; a wise man sees shade.
He who sullies the earth sullies himself; he who dulls the sun dulls his senses.
The future is the reversal of destruction.
Even a bee's too busy.
Profits are measured by the dollar, but real profit cannot be measured.
A wholesome food comes in fewer than sixteen pieces from seven states.

Prisons are built with the bricks of luxury items.

Let man wear the fell of the hemp seed, woman the fleece of cotton.
The bird a thought, the spider a path, the mind the means.

What was once proved and known is now only rarely imagined.
What was once used to imagine now operates software.
The rat, the mouse, the starling, the squirrel; the lion, the tyger, the
elephant, the whale—only the useless, or rootless, survive, otherwise:
extinction porn.

The cistern pollutes; the fountain overflows, is of no use to itself.
Once thought filled immensity; now it purchases goods.
To speak your mind is to be unpatriotic; to be human, then, is to be unpatriotic.
All things imagined must be images of truth; all things created must be fragments of our imagination.
The eagle never wreaked so much havoc as when he submitted to whims of profit.
The eagle provides for himself, but the air provides for the eagle.
Want in the morning. Buy at noon. Buy in the evening. Buy in your sleep.
He who has suffered you to impose on him knows the market.
As the plow follows markets, so the market follows itself.
The tygers of the market are no wilier than the corporate dogs.
Expect poison from the standing mind.
The coals of Wall Street, the bricks of despair, the last drop, the last grain.
As the cat chooses the warmest place to curl her bones so the wise man seeks home.
To create a new kind of flower is the splice of genes.
The best wine is the oldest, the best thought is the first.
Cheerfulness is the hammer of the right.

The expressway is a straight line, but the crooked road remains the road of genius.

Where man is, nature is bereft.
Where nature is not man, is not known.
Where nature is not natural, man is not man.
As a dog returns to his vomit, so a citizen to his belief in separation.
More is destruction.
Less is the wisdom of the future.
Abundance is all context.
The end of thought is the end of man is the end of earth.
In absentia, in absence, in obsolesce, or obnoxious.
Where nature is, man is not enough.
Enough, or too much. Too much.

Go forth and undo harm.

Go forth and do.

Carmine Starnino

(b. 1970)

Carmine Starnino was born in Montreal. He studied at Dawson College, where he benefited from the tutelage and poetic example of Michael Harris, and at Concordia University. His poetry collections include *The New World* (1997), *Credo* (2000), *With English Subtitles* (2004), and *This Way Out* (2009). In addition to authoring *A Lover's Quarrel* (2004), a collection of spirited essays on Canadian poetry, and editing *The New Canon: An Anthology of Canadian Poetry* (2005), he is poetry editor for Signal Editions at Véhicule Press and senior editor for *Reader's Digest Canada*. His work has been enthusiastically received, winning the Irving Layton Prize at Concordia, the Canadian Author's Association Prize, the F.G. Bressani Prize, and the A.M. Klein Award. *This Way Out* was shortlisted for the Governor General's Award.

In an interview conducted by Dani Couture, which appeared online in *Northern Poetry Review*, Starnino insists on the fusion of form and content in poetry:

> If anything I've written has given pleasure I'd like to think it was a pleasure that took readers by surprise . . . I always try, one way or another, to provide a fresh entry into things; to offer something readers don't already have, or can't find elsewhere. Providing this sort of delight (or trying to, at least) seems to me incontestably important, or why else would readers, with all the other things fighting for their attention, take the time to read a poem? I'm always reminded of e.e. cummings' remark that his poetry was in competition with "roses and locomotives (not to mention acrobats Spring electricity Coney Island the 4th of July the eyes of mice and Niagara Falls)."
>
> Auden is, of course, right to suggest that form in poetry can be enjoyed partly for the curiosity of the form itself (the sonnet as a sonnet can be an occasion of relish). But bacchics and choriambs are worthless unless they're intrinsic to the perception that sought them out: unless they're necessary for creating a specific kind of meaning, a meaning that those forms—and only those forms—can transform into something recognizable and strange. Somewhere in that realm of recognition and strangeness is, I'd argue, where our best poems exist. But these poems aren't the sort that a reader

> can "look out" for because you never know what shape they'll take ("Ecstasy affords the occasion," quipped Marianne Moore, "and expediency determines the form.") I believe in providing certain core satisfactions for the reader: a locus of linguistic energy, a life-line between subject matter and language.

A provocative piece from Starnino's book of essays *Lazy Bastardism* (2012) is available online: www.poetryfoundation.org/poetrymagazine/article/238414.

Lullaby

My mother is standing
with her back to me, and all I can see
of Anthony is his large head balanced upon
her bare shoulder, one arm
folded neatly beneath

his chin, and the other,
with its blunt fist, raised as it rests
against the base of her throat. The lullaby she is singing
is something I remember
from my own childhood,

when she would sit
on the edge of my bed, her hand
motionless upon my chest, humming. Closing my eyes, then,
I tried to follow her as she slipped in
and out of a dozen tunes,

often running back over
the same stretch of melody, again
and again, as if searching for the right song,
the right spell, that would put me to sleep.
And I listened so intently

that I was unaware
of the drowsiness settling over me
like a dark weight, my breathing growing heavy and slow.
But tonight I watch the nape
of her neck crease

as she brings the song
closer to his ear, her breath warming

his soft temple, her arms anchoring the small, limp body
which has already begun drifting
from itself, moving

outward, beyond
the slow, measured pull
of her voice. Until all that remains is the sleep
that fills his head like warm water,
and gently washes against its
delicate shell of bone.

After Caravaggio's "The Crucifixion of Saint Peter"

The executioners, it's true, look a little oafish—
but surely, deep down, they're trustworthy men.
Reliable, hardworking fellows, maybe hired
for the day, who don't see themselves so much

as crucifying an old man, but as earning
an honest wage. At this point in the execution
they've just finished hammering, and are now
turning Peter upside-down. (Peter, it's said,

requested this, so as not to mimic Jesus's death).
The first man, facing away, strains at the rope he is
pulling across his back. The second squats
underneath, tired shoulder against the wood,

and pushes up. The third stands between them,
steadying the cross as they slowly flip it over
Peter, however, seems somewhat confused.
Where's the daub of sunlight striking his face

from some invisible rift in the clouds, the woozy
peacefulness being poured into his body
by God? He tries to lift his hand in blessing, a spike
holds his palm down. The sky is darkening,

and as Peter hangs there—the pain muscling itself
into his arms and legs—the executioners
work as fast as they can (after all, it's getting late
and there are still so many others to attend to).

What My Mother's Hands Smell Like

Right now it's obviously garlic. She's chopping
a little of it for tonight's *pasta con alice*, my father's
favourite dish. The sauce calls for three cloves
and three fillets of anchovies, mashed with a fork,
all brought together to fry in some oil for about
two minutes. But after dinner—after she's scoured
the mucked pan and scrubbed the smeared plates,
after she's flushed the glasses free of wine-stains
and wiped the grease speckling the top of the oven—
take her hands, ruddy with the scalded burnish
of hot water, bring them to your face, breathe deeply,
and somewhere, worked into her red knuckles,
is the cool stowed in a pile of sheets just off the line,
is the scent of one's soul in a dry dwelling-place.

Song of the House Husband

Cherish it most when it steams—
"steam," though, fails to praise
its seethe of vapour, or, propped
upright, the suspirating hush as it catches
its breath. Flanks like the shins
of a ship or open halves of a mussel,
and, on its brow, the spirit-level's
impressionable bubble. Fructifying flatness,
it takes my trouser's frown, gives
back pleats. Takes my tired, tucked-in shirt,
makes it newly dapper. And really,
nothing's like the hiss of its hull
kissing a dampened dent (releasing
that rich, road-side scent of rain
on dust). Hope for the linens freckled
with folds. Hope for the crimped,
the crumpled, the crinkled, the crushed.
Hope for the rippled, the ruffled,
the rumpled, the rucked. O coffer
of creaselessness! I do not know
how to cut a straight furrow. I do not know
how to drive a batch of nails. But
grip your handle as I would a spade,
your heft the heft of a hammer.

Pugnax Gives Notice

He's done with it, the tridents and tigers,
the manager's greed, the sumptuous beds
of noble women who please their own moods.
He's done with dogging it for the crowds,
the stabbing, the slashing, the strangling,
the poor pay, the chintzy palm branch prizes.
Make no mistake. Pugnax is a real fierceosaurus.
Winner of 26 matches, a forum favourite.
Yet his yob genes have, it seems, gone quiet.
Fatigue has called his soul back to his body.
Circles under his eyes; he sleeps badly.
Late-night cigs lit from the dog-end of the last,
cutwork of the clock nibbling him small.
In the barracks around him his friends snore,
lucky returnees of the last hard hacking,
dead to the world, free of a weapon in the fist.
Priscus face-down in the crook of his arm.
Triumphus flung open, caught on a bad turn.
Verus collapsed, whacked, against the cot.
Flamma, doomed by down-thumbing shadows,
lies in a stain of his final shape and size.
Pugnax loves them all, chasers and net-fighters,
fish-men and javelin-throwers, carefree
despite punishing practices, screaming orders,
despite limbs trained to turn lethal for mobs
unable to bear the thought of two men
clinging to life, but here it's only the thock
of wooden sword against wooden sword,
the racket as they fall on each other's shields
in joy. Pugnax's heart breaks for them.
Understand, he has inflicted pain and felt pain,
but now wants to go native, move into a flat,
experiment with fashionable clothes,
dawdle at the baths, tame his nights with tea,
be spellbound by the smell of soap, find a wife.
Our boy dreams of joining the crowd,
shouting himself hoarse as some bonehead
gets knocked down and the blade pushed
through his chest, stapling him to the ground.
At intermission, he'll watch as the blood
is raked over with sand, thinking chore thoughts:
yard work, paint jobs, weekend projects.

Ken Babstock

(b. 1970)

Ken Babstock was born in Burin, Newfoundland, but raised mostly in Pembroke, Ontario. His father was a United Church minister; his mother, a nurse who enrolled in graduate studies, making literature an important element in her son's growing up. Babstock dropped out of Concordia University, travelling to BC and Ireland, working at odd jobs to support the angry young man's poems that would emerge in his first book, *Mean* (1999). *Days into Flatspin* followed in 2001, creating a stir amongst both traditional and experimental poets, for its energy and willingness to push formal experiment, which seems to involve deconstructing the lyric.

Babstock is intent on making sound a central element in his poetry. As he says in an interview for the *National Post* (22 April 2011), "It's about reading the poem as a poem. . . . I'm one of those people that has sort of invested everything in sound, except that meaning won't leave me alone." It's the issue of meaning that seems to trouble some of his readers.

On the subject of poetic fragmentation, Babstock says: "I wanted to be honest about how little I understood. It's a portrayal of a mind failing a lot of the time. I wasn't trying to be deliberately obfuscating, or to throw a veil over things" (interview conducted by E. Martin Nolan, *Puritan* No. 13). Expanding on this matter, he says:

> There is a kind of impossibility in casually making connections. Whatever cutting-edge physics is telling us right now, what biogenetics is telling us, or chemistry, what political theory is telling us, it's incredibly difficult to keep abreast of, even for the specialists in the field. So there is a blasting apart of information that makes it close to impossible to get a handle on the reality of the world we walk around in every day . . . fragmentation and the confusion are inherent to social reality right now. So I hope the poems are allowing for that, but at the same time insisting . . . that connections can be made, that interactions can be made . . . an insistence on some semblance of order against a backdrop of chaos.

Babstock's work can be personal and universal, introspective and comic, cerebral and emotional, serious and outrageous. His wiring is unique, with a button in his brain that triggers wordplay, puns, rapid-fire verbal associations, and imaginative leaps that try to defy, or at least delay, logic. The best of those leaps recall Brecht's use of alienation techniques, devices to pull the plank out from under us, to make us think rather than take refuge in familiar emotions such as nostalgia and empathy.

Essentialist

Snug underground in the civic worm burrowing
west, I was headed to class when a cadet
in full combat dress got on my train.

But for a pompom sprucing up the beret,
his age, the fact he was alone, and here,
this boy could've been boarding amphibious

landing craft. I checked for guns, grew pious
of this spinning orb's hotter spots. He
was all camo, enactment-of-shrubbery, semblance

of flora in varying shades, hues, mottlements
of green. A helmet dangled on his back, a hillock
in spring, sprouting a version of verdant grasses

in plastic. I got past enjoying a civilian's recoil
from things military, brutal, conformist, and took
a peek at what my soldier was so engrossed in—

Thoreau's *Walden*—imagine him, rubbing oil
into a Sten gun's springed bolts, working through
his chances at a life away from men: berries

plumping in among their thorns, night's
curtain drawn across the window of the lake . . .
We must reconcile the contradictions as we

can, but their discord and their concord
introduce wild absurdities into our thinking
and speech. No sentence will hold the whole

truth, and the only way in which we can be just
is by giving ourselves the lie; speech is better
than silence; silence is better than speech;—

All things are in contact; every atom has
a sphere of repulsion;—Things are, and are
not, at the same time;—and the like. There are other

minds. Surfacing at St George, I cupped my hands
and blew—bodies scattering among museums,
bank towers, campus rooms, and shops, each

to where they're thinking of or not, seemed
to prove a law we're locked into, demonstrable
with iron filings, magnets, and clean tabletop.

I can watch their faces go away. The singing's not
to record experience, but to build one viable
armature of feeling sustainable over time.

The stadium's lit, empty, and hash-marked
for measuring the forward push. On the surface
of the earth are us, who look in error, and only seem.

Explanatory Gap

Would Form, Colour, and Motion please report to Area 17
where you'll be met by Memory and Recognition. An unbroken
field of light is uninformative. The cracks,

the jinks, what won't cohere or blend but bends, fissures,
falls to the field
or becomes figure. A visual percept is degraded light.
We all like to sound important. I was convinced I'd actually loved

by a hot tinny pain spreading downward from the sternum. She
was gone, though,
by the time the evidence appeared, and I'd moll around the train ditch
of an evening, reading German dictionaries and pulling
loosened spikes

from the tie braces, designing industrial versions of croquet.
Home shot:
through the St Louis Arch to the CN tower. Oil derricks and
wrecking balls.

I had no friends for a time. Whether

it happened or didn't it felt as it did and affected the weather. I
was being fleeced, still I paid
for entertainment. It helped me feel worse, and worse was where

lovely numb wet its tongue. I sucked it like a strip of dripping lamb—

As Marginalia in John Clare's *The Rural Muse*

I wasn't finished. From as far back
as I can recall having heard a voice in my skull

I've wanted to die, or change, or die
changing. Hexagonal window, the moon

penned in it, and a segmented swarm sucking
up peonies. Heat off tar shingles

in June as the blood in one arm
blackened, thickened, went blearily toxic,

I exited earth up an IV tube.
The wall-mounted paper dispenser

narrating nightmares of scale, sores fell
from fingers—get well petals—and grew

back puce. Slug of little light, the bedrail
gleamed. Warmed yoghurt, a summons

button and visual aphasia. Now I've no spit,
no hospice and admit nothing, or

for long stretches, only that what happened
was all that ever could have happened.

Reeds curtain where land abuts lake,
if such limit exists, if ducks aren't taken

by pike mid-thought.

Carolinian (Crosscut with Sound)

Colander, canopy, colander. Contrivance
of green light-spots we're leoparded by.
Wild grape ampersand.

Joining land with how we see the land, walk softly
over the mudded impress shod horses
made earlier—

their dung looks fungal, very "forest floor."
Mid-trunk, one or more twig buds
whose cells continue to multiply

but never differentiate.
Atop a paper-bag groundcover,
tympany of deer deciding gone's best,

"patter of Delia's feet."
Burl Ives puns follow hard on the heels
of calling Kentucky blue timothy, and timothy

red fescue, and fescue not Kentucky
blue, not panic grass, but some kind of wheat.
None of it native and the six of us six

pages of *Murphy* or *Watt*.
Trail attendants made cordwood of the blowdown.
If we had growths that big we'd be televisually

famous. It's here the trail splits, loops back,
past the Z of a fawn's foreleg
portending not much from the black mulch,

to where squat cars are themselves slubs
on the bolt of horseradish field trimmed with purple phlox.
They'd shave or slice those monstrous,

boxed-ear excrescences to make Vermeer . . .
I mean, "veneer." I was back on the light.
Decorative veneer. It's so not quiet in here.

Karen Solie

(b. 1966)

Karen Solie was born in Moose Jaw, Saskatchewan, and grew up on the family farm. She worked at a variety of jobs, including espresso jerk, farm hand, reporter/photographer, research assistant, and English teacher. Her poems and stories have appeared in numerous magazines and anthologies, including *Breathing Fire* and *Introductions: Poets Present Poets*. Solie's poetry books include *Short Haul Engine* (2001, Dorothy Livesay Poetry Prize, Griffin Prize shortlist), *Modern and Normal* (2005), and *Pigeon,* (2010, Griffin Prize). She has taught at the University of Victoria, and for the Optional Residency MFA program at the University of British Columbia.

The Griffin Prize jury had this to say of "An Acolyte Reads *The Cloud of Unknowing*":

> It's this particular affliction of desire—and the corrosive effects of human desire both upon ourselves and the world we inhabit—that Solie most often meditates upon in poems as humorous, often, as they are sobering. "Gone are the bad old good old days. Before us, / vast unfenced acres of decline," she says in "Prayers for the Sick." Solie forces us to look squarely at that decline, the landscapes we've ruined, the vistas we've cluttered, in service to a longing that, as she puts it, "hovers like billboards / over the expressway." The vision here is powerful, philosophical, intelligent, especially adept at pulling great wisdom from the ordinary—as when a tractor is found to manifest "fate, forged / like a pearl around the grit of centuries." It may be, as Solie suggests, that "the honourable life / is like timing. One might not have the talent for it." Among the greatest of Solie's talents, evident throughout the poems of *Pigeon*, is an ability to see at once into and through our daily struggle, often thwarted by our very selves, toward something like an honourable life.

Real Life

A woman, walking in her city,
sees something beautiful.
It may not be the preludes and fugues

of harbourfront or breakwater, nor
that great blue heron who rests
year after year in the big cedar
bordering a popular park. Sometimes,
small things give themselves up to us,
or we to them: a delicate lettuce
of spearmint moss on a bus stop bench,
a length of pipe rusted in baroque filigree.
Whatever it is, seeing it, the woman
thinks that if ever there were a time
to fall on her knees, this is it;
but doesn't, seeing that it's mid-morning
and the street full of bachelors.

Determinism

Someone's walking toward you, tree to tree, parting leaves
with the barrel of a rifle. There's a scope
on it. He's been watching awhile
through his good eye, you, washing dishes, scouring
what's burned with a handful of salt, so your shoulders shake
a little. Keep your back to him. It's sexier
under the bulb, light degraded,
like powder. The kitchen screens
are torn. You've worn something
nice. There's a breeze he's pressing through, boots
in the grass. There's a breeze and you smell him
blowing in on it. As if this has always
been happening and you've entered the coincidence of your life
with itself, the way a clock's ticks will hit the beat of a Hank Williams song,
the best one, on the radio, fridge hum tuned without a quaver
to the sustained notes of the bridge. As if
you've arrived at where the hinge
articulates. An animal
may be bleeding in the woods. He could be carrying a pair of grouse
by the feet. Only details are left, bruises of gesture, style's aspirin
grit. He shuts the door and leans the gun against the wall
like a guitar. You keep your back to him because
it's sexier. Because in turning
you will see the dinner in all its potential
as you speak, spring the catch, finish this, the weighted moment
buckling into consequence. The place
where you can face your history and see it coming.

Pest Song

Your habits drew me. I could tell by the way
you leave the milk out at night, bread box open
and grains untied, that you are passionate
and I was smitten, lived with you for months

before you knew I was alive, learned the wiring
of your moods, drinking from your cups
and tasting leaves of every book you've read, sly
and devoted as a friend. Forgetting the wisdom

of my kind, I cried out one night when you walked
through the door, and the set of your mouth
was a new kind of poison. You say
there can never be just one. It's understood.

But be assured, you don't know everything. I am
alone. When you bring others to our home
I make a scene. If they really loved you, they
would stay. I rest on your pillow, lick your soap,

embrace your toothbrush while you're gone. Now,
you're setting traps, eyes mean as bleach,
but I can't believe you really want to do me harm.
You'd miss me and not know why, my voice,

the grace notes of my feet. So I keep my hunger
wrapped up tight, watch my step, come out late
to stare at you from some dark place, and wait
until you're fast asleep before kissing you goodnight.

Tractor

More than a storey high and twice that long,
it looks igneous, the Buhler Versatile 2360,
possessed of the ecology of some hellacious
minor island on which options
are now standard. Cresting the sections
in a corona part dirt, part heat, it appears
risen full-blown from our deeper needs,
aspirating its turbo-cooled air, articulated
and fully compatible. What used to take a week
it does in a day on approximately

a half-mile to the gallon. It cost one hundred
fifty grand. We hope to own it outright by 2017.
Few things wrought by human hands
are more sublime than the Buhler Versatile 2360.

Across the road, a crew erects the floodlit
derricks of a Texan outfit whose presumptions
are consistently vindicated.
The ancient sea bed will be fractured to 1000 feet
by pressuring through a pipe literal tons
of a fluid—the constituents of which
are best left out of this—
to tap the sweet gas where it lies like the side
our bread is buttered on. The earth shakes
terribly then, dear Houston, dear parent
corporation, with its re-broken dead and freshly
killed, the air concussive, cardiac, irregular.
It silences the arguments of every living thing
and our minds in that time are not entirely elsewhere.

But I was speaking of the Buhler Versatile 2360
Phase D! And how well recognized it is
among the classics: Wagner,
Steiger, International Harvester, John Deere, Case,
Minneapolis-Moline, Oliver, White, Allis-Chalmers,
Massey-Ferguson, Ford, Rite, Rome.
One could say it manifests fate, forged
like a pearl around the grit of centuries. That,
in a sense, it's always been with us,
the diesel smell of a foregone conclusion.
In times of doubt, we cast our eyes
upon the Buhler Versatile 2360
and are comforted. And when it breaks down, or thinks
itself in gear and won't, for our own good, start,
it takes a guy out from the city at 60 bucks an hour
plus travel and parts, to fix it.

Casa Mendoza

On public transit, I rode to meet him in the lounge
of an old motel on a busy through-road
in east Etobicoke, south of the Nabisco factory
and water treatment plant amid sports bars,

tarp shops, dealerships, and self-
storage, one of a strip doomed by the geologic
headway of condominiums aspiring to Miami
or Neo-Deco via Vegas. CCTV and gated
courtyards, lakeside. I was committed
to change. Lingered in the parking lot and thought it oddly
gracious, appropriate, private, with its rear

views of The Beach and Silver Moon, both earmarked
for demolition, disused antennas upholstered
in birds and the big oaks throwing their overcoats
over everything: weeds
flowering in vacant lots, heaved sidewalk
from which I'd just seen a pair of Scooby-Doo
underpants, men's, size XXL, in the gutter. Nearby,
the Hillcrest and North American, in hourly
throes of cost-to-profit ratios, were going down
in a blaze of filmic neon. The dark little lobby
was Spanish-themed, with something German

about it, and anachronistically panelled. I was out
of my depth. Running hot and cold. From the patio
overlooking the water, the city core
appeared as background and setting
for what we were mixed up in. Even then,
a Demonstration Centre had cropped up on the long
lawn, pink to orange in the failing light like a patient,
worsening, a woman inside manning
the phones. Above that, little brown bats,
though they flew in dwindling numbers, flew nonetheless.
We knew it couldn't last, and then it did.

An Acolyte Reads *The Cloud of Unknowing*

Aspiring, not to emptiness, but to continually empty
one's self as a stream pours into a larger body
what it receives from the watershed—how midway
it carves a bed in this life, a clarity of purpose—
never ends. Simone Weil starves herself to death
again and again in London while the great mystery
appears to me as through a pinhole camera: reduced,
inverted, harmless. It's hard to concentrate, living
between Fire Station 426 and the Catholic hospital,

though the man shouting on the steps of the drop-in centre
appears, as much as anyone could, to be heroically
wrestling himself free from reality, his pain the soul's
pain in knowing it exists. I have dissolved
like an aspirin in water watching a bee walk into
the foyer of a trumpet flower, in the momentary
solace of what has nothing to do with me, brief
harmony of particulars in their separate orbits,
before returning to my name, to memory's warehouse
and fleet of specialized vehicles, the heart's
repetitive stress fractures, faulty logic, its stupid
porchlight. If virtue is love ordered and controlled,
its wild enemy has made a home in me. And if
desire injures the spirit, I am afflicted. Rehearsing
philosophy's different temperaments—sanguine, contrary,
nervous, alien—one finds a great deal to fear.
A lake-effect snowstorm bypasses the ski hills,
knocks the power out of some innocent milltown.
The world chooses for us what we can't, or won't.

Sue Sinclair

(b. 1972)

Sue Sinclair, who claims to write out of "melancholy and bitter-sweetness," grew up in St. John's, Newfoundland. She studied at Mount Allison University, the University of New Brunswick, and the University of Toronto, where she recently completed a doctorate in philosophy. Raised by parents who were avid readers, she says she wanted to be a writer since she was "yay high," and lists as her favourite writers and principal influences Tomas Tranströmer, for his deep images, dream logic, and imaginative leaps; Rainer Maria Rilke, for inventing the "thing" poem, in which the poet steps back from the self of Romantic poetry to focus on the people, places, and objects of this world; Don McKay, for his quirky, often humorous, but deeply engaging nature poems; and Jan Zwicky, from whom she learned a passion for lyric philosophy.

Poetry, Sinclair says, makes us slow down, take things more seriously. About where poems come from, she has this to say:

> Inspiration often gets a bad rap, perhaps because emphasizing inspiration can imply that writing doesn't also involve hard work. Nevertheless, poems for me tend to begin with something like inspiration: those moments of being struck by something, moments we all have as we go about the day. Some—watching a giant breaker crash on shore—are more obviously striking than others—the fridge suddenly taking on the aspect of a companion. These moments of being struck are rich, and the poems are about trying to tune myself in to these moments as deeply as I can. Obviously you may not be struck if you're not receptive, willing to be struck, and often it means allowing yourself to be sidetracked from other agendas. And then there's the hard work: the hard work of staying open and attentive, which isn't always easy, and the hard work of becoming a skilled enough wordsmith to respond by way of a poem. But working hard often feels good—whether I'm working on poetry or philosophy or lifting boxes on moving day.

Sinclair is much admired by fellow poets and in demand as a reader. Her books of poetry include *Secrets of Weather and Hope* (2001), *Mortal Arguments* (2003), *The Drunken Lovely Bird* (2005), and *Breaker* (2008). She was a finalist for the Gerald Lampert Memorial Award and the Atlantic Poetry Prize, won the International Independent Publishers' Award for Poetry and has appeared twice in the *Best Canadian Poetry* anthologies. She was writer-in-residence at the University of New Brunswick in 2011–12 and now resides in Montreal.

Saskatchewan

The cows have come
to see us, leaning
their soft, muscoussy noses
over the fence, their breath
heavy and smelling
of the ocean—salt, mollusc,
seaweed—it's not difficult
to imagine them, hooves and horns
rising out of the waves. Testing
their footing, they clomp
up the beach and wander
out to the prairie, looking for a place

to lie down. Their eyes show
how far they have travelled
but not what they have
seen. They have the look
of all lost peoples:
everything, even intelligence,
submerged, they peer
at us, wait for us to make
the first move. Only at dusk,
near the salt lick, do they
reveal themselves. We overhear
their rough tongues scraping
the block, as if that
were the way home.

Departure

Sometimes, autumn reveals the inward
light of things we call *glowing*.
A handful of red maple leaves.
A light that doesn't exceed itself
and has something to do

with departure. Think of a church,
the long, slow, sad colours, the way
they linger, miles from the sun, with no thought
of lingering. Again the red leaves.

Lay them on a table.
The dead have come back
to haunt the surface of the wood.
They can see themselves in the polish,
appear and disappear, something more than
and less than a face.

At the end of everything, you think,
there is this—this quickness,
this vanishing, this brilliance. The unseen
glimmer that bound it all together
escapes and is forgiven.

And everyone knows that forgiveness
gives off light, that healing

is the next thing to fire. It calls you
as it goes. You lay your
hand on the table.

Prime

Dragonflies hover in tandem, glued
together at the ends
like the trees reflected in the pond, everything
in pairs,
    multiple,
        lily pads
rucked up against
each other, some lifted
from the water
like heroes carried home
on shoulders: frogs
ping like rubber bands,

the buzz, the glitter, flashbulbs
popping, so this
is where media was born,

its meaning asway
in the lushness of place,
full of ears, alert:

the world sits up, attentive,
listens to the story of itself from
beginning to end,

applauds wildly.

Jellyfish

Stranded, they shrink slowly into the sand,
and you have the uncomfortable feeling
of knowing more than you should,
like watching a man pretend
he isn't fat, isn't lonely, can't cry.

Mortality works itself out on the beach.
Vulnerable, it lets you touch the soft jelly of its least

protected parts. How every kind of beauty collapses
and begins again. Time waits at the centre,
almost transparent, its illegible abstractions barely
visible in the lucid, wet span of the shore. Read them
before they disappear. Bodies vanishing like the body
of this light, which dissolves without telling us why.

Before You Were Born

They have taken a step away
from the familiar. Their lives so far
peel like paint, behind it their real existence.
Your father, at the bar,
buys your mother a drink. You are hidden,
painted into the picture but camouflaged.
No one has seen you yet.

They watch the bartender
pull the tap. It shines
like the places they hope to visit,
the plans they don't have yet.

She is a room in a house that lets the light
in slowly. His inner life rests on his face
like a lamp
he's forgotten to turn off.

The visible makes love
to the invisible. People gather
around tables, quivering,
wanting to be taken from darkness
into the flame.

The bartender keeps his wings folded
at his back. Watches. A bottle opener
hangs from a chain on his belt.
The dust on his wings glitters,
rubs off if he's not careful.

The lights are dim, but the mirrors
multiply their faces, send them down
a long corridor. They emerge, repeated,
confirmed. Your mother, your father. Yourself.

Here it is, the secret
they didn't dare believe.
They don't know how it will show them home.
They feel their way in the dark.

Orpheus Meets Eurydice in the Underworld

Still limping, she has come. She waits at the foot of the hill, doesn't dare go further, remembers how it once vanished under her feet.

She has spent the time thinking about her wedding day, tracing the mark on her ankle where the serpent bit. It hasn't healed yet; perhaps it won't until he comes back. She has never desired his death, but wished for it as one wishes for rain.

The steep hill, where it led and couldn't lead. So many times.

When he arrives he looks more tired than she can understand. The lyre has vanished; they stand together silently.

Even as she remembers his face, she loses something else. She has been alone so long now; how often she has stood here, how much she has wanted to climb.

She takes him home, puts him to bed, then slips in beside him. His childhood bed, too short for him now; they will have to find another.

They waken slowly. As ghosts they pass through each other's bodies, she puts her hand into his heart. He had been worried she would forget.

They play in the fields, run races, drift through tall grasses carelessly, as only those who have had to wait forever can. They have a private sign language; no one speaks in this place, even the streams are still.

Sometimes when they are walking she teases him, falls behind. He looks over his shoulder again and again: there she is. They never tire of this game.

Anne Compton

(b. 1947)

Anne Compton was born and raised in Bangor, a farming community in Prince Edward Island. She completed her BA at Prince of Wales College, her MA at York University, and her PhD at the University of New Brunswick. She was Lorenzo Writer-in-Residence at the Saint John Campus of UNB, director of the Lorenzo Reading Series, and taught literature and creative writing. Her scholarly publications include *A.J.M. Smith: Canadian Metaphysical* (1994), *The Edge of Home: Milton Acorn from the Island* (editor, 2002), *Coastlines: The Poetry of Atlantic Canada* (co-editor, 2002), and *Meetings with Maritime Poets* (2006). Her poetry publications include *Opening the Island* (2003, Atlantic Poetry Prize), *Processional* (2005, Governor General's Award, Atlantic Poetry Prize), and *Asking Questions Indoors and Out* (2009, shortlisted for the Atlantic Poetry Prize). She is also the recipient of the Alden Nowlan Award for Excellence in the Literary Arts and a National Magazine Award.

In an interview with *Open Book Toronto*, Compton explains what first sparked her interest in poetry:

> What contributed to my becoming a poet was not so much an experience as an attitude. In the household that I grew up in, there was an attitude of awe in regard to the poetry of the psalms. It wasn't so much the religious content of the psalms that made my father's face radiant when he referred to them. In fact, he never talked about their content, but when he used that phrase "the poetry of the psalms," I understood, from his voice and look, that there was something about poetry that set it apart from other kinds of writing.

In the same interview, she describes what she likes best about poetry:

> The best thing about being a poet is the change it makes in the brain so that you become daily alert and noticing, wide awake to what your senses are picking up—the sights and sounds of everything around you. The feel of things. In terms of the senses, writing makes you greedy. Even if I were never to write another poem, I'll always be grateful that poetry, and the note-scribbling that precedes it, came along and revved up my attentiveness.

The House after Dark, Winter

The lamps extinguished, moonlight carouses the kitchen,
takes a shine to the fridge, a lick of the butter knife.

On the table, the day folded back into envelopes.
Never as neat as the news when it came. Bulkier.

Slow walk of the hallway. A sconce fixing the west
wall, the coolness of it. The cellar conferring its air.

The body, aware of itself because it needs sleep, takes
precautions up the stairs. A dark landing.

The book marked and put down for the night. The house
settling on its plot: midnight, a woman in conclusion.

Home and house are not the same. We miss one (who lives
there now), wed the other. Wife to the *hus*, hussy.

Though room & board can be bought, it's not the same.

Upstairs, downstairs, rooms for this and that.
Why aren't there better words for what we love?

If we were grander we'd have an aerie, solarium, cupola
but I'd not leave a pantry for that prospect.

Emily was in the pantry, skimming milk, when a poem came down.
Anyone who's worked in a milk room knows about the scalding.

Asked if it was going to be a maid or an icebox,
Virginia Woolf chose the maid. Time spoils fastest.

I think of all those women who wrote in a house near water
their words tilting lanterns over distance.

In the morning,
my breath'll be in the hall before me

the light will not stall once on the river.

After Reading a Poem by Stanley Kunitz

I ask you, Why do the good words build houses
in air? Swing open a door, take you down a hallway?
Why is *back* the most beautiful direction?

Knowing no one's there, why do you want to go at all?
Why—with all that's here, this soft summer evening—
are you tense as a child hurrying down a road, the west ditch
waving vetch and Queen Anne's lace, small purple heart
at the centre, dozens of them. We were a dozen, almost.
A dozen if you counted the one who didn't live.
What would that be like? The question we pitched back and forth.

Opening book after book—their covers, small doors—
and what do you hope to find anyway? Some handle, or what?

More if you counted the ones who came to stay. Tubercular cousins
and other convalescents. Refuge for the sick. Rheumatic fever.
Upstairs, the room with blinds down. Through all sorts of weather,
she slept the afternoon away. Afternoons to heal a heart. House
to mend.

All words, roads
                    making their way there.

Go up and see Rose, our mother said, and we did. The knitting
asleep in her lap. Her hands, slugs on the spread.
Hi, Rose. Bye, Rose: Brutal children, we rounded the bed
at a gallop, John and me. I've seen him now as still. Hands on a coverlet
stiff with knowing. What we threw carelessly in air, answered.

Some words, by God, shouldn't be spoken.

What Light Decays

I make my way down the shingle to my father. He's by the rowboat
smoking a cigarette. You'd think he'd be wayworn at his age but no,
he's quick to my step, except his eyes have the look of the overslept—

Where's your mother? I'm not sure what he means, or means to do.
He oughn't to be here so late in the season, water levels rising.
Gone gatewards, I gesture, using his expression. She went before.

It's like nights were, he says, *and the forgetting that followed—*
mornings, no effort could stay what scattered. But more so.
I know I'm from here, but I've only scraps. Those, and the river.

His voice hollows off—how words sound in a silo come spring,
the silage gone. There's a sea smell to his clothes though he's come,
he claims, from the headpond. Where herons nest.

One time—this was long ago—he told us, *They have two elements.*
Neither's earth. From the crowd of us, he called my name, or so
I thought. For *me*, he'd tell. It's easy to be mistaken so near to sleep.

We stayed that way—in prow and stern—the better part of an hour
or a minute. It wasn't my time, and what he had of here was soon spent.
Hauled ashore, a boat's unsteady. Small stones shift beneath its weight,

clatter in the suck of a current coming in. A grackle-rasp
of wind had started up. And in that wind he stood to go,
a black-crowned night heron near us on the bank.

What are you? he wants to know—his valedictory words. I wish for *how,*
not *what*, the old sweetness of tone. Had he something to tell—even then—
I could not lose the daughter to gain a guide.

The light on the far shore, where larch braid spruce, was opening morning,
one shutter
at a time. Night and his oarsman, along the river Oblivion, headed out to sea.
Up the hill home, the highbush cranberries were flushed with frost.

The Intelligent Man's Guide to the Shore

Up near the dunes, a summer storm has packed the seaweed solid.
Sun-dried divan, I think. Some part of my mind, sixteen and sexual.
Late-day sun on the slope of your shoulder, a heat I imagine
through loose clothes when thought slips under. Stepping in surf.

Mattress of kelp and algae that could support the weight of us—
leathery Laminaria approving in briny breath if we went there.

Down shore, in the ebb, the moss rakers' horses look a blur.
Everything here runs together, joins.
You're out of your element

and in mine. I would have you deeper: The ocean tugging at our ankles
is a compulsion that takes and leaves, scours the sand in its own image
and beds the seaweed. Water remembers what air forgets: How it rose,

surged ashore. In the great refusal I'm good at, I rehearse the uses of
kelp and bladder wrack (genus, *fucus*), explain the role of the holdfast
in underwater kelp forests—what anchors the beautiful 'til broken.

The Library, Nova Scotia

Sometime, after you've gone, someone will happen upon John Donne's poems;
read for the first time a novel by Virginia Woolf. *To the Lighthouse* perhaps.
It'll remind her of the grey gloves her mother wore. Gone in the seams, chafed soft.
In the evening she'll walk a poplar-lined street to the library. *The Voyage Out*,
she'll say, *The Waves*. At the checkout, record the argent air of her afternoon—
so like the air, years past, altered by your asking, *Why did Mrs. Ramsay have to die?*
A death occurring, even now, to the girl whose mother's gloves were grey, pale as
the underside of poplar leaves. How it goes on—will go on—in your absence.
That daring when words open seaways, and the imperfect becomes a room more navigable.

Behind her, the library in the Annapolis is a ship asail. Rain shrinking the endpapers.

Suzanne Buffam

(b. 1972)

Suzanne Buffam was born in Montreal. She earned her MA from Concordia University and her MFA from the Iowa Writers' Workshop. She won the CBC Literary Award for poetry and the Gerald Lampert Memorial Award. Her two poetry collections are *Past Imperfect* (2005) and *The Irrationalist* (2010, Griffin Poetry Prize shortlist). She teaches creative writing at the University of Chicago.

Buffam likes to approach poetry from a point of not-knowing, which is not the same as deductive reasoning, but rather a lyrical prospecting, getting a sense of what you think or feel about something by seeing what you dredge up, what you say, and how you say it. In short, the poem as a dance of ear, eye, and mind—a process of discovery. Even then, she resists closure: "I think, with poems, the endings that I like the most are the ones that puzzle me, and leave me to sit with the poem over the course of several decades, revisiting them. Stevens has a way of ending poems that are deeply puzzling" (*Canadian Interviews*, 26 May 2011).

In another interview, she explains her resistance to the poem sequence or "project" book: "I've tried to write from that approach before, partly because I think it might spare me the terror of starting afresh each time I sit down, but for the most part I seem to need that rudderless terror to really feel invested." When the interviewer, Sina Queyras, asks about the interiority of her work, Buffam says:

> "Interiority" and "spaciousness" is a lovely pair of words to describe any book of poems. They speak directly to what poetry can do, perhaps like no other medium, or at least the kind of poetry I want to write: create a kind of expansive interiority that allows for contemplation. A poem, a book of poetry, is a literal space that provides a reader—or a writer—with a site for genuine encounter, in Buber's sense of the word. An occasion to glimpse, however fleetingly, a window that opens beyond time and self . . . onto what? timelessness? selflessness? Something vastly more expansive, in any case, than I typically glimpse in my daily routine. (*Maisonneuve*, 15 Nov. 2010)

Buffam also compares poetry to dreams, where "anything can happen." Her poems are the work of an elegant ironist—polished, witty—and she is as capable of self-mockery as she is of looking askance at the world and its contradictions. Very little escapes her critical intellect, but even the angry poems are driven by a strong lyrical impulse and rigorous attention to detail. Even in what she calls a "little commentary" in *The Irrationalist*—"The first line should pry up / A little corner of the soul / As the first ray of daylight / Pries open the sleeper's lids"—a meticulous attention to sound is evident, in the recurring consonants and the intricate pattern of stresses.

Mariner

Sometimes I eat an orange and completely forget about dying. Nonetheless, the thought of home can reliably be said to bring tears to the eyes of any traveller. When the sailor travels inland, he misses not so much the sight of the ocean as the sound it makes beneath him at night when the world has disappeared and there are only stars above to guide him. Perhaps he also misses the smell of creosote in the breeze, but it remains so utterly abstract in its absence he cannot properly be said to *feel* the lack. On the other hand, I find it possible to miss what I have never known. My voice has been described as nondescript, yet I continue to use it. I call to the hills and to the good people in them. I call to hear the sound of my own voice. The truth is, I seldom think about home at all. To grow up at sea is a mixed blessing, granted, but show me a blessing that isn't.

The Starfish

A wave reached up to tug my hem.
Because of you I let it pull me in.
And then I turned from where you stood
delighting in my own delight at yours
in my soaked skirt, and swam towards
the middle of the lake. Between my strokes,
erratic, slack, small buffetings
that gave the day, your laughter
from the shore, their shape. Your skipped
voice lit across the waves and gave me
something vanishing to aim for, something solid
to outreach. Did I want you to lose sight of me?
Just long enough for me to learn
how being lost would feel? I felt your watching
for my face, my wave, for any solid part

of what I'd led you to believe. I leaned
back in the lake and let it take me, almost,
under. Above my waist, fanned out around me
in the waves, my skirt rose up and made of me
a shape I couldn't take on shore or keep.

The New Experience

I was ready for a new experience.
All the old ones had burned out.

They lay in little ashy heaps along the roadside
And blew in drifts across the fairgrounds and fields.

From a distance some appeared to be smouldering
But when I approached with my hat in my hands

They let out small puffs of smoke and expired.
Through the windows of houses I saw lives lit up

With the otherworldly glow of TV
And these were smoking a little bit too.

I flew to Rome. I flew to Greece.
I sat on a rock in the shade of the Acropolis

And conjured dusky columns in the clouds.
I watched waves lap the crumbling coast.

I heard wind strip the woods.
I saw the last living snow leopard

Pacing in the dirt. Experience taught me
That nothing worth doing is worth doing

For the sake of experience alone.
I bit into an apple that tasted sweetly of time.

The sun came out. It was the old sun
With only a few billion years left to shine.

Please Take Back the Sparrows

Please take back the sparrows. They are bothersome and cute. They are brown and daily all year long. They make a plaything of the wind and the spruce. They come too close. They look right at me with their tiny black eyes. They dart through spaces. They pick up the pieces and the pace. From rooftop to eaves trough to wire to branch—they spring spring spring spring spring spring spring. They are not sorry. They are not singing. Many they are one they are never not somewhere. They are not not singing. They are not slack. They fear the bluejay and the airedale. They drink from the pond! They scatter thinking. They are not asking or telling they are scattering thinking they are shivering. They are awake or they are shivering. Please, take back the sparrows. They bathe in dust.

The Wise Man

I am not a wise man. This makes my life difficult in certain ways. But in other ways it simplifies things. I find it hard to sit still very long before I get up and wander the halls in my hat for example. On the other hand I stay warm and keep moving. Could these ways be the same way? A wise man could tell you. A wise man would look out his window and see not a row of low clouds rolling east like a trainload of coal through a crossroads, but a lit glimpse of the infinite, the wise man's only home. A wise man might think of his childhood and smile. Often in a quandary I ask myself what would a wise man do? A fool sees not the same tree that a wise man sees, said a wise man, and when I look out at the spruce I wonder what a wise man sees. A wise man might laugh at such questions. As for me I laugh often, but I don't get the joke.

Enough

I am wearing dark glasses inside the house
To match my dark mood.

I have left all the sugar out of the pie.
My rage is a kind of domestic rage.

I learned it from my mother
Who learned it from her mother before her

And so on.
Surely the Greeks had a word for this.

Now surely the Germans do.
The more words a person knows

To describe her private sufferings
The more distantly she can perceive them.

I repeat the names of all the cities I've known
And watch an ant drag its crooked shadow home.

What does it mean to love the life we've been given?
To act well the part that's been cast for us?

Wind. Light. Fire. Time.
A train whistles through the far hills.

One day I plan to be riding it.

Acknowledgements

MILTON ACORN "Offshore Breeze", "Charlottetown Harbour", "The Island", "Knowing I Live in a Dark Age", "The Natural History of Elephants", and "I've Tasted My Blood" from *Dig Up My Heart, Selected Poems: 1952-1983*, (Toronto: McLelland & Stewart, 1983). Reprinted with permission of the estate of Milton Acorn.

MARGARET ATWOOD "Progressive Insanities of a Pioneer", "Death of a Young Son by Drowning", "Notes Towards a Poem That Can Never Be Written", and "A Women's Issue" from *Selected Poems 1966–1984* (Toronto: Oxford University Press Canada, 1990). Copyright © Margaret Atwood 1990. Reprinted by permission. "They eat out" from *Power Politics* copyright © 1971 by Margaret Atwood. Reprinted by permission of Stoddart Publishing Co. Limited.

MARGARET AVISON "Snow", "To Professor X, Year Y", "The Swimmer's Moment", "Voluptuaries and Others", "Pace", "Black-White Under Green: May 18, 1965", and "In a Season of Unemployment" reprinted from *Always Now* (in three volumes) by Margaret Avison by permission of the Porcupine's Quill. Copyright © The Estate of Margaret Avison, 2003.

KEN BABSTOCK "Essentialist" and "Explanatory Gap" from *Airstream Land Yacht* (Toronto: House of Anansi, 2011); "As Marginalia in John Clare's The Rural Muse" and "Carolinian (Crosscut with Sound)" from *Methodist Hatchet* (Toronto: House of Anansi, 2012).

EARLE BIRNEY "From the Hazel Bough", "David", Bushed", and "The Bear on Delhi Road" from *The Collected Poems of Earle Birney* by Earle Birney. Used by permission of Wailan Low, executor of the estate of Earle Birney.

ROBIN BLASER "Winter Words", "Dreams, April 1981", "The Iceberg", "Home for Boys and Girls", "For Barry Clinton, d. 17, June, 1984, of AIDS", "Praise to Them, December 30, 1984", and "Of the Land of Culture" from *The Holy Forest* (Vancouver: Talonbooks, 1993). Copyright © Robin Blaser.

ROO BORSON "Talk", "Waterfront", "Flowers", and "A Sad Device" reprinted by permission of the author.

GEORGE BOWERING "Grandfather" from *Points on the Grid* (Contact Press, 1964); "Bones Along Her Body" from *The Catch* by George Bowering (Toronto: McClelland & Stewart, 1976); "From Kerrisdale Elegies, One" from *Kerrisdale Elegies* by George Bowering (Toronto: Coach House Press, 1984). All poems reprinted by permission of the author.

DIONNE BRAND "Ossuary I" and "Ossuary XV" excerpted from *Ossuaries* by Dionne Brand. Copyright © 2010 Dionne Brand. Reprinted by permission of McClelland & Stewart.

DI BRANDT "nonresistance, or love Mennonite style" from *Agnes in the Sky* by Di Brandt (Winnipeg, MB: Turnstone Press, 1990), used by permission of the publisher; "Jerusalem, the golden, city of my dreams" and "there are no words in me for Gaza, for what i saw" from *Jerusalem, beloved* by Di Brandt (Winnipeg, MB: Turnstone Press, 1995), used by permission of the publisher; "Dog Days in Maribor, 1, 7, 8, 9, 10, 11" from *Now You Care* (Toronto: Coach House Books, 2003); "let me tell you, dear reader" from *mother, not mother*, reprinted by permission of the author.

ROBERT BRINGHURST "The Beauty of Weapons", "Anecdote of the Squid", "For the Bones of Josef Mengele, Disinterred June 1985" and "The Occupation" from *Selected Poems* (Kentville, NS: Gaspereau, 2009). Reprinted with permission.

SUZANNE BUFFAM "Mariner" and "The Starfish" from *Past Imperfect* (Toronto: House of Anansi, 2006); "The New Experience", "Please Take Back the Sparrows", "The Wise Man", and "Enough" from *The Irrationalist* (Toronto: House of Anansi, 2010).

ANNE CARSON "The Truth About God" by Anne Carson, from *Glass, Irony and God*, copyright © 1995 by Anne Carson. Reprinted by permission of New Directions Publishing Corp.

GEORGE ELLIOTT CLARKE "Look Homeward, Exile", "The Lover's Argument with Shelley", "The Wisdom of Shelley", and "Blues for X" from *Whylah Falls* (Kentville, NS: Gaspereau, 2010); "Ballad of a Hanged Man" from *Blues and Bliss: The Poetry of George Elliott Clarke* (Gaspereau, 2001). "IX/XI" from *Black* (Gaspereau, 2012). All poems reprinted by permissin of Gaspereau Press.

LEONARD COHEN "Elegy" excerpted from *Let Us Compare Mythologies* by Leonard Cohen. Copyright © 1969 Leonard Cohen. Reprinted by permission of McClelland & Stewart. "The Genius" and "Now of Sleeping" excerpted from *Selected Poems, 1956–1968* by Leonard Cohen. Copyright © 1964, 1966, 1968 Leonard Cohen. Reprinted by permission of McClelland & Stewart. "You Have the Lovers", "As the Mist Leaves No Scar", "Style", and "The Music Crept by Us" excerpted from *Stranger Music: Selected Poems and Songs by Leonard Cohen*. Copyright © 1993 Leonard Cohen. Reprinted by permission of McClelland & Stewart.

ANNE COMPTON "The House After Dark, Winter", and "After reading a poem by Stanley Kunitz" from *Processional* (Fitzhenry & Whiteside, 2005); "What light decays", "The Intelligent Man's Guide to the Shore", "The Library, Nova Scotia" from *asking questions indoors and out* (Fitzhenry & Whiteside, 2009). All poems © Anne Compton.

LORNA CROZIER "A Brief History of the Horse" and "Packing for the Future: Instructions" from *Inventing the Hawk* by Lorna Crozier. Used by permission of the author. "Watching My Lover" and "The Sex Lives of Vegetables" excerpted from *The Blue Hour of the Day: Selected Poems*. Copyright © 2007 Lorna Crozier. Reprinted by permission of McClelland & Stewart. "Taking the Measure" excerpted from *Small Mechanics* by Lorna Crozier. Copyright © 2011 Lorna Crozier. Reprinted by permission of McClelland & Stewart.

MARY DALTON "A Question of Narrative", "Backhome Blues: Another Tune", and "The Great Big Sea and Lost Speech" from *Red Ledger* (Montreal: Signal Editions, 2006); "Conkerbells", "Janneying", "Merrybegot", "My One Brother", and "Yet" from *Merrybegot* (Montreal: Vehicule Press, 2003).

DON DOMANSKI "Untitled with Invisible Ink" and "A Hummingbird's Heart Beats 1260 Times a Minute" from *All Our Wonder Unavenged* (London, ON: Brick Books, 2007); "Biodiversity is the Mother of All Beauty" and "For the Pure Mother Bee" from *Bite Down Little Whisper* (London, ON: Brick Books, 2013).

PATRICK FRIESEN excerpt from "Anna" and "a woman from jamaica" from *You Don't Get to Be a Saint* copyright © 1992 Patrick Friesen. Reprinted by permission of the author and the publisher. "Koestler's Window" from *Jumping in the Asylum* (Toronto: Quattro Books, 2011); "Caught in the Sky" from *Carrying the Shadow* (Erin, ON: Porcepic Books, 1999).

GARY GEDDES "Sandra Lee Scheuer", "Jimmy's Place", and "Philip Larkin" reprinted by permission of the author.

SUSAN GLICKMAN "For My Students In English 108 Who Complain That All Modern Literature Is Too Depressing" from *The Power to Move* (Montreal: Signal Editions, 1986); "Families" from *Henry Moore's Sheep and Other Poems* (Montreal: Signal Editions, 1990); "When They Are Asleep In Their Nimbus of Flame" and "Know Your Audience" from *Running in Prospect Cemetery: New and Selected Poems* (Montreal: Signal Editions, 2004); "On Finding a Copy of 'Pigeon' in the Hospital Bookstore" from *The Smooth Yarrow* (Montreal: Vehicule Press, 2012).

RALPH GUSTAFSON "'S.S.R., Lost at Sea' The Times", "Now at the Ocean's Verge", "The Newspaper", "Wednesday at North Hatley", "In the Yukon", "Ramble on What in the World Why", "The Arrival of Wisdom", and "State of Affairs" from *The Moment Is All: Selected Poems, 1944–1983* by Ralph Gustafson. All poems used by permission from McClelland & Stewart, Ltd. *The Canadian Publishers.*

LOUISE BERNICE HALFE Published by Coteau Books, Regina, Canada: "Wagon Ride", "Body Politics", "Lizard's Curse", "Hamilton's Graveyard", and "So Sorry" from *Bear Bones and Feathers*; "Manyberries" from *The Crooked Good*. Used with permission of the publisher.

MICHAEL HARRIS "Siren Songs", "After Rodin's *The Kiss*", "Uncle Edward", and excerpt from "Turning Out the Light" from *New and Selected Poems* by Michael Harris (Montreal:

Signal Editions, 1992). "Concentrate" from *Circus* by Michael Harris (Montreal: Signal Editions, 1992).

STEPHEN HEIGHTON "The Machine Gunner" and "Were You to Die" from *The Ecstasy of Skeptics: Poems* (Toronto: House of Anansi, 1994); "Constellations" from *The Address Book: Poems* (Toronto: House of Anansi, 2004); and "Herself, Revised" from *Patient Frame: Poems* (Toronto: House of Anansi, 2010).

D.G. JONES Used by permission of the author: "Beautiful Creatures Brief as These", "For Françoise Adnet", "These Trees Are No Forest of Mourners", "The Stream Exposed With All Its Stones", and "Words from the Aviary" from *A Throw of Particles* (Toronto: Stoddart, 1983).

A.M. KLEIN, "Heirloom", "Autobiographical", "For the Sisters of the Hotel Dieu", and "Portrait of the Poet as Landscape" from *Complete Poems*, Zailig Pollack, ed. (Toronto: University of Toronto Press, 1990). Reprinted by permission of University of Toronto Press Inc.

ROBERT KROETSCH "Meditation on Tom Thomson" from *Stone Hammer Poems 1960-1975* by Robert Kroetsch (Fernie, BC: Oolichan books, 1975). Copyright © 1975 Robert Kroetsch. With permission of the author's estate. Excerpt from "Seed Catalogue" copyright © Robert Kroetsch 1989. From *Completed Field Notes: The Long Poems of Robert Kroetsch* (originally published by McClelland & Stewart, now available from University of Alberta Press). Reprinted by permission. "For a Poet Who Has Stopped Writing" from *Advice to My Friends: A Continuing Poem* by Robert Kroetsch (Toronto: Stoddart, 1985). Copyright © 1985 Robert Kroetsch. With permission of the artist's estate. "Are We There Yet?" from *Snowbird Poems*, by Robert Kroetsch (Edmonton, AB: University of Alberta Press, 2004). Copyright © 2004 Robert Kroetsch. With permission of the author's estate.

PATRICK LANE "Passing into Storm", "Elephants", "Albino Pheasants", "Fathers and Sons", and "The Spoon" are reprinted by permission of the author.

IRVING LAYTON "Look, the Lambs Are All Around Us", "The Cold Green Element", "The Fertile Muck", "Whatever Else Poetry Is Freedom", "Berry Picking", and "Keine Lazarovitch 1870–1959" excerpted from *A Wild Peculiar Joy: The Selected Poems by Irving Layton*. Copyright © 1982, 2004 Irving Layton. Copyright © Estate of Irving Layton. Reprinted by permission of McClelland & Stewart.

DENNIS LEE "400: Coming Home" and excerpt from "Civil Elegies/1" from *Civil Elegies and Other Poems* by Dennis Lee (Toronto: House of Anansi Press, 1972) Copyright © 1972 Dennis Lee. With permission of the author. "Coming Becomes You" from Nightwatch: New & Selected Peoms 1968-1996 by Dennis Lee (Toronto: McClelland & Stewart, 1996). Copyright © 1996 Dennis Lee. With permission of the author. "Home" from *Testament* (Toronto: House of Anansi Press, 2012).

TIM LILBURN Used by permission, McClelland & Stewart, Ltd. *The Canadian Publishers*: "In the Hills, Watching" and "How To Be Here?" from *Moosewood Sandhills* by Tim Lilburn (2004); "Orphic Disgorgement, Anti-Colonial Disgorgement" excerpted from *Orphic Politics* by Tim Lilburn. Copyright © 2008 by Tim Lilburn. Reprinted by permission of McClelland & Stewart. "Names of God" and "Pumpkins" are reprinted by permission of the author.

DOROTHY LIVESAY, "Spain", "Comrade", "The Unquiet Bed", "Bartok and the Geranium", and "Without Benefit of Tape" from *Collected Poems: The Two Seasons* by Dorothy Livesay (Toronto: McGraw-Hill Ryerson, 1972). Reprinted by permission; "'First Fisherman' from *Call My People Home*", from *Collected Poems: The Two Seasons* by Dorothy Livesay (Toronto: McGraw-Hill Ryerson, 1972). Reprinted by permission.

PAT LOWTHER "Touch Home" from *Milk Stone* by Pat Lowther (Ottawa: Borealis Press, 1974). Reprinted by permission. "Coast Range", "Octopus", and "The Dig" from *A Stone Diary*. Copyright © Oxford University Press Canada 1977. Reprinted by permission.

GWENDOLYN MACEWEN "Manzini: Escape Artist", "Poems Improvised Around a First Line", "Memoirs of a Mad Cook", and "The Child Dancing" from *Magic Animals: Selected Poetry of Gwendolyn MacEwen* (Toronto: Stoddart, 1984). Reprinted by permission of the Estate of Gwendolyn MacEwen. Excerpt from "The T.E. Lawrence Poems" from *The T.E. Lawrence Poems* by Gwendolyn MacEwen (Oakville, ON: Mosaic Press, 1982, www.mosaic-press.com). Reprinted by permission of Mosaic Press.

DON MCKAY "The Great Blue Heron", "Fridge Nocturne", and "Waking at the Mouth of the Willow River" excerpted from *Camber* by Don McKay. Copyright © 2004 Don McKay. Reprinted by permission of McClelland & Stewart. "Adagio for a Fallen Sparrow" excerpted from *Birding, or Desire: Poems by Don McKay.* Copyright © 1983 Don McKay. Reprinted by permission of McClelland & Stewart; "Nocturnal Migrants" excerpted from *Another Gravity.* Copyright © 2000 Don McKay. Reprinted by permission of McClelland & Stewart. "Loss Creek" and "Philosopher's Stone" excerpted from *Strike/Slip* by Don McKay. Copyright © 2006 Don McKay. Reprinted by permission of McClelland & Stewart.

ELI MANDEL "Thief Hanging in Baptist Halls", "Pictures in an Institution", and "On the 25th Anniversary of the Liberation of Auschwitz: Memorial Services, Toronto, YMHA, Bloor & Spadina, January 25, 1970", reprinted by permission of the estate of Eli Mandel.

DAPHNE MARLATT Reprinted by permission of the author: "Imagine: A Town" and "A by-channel; a small backwater" from *Steveston*, Third Edition, by Daphne Marlatt, photographs by Robert Minden (Vancouver: Ronsdale Press, 2000); "listen" from *Network* (Vancouver: Talonbooks, 1980); "a lapsed" and "this city: shrouded" from *Vancouver Poems Then and Now* (Vancouver: Talonbooks, 2013).

A.F. MORITZ "Dark Man" and "Stabbing" from *Early Poems* (Insomniac Press, 2009); "Woman in Astrakhan" from *Night Street Repairs: Poems* (Toronto: House of Anansi Press, 2011); "The Tidal Wave" from *The Sentinel* (Toronto: House of Anansi Press, 2008); and "News" from *The New Measures* (Toronto: House of Anansi Press, 2012).

ERIN MOURÉ "Postmodern Literature" reprinted by permission of Stoddart Publishing Co. Limited, "For Mitterand's Life, For My Life, For Yours" from *Search Procedures*. Copyright © Erin Mouré. "The Cooking" from *Sheepish Beauty, Civilian Love* (Montreal: Véhicule Press, 1992). Reprinted by permission of the publisher. "XVI / What I'd give for my life to be my neighbour's old car" from *Sheep's Vigil by a Fervent Person*; excerpt from "The Unmemntioable" from *The Unmemntioable* (Toronto: House of Anansi Press, 2012).

SUSAN MUSGRAVE "Arctic Poppies", "The Laughter in the Kitchen", and "The Moment" from *Things that Keep and Do Not Change* copyright © 1999 by Susan Musgrave. Published in Canada by McClelland & Stewart, a division of Random House of Canada. Reprinted by permission of the author. "Origami Dove" and "Winter" from *Origami Dove* copyright © 2011 by Susan Musgrave. Published in Canada by McClelland & Stewart, a division of Random House of Canada. Reprinted by permission of the author.

JOHN NEWLOVE "Then, If I Cease Desiring", "Crazy Riel", "Verigin, Moving In Alone", and "Ride Off Any Horizon" from *The Fat Man: Selected Poems 1962 –1972* by John Newlove. Used by permission, McClelland & Stewart, Ltd. *The Canadian Publishers*. "Such Fun, Such Fun" from *Apology for Absence: Selected Poems 1962–1992* (Erin, ON: Porcupine's Quill, 1993). Reprinted by permission.

bp NICHOL "Blues", excerpt from "The Captain Poetry Poems", "Landscape: 1", and "The Mouth" are reprinted by permission of the Estate of bp Nichol.

ALDEN NOWLAN "Beginning", "Warren Pryor", and "For Claudine Because I Love Her" are reprinted by permission of the Estate of Alden Nowlan. "And He Wept Aloud, So That the Egyptians Heard It" copyright © 1967, 1969, 1982 by Irwin Publishing Inc. Reprinted by permission House of Anansi. "The Mysterious Naked Man", and "Ypres: 1915" copyright © 1967, 1969, 1982 by Irwin Publishing Inc. Reprinted by permission of House of Anansi.

MICHAEL ONDAATJE "Early Morning, Kingston to Gananoque", "Elizabeth", and "The Gate in His Head"; from *Billy the Kid*, copyright © 2008 by Michael Ondaatje. Reprinted by permission of Michael Ondaatje. "Bear Hug"; from *The Cinnamon Peeler*, copyright © 1989 by Michael Ondaatje. Reprinted by permission of Michael Ondaatje. "Letters & Other Worlds" copyright © 1971 by Michael Ondaatje. Reprinted by permission of Michael Ondaatje.

P.K. PAGE "The Stenographers", "Landlady", "Stories of Snow", "Photos of a Salt Mine", "After Rain", and "Planet Earth" reprinted from *The Hidden Room (in two volumes)* by P.K. Page by permission of The Porcupine's Quill. Copyright © The Estate of P.K. Page, 1997.

ELIZABETH PHILLIPS "Oxbow" from *Torch River* (London, ON: Brick Books, 2007); "November: Far Past", "The Night Before", and "Wings" from *A Blue with Blood in it* (Regina, SK: Coteau, 2000).

E.J. PRATT "The Shark", "Sea-Gulls", "The Man and the Machine", "Erosion", and excerpt from "The Titanic" from *EJ Pratt: Complete Poems*, ed. Sandra Djwa and R.G. Moyles (Toronto: University of Toronto Press, 1989). Reprinted by permission of University of Toronto Press Inc.

AL PURDY "Home-Made Beer" from *Rooms for Rent in the Outer Planets* by Al Purdy (Madeira Park, BC: Harbour Publishing, 1996). Reprinted by permission. Used by permission, McClelland & Stewart, Ltd. *The Canadian Publishers*: "The Country North of Belleville", "The Cariboo Horses", and "Wilderness Gothic" from *The Cariboo Horses* (Toronto: McClelland & Stewart, 1972); "Arctic Rhododendrons" from *North of Summer* (Toronto: McClelland & Stewart, 1967); "Lament for the Dorsets" from *Wild Grape* (Toronto: McClelland & Stewart, 1968).

SINA QUERYAS "Even the idea of river", "With or without rivets", and "On the scent" from *Lemon Hound* (Toronto: Coach House Books, 2006); "Divining Rod, or How to Find a Neural Pathway..." and "The Proverbs of Hell" from *Expressway* (Toronto: Coach House Books, 2009).

LISA ROBERTSON "She Has Smoothed Her Pants to No End" from *Debbie: An Epic* (Vancouver: New Star Books, 1997); "Give me hackneyed words" and "My Purpose Here" from *The Weather* (Vancouver: New Star Books, 2002); "Essay on Heaven" from *Magenta Soul Whip* (Toronto: Coach House Books, 2011).

ROBYN SARAH "Fugue", "A Meditation Between Claims", and "Scratch" from *The Touchstone: New and Selected Poems* copyright © 1992 by Robyn Sarah. Reprinted by permission of Stoddart Publishing Co. Limited. "On Closing the Apartment of My Grandparents of Blessed Memory" from *Questions About the Stars* (London, ON: Brick Books, 1998). Reprinted by permission of the author. "Riveted" reprinted from *A Day's Grace* by Robyn Sarah by permission of The Porcupine's Quill. Copyright © Robyn Sarah, 2004.

F.R. SCOTT "Lakeshore", "Laurentian Shield", "Overture", "Charity", "Saturday Sundae", "Bonne Entente", and "For Bryan Priestman" from *Collected Poems* by F.R. Scott (Toronto: McClelland & Stewart, 1981). Reprinted with the permission of William Toye, Literary Executor for the Estate of F.R. Scott.

SUE SINCLAIR "Saskatchewan" and "Departure" from *Secrets of Weather and Hope* (London, ON: Brick Books, 2001); "Prime" from *Mortal Arguments* (London, ON: Brick

Books, 2003); "Jellyfish," "Before You Were Born," and "Orpheus Meets Eurydice in the Underworld" were originally published in *The Drunken Lovely Bird* © 2004 by Sue Sinclair. Reprinted by permission of Goose Lane Editions.

A.J.M. SMITH "Like an Old Proud King in a Parable", "A Hyacinth for Edith", "The Lonely Land", "The Plot against Proteus", "News of the Phoenix", "Prothalamium", and "The Wisdom of Old Jelly Roll" reprinted with the permission of William Toye, literary executor for the estate of A.J.M. Smith.

KAREN SOLIE "Real Life" from *Short Haul Engine* (London, ON: Brick Books, 2001); "Determinism" and "Pest Song" from *Modern and Normal* (London, ON: Brick Books, 2005); "Tractor", "Casa Mendoza", and "An Acolyte Reads *The Cloud of Unknowing*" from *Pigeon: Poems* (Toronto: House of Anansi, 2011).

DAVID SOLWAY "Bedrock" from *Bedrock* (Montreal: Signal, 1993); "Stones in Water" from *Stones in Water* (Rockside, MA: Wildside, 1994); "Modern Marriage" from *Modern Marriage* (Montreal: Signal, 1987), and "Undertow" from *Reaching for Clear: The Poetry of Rhys Savarin* (Montreal: Véhicule, 2006).

CARMINE STARNINO "Lullaby" and "After Caravaggio's 'The Crucifixion of Saint Peter'" from *The New World* (Montreal: Véhicule Press, 1997). "What My Mother's Hands Smell Like" from *Credo* (McGill-Queen's University Press, 2007), p. 33; "Song of the House Husband" from *With English Subtitles*, (Montreal: Gaspereau, 2004); and "Pugnax Gives Notice" from *This Way Out* (Gaspereau, 2009), reprinted by permission of Gaspereau Press.

JOHN STEFFLER "Monster Bait" reprinted by permission of the author; "That Night We Were Ravenous" excerpted from *That Night We Were Ravenous* by John Steffler. Copyright © 1998 John Steffler. Reprinted by permission of McClelland & Stewart; "After the Dance-Filled Rooms, the Smoke" and "The Cat Sleeps" from *The Wreckage of Play: Poems* (Toronto: McLelland & Stewart, 1998); "Beating the Bounds" excerpted from *Lookout* by John Steffler. Copyright © 2010 John Steffler. Reprinted by permission of McClelland & Stewart.

ANNE SZUMIGALSKI "Victim" from *Woman Reading in Bath* (Toronto: Doubleday Canada, 1974). "Fishhawks" and "The Lullaby" from *A Game of Angels* (Winnipeg, MB: Turnstone Press, 1980). "The Arrangement" and "Shrapnel" from *Dogstones* (Saskatoon, SK: Fifth House, 1986). "Third Trimester" from *Voice* (Regina, SK: Coteau Books, 1995). All poems reprinted by permission of the Literary Executor for the Estate of Anne Szumigalski.

RAYMOND SOUSTER "Young Girls", "Lagoons, Hanlan's Point", "Downtown Corner News Stand", "Study: The Bath", "All This Slow Afternoon", "The Six-Quart Basket", and "Somalia" from *Collected Poems of Raymond Souster* (Ottawa: Oberon Press, 1980). Reprinted by permission of Oberon Press.

SHARON THESEN "Elegy, the Fertility Specialist", "September, Turning, the Long Road Down to Love", "Animals", "Afternoon With Liver", and "The Torturer's Horse" reprinted by permission of the author.

JOHN THOMPSON "Wife" and "Horse" from *At the Edge of Chopping There Are No Secrets* (Toronto: House of Anansi Press, 1973); "II / In this place we might be happy", "VIII / I forget: why are there broken birds", "XVI / The barn roof bangs a tin wing", "XXV / In a dark wood", and "XXXVII / Now you have burned your books" from *Stilt Jack* (Toronto: House of Anansi Press, 1978).

RHEA TREGEBOV "At 3:00 or 4:00 or 5:00 a.m. March-June 1987" and "Intelligent Life: Elegy" from Selected and New Poems, (Hamilton, ON: Wolsak & Wynn Publishers Limited, 2004); "Edge Zone" and "Wherever You Are" from *Mapping the Chaos* (Signal Editions, 1995); "Family Dinners: Gordie" from *All Souls* (Montreal: Signal Editions, 2012).

FRED WAH "From Pictograms from the Interior of BC", excerpt from "Waiting for Saskatchewan", "Elite 2", and "Father/Mother Haibun" (#4 and #11) are reprinted by permission of the author. "Hamill's Last Stand" from *The False Laws of Narrative: The Poetry of Fred Wah*, (Montreal: Wilfrid Laurier University Press, 2009).

BRONWEN WALLACE "The Woman in This Poem", "A Simple Poem for Virginia Woolf", and "Common Magic" from *Signs of the Former Tenant* by Bronwen Wallace (Ottawa: Oberon Press, 1983). Reprinted by permission of Oberon Press.

TOM WAYMAN "Wayman in Love" from *For and Against the Moon: Blues, Yells, and Chuckles*, Macmillan of Canada, 1974. "Did I Miss Anything", from *Did I Miss Anything? Selected Poems 1973–1993*, Harbour Publishing, 1993. "Cup" from *My Father's Cup*, Harbour Publishing, 1993. "Air Support" from *Dirty Snow*, Harbour Publishing, 2012. www.harbourpublishing.com

PHYLLIS WEBB "Love Story", "Sitting", "Poetics Against the Angel of Death", "Eschatology of Spring", "Prison Report", "Treblinka Gas Chamber", and "Cornflowers and Saffron Robes Belittle the Effort" from *Selected Poems* (Vancouver: Talonbooks, 1982). Copyright © Phyllis Webb. Reprinted by permission of the author and Talon Books Ltd. "Peacock-Blue: An Anti-Ghazal" from *Water and Light: Ghazals and Anti-Ghazals* (Toronto: Coach House Press, 1984).

JAN ZWICKY "The Geology of Norway" and "Border Station", from *Songs for Relinquishing the Earth* (London, ON: Brick Books, 1998). All poems reprinted by permission of the author. "Small Song: Prairie" from *Thirty-seven Small Songs & Thirteen Silences*, (Kentville, NS: Gaspereau, 2005); "Autobiography" from *Forge* (Gaspereau, 2011).

Index